T0305950

"On the heels of a world-wide pandemic when both individuals and organizations are dealing with economic upheaval and uncertainty, a reconsideration of the notion of resilience is both important and timely. In *Resilience in Modern Day Organizations*, the editors have produced such a review. The international slate of chapter authors consider the nature and effects of resilience at different levels of the organization, apply these considerations to specific occupations and occupational contexts and conclude by pointing to the implications of their review for individuals, organizations and researchers. The book will be a welcome addition to the library of anyone interested in fostering healthy workplaces and resilience in organizations."

E. Kevin Kelloway, *Ph.D., University Research Professor,*
Saint Mary's University, Halifax, NS, Canada

"Fotinatos-Ventouratos, Sir Cary Cooper, and Antoniou have edited a valuable volume on resilience in modern organizations. The post-COVID work world demands the scientific, professional, and applied information offered by these leading global scholars. This volume is essential reading!"

James Campbell Quick FSAScot FAPA, *Distinguished University Professor,*
Emeritus, The University of Texas at Arlington, USA Colonel,
United States Air Force (Ret.), LOM Arlington Veterans Park
Foundation Fort Worth Air Power Council

RESILIENCE IN MODERN DAY ORGANIZATIONS

This international and thought-provoking volume addresses both theoretical and conceptual issues of resilience in modern organizations, looking at areas of concern and providing suggestions for future preventative measures.

In recent years, organizations across the world have been subjected to major upheavals as several crises, including the COVID-19 pandemic, the World Economic Crisis, and the Migratory Crisis, have contributed to the changing landscape of work. Individuals, organizations, and societies have been forced to re-think, re-adjust, and re-align in the face of adversity. The "survivors" of such upheavals are those who come to grips with the new realities of our times and encompass resilience in its entirety. This timely collection assesses resilience on critically important variables, such as socio-economic status, occupational type, and gender differences, and highlights preventative measures that organizations and individuals should take to maximise wellbeing and adjustment in these ever-changing and challenging times.

Essential reading for students, scholars, practitioners, and policy makers, this volume sheds light on the multi-faceted ways to enhance the resilience paradigm and offers insights into implications for future research in the area.

Ritsa S. J. Fotinatos-Ventouratos is a Professor of Psychology at Deree College, The American College of Greece, where she has been lecturing for over 20 years. She obtained her Doctorate Degree in Organizational Psychology from UMIST (University of Manchester Institute of Science & Technology), UK. Her areas of research lie in the field of psychological wellbeing at work, occupational stress, gender differences, as well as investigating the social impact on the changing and diverse nature of the world of work.

Sir Cary L. Cooper is the 50th Anniversary Professor of Organizational Psychology and Health at the Alliance Manchester Business School, University of Manchester. He is a founding President of the British Academy of Management, Immediate Past President of the Chartered Institute of Personnel and Development (CIPD), former President of RELATE, President of the Institute of Welfare, and Chair of the National Forum for Health and Wellbeing at Work (comprised of 50 global employers).

Alexander-Stamatios G. Antoniou is Professor of Psychology at the National and Kapodistrian University of Athens/Greece and director of the Social and Organisational Psychology Lab. He holds undergraduate and postgraduate degrees and three PhDs in Psychology, Philosophy, and Management from universities in Greece and in the UK (The University of Manchester and UMIST). He is the director of two academic series and editor/co-editor with distinguished scholars of 22 edited books. His main research interests include work well-being, business ethics, moral leadership, and vulnerable groups at work.

Current Issues in Work and Organizational Psychology

Series Editor: Cary L. Cooper

Current Issues in Work and Organizational Psychology is a series of edited books that reflect the state-of-the-art areas of current and emerging interest in the psychological study of employees, workplaces and organizations.

Each volume is tightly focused on a particular topic and consists of seven to ten chapters contributed by international experts. The editors of individual volumes are leading figures in their areas and provide an introductory overview.

Example topics include: digital media at work, work and the family, workaholism, modern job design, positive occupational health and individualised deals.

Towards Inclusive Organizations: Determinants of successful diversity management at work
Edited by Sabine Otten, Karen Van Der Zee, and Marilynn Brewer

Burnout at Work: A Psychological Perspective
Edited by Michael P. Leiter, Arnold B. Bakker, and Christina Maslach

New Frontiers in Work and Family Research
Edited by Joseph G. Grzywacz and Evangelia Demerouti

The Psychology of Digital Media at Work
Edited by Daantje Derks and Arnold B. Bakker

A Day in the Life of a Happy Worker
Edited by Arnold B. Bakker and Kevin Daniels

For more information about this series, please visit: https://www.routledge.com/ Current-Issues-in-Work-and-Organizational-Psychology/book-series/CURRENTISSUES

RESILIENCE IN MODERN DAY ORGANIZATIONS

*Edited by Ritsa S. J. Fotinatos-Ventouratos,
Cary L. Cooper, and
Alexander-Stamatios G. Antoniou*

LONDON AND NEW YORK

Designed cover image: © Getty Images

First published 2024
by Routledge
4 Park Square, Milton Park, Abingdon, Oxon OX14 4RN

and by Routledge
605 Third Avenue, New York, NY 10158

Routledge is an imprint of the Taylor & Francis Group, an informa business

British Library Cataloguing-in-Publication Data
A catalogue record for this book is available from the British Library

Library of Congress Cataloging-in-Publication Data
Names: Fotinatos-Ventouratos, Ritsa, editor. | Cooper, Cary L., editor. |
Antoniou, Alexander-Stamatios G., editor.
Title: Resilience in modern day organizations /
edited by Ritsa S.J. Fotinatos-Ventouratos, Cary L. Cooper,
and Alexander-Stamatios G. Antoniou.
Description: Abingdon, Oxon ; New York, NY : Routledge, 2024. |
Series: Current issues in work and organizational psychology |
Includes bibliographical references and index.
Identifiers: LCCN 2023016199 (print) | LCCN 2023016200 (ebook) |
ISBN 9781032263441 (hardback) | ISBN 9781032258041 (paperback) |
ISBN 9781003287858 (ebook)
Subjects: LCSH: Organizational resilience. | Organizational effectiveness. |
Organizational change.
Classification: LCC HD58.9 .R468 2024 (print) | LCC HD58.9 (ebook) |
DDC 658.4/06--dc23/eng/20230407
LC record available at https://lccn.loc.gov/2023016199
LC ebook record available at https://lccn.loc.gov/2023016200

ISBN: 978-1-032-26344-1 (hbk)
ISBN: 978-1-032-25804-1 (pbk)
ISBN: 978-1-003-28785-8 (ebk)

DOI: 10.4324/9781003287858

Typeset in Times New Roman
by KnowledgeWorks Global Ltd.

Ritsa S. J. Fotinatos-Ventouratos

I would like to dedicate this book to my cherished family—my husband and children—who have given me the immense love, support, and encouragement to keep writing—thereby turning this book into a reality.

My dedication also goes in loving memory of my dear wonderful mum, whom I lost during the COVID era, and who was not able to see the completion of this volume. She would have been extremely happy and proud.

Alexander-Stamatios G. Antoniou

To the memory of my beloved father... I miss you dad...

Cary L. Cooper

I would like to dedicate this book to all my former and present Ph.D. students for keeping me up-to-date and energised!

CONTENTS

PART III
**Enhancing the resilience paradigm: Scientific
implications for future research** **213**

CONTRIBUTORS

Virginia-Eirini Angelou, National and Kapodistrian University of Athens, Greece.

Alexander-Stamatios G. Antoniou, National and Kapodistrian University of Athens, Greece.

Felicity R. L. Baker, Clinical Psychologist and Founder of Ultimate Resilience, UK.

Kevin L. Baker, Clinical Psychologist, Nottinghamshire Healthcare NHS Trust, UK.

Nick Banerjee, Rice University, USA.

Sakshi Bansal, Senior Consultant at ARUP in London, and Founder of Project LEAP, UK.

Tammy Beck, University of Nebraska-Lincoln, USA.

Jo Burrell, Clinical Psychologist and Founder of Ultimate Resilience, UK.

Andrew James Clements, Aston University, UK.

Cary L. Cooper, Manchester Business School, University of Manchester, UK.

Ingrid K. Covington, Chartered Psychologist (CPsychol, HCPC) and Founder of Staying Well Together, Belgium.

Thomas A. de Vries, University of Groningen, The Netherlands.

Nikos Drosos, European University Cyprus, Cyprus.

Ida Du, Rice University, USA.

Vicki Elsey, Northumbria University, UK.

Denis Fischbacher-Smith, University of Glasgow, UK.

Ritsa S. J. Fotinatos-Ventouratos, The American College of Greece, Greece.

Louise Grant, University of Bedfordshire, UK.

Nevena Ivanovic, University of Groningen, The Netherlands.

Tisnue Jean-Baptiste, Rice University, USA.

Danielle King, Rice University, USA.

Gail Kinman, Birkbeck University, UK.

Cynthia Lengnick-Hall, The University of Texas at San Antonio, USA.

Wika Malkowska, Northumbria University, UK.

Evangelia Markopoulou, National and Kapodistrian University of Athens, Greece.

D. M. Pestonjee, Pandit Deendayal Petroleum University, India.

Radhika Thanki, Pandit Deendayal Petroleum University, India.

Gerben S. van der Vegt, University of Groningen, The Netherlands.

Kate van Heugten, University of Canterbury, New Zealand.

Haley Myers Woznyj, Longwood University, USA.

AUTHOR BIOGRAPHIES

Professor Ritsa S. J. Fotinatos-Ventouratos obtained her Doctorate Degree in Organizational Psychology from UMIST (University of Manchester Institute of Science & Technology), UK, under the supervision of Professor Sir Cary L. Cooper. Her areas of research lie in the field of psychological wellbeing at work, occupational stress, gender differences, as well as investigating the social impact on the changing and diverse nature of the world of work. As a professor employed at Deree College, The American College of Greece, she has been lecturing at this university for over 20 years in the areas of Industrial-Organizational Psychology, Social Psychology, and Stress and Wellbeing domains. In addition to presenting her research at international conferences and congresses, she is also a member of the British Psychology Society and has chaired the International Relations Committee for the Division of Occupational Psychology, UK. She has published extensively in the domain of Organizational Psychology, focusing primarily on issues related to stress and wellbeing. Her international contributing works include the book, co-authored with Professor Sir Cary Cooper, entitled *The Economic Crisis and Occupational Stress*, as well as a contributing book chapter entitled "The Psychological and Social Implications of the Gender Wage Gap." In 2021, Professor Fotinatos-Ventouratos wrote a further contributing book chapter entitled "The Causes and Consequences of Organizational Stress: The Case of Greece" in the edited book *Organizational Stress Around the World*. Professor Fotinatos-Ventouratos frequently serves as a scientific reviewer for European and International conferences and is currently a member of the Scientific Committee for the European Congress of Psychology. Professor Fotinatos-Ventouratos is also an appointed Editor for the *International Journal of Stress Management*, an American Psychological Association (APA) journal, and the official journal of the International Stress Management Association.

Cary L. Cooper is the 50th Anniversary Professor of Organizational Psychology and Health at the Alliance Manchester Business School, University of Manchester. He is a founding President of the British Academy of Management, Immediate Past President of the Chartered Institute of Personnel and Development (CIPD), former President of RELATE, President of the Institute of Welfare, and Chair of the National Forum for Health and Wellbeing at Work (comprised of 50 global employers). He was the Founding Editor of the *Journal of Organizational Behavior*, former Editor of the scholarly journal *Stress and Health*, and is the Editor-in-Chief of the Wiley-Blackwell *Encyclopaedia of Management*, now in its 3rd edition. He has been an advisor to the World Health Organization, ILO, and the EU in the field of occupational health and wellbeing, was Chair of the Global Agenda Council on Chronic Disease of the World Economic Forum (2009–2010) (then served for 5 years on the Global Agenda Council for mental health of the WEF), and was Chair of the Academy of Social Sciences 2009–2015. He was Chair of the Sunningdale Institute in the Cabinet Office and National School of Government 2005–2010. Professor Cooper is currently the Chair of the National Forum for Health & Wellbeing at Work (comprised of 40 global companies, e.g., BP, Microsoft, NHS Executive, UK government [wellbeing lead], Rolls Royce, John Lewis Partnership, etc.). Professor Cooper is the author/editor of over 250 books in the field of occupational health psychology, workplace wellbeing, women at work, and occupational stress. He was awarded the CBE by the Queen for his contributions to occupational health; and in 2014, he was awarded a Knighthood for his contribution to the social sciences.

Alexander-Stamatios G. Antoniou is Professor of Psychology at the National and Kapodistrian University of Athens (NKUA), Greece, and holds undergraduate and postgraduate degrees in Psychology, Philosophy, Education, and Management from universities in Greece and in the UK (The University of Manchester & UMIST). He teaches Social Psychology, Organisational and Work Psychology, Psychology of Personality and Individual Differences-Psychometrics, and Mental Health of Children and Adolescents. Professor Antoniou has taught in a number of undergraduate and postgraduate programmes, including at the School of Medicine, the School of Philosophy and the Department of Psychology (NKUA), the National School of Public Health, the Panteion University of Social and Political Sciences. Apart from undergraduate and postgraduate students, he has taught hospital doctors, nursing staff, psychologists, teachers, and staff of Ministry of Health and Welfare on areas of health promotion, work-related aspects of personality, stress and time management, interpersonal relationships, professional burnout, and special education. Professor Antoniou has received a number of awards and scholarships and he is a member of many scientific associations. He has participated as national coordinator and researcher in many national and European research programmes (e.g., OSHA, EQUAL, PSYCHARGOS). His professional experience also includes being a director of the organization "Epanodos" of the Ministry of Justice, scientific advisor at the National Committee of Greek Radio-Television, and coordinator of the Division of Organisational Psychology of the Hellenic Psychological Society. Professor Antoniou has served as director/member of many scientific and administrative committees of the NKUA, Ministry of Education, and other organizations. He has served as a human resource consultant for public and private organizations and delivered seminars to personnel on professional wellbeing, occupational health, communication at work, and leadership. He has presented his work at more than 300 national and international conferences and he is the author of 8 books and more than 100 research papers in peer reviewed journals and 150 chapters in edited books. He has translated 40 books into Greek in the fields of psychology, education, and philosophy. He is director of 2 academic series and editor/co-editor of 22 edited books (10 Greek and 12 international editions) with distinguished scholars such as Sir C. Cooper, C. Spielberger, H. Eysenck, R. Burke, B. Kirkcaldy, and C. Gatrell (with more than 330 academics and researchers as contributors). His main research interests include occupational stress and professional burnout, moral leadership, work values, organizational politics, communication networks, and special educational needs.

ACKNOWLEDGEMENT

Professor Ritsa S. J. Fotinatos-Ventouratos would like to say a big Thank You, with immense gratitude and appreciation, to my co-editor Professor Sir Cary. L. Cooper. Spanning over 30 years of knowing each other, he has been my Professor and Supervisor of my doctorate degree, teaching me the "ropes" and expertise of our field and, at the same time, he has been my mentor in academia. Thank you for your words of wisdom, scientific advice, and dear friendship. You have been my inspiration to continue in the scientific field.

INTRODUCTION

Resilience in Modern Day Organizations

Ritsa S. J. Fotinatos-Ventouratos, Cary. L. Cooper, and Alexander-Stamatios G. Antoniou

The thematic topic of resilience has been studied for many consecutive years and by numerous scientists across the globe (see, for example, Baker et al., 2021; Crane, 2017; Robertson et al., 2015). Indeed, it is a construct that not only has been studied by a variety of scholars, spanning many professional fields, but also with a multi-faceted variety of meanings depending on the context and content under investigation. In fact, Meredith et al. (2011) reviewed the broad literature on resilience and noted that prior researchers had offered 104 definitions of the construct. However, what has generally been agreed upon is that the term "resilience" per se is considered a positive construct and is often described in the literature as "the ability to bounce back in times of adversity" (Garcia-Dia et al., 2013 cited in Rees et al., 2015). Simultaneously, it is widely acknowledged to be a complex, dynamic and multi-dimensional phenomenon (Armaou & Antoniou, 2015a; Waugh & Koster, 2014 cited in Rees et al., 2015). Further, and on closer examination, a historical trace indicates that the word was introduced into the English language in the early 17th century from the Latin verb "resilire" meaning to "rebound" or "recoil" (Concise Oxford Dictionary, Tenth Edition, 1999).

Despite this current plethora of literature aiming to grapple with an understanding of the construct itself, the "psychology" of resilience has also generated scientific support, with the APA (2016) suggesting that resilience refers to the ability to adapt to stress and adversity. Moreover, the scientific topic of resilience has rendered itself of pivotal importance amongst organizational psychologists and on a global scale. Perhaps one may suggest that this scrutiny could not have come at a more crucial time, given the current turbulent eras that citizens and employees have witnessed; first as a consequence of the world economic crisis (Fotinatos-Ventouratos & Cooper, 2015), and subsequently due to the effects of the COVID-19 pandemic (Fotinatos-Ventouratos & Clements, 2022). Thus, one may propose that

DOI: 10.4324/9781003287858-1

the issue of resilience has become almost a necessity to research and evaluate given the many embedded individual and organizational challenges to consider.

In alignment with the above introductory remarks, it is without a doubt that organizational psychologists have produced an established body of research that has until now primarily given emphasis on the *individual characteristics* that are needed to enhance resiliency in the job. For example, Kakkar (2019) commented on "how research indicates that resilient individuals can deal with stress and cope with adverse conditions, and further "that organizations with resilient employees are more likely to thrive in uncertain business environments." Similarly, and as well noted by King et al. (2016), there has been considerable support that has focused on the first wave of individual protective factors such as self-esteem, self-efficacy, and optimism, which relate to resiliency. Another example of a trait that has been associated with resilience is coping, which refers to cognitive and behavioural efforts aiming to reduce the intensity of stressful events and recover one's resources (Armaou & Antoniou, 2015b). Moreover, other positive psychosocial resources, such as hope, optimism, and meaning in life have a negative correlation with psychological distress (Drosos & Antoniou, 2016) and can play a protective role for the individual enhancing resilience. One may suggest, therefore, that this abundance of research has been valuable and has indeed shed important light on *employee–personal* factors in relation to improving resilience in the job. Such factors could be found in the way that leaders, one of the most important factors in an organizational environment, interact with employees and shape a dynamic that is valuable in increasing performance rates and handling crises (Antoniou, 2021). However, after reviewing the literature for considerable time, it became apparent to us, as Editors, that there appears to be a somewhat underrepresentation in the literature in relation to what *organizations* can, and should do, in enhancing resiliency in the business domain. Furthermore, little-to-no attention has been given regarding (the necessity of) state or/and EU-funded initiatives to mitigate the negative effects of both the recent economic crisis and the COVID-19 pandemic and foster resilience and mental health (e.g., Drosos et al., 2021).

Hence, as the Editors of this volume, we comment that there still appears to be a limited amount of scholarly work examining the *organizational factors* that may promote resilience; what appears to have been done is research focusing primarily on identifying individual personality characteristics that may predict individual resilience within the working arena. Although, to allow people to flourish in the job, and especially given our turbulent times, there is a critical need to also address the *organizational factors* and *organizational resources* that will allow people to thrive and become resilient in the world of work. Only then, when *both* sides of the coin are equally examined, and equally represented, may the total picture be formed with robustness and thoroughness.

It was at this point, that the Editors, all of whom are organizational psychologists, decided to contact scholars across the globe, to contribute to our volume on *Resilience in Modern Day Organizations.*

With the above in mind, we encourage readers to view each part of the volume as complementary. Part I of the book addresses critical theoretical, conceptual, and scientific factors of concern. Part II of the book places the resilience thematic topic under examination, by scientifically assessing both occupational and contextual issues of importance in today's world. In Part III, the authors address the scientific implications for future research, with a vision to enhancing the resilience paradigm, and revisit assumptions about resilience effects.

Taken together, and looked in a complementary yet complete format, we hope that readers will appreciate that given our turbulent individual organizational and societal challenges, resiliency is surely needed, and perhaps more so than ever. One may suggest, that after the recent world upheavals faced by citizens across the globe, we need to "move forward with resilience" and this can only be achieved successfully, if all forces join equally together in both strength and stamina for wellbeing, mental toughness, and harmony to prevail.

References

American Psychological Association. (2016). *The road to resilience.* Retrieved online from http://www.apa.org/helpcenter/road-resilince.aspx

Antoniou, A.-S. (2021). *Sigxroni igesia ke ekpaideutiko plaisio [Contemporary leadership and educational context].* Gutenberg.

Armaou, M., & Antoniou, A.-S. (2015a). Hardiness and resilience at work. In A.-S. Antoniou (Ed.), *Current perspectives in occupational health psychology* (pp. 19–35). Broken Hill.

Armaou, M., & Antoniou, A.-S. (2015b). Investigating teachers' well-being and the role of resilience. In A.-S. Antoniou & C. L. Cooper (Eds.), *Coping, personality and the workplace: Responding to psychological crisis and critical events* (pp. 177–191). Gower.

Baker, F. R. L., Baker, K. L., & Burrell, J. (2021). Introducing the skills-based model of personal resilience: Drawing on content and process factors to build resilience in the workplace. *Journal of Occupational and Organizational Psychology, 94*(2), 458–481.

Concise Oxford Dictionary (1999). (10th ed.). Oxford University Press.

Crane, M. F. (2017*). Managing for resilience: A practical guide for employee wellbeing and organizational performance.* Taylor & Francis Group.

Drosos, N., & Antoniou, A.-S. (2016). Subjective psychological well-being of the aging workforce in times of economic crisis: The case of Greece. In A.-S. Antoniou, R. J. Burke, & C. L. Cooper (Eds.), *The aging workforce handbook* (pp. 85–107). Emerald Group Publishing Limited.

Drosos, N., Theodoroulakis, M., Antoniou, A.-S., & Cernja Rajter, I. (2021). Career services in the post-COVID-19 era: A paradigm for career counseling unemployed individuals. *Journal of Employment Counseling, 58*(1), 36–48. https://doi.org/10.1002/joec.12156.

Fotinatos-Ventouratos, R. S. J., & Clements, A. (2022). *From poverty to flourishing: Covid perspective.* British Psychological Society, BPS Briefing Paper, March 2022.

Fotinatos-Ventouratos, R. S. J., & Cooper, C. L. (2015*). The economic crisis and occupational stress.* Edward Elgar Publishing.

Kakkar, S. (2019). Leader-member exchange and employee resilience: The mediating role of regulatory focus. *Management Research Review (MRR)*, *42*(9) 1062–1075. https://doi.org/10.1108/MRR-03-2018-0116

King, D. D., Newman, A., & Luthans, F. (2016). Not if, but when we need resilience in the workplace. *Journal of Organizational Behavior*, *37*, 782–786.

Meredith, S., Sherbourne, C., Gaillot, S. J., Hansall, L., Ritschard, H. V., Parker, A. M., & Wrenn, G. (2011). *Promoting psychological resilience in the U.S. military*. RAND Corporation.

Rees, C. S., Breen, L. J., & Hegney, D. (2015). Understanding individual resilience in the workplace: The international collaboration of workforce resilience model. *Frontiers in Psychology*, 6, Article 73.

Robertson, I. T., Cooper, C. L., Sarkar, M., & Curran, T. (2015). Resilience training in the workplace from 2003 to 2014: A systematic review. *Journal of Occupational and Organizational Psychology*, *88*, 533–562.

Resilience in Perspective

Theoretical, Conceptual, and Scientific Factors

PART I

1

WHAT ARE YOU THINKING?

Understanding the Cognitive Dimension of Resilience Capacity

Cynthia Lengnick-Hall, Tammy Beck, and Haley Myers Woznyj

Resilience is a system's ability to return to a renewed equilibrium and regain reliable functioning after experiencing a disruptive, often unexpected, adverse event (Bhamra et al., 2011) as well as to learn and develop new capabilities, thereby emerging stronger and better able to thrive as a result of the experience (Lengnick-Hall & Beck, 2005; Weick & Sutcliffe, 2015). Resilience is a little different at every level (individual, group, organization, or system), reflecting the particular dynamics of each grouping. Regardless of level, the concept of resilience encompasses processes, outcomes, and characteristics or capabilities.

First, the process of organizational resilience includes developing resilience capacity (cognitive, behavioural, contextual, relational capabilities, and assets) (Lengnick-Hall & Beck, 2005; Williams et al., 2017), noticing and responding effectively to serious disturbances to the system (Williams et al., 2017), developing new capabilities and resources as part of the response (Hollnagel et al., 2006; Lengnick-Hall & Beck, 2005, 2009), and attending to feedback to learn from the experience (Rudolph & Repenning, 2002). Most scholars acknowledge that resilience is a dynamic process and evolves over time (Duchek, 2020; Wildavsky, 1988). The process often begins with a recognition that developing the organization's ability to withstand relentless stressors (Gittell et al., 2006; Lengnick-Hall & Beck, 2009) and to be able to respond effectively to unexpected disaster scenarios (Sutcliffe & Vogus, 2003) requires investment and strategic action prior to the time when these capabilities are actually needed. From a process perspective, resilience begins with developing resilience capacity and is triggered when a situation or event takes place. At that point, those involved need to decide what actions to take, how to implement key capabilities and activate crucial relationships as needs arise, and how to learn from the experience.

DOI: 10.4324/9781003287858-3

Second, as an outcome, resilience is the realisation of renewed equilibrium and desirable functioning following a trigger event accompanied by the acquisition of new capabilities and revised perspectives. As we have argued in prior works, resilience as an outcome goes beyond simply bouncing back to an earlier state but encompasses renewal, learning, and a foundation for thriving in the future (Lengnick-Hall & Beck, 2005). At an individual level, resilience is often tied to hardiness (Kossek & Perrigino, 2016), and to persistence and emotional stability despite adversity (Ong et al., 2006). At a group or team level, resilience outcomes are often tied to collective accomplishment, cohesion, and mastery, as well as a self-reinforcing spiral of improvement (Stoverink et al., 2020). At an organizational level, resilience outcomes are characterised by the maintenance or restoration of high-level functioning (Williams et al., 2017) along with robust transformations that enhance established capabilities (Lengnick-Hall & Beck, 2005).

Third, as a characteristic of an individual, group, or organization, resilience focuses on the capabilities or competencies needed to withstand, and often benefit from, adversity that is both relentless and familiar or unexpected. We refer to this as resilience capacity (Lengnick-Hall & Beck, 2005). As others have pointed out, resilience capacity is the distinction between the process of *being* resilient and outcomes that demonstrate resilience (Stoverink et al., 2020). Resilience capacity is evident in the prior knowledge base and resource availability portions of process models of resilience (e.g., Duchek, 2020). That is, resilience capacity affords the organizations with the capabilities to effectively anticipate, cope with, and adapt to adverse events. Scholars of individual resilience often emphasise such personal characteristics as adaptation, emotional stability, hardiness, psychological elasticity, coping capabilities, and positive psychological and physical functioning (Bonanno et al., 2011; Kossek & Perrigino, 2016; Lester et al., 2018; Ong et al., 2006). Those examining team or group resilience often emphasise characteristics such as effective leadership, coordination, social capital, role flexibility, improvisation, and shared mental models (Alliger et al., 2015; Lester et al., 2018; Stoverink et al., 2020).

At the organizational level, we argue that resilience capacity is comprised of cognitive resilience, behavioural resilience, and contextual resilience (Lengnick-Hall & Beck, 2005). Other scholars have added attributes that govern system dynamics (Williams et al., 2017) and financial resources (Bradley et al., 2011) to the mix. Resilience capacity encompasses the cognitive, behavioural, and contextual capabilities that enable members to individually and collectively recognise, acknowledge, and effectively interpret or understand an adverse situation, figure out how to respond in a way that meets or resolves the immediate challenge, act to implement the response, and enables the individual or system to thrive in the future. While resilience capacity includes several individual and collective capabilities (Lengnick-Hall & Beck, 2005; Sutcliffe & Vogus, 2003; Williams et al., 2017), in this chapter, we focus on cognitive resilience and emphasise the collective level of analysis.

Understanding cognitive resilience

Cognitive resilience is defined as a conceptual orientation and set of capabilities that enables an individual, group, team, or organization to quickly notice and make sense of disruptive events and to use their knowledge and insights to formulate and select responses that "go beyond simply surviving an ordeal" (Lengnick-Hall & Beck, 2005, p. 750; Williams et al., 2017). We see cognitive resilience as a foundation of other elements of resilience capacity since it provides the mental platform needed to interpret events, develop effective action repertoires, communicate ideas, and engage with essential internal and external actors. Cognitive resilience enables problems to be noticed early when they can be more easily avoided or managed, and for new information to be assimilated quickly to shape the way that events are understood.

Components of cognitive resilience

While they have slightly different forms at each level, there are at least seven specific elements key to creating cognitive resilience within individuals, teams/groups, and organizations. These crucial components include (1) realistic wisdom, (2) constructive sensemaking, (3) learned confidence, (4) an entrepreneurial or problem-solving orientation, (5) virtual role systems, (6) a clear and robust ideological identity, and (7) an ability to both absorb and reduce complexity (Lengnick-Hall & Beck, 2005, 2009).

Realistic wisdom

Resilience requires a firm grounding in reality. Weick (1993) defines wisdom as blending confidence, caution, and expertise in a way that yields understanding and diagnosis as well as curiosity and a search for new information. Resilience suffers from either excessive caution or excessive confidence. Minimal knowledge leads to oversimplification, whereas learning more encourages an awareness of nuances, complexities, and unanswered questions. However, too much information can be overwhelming and make it more challenging to separate key insights from background noise. Wisdom is a recognition that situations are unique, and even very subtle differences can lead to powerful variations in relationships, consequences, and actions. Resilience often relies on effective but unconventional solutions that are neither reckless nor timid. A firm grasp on reality helps weed out infeasible paths. Questioning assumptions helps to create innovative options.

Constructive sensemaking

Resilience requires insight and understanding of novel and complicated, dynamic, situations. Thomas et al. (1993) describe constructive sensemaking as "the reciprocal interaction of information seeking, meaning ascription, and action" (p. 240). Sense-making has both individual and social dimensions (Weick, 1995). Since resilience is a response to unexpected and often unfamiliar events, understanding and inter-preting these events stretches the normal repertoire of individuals and organiza-tions. Sensemaking is particularly constructive when it provides sufficient certainty to accomplish immediate objectives and cope with an emergency, while preserving longer-term flexibility to act based on new insights and opportunities (Lengnick-Hall & Beck, 2005). At the individual level, constructive sensemaking comes from an empowering world view (Aitken, 1999), an enactment orientation (Weick, 1988), and a tolerance for uncertainty (Mallak, 1998). At a collective level, constructive sensemaking is tied to scanning and interpretation skills (Thomas et al., 1993), pur-pose and vision (Collins & Porras, 1994), and the ability to effectively frame, label, and communicate information, situations, and decisions (Dutton et al., 1983).

Learned confidence

Resilience often requires bold action. Learned confidence is a comprehensive as-sessment of ability based on demonstrated mastery and experience in successfully dealing with certain types of situations (Gist & Mitchell, 1992). Efficacy enables action and mobilises individuals to make decisions and assign resources (Bandura, 1988). As Gist and Mitchell (1992) point out, this can have a strong influence on behavioural choices including effort, persistence, and goal selection, which, in turn, influences performance. Since resilience often requires unconventional or innova-tive responses, learned confidence contributes to the calculated risk-taking needed for effective choices and actions. Confidence cannot be learned in a vacuum. It requires attempts to achieve goals that may be out of reach and, as is shown in the hardiness literature (e.g., Maddi, 1987), when dealing with adverse situations too many buffers or too much slack diminishes the opportunity to develop confidence.

Problem-solving orientation

Resilience requires making difficult choices. A problem-solving orientation entails taking initiative as well as taking responsibility for the results of actions that are pursued and those that are not instigated. This cognitive frame is tied to steward-ship (Davis et al., 1997), double-loop learning (Argyris, 1976) and entrepreneur-ship (Williams et al., 2017). A problem-solving, entrepreneurial orientation helps create a balance between collaboration and independence and between inquiry and commitment. Ambidexterity like this has been shown to be important for organi-zational success and an ability to navigate challenging situations (Birkinshaw & Gupta, 2013). As Kahneman (2011) points out, it is easy to get trapped in thinking more about potential losses than recognising the possible costs of foregoing poten-tial gains. This imbalanced orientation undermines problem-solving and entrepre-neurial efforts.

Robust ideological identity

Resilience relies on a clear sense of mission and core values (Freeman et al., 2003). A strong ideological identity provides a basis for making difficult choices in uncertain circumstances (Collins & Porras, 1994). Identity helps to motivate individuals to act, assists in developing deep social capital, and encourages viewing situations more opportunistically despite adverse conditions. Moreover, a strong identity can ignite exceptional psychological resources and attract help from untapped sources (Freeman et al., 2003). In many ways, a clear value-driven identity enables individuals, teams, and organizations to find meaning in unprecedented situations as well as the courage to take necessary actions.

Knowing when to absorb complexity and when to reduce it

Resilience is complicated and requires skill at both reducing and absorbing complexity (Boisot & Child, 1999). It also requires the cognitive ability to determine which is the correct course of action. At times, such as when a disruption is temporary and a new equilibrium is on the horizon, the most effective route may be to reduce complexity and attempt to re-establish fit (Chakravarthy, 1982; Lengnick-Hall & Beck, 2005). In other situations when a disruption appears to be evolving and turbulent, actions to absorb complexity and develop new paths and skills are most effective (Lengnick-Hall & Beck, 2005). Cognitive resilience encompasses the ability to diagnose the situation and make an appropriate choice rather than relying on habit or succumbing to threat rigidity or escalation of commitment behaviours.

Virtual role systems

Resilience requires an ability to make choices even if all the relevant decision makers cannot be gathered to make sense of the situation and decide how to proceed. Weick (1993) recommends the social construction of a virtual role system that enables individuals to fill in the missing perspectives in their own minds. This is a cognitive skill that requires a deep understanding of individual roles and relationships and a comprehensive knowledge of organizational activities. Virtual role systems require comprehensive social capital and clear knowledge of organizational roles. They also require an ability to anticipate and share perspectives from diverse vantage points.

In summary, cognitive resilience provides the conceptual skills and orientation that enables those dealing with adverse circumstances to anticipate events, notice important features quickly, interpret conditions accurately, analyse thoroughly and realistically, and devise responses that go beyond simply coping with an ordeal. Next, we discuss how cognitive resilience is related to other elements of resilience capacity.

The role of cognitive resilience in the capacity for resilience

Overall, cognitive resilience enables and shapes behavioural and contextual resilience—the other two dimensions of resilience capacity (Lengnick-Hall & Beck, 2005). Behavioural resilience captures a type of resourcefulness where organizations gain further insight about the problem and use established routines and resources, as well as develop new ones, to effectively respond to events (Lengnick-Hall et al., 2011). Further, contextual resilience consists of interpersonal connections and resources that allow quick responses to surprising and disruptive events (Lengnick-Hall et al., 2011). Cognitive resilience provides the basis for determining what behaviours are needed to be resilient and how to interact with those within and beyond the immediate system. Achieving resilience is challenging and requires deliberate, thoughtful, insightful analysis and response.

Cognitive resilience is the foundation for crafting, selecting, and activating desired behaviours, resource allocations (aspects of behavioural resilience), and relationships (important for contextual resilience). As Weick et al. (2005) explain, sensemaking and related cognitive resilience components organize flux, notice and bracket experiences, create stabilising categorisations, help articulate assumptions, provide a basis for social interactions, and focus attention on action. Weick's (1988) term for this concept is enactment. Enactment is the idea that people create the parameters of many of the circumstances they encounter as a consequence of the assumptions and organizing structures they develop. Disruption and adversity are by their very nature ambiguous, often encompassing contradictory, equivocal, and unfamiliar forces. Enactment enables individuals and organizations to make sense of what is happening so they are able to act. Cognitive resilience provides the tools needed to do this effectively.

Cognitive resilience promotes robust transformation, which means that an organization can capitalise on environmental change in ways that foster new capabilities and options (Lengnick-Hall & Beck, 2005). In other words, this approach sees uncertainty as a mechanism that can enable future viability (Sutcliffe & Vogus, 2003). Cognitive resilience encourages ingenuity and a search for inventiveness and new opportunities, resists the temptation to emphasise control and invoke standard responses, and promotes resourcefulness (i.e., behavioural resilience). Further, cognitive resilience increases the range of viable, diverse routines that an individual or collective system can consider for dealing with complexity, uncertainty, and adversity. It improves the likelihood for preventing small challenges from becoming big disasters (Williams et al., 2017). It increases the potential for accurately diagnosing and understanding unfamiliar events and circumstances. Cognitive resilience facilitates absorptive capacity and information assimilation (Cohen & Levinthal, 1990). It encourages logical and firm-specific options for action (Weick & Sutcliffe, 2006). And as we discuss in a subsequent section, cognitive resilience provides the language and communication patterns that promote system level resilience.

Moving from individual to collective cognitive resilience

It is important to recognise that resilience at one level does not necessarily mean resilience at another level (Alliger et al., 2015). Not only does each level reflect unique attributes, dynamics, and interactions common to that system level, the ways in which individual attributes emerge into collective capabilities also matters. For example, in their study of how dual-earner couples made sense of and responded to work-life shock events, Crawford et al. (2019) explain how each partner's sense-making shapes couple-level sensemaking, which thereby shapes both individual and couple-level investments and behaviour. In this section, we discuss three aspects of creating collective cognitive resilience: (1) generating shared knowledge and understanding from a knowledge management perspective, (2) consequences of composition versus compilation processes for creating collective cognitive resilience, and (3) implications of equifinality.

Cognitive resilience as knowledge-in-practice

Knowledge-in-practice (KIP) is the information and know-how involved in the sequences, routines, capabilities, and activity systems for conducting work in organizations (McIver et al., 2013). Collective cognitive resilience is the shared information and know-how needed to do the work of noticing, making sense of, and deciding how to respond to adverse situations. Resilience work requires different kinds of tasks and routines and, therefore, variety in the types of KIP required. McIver et al. (2013) describe four distinct kinds of KIP that vary in terms of the extent to which the requisite knowledge is easily learned and the extent of tacit knowledge involved. *Enacted information* has a low level of tacitness and can be easily learned. Ideological identity is typically this type of KIP. *Accumulated information* KIP also has relatively low tacitness but can be quite difficult or time-consuming to learn. Tools for developing a problem-solving or entrepreneurial orientation, analysis techniques for deciding whether to reduce or absorb complexity, and virtual role systems are typically accumulated information KIP. *Apprenticed know-how* KIP has a high level of tacitness but remains relatively straightforward to learn as long as sufficient time and effort is applied. Apprenticed know-how is following routines and learning-by-doing so learned confidence is largely apprenticed know-how KIP. Finally, *talent and intuitive know-how* is KIP that has a high tacit component and can be very difficult to learn. While elements of realistic wisdom and constructive sensemaking can be learned in other quadrants, the integrated capabilities often fall into the intuitive know-how category.

The distribution of cognitive resilience components across the spectrum of KIP suggests several implications. First, since tacit knowledge is most easily learned through experience, providing opportunities for individuals throughout the organization to practice their sensemaking skills and making wise decisions under the apprenticeship of those who already possess the tacit knowledge needed can expand these capabilities across the organization. Further, articulating assumptions and contingencies to ensure these are widely known and understood can help develop collective cognitive resilience. Second, designing opportunities for individuals and teams to develop and hone their problem-solving skills and their judgements regarding how to manage complexity can enhance those aspects of cognitive resilience across the organization. Information storage and dissemination, routines, templates, and procedures can lead to collective expertise in these areas. Third, collective cognitive resilience can be enhanced by designing ways to leverage those in the organization who have the requisite tacit knowledge by developing routines for gathering and disseminating information these individuals can use to develop insight and judgements. Data that is unambiguous and evidence-based decisions can be codified and disseminated fairly broadly, but tacit information sharing requires interaction and experience. Designing a menu of knowledge management tools and techniques that accommodates the full spectrum of knowledge types needed to attain cognitive resilience is a crucial investment in preparedness.

Processes for generating collective cognitive resilience

Moving from individual to collective cognitive resilience is a process of knowledge and practice integration. Kozlowski and Klein (2000) propose two distinct integration mechanisms: composition and compilation. The most important distinction between these two processes is whether individual differences are amplified or diminished during the aggregation process. With composition integration processes individual contributions are primarily isomorphic and collective understanding is generally additive and linear. Composition processes use repetition and replication to reinforce consistency. Organizations with strong institutionalised communication structures and organizational routines typically rely on composition to move from individual to collective capabilities. Composition integration activities are particularly well suited for developing a robust ideological identity and sharing the information needed to construct virtual role systems.

Compilation integration processes are emergent, non-linear, and highlight individual differences. Specifically, they suggest that unique individual contributions combine in a complex, configurational manner that results in wide variations but also encourages reconsideration of assumptions and engaging in double-loop learning (Carlile, 2004). Compilation processes encourage innovation and resourcefulness. Creating collective resilience capabilities through compilation processes reflects the idea that integrating complementary but diverse ideas, perspectives, knowledge, and skills yields the most effective results. Rather than relying on institutionalised norms and established routines, compilation integration efforts typically depend on leadership, self-management mechanisms, and social capital to take place. Compilation integration processes are typically beneficial to efforts to develop collective problem-solving and entrepreneurial competencies, to determine how to manage complexity, and to cultivate realistic wisdom.

What this suggests is that collective cognitive resilience capacity requires both composition and compilation integration processes over time and across issues. Different types of routines need to be developed and organizational members need to develop expertise and understanding of which forms of integration are appropriate to achieve the various desired outcomes.

Equifinality

Resilience is firm-specific. The cognitive attributes and talents that are essential for one organization, may not be relevant in another firm with a very different set of goals, culture, or strategic capabilities. As noted, context matters so the specific conditions, speed, and patterns of disruption also influence what factors are most crucial for effective cognitive resilience. Equifinality also means that there is more than one viable route to establishing resilience. Different blends of cognitive, behavioural, and contextual factors can be successful. The interactions across these capability sets also influence the particular dimensions and competencies that are needed.

Multi-level communication mechanisms for developing cognitive resilience

Improved understanding of the process by which resilience develops in organizations continues as a central question for managers and researchers alike (Van der Vegt et al., 2015; Williams et al., 2017). Since the operational reality for many organizations includes facing challenges and adversity, response options that build and leverage resilience are becoming more important for sustainability. Questions remain, however, regarding *how* organizational leaders proceed to first build resilience capacity in themselves and others and then to take advantage of the resource when conditions demand (Williams et al., 2017). How do leaders hone their cognitive capabilities in diagnosing unexpected and unusual events? What processes allow leaders to build their sensemaking skills or problem-solving ingenuity and then ensure similar capability development across all levels of the organization, thereby promoting greater organizational resilience? What are the ingredients that enable collective cognitive resilience? We focus our attention on one useful mechanism by which organizations and its members can build a capacity for cognitive resilience—that is, through the use of communication. We consider the role of communication in fostering cognitive resilience at the individual level initially, and then through multi-level emergent processes whereby individual attributes become manifest as a collective phenomenon (Ployhart & Moliterno, 2011), ultimately transforming into a collective capability.

Communication is a cornerstone of collective cognitive resilience. Buzzanell (2010, 2018) and Long et al. (2015) argue that resilience can be developed, nurtured, maintained, and constituted through discourse, communication, narratives, and interactions. Further, Baran and Woznyj (2020) found that slow, siloed, or non-existent communication are prime obstacles to an organization's ability to quickly respond to events. This perspective suggests that resilience is not merely something that individuals characteristically possess, but that it develops through a process built on a foundation of interpersonal communication. Resilience is therefore emergent, and according to this communication theory approach, resilience can be talked into being (Buzzanell, 2010). Consistent with other views of resilience noted earlier, a communicative resilience process begins subsequent to a trigger or adverse event, which sets in motion attempts to make sense of the situation. However, this perspective relies on communication to build and leverage the cognitive structures needed to effectively withstand the challenge. According to Buzzanell (2010, 2018) and Long et al. (2015), five communicative processes promote resilience development: (1) crafting normalcy, (2) affirming identity anchors, (3) maintaining and using communication networks, (4) putting alternative logics to work, and (5) legitimising negative feelings while foregrounding productive action. We describe each of these communicative processes briefly and then suggest how each process is linked to the components of cognitive resilience discussed in a prior section of this chapter.

Crafting normalcy

The words that organizational members use to describe their circumstances following an adverse event contribute to their interpretation of the event and associated conditions; that is, members can use language to talk normalcy into being (Buzzanell, 2010). We create the new normal by saying it is so. The resulting new normal is shaped by the discourse shared between those impacted by adversity as they discuss the parameters of the event, the impact of the event, and the operational changes (if any) made subsequent to the event. Bottom-up communication can help craft normalcy (Brykman & King, 2021). Specifically, when leaders create a voice climate, or an environment where employees are encouraged to share knowledge, concerns, and ideas and feel comfortable doing so, it can create alignment among the team and organization (Baran & Woznyj, 2020; Brykman & King, 2021). In this process, when members make statements like "that wasn't so bad" or "we are better off because of the challenge we faced," it allows for cognitive processing and interpretation to take place where conditions are viewed as manageable, and members exude a confidence in their ability to move forward productively. Leaders can even use language to coach others in the organization to respond to challenges by talking about opportunity maximisation even when losses are likely (Solansky et al., 2014). Doing this creates a new normal where potential gains receive more attention than potential losses, and members are not paralysed by the fear of failure. Creating a new normal through communication provides an ongoing construction of the future; that is, a post-adversity vision of possible futures (Buzzanell, 2018).

Actively crafting normalcy contributes to several dimensions of cognitive resilience. First it emphasises *constructive*, rather than intimidating, sensemaking in that it focuses on actionable interpretations. Second, crafting normalcy enables individuals and groups to believe they have the understanding and the ability needed to effectively deal with the situation at hand. In this way, crafting normalcy contributes to problem-solving and entrepreneurial activities. Third, crafting normalcy puts situations and responses into a perspective that can be more easily accepted. This enables new information to be assimilated more readily since it is not perceived as a great threat. The resulting reassurance that individuals and groups can move forward on a productive and beneficial trajectory contributes to developing learned confidence.

Affirming identity anchors

Organizational discourses that members use to explain "who we are" and "what we do" as individuals or as a collective help to serve as anchors during times of adversity. Members can return to the enduring, stable identity phrases when the environment around them is less certain and perhaps shifting. For organizations, such discourse can include a refocus and articulation of the firm's mission, its values, primary objectives, and/or brand. Strong leadership will be important in this endeavour because top management can communicate the mission, role model its values, and otherwise provide clear direction to employees (Baran & Woznyj, 2020). These anchors that reiterate who we are and what we do can serve to foster resilience in adverse times by engendering renewal (Buzzanell, 2010), attracting support from external others, or perhaps by suppressing internal resistors (Long et al., 2015). When the owners at Malden Mills responded publicly to a devastating fire that destroyed their plant, they announced their commitment to rebuild and pay displaced workers (Seeger & Ulmer, 2002). These welcome messages resonated well with employees, not just for the needed financial security, but because they were consistent with the previous company messaged values that identified employees as "the company's most valuable assets" (p. 131). Such identity anchors form the clear and robust ideological identity needed for cognitive resilience, and in this case, served to motivate employees to remain committed to the organization despite the uncertain future.

As discussed, a robust ideological identity is a key ingredient in cognitive resilience capacity. Reinforcing identity anchors by reaffirming values, beliefs, priorities, and guiding principles enables organizational members to confront brutal facts and depart from comfortable routines that may be inconsistent with the current and future reality (Collins, 2001). A strong identity not only helps determine when to reduce complexity by striving for fit and when to absorb complexity by embracing divergent forces and searching for a novel path forward. A robust ideological identity also aids in developing virtual role systems by grounding relationships in ways that highlight organizational priorities.

Maintaining and using communication networks

Organizations rarely possess all the resources and capabilities needed to operate effectively under all circumstances. As such, they often find strategic value in collaborating with other organizations to gain timely access to needed resources. As indicated, contextual resilience capacity is an essential ingredient for individuals, groups, and organizations to be resilient and thrive. The complexity, uncertainty, and unprecedented challenges make collaborative relationships essential for survival (Beck & Plowman, 2014). Consistent with a process perspective on resilience, enduring types of collaboration take time to build, and investments in relationship building are needed to establish communication networks long before they are accessed. But once these connections are built, such communication networks, and the social capital embedded within the accompanying relationships, can provide resources and support during times of challenge (Buzzanell, 2010; Lengnick-Hall & Beck, 2005). The web of interrelationships found among communication network partners may provide access to financial and physical resource support (such as that found in contextual resilience), but equally important, access to needed information for sensemaking and problem-solving activities (Long et al., 2015).

Within a team, sharing knowledge, information, and ideas can facilitate decision-making (Baran & Woznyj, 2020). In addition, Brykman and King (2021) argue that information elaboration within teams is an iterative process where team members exchange, discuss, and integrate ideas and knowledge. This information exchange can enhance the capacity for resilience. External stakeholders and key communication network partners may possess new or different knowledge about the environmental conditions or may even have valuable experience in facing similar adversities. The established communication network can be accessed and leveraged to provide essential learning or shared wisdom among the network partners. In this way, an organization gains confidence in their own abilities to respond to challenges via the learning that took place by others in their communication network.

Putting alternative logics to work

Sometimes, the best option for dealing with challenging circumstances may be to reframe or relabel the situation and use language and terminology to describe the circumstances in ways that may seem to contradict reality. However, such relabelling does not necessarily mean ignoring the existing conditions, but instead choosing to use descriptive communication construction in ways that reframe the setting to allow individuals to co-exist and thrive within the adverse environment (Buzzanell, 2010). According to Weick and Sutcliffe (2001), the way that you label adverse conditions can impact the manner in which others respond, and certain language (in their case using "near miss" versus using "close call"; p. 165) provided more beneficial warning of potential system risks. The result is a reorientation that makes the event more vivid, salient, and memorable and motivates others to take action in spite of the threat. These types of communications help build realistic wisdom as well as constructive sensemaking broadly within an organization. Long et al., (2015) found that when a struggling Chinese NGO (who previously lacked legitimacy due to their organizational form) chose to relabel their organization type via self-descriptions, they were able to attract needed support from external others and suppress internal resistance that could have undermined sustainable development. In both examples, reframing and relabelling something about the circumstance or organization itself allowed for improved constructive sensemaking and learning and the realisation of subsequent investments and actions needed for survival.

Legitimising negative feelings while foregrounding productive action

Moving forward, post-adversity may require relinquishment of past feelings of self-doubt or prior resignation to defeat associated with adversity; at least temporarily. This tactic places such negative feelings in the background while energy and attention are redirected to focus instead on more positive productive action. This process of "foregrounding" (Buzzanell, 2010) allows individuals to simultaneously acknowledge the real, threatening conditions and the insecurities they provoke (realistic wisdom), while also deliberately choosing to focus on the positive potential of what may come and to use language and framing that evokes hopefulness and possibilities (learned confidence and entrepreneurial orientation). Chen and Zhang (2021) argue that behavioural integration (i.e., interactions like sharing information and collaborating) in teams results in changes in cognitions that allow for foregrounding productive action. For instance, behavioural integration can reduce resistance to change and increase a tolerance for newness. This can "lay the foundation of forming efficacious beliefs" (p. 784). When used to replace language that emphasises status quo or is crisis-centred, discourse focused on expansion, growth, and new opportunities provides a fertile environment for the type of innovative and entrepreneurial decision-making evident in cognitive resilience.

Negative emotions and feelings of loss or defeat naturally occur when individuals and organizations experience disastrous events, but such emotions can stifle goal attainment (Buzzanell, 2010). The task here is not to disregard or eliminate the feelings evoked by adversity, but instead to change the way that we talk about them, think about them, and act on them (Buzzanell, 2018). When individuals and teams contextualise their struggles through narrative depictions, they can detach themselves from the struggle and view the struggle as separate from the team. This detachment allows members to redirect cognitive processing and teamwork toward solving the shared problem at hand instead (Lawrence & Maitlis, 2012). Communication narratives based on this technique promote future-oriented thinking and empower organizational members to imagine new, possible paths forward.

In summary, a communication theory view on resilience suggests that cultivation of resilience is possible through communication that: constructively reframes adverse experiences, builds stable organizational connections, includes discursive discussion opportunities for developing contingency plans, uses interpersonal interactions to reinforce collective identities and co-create the new normal, and spans multiple levels (micro, meso, and macro). Communication is a vital mechanism for undertaking both composition and compilation integration processes. And as with other aspects of cognitive resilience capacity, selecting the best integration approach to promote the focal process is a crucial factor. For example, since diverse perspectives enhance the ability to put alternative logics to work, compilation integration processes will be most helpful for these communication processes. In contrast, composition integration processes are most likely to yield the desired affirmation of identity anchors. Overall, these five communication activities are the engine driving collective development of the seven components of cognitive resilience.

Implications for future research and theory development

As with any multidimensional construct, it is important to understand how the various components work together, whether any elements are particularly dominant, and whether cognitive components benefit from being developed sequentially or simultaneously. In addition, it will be useful to gain a better understanding of the threshold necessary to attain for each element. For example, can an organization have adequate cognitive resilience capacity when there are high degrees of realisation for some of the components with only modest achievement in others? Are some components required while others are more discretionary? How do different configurations of cognitive resilience influence the types of disruptions that can be effectively addressed? Examining the boundary conditions and variations in cognitive resilience configurations will provide useful insights for making investment choices.

Similarly, it is important to specify more precisely the influential links between the context in which resilience unfolds and cognitive resilience capacity so these connections can be managed more directly. Stated differently, we have a solid understanding of the elements that comprise cognitive resilience but do not have sufficient mastery of the specific patterns of interaction or the contextual forces that drive these relationships. One aspect of this dynamic balance that would be particularly useful to understand better relates to the tension and reciprocal interactions between emergent processes and established structures. For example, an organization's technology-in-practice, which contends that through recurrent engagement with technology, organizations can enact emergent structures as a function of organizing and action (Orlikowski, 2000), may influence cognitive resilience development in unexpected ways. Further, cognitive resilience can reshape an organization's communication practices while information and communication structures simultaneously redesign aspects of cognitive resilience.

We recognise that both institutionalised and emergent forces are in play in each direction, but only have limited understanding of the relative strength and patterns that determine various outcomes. For example, how do organizations integrate technology structures into the activities surrounding sensemaking and diagnosing unexpected and unusual events, and how does this integration strengthen subsequent iterations of the structures and systems needed to address the next occurrence of organizational adversity? Incorporating a technology-in-practice perspective (Orlikowski, 2000) into the discussion of cognitive resilience would heed the call from Williams et al. (2017) to better understand how leaders build resource endowments that promote greater resilience.

Implications for practice

Perhaps one of the most important implications for management practice is that cognitive resilience capacity takes time, effort, and investment to develop. It doesn't spring into being once a crisis has appeared. Most of the elements of cognitive resilience rely on knowledge that is complicated, challenging to learn, or tacit. Collective cognitive resilience requires both compilation and composition aggregation activities as well as extensive communication mechanisms. Understanding must not only be assimilated within an organization, it must be integrated within individual and group frameworks for understanding to provide the necessary guidance for designing organization routines and information processing tools. This suggests that firm-specific, evidence-based decision-making should be the foundation for designing an organization's cognitive resilience repertoire. Further, this suggests that organizations need to think about and invest in developing resilience capacity long before any disaster strikes. Cognitive resilience is part of a crucial safety net for organizational survival and success, but like an insurance policy, it cannot be put together after a need materialises.

A second implication for practice is based on the observation that cognitive resilience capacity relies on balancing competing perspectives and forces. As discussed, realistic wisdom is neither too cautious nor overconfident. Problem-solving is often unconventional but grounded in a realistic understanding of resources and capabilities. Often, complexity must be reduced in some areas while absorbed in others. This means that cognitive resilience capacity requires a certain degree of organizational and individual ambidexterity. This is not an easy competence to develop and honing ambidextrous skills requires clear objectives, practice, and effective leadership.

Weick (1984) introduced a small wins approach to accomplishing large scale objectives. He suggests that reframing major challenges into smaller events viewed as series of controllable opportunities limits the fear that can interfere with effective diagnosis and problem-solving and encourages a more resourceful and engaged perspective. We believe this has important lessons for managers in their efforts to achieve organizational resilience as well. A small-wins approach relies on building upon a sequence of incremental successes to facilitate learned confidence and provide new insights. Communication strategies such as crafting normalcy and engaging in a variety of communication networks can provide a context for implementing small wins initiatives.

A third recommendation for developing cognitive resilience is to avoid making organizational operations run too smoothly or set goals that are too easy to reach. While this may seem counterintuitive given the pressures on efficiency and effectiveness in many organizations, the contrast between Costa Rica and Hawaii in terms of the resilience of their respective ecosystems illustrates why this is crucial (Moore, 1996). Both countries have very similar source biology, but they developed into profoundly different ecosystems in terms of resilience capacity. Hawaiian plants and animals have evolved into exotic and fragile systems that are quite vulnerable when exposed to unfamiliar influences. The plants and animals of Costa Rica, in contrast, are vigorous and tenacious. A primary factor that accounts for this difference is that Hawaii is relatively isolated, so its biological systems are buffered from problems and predators. Costa Rica, in contrast, is a land bridge experiencing relentless threats to survival. Creating cognitive resilience capacity can help organizations become more like a causeway and less like a fragile organism.

A final recommendation to develop cognitive resilience follows Baran and Woznyj's (2020) suggestion to use both high and low technology tools to facilitate communication. Information technology serves as one tool that can support the development of cognitive resilience via the communication activities that take place in organizations. Such technology aids communication processes by serving as an efficient platform for sharing descriptions of events and their impact to operational activities (which are needed when leaders craft a new normal), distributing reminder messages about the mission and values (which are needed when affirming identity anchors), or even storing shared knowledge from network partners (which is needed when leveraging communication networks for sensemaking purposes). Information technology also facilitates setting task agendas, generating solutions, supporting interpersonal relationship development, and facilitating other group functioning. Lower-tech solutions may include drawing on best-practices to lead meetings and aspects of Scrum (such as the Daily Scrum event [Baran & Woznyj, 2020]) efficiently and effectively.

Beyond these limited instrumental functions, however, research at the intersection of technology and organizational studies suggests that information technology also contributes to structure development (e.g., organizational rules, routines, resources, procedures, and social exchange practices) through its use by those that interact with it (Orlikowski & Barley, 2001). Cognitive resilience strengthens the development of productive technologies-in-practice because as sensemaking, problem-solving, and realistic wisdom increase, the choices about which structural features of the technology to keep and which to jettison become clear.

References

Aitken, S. (1999). How Motorola promotes good health. *The Journal for Quality and Participation, 22*(1), 54–57.

Alliger, G. M., Cerasoli, C. P., Tannenbaum, S. I., & Vessey, W. B. (2015). Team resilience: How teams flourish under pressure. *Organizational Dynamics, 44*, 176–184.

Argyris, C. (1976). Single-loop and double-loop models in research on decision-making. *Administrative Science Quarterly, 21*(3), 363–375.

Bandura, A. (1988). Organizational applications of social cognitive theory. *Australian Journal of Management, 13*, 137–164.

Baran, B. E., & Woznyj, H. M. (2020). Managing VUCA: The human dynamics of agility. *Organizational Dynamics*. doi: 10.1016/j.orgdyn.2020.100787.

Beck, T. E., & Plowman, D. A. (2014). Temporary, emergent interorganizational collaboration in unexpected circumstances: A study of the *Columbia* Space Shuttle response effort. *Organization Science, 25*(4), 1234–1252.

Bhamra, R., Dani, S., & Burnard, K. (2011). Resilience: The concept, a literature review and future directions. *International Journal of Production Research, 49*(18), 5375–5393.

Birkinshaw, J., & Gupta, K. (2013). Clarifying the distinctive contribution of ambidexterity to the field of organization studies. *The Academy of Management Perspectives, 27*(4), 287–298.

Boisot, M., & Child, J. (1999). Organizations as adaptive systems in complex environments: The case of China. *Organization Science, 10*, 237–252.

Bonanno, G. A., Westphal, M., & Mancini, A. D. (2011). Resilience to loss and potential trauma. *Annual Review of Clinical Psychology, 7*, 511–535.

Bradley, S. W., Shepherd, D. A., & Wiklund, J. (2011). The importance of slack for new organizations facing 'tough' environments. *Journal of Management Studies, 48*(5), 1071–1097.

Brykman, K. M., & King, D. D. (2021). A resource model of team resilience capacity and learning. *Group & Organization Management, 46*(4), 737–772.

Buzzanell, P. M. (2010). Resilience: Talking, resisting, and imagining new normalcies into being. *Journal of Communication, 60*, 1–14.

Buzzanell, P. M. (2018). Organizing resilience as adaptive-transformational tensions. *Journal of Applied Communication Research, 46*(1), 14–18.

Carlile, P. R. (2004). Transferring, translating, and transforming: An integrative framework for managing knowledge across boundaries. *Organization Science, 15*(5), 555–568.

Chakravarthy, B. S. (1982). Adaptation: A promising metaphor for strategic management. *Academy of Management Review, 7*, 35–44.

Chen, Y., & Zhang, Y. (2021). Fostering resilience in new venture teams: The role of behavioral and affective integration. *Group & Organization Management, 46*(4), 773–816.

Cohen, & Levinthal (1990). Absorptive capacity: A new perspective on learning and innovation. *Administrative Science Quarterly, 35*(1), 128–152.

Collins, J. C., & Porras, J. I. (1994). *Built to last: Successful habits of visionary companies*. HarperBusiness.

Collins, J. C. (2001). *Good to great: Why some companies make the leap and others don't*. HarperCollins.

Crawford, W. S., Thompson, M. J., & Ashforth, B. E. (2019). Work-life events theory: Making sense of shock events in dual-earner couples. *Academy of Management Review, 44*(1), 194–212.

Davis, J. H., Schoorman, F. D., & Donaldson, L. (1997). Toward a stewardship theory of management. *Academy of Management Review*, *22*(1), 20–47.

Duchek, S. (2020). Organizational resilience: A capability-based conceptualization. *Business Research*, *13*(1), 215–246.

Dutton, J. E., Fahey, L., & Narayanan, U. K. (1983). Toward understanding strategic issue diagnosis. *Strategic Management Journal*, *4*, 307–323.

Freeman, S. F., Hirschhorn, L., & Maltz, M. (2003). Moral purpose and organizational resilience: Sandler O'Neill & Partners, L.P. in the aftermath of September 11, 2001. *Academy of Management Proceedings*, *2003*(1), B1–B6. doi: 10.5465/ambpp.2003.13792457

Gist, M. E., & Mitchell, T. R. (1992). Self-efficacy: A theoretical analysis of its determinants and malleability. *Academy of Management Review*, *17*(2), 183–211.

Gittell, J. H., Cameron, K. S., Lim, S., & Rivas, V. (2006). Relationships, layoffs, and organizational resilience. *Journal of Applied Behavioral Science*, *42*(3), 300–329.

Hollnagel, E., Woods, D., & Leveson, N. (2006). *Resilience engineering: Concepts and precepts*. Ashgate Publishing.

Kahneman, D. (2011). *Thinking fast and slow*. Farrar, Straus & Giroux.

Kossek, E. E., & Perrigino, M. B. (2016). Resilience: A review using a grounded integrated occupational approach. *Academy of Management Annals*, *10*(1), 729–797.

Kozlowski, S. W. J., & Klein, K. J. (2000). A multilevel approach to theory and research in organizations: Contextual, temporal, and emergent processes. In K. J. Klein & S. W. J. Kozlowski (Eds.), *Multilevel theory, research and methods in organizations: Foundations, extensions, and new directions* (pp. 157–210). Jossey-Bass.

Lawrence, T., & Maitlis, S. (2012). Care and possibility: Enacting an ethic of care through narrative practice. *Academy of Management Review*, *37*(4), 641–663.

Lengnick-Hall, C. A., & Beck, T. E. (2005). Adaptive fit versus robust transformation: How organizations respond to environmental change. *Journal of Management*, *31*(5), 738–757.

Lengnick-Hall, C. A., & Beck, T. E. (2009). Resilience capacity and strategic agility: Prerequisites for thriving in a dynamic environment. In C. Nemeth, E. Hollnagel, & S. Dekker (Eds.), *Preparation and restoration*. Ashgate Publishing.

Lengnick-Hall, C. A., Beck, T. E., & Lengnick-Hall, M. L. (2011). Developing a capacity for organizational resilience through strategic human resource management. *Human Resource Management Review*, *21*(3), 243–255.

Lester, P. B., Lester, G. V., & Saboe, K. N. (2018). Resilience in the workplace: Taking a cue from the U.S. Military. *Organizational Dynamics*, *47*(4), 201–208.

Long, Z., Buzzanell, P. M., Wu, M., Mitra, R., Kuang, K., & Suo, H. (2015). Global communication for organizing sustainability and resilience. *China Media Research*, *11*(4), 67–77.

Maddi, S. R. (1987). Hardiness training at Illinois bell telephone. In *Health promotion evaluation: Measuring the organizational impact* (pp. 101–115). National Wellness Association.

Mallak, L. A. (1998). Putting organizational resilience to work. *Industrial Management*, *40*(6), 8–13.

McIver, D., Lengnick-Hall, C. A., Lengnick-Hall, M. L., & Ramachandran, I. (2013). Understanding work and knowledge management from a knowledge-in-practice perspective. *Academy of Management Review*, *38*(4), 597–620.

Moore, J. F. (1996). *The death of competition*. HarperCollins.

Ong, A. D., Bergeman, C., Bisconti, T. L., & Wallace, K. A. (2006). Psychological resilience. Positive emotions, and successful adaptation to stress in later life. *Journal of Personality and Social Psychology, 91*(4), 730–749.

Orlikowski, W. J., & Barley, S. R. (2001). Technology and institutions: What can research on information technology and research on organizations learn from each other? *MIS Quarterly, 25*(2), 145–165.

Orlikowski, W. J. (2000). Using technology and constituting structures: A practice lens for studying technology in organizations. *Organization Science, 11*(4), 404–428.

Ployhart, R. E., & Moliterno, T. P. (2011). Emergence of the human capital resource: A multilevel model. *Academy of Management Review, 36*(1), 127–150.

Rudolph, J. W., & Repenning, N. P. (2002). Disaster dynamics: Understanding the role of quantity in organizational collapse. *Administrative Science Quarterly, 47*(1), 1–30.

Seeger, M., & Ulmer, R. (2002). A post-crisis discourse of renewal: The cases of Malden Mills and Cole Hardwoods. *Journal of Applied Communication Research, 30*, 126–142.

Solansky, S. T., Beck, T. E., & Travis, D. (2014). A complexity perspective of a meta-organization team: The role of destabilizing and stabilizing tensions. *Human Relations, 67*(8), 1007–1033.

Stoverink, A. C., Kirkman, B. L., Mistry, S., & Rosen, B. (2020). Bouncing back together: Toward a theoretical model of work team resilience. *Academy of Management Review, 45*(2), 395–422.

Sutcliffe, K. M., & Vogus, T. J. (2003). Organizing for resilience. In K. S. Cameron, J. E. Dutton, & R. E. Quinn (Eds.), *Positive organizational scholarship: Foundations of a new discipline* (pp. 94–110). Barrett-Koehler.

Thomas, J. B., Clark, S. M., & Gioia, D. A. (1993). Strategic sensemaking and organizational performance: Linkages among scanning, interpretation, action, and outcomes. *Academy of Management Journal, 36*(2), 239–271.

Van der Vegt, G., Essens, P., Wahlstrom, M., & George, G. (2015). Managing risk and resilience: From the editors. *Academy of Management Journal, 58*(4), 971–980.

Weick, K. E. (1984). Small wins: Redefining the scale of social problems. *American Psychologist, 39*(1), 40–49.

Weick, K. E. (1988). Enacted sensemaking in crisis situations. *Journal of Management Studies, 25*(4), 305–317.

Weick, K. E. (1993). The collapse of sensemaking in organizations: The Mann Gulch disaster. *Administrative Science Quarterly, 38*(4), 628–652.

Weick, K. E. (1995). *Sensemaking in organizations.* SAGE.

Weick, K. E., & Sutcliffe, K. M. (2001). *Managing the unexpected: Assuring high performance in an age of complexity.* Jossey-Bass.

Weick, K. E., & Sutcliffe, K. M. (2006). Mindfulness and the quality of organizational attention. *Organization Science, 17*(4), 514–524.

Weick, K. E., & Sutcliffe, K. M. (2015). *Managing the unexpected: Sustained performance in a complex world.* John Wiley & Sons.

Weick, K. E., Sutcliffe, K. M., & Obstfeld, D. (2005). Organizing and the process of sensemaking. *Organization Science, 16*(4), 409–421.

Wildavsky, A. B. (1988). *Searching for safety.* USA Transaction Books.

Williams, T. A., Gruber, D., Sutcliffe, A., Shepherd, K. M., & Zhao, A. (2017). Organizational response to adversity: Fusing crisis management and resilience research streams. *Academy of Management Annals, 11*(2), 733–769.

2

INDIVIDUAL, TEAM, AND ORGANIZATIONAL RESILIENCE[1]

A Multi-Level Dynamic Relationship

Andrew James Clements and Gail Kinman

Introduction

Interest in resilience has grown as a result of observations that some individuals appear to endure negative experiences without exhibiting detrimental outcomes (Chapman et al., 2020). Early research on resilience focused on children who had experienced adversity (Pangallo et al., 2015), but more recent work has considered other contexts, including the world of work. With rapidly changing socio-economic conditions and emerging health threats, there is growing interest in why some individuals, teams, organizations, and societies appear to be more "resilient" in coping with crises (Chapman et al., 2020; Raetze et al., 2022; Rice & Liu, 2016; Vanhove et al., 2016) or even thrive under such conditions (Amiri et al., 2021; Krishnan et al., 2022). Previous research on resilience has focused on economic and social challenges such as economic downturns (Strycharczyk & Elvin, 2014), but there is a growing recognition that the "new normal" is marked by an increasing risk of life-threatening events such as natural disasters—especially in the context of climate change (Tisch & Galbreath, 2018), pandemics, and terrorist attacks (Mithani, 2020). This may reflect a combination of acute hazards (such as natural disasters) and the more chronic stressors associated with ongoing periods of uncertainty. Events such as the COVID-19 pandemic threaten the survival of organizations as well as individuals, highlighting the importance of identifying the characteristics that underpin resilience in different contexts (Do et al., 2022; Nava, 2022). In this chapter, we explore the challenges inherent in conceptualising resilience, approaches to theorising resilience at multiple levels (e.g., individual, team, and organizational), and emerging empirical research that examines links between these levels. We conclude by discussing limitations of the current literature and identifying potential avenues for future empirical work.

DOI: 10.4324/9781003287858-4

What is resilience?

Although there is an extensive body of research on resilience, there is still considerable disagreement about its nature (Hartmann et al., 2020; Hillmann, 2021). The original inspiration for resilience came from materials engineering and complex ecosystems, reflecting the notion of a system able to change shape, to bend, and to withstand stresses produced by environmental changes (Home & Orr, 1998). Since then, resilience has been defined variously as (Raetze et al., 2022):

- An attribute of entities: e.g., a property that enables the entity to remain unchanged, to "bounce back" to an original condition, or to thrive.
- A process: e.g., a response to a generally challenging environment a specific adverse event or challenge, or to more chronic conditions of adversity.
- An outcome: e.g., becoming resilient.

In other words, there is major disagreement about what resilience is, the circumstances under which it can be observed, and (if resilience is conceptualised as an outcome) the outcomes that capture resilience in action. The lack of consensus in definition means there is also no consistent approach to measuring resilience, with both issues presenting barriers to the development of an evidence base.

Reflecting debates about the nature of resilience in general (Hartmann et al., 2020; Hillmann, 2021), resilience has been examined at the individual (Pangallo et al., 2015), team (Chapman et al., 2020), and organizational levels (Conz & Magnani, 2020). Interestingly there are some patterns of focus at particular levels; for example trait-based approaches are common in research at the individual level (Oshio et al., 2018; Pangallo et al., 2015), while research at the organizational level often treats resilience as an outcome (Duchek, 2020).

The individual level—and beyond

Much of the psychological literature on resilience in organizations has focused on the individual level. Many reviews have operationalised it as a personality trait reflecting individual characteristics such as equanimity, flexibility, and perseverance (Liu et al., 2020; Oshio et al., 2018; Pangallo et al., 2015). Some scholars, however, have treated resilience as a "bundle" of traits and qualities that enable an individual to thrive in a particular organizational context (Kinman & Grant, 2017). Meta-analysis has shown that trait resilience is negatively related to indicators of poor mental health, and positively associated with good mental health (Hu et al., 2015). Other meta-analysis has also highlighted positive relationships between trait resilience and personality characteristics such as extraversion, openness to experience, agreeableness, and conscientiousness and low levels of neuroticism (Oshio et al., 2018). Taken together, this may suggest a dispositional quality to individual resilience (or that resilience is a higher order latent construct), with implications for people's response to adversity. Consequently, many organizations are seeking to select individuals who have the qualities that might enable them to cope with challenging working conditions (King et al., 2021) or implement interventions to increase resilience among their employees (Vanhove et al., 2016). However, two meta-analytic reviews have identified only small effects on wellbeing (Liu et al., 2020; Vanhove et al., 2016) that diminish over time (Vanhove et al., 2016). Both reviews have noted inconsistency in the way that resilience has been operationalised and the interventions that have been implemented and evaluated, making it difficult to assess the relevance and effects of individual resilience. Liu et al. (2020) have called for more sophisticated models of resilience incorporating traits, coping styles, interpersonal factors and socio-economic factors to help practitioners identify what to target in capacity-building activities at the individual level. Incorporating different approaches to resilience may enable the development of a more sophisticated models, as we explore later in this chapter.

However, focus on individual-level resilience has been subject to criticism. Some scholars have argued that the prevailing discourse around resilience emphasises the role of the individual in coping with challenging circumstances and "bouncing back" from adversity, which minimises or overlooks entirely the political and economic systems, and working conditions, that cause that adversity (Davis, 2016; Gill & Orgad, 2018). In this discourse, it is maintained that the individual must be resilient in response to adversity (Price et al., 2012) and the role of institutions in supporting the wellbeing of employees is rendered invisible (Ferris, 2021). Thus, resilience may be presented as a way of enduring management practices that contribute to workplace psychosocial hazards (Webster & Rivers, 2019) and thereby impact wellbeing. There are signs that individuals may indeed internalise this sense of personal responsibility. For example, a narrative analysis undertaken with nurses working in the early stages of the COVID-19 pandemic suggested that accounts of resilience as an individual quality had been internalised, leading to participants blaming themselves or colleagues for a perceived lack of resilience rather than systemic failings (Conolly et al., 2022). Conolly and colleagues also found that nurses expressed a sense of martyrdom, but were reluctant to seek support, suggesting a preference to "cope" on an individual basis. However, while Conolly and colleagues interpreted this as a preference, it may also reflect external pressures (e.g., cultural expectations).

It is important to note that differences in access to resources that enable one to "bounce back" from adversity may be overlooked in favour of meritocratic assumptions that those who thrive are "naturally" more resilient and deserving (Bal et al., 2020). Consequently there have been calls to examine not only individual resilience, but also the system-level challenges that demand coping or demonstrating resilience in action (Shaw et al., 2016). We suggest that a multi-level approach to resilience can provide insight into how individuals navigate challenging environments whilst also examining (and challenging) the environments themselves. This would be consistent with the view that resilience is emergent, reflecting the interaction of an entity with its environment (Pangallo et al., 2015). Such an approach may also identify that what makes an entity resilient to one challenge (e.g., market changes) may not make it resilient to another (e.g., the outbreak of war; Kuldas & Foody, [2021]). Further, in an individual context, a recognition that "bouncing back" from adversity is easier for those with access to greater resources as highlighted above (Ferris, 2021), whether internal (e.g., optimism) or external (e.g., support), highlights the importance of examining resources at individual and contextual levels (e.g., team, organizational, and geographical region).

Varied concepts: Causes and consequences

A review by Hillmann (2021) demonstrated that, to some degree, the differences in how resilience is conceptualised reflects its multidisciplinary nature. For example, a trait or state approach to resilience is associated with the positive organizational behaviour field, whereas in engineering resilience could be reflected in employee safety behaviours. Like "stress," the flexibility of the term resilience may have contributed to its appeal and spread (Raetze et al., 2022) and application to various agendas. A consequence is that scholars use the term to mean different things, i.e., the jingle fallacy; however, there has also been a proliferation of other concepts similar to resilience, such as grit (Ion et al., 2017), mental toughness (Lin et al., 2017), and hardiness (Srivastava & Dey, 2020), i.e., the jangle fallacy (Raetze et al., 2022). To complicate matters, researchers often do not specify how they are conceptualising resilience in their work, assuming a shared understanding (Chapman et al., 2020; Hartmann et al., 2020). Clearly, the lack of consistency in how resilience is defined and measured is a potential barrier to meta-analytic reviews, (Hartmann et al., 2020). In an attempt to provide conceptual clarity, some scholars have produced reviews by integrating different resilience perspectives into a framework (e.g., Conz & Magnani, 2020; Hartwig et al., 2020; Raetze et al., 2022; Tasic et al., 2019).

The lack of consensus highlighted above (and reflected in Table 2.1) means that there are implications for researchers. First, given the heterogeneous nature of the literature, it is perhaps necessary for scholars to acknowledge the disciplinary approach they take to the topic. Second, in the absence of consensus, it will be useful for authors to identify whether they are conceptualising resilience as a trait or capacity, a process, or an outcome. There are also implications for how resilience is measured, which should also be made explicit by researchers. For example, an individual trait approach may require a single self-report measure, whereas a process approach will require measures of multiple constructs such as predictors (such as organizational demands, support, etc.) and outcomes (such as wellbeing, satisfaction, retention). By contrast, resilience treated as an outcome requires the precise identification of that outcome (e.g., financial performance or sickness absence rates) and a prior justification of the pattern that would demonstrate a resilient response. Nevertheless, some consistency in the treatment of resilience could

TABLE 2.1 Conceptualisations of resilience

	Example conceptualisation	Example construct
Individual	Trait	Adaptability
	Coping style	Emotional stability
		Emotional resilience
		Active coping
Team	Team characteristics	Team culture
	Team processes	Communication, support, conflict management
	Team outcomes	Performance, resistance
Organization	Dynamic capability	Firm resilience, supply chain resilience
	Ecological	Capacity of system to absorb disruption
	Resource-based	Availability of financial resources

enhance the ability to develop interdisciplinary research. For example, if psychologists (drawing on trait resilience) were to work with engineers (treating resilience as safety behaviours), an agreement may be needed on which disciplinary approach would be used to defining resilience. Precise specification can also aid scholars in identifying which approach is being taken from those available.

We suggest that a process-based or transactional approach has advantages over attribute (e.g., trait or capacity) and outcome perspectives. An issue in common to treating resilience as an attribute or an outcome (or desired state) is that it draws attention away from what entities (e.g., organizations) do to be (or not be) resilient (Duchek, 2020). Selecting an organization for study on the basis that it appears to have demonstrated resilience involves ex post facto design, which prevents the establishment of causality (Giuffre, 1997). In other words, it is difficult to identify why the organization was resilient and what made it resilient. There is instead a risk that any positive change is treated as evidence of resilient functioning (Liu et al., 2020) as opposed to "luck" or other external factors such as market forces. By contrast, a process model in which we consider resources available to, for example, an organization, the actions the organization takes, and the nature of the specified outcome provides greater insight into important boundary conditions (i.e., conditions that enable or inhibit expected outcomes). For example, an organization might invest in widespread training of critical skills (rather than relying on one or two individuals possessing crucial capabilities), which, in turn, protects the organization against the impact of staff sickness. However, the benefits of this strategy may be stronger for outcomes more closely linked to employee productivity than for those linked to other factors (e.g., firm reputation). Due to the complex nature of these processes, we argue that a systems approach is needed, which we discuss later in this chapter.

Process models

Some recent reviews have attempted to consolidate the disparate literature on resilience by proposing a temporal approach in which different concepts (e.g., proactive and reactive resilience), are pertinent at different stages of crisis (Conz & Magnani, 2020; Duchek, 2020; Raetze et al., 2022; Stoverink et al., 2020). These reviews focus on resilience at a collective level, with some examining organizational resilience (Conz & Magnani, 2020; Raetze et al., 2022), and another addressing team resilience (Stoverink et al., 2020). While the models proposed have important differences, common features are a distinction between pre-adversity and post-adversity. In other words, distinction can be made between a preparatory phase, which includes preventative measures, and the reactive phase in which action is taken in response to an adverse event (Denyer, 2017). Conz and Magnani, Duchek, and Stoverink et al. include stages set during the adversity, while Raetze and colleagues examine developmental resilience as part of their model, focusing on entities exhibiting healthy functioning despite the early presence of risk factors. In Conz and Mangani, Duchek, and Raetze et al.'s models, the pre-adversity phase is treated as a proactive stage, in which the entity (e.g., organization) prepares for adversity (e.g., by acquiring resources or anticipating crises). For example, an organization might prepare for disruption to face-to-face working by enhancing its remote working capabilities and developing manager and employee skills to support this change. In Stoverink et al., the pre-adversity stage is described in terms of the capacities that teams have for resilience (but are not enacted until circumstances demand it). For example, a team might have flexible decision-making capacities, but these may not be required until typical processes are shown to be unhelpful.

The models discussed above differ in their treatment of outcome trajectories. Raetze et al.'s reactive phase emphasised the possibility for different trajectories, namely recovery ("bouncing back to normal"), resistance (remaining unchanged), and thriving (improving). By contrast, Conz and Magnani focused on two resilience capabilities, absorption and adaptation, with two different pathways. The absorptive path, as theorised, is marked by redundancy of resources in the proactive phase and robustness at the time of crisis and agility in the reactive phase. In this path, the emphasis is on remaining unchanged in the face of adversity. The adaptive path is marked by resourcefulness (i.e., a diversity of resources that are utilised appropriately) in the proactive phase, whereas the reactive phase is characterised by adaptability at the time of crisis (e.g., opening new pathways for action), and flexibility. The emphasis in this path is on changing in response to adversity. Stoverink et al., on the other hand, assumed that resilience would involve a decline in performance, followed by a return to previous performance or a net increase to performance. Like Conz and Magnani, Stoverink et al. theorised two team responses to adversity, through adaptation or persistence, the latter of which was defined in terms of "staying the course." Unlike Conz and Magnani, this model specifies that the distinct pathways appear only after adversity.

Munoz et al. (2022) propose an alternative framework in which resilience reflects a single trajectory, namely "bouncing back," proposing that the ability to withstand adversity without harm should be termed "robustness" and performance gains resulting from adversity should be labelled "antifragility." However, in line with Conz & Magnani (2020), we argue that it is more useful to examine how different resilience pathways may yield different outcomes. Attention to pathways to resilience, e.g., absorption versus adaptation (Conz & Magnani, 2020), might also account for different outcome trajectories that have been identified (Munoz et al., 2022; Raetze et al., 2022). For example, the absorptive pathway might be more pertinent to the resistance trajectory (e.g., being more or less unaffected by a sudden change in workload), while the adaptive pathway might have greater implications for thriving (e.g., by pivoting to a more competitive business model). For example, a manufacturing organization might pivot to an emphasis on customer service in the face of reduced sales. Interestingly, in the models of Duchek (2020) and Stoverink et al. (2020), a key outcome includes learning and change within the organization, whereas the other models discussed have focused on performance outcomes. This learning may be crucial for the performance outcome; for example, for a firm to "pivot" it may need to identify strategies for its new business model. Drawing on the process models so far, we provide a framework drawing on themes from across the approaches taken (Figure 2.1).

Conz & Magnani (2020) noted a need for research to explore how different resilience capacities might relate to crucial outcomes such as financial performance and sustainability. Factors (or resources) that enable entities to

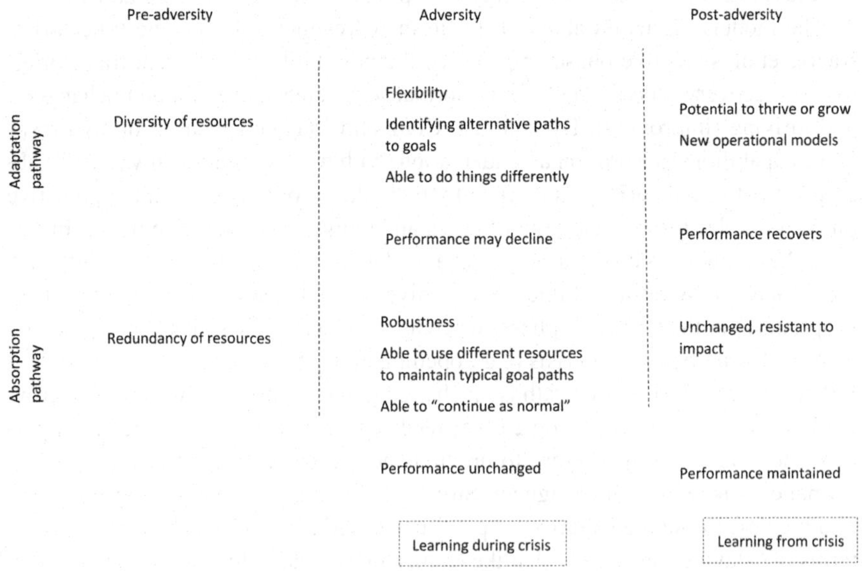

FIGURE 2.1 The adaption and absorption pathways across the adversity process

"bounce back" are likely to differ across the levels; for example, individual, team, organizational, community (Thibodeaux, 2021). For instance, a resilient "mindset" may help an individual cope with adversity through, for example, persistence and active coping, but an organization bouncing back from adversity may need financial resources. Similarly, for a team to function well under adversity, we may expect communication styles to play a crucial role. There may be interlinkages between levels—for example, an organization with financial resources may also benefit from having employees with a resilient mindset. Organizational resources are also likely to be needed to enable individual level resources to be replenished. We may also expect that factors associated with positive outcomes are likely to depend on context (e.g., the nature of the adversity [Gucciardi et al., 2018]) and the culture of the organization (e.g., which solutions are "acceptable").

At the team level, Stoverink et al. (2020), drawing on Weick (1993), identify four sources of team resilience:

- Team potency, reflecting the team's belief it can perform any task.
- The team's mental model of teamwork; i.e., team members' understanding of how their work connects with that of others.
- Team capacity to improvise.
- Team psychological safety; i.e., the perception that it is safe to take risks.

These may be inter-linked because psychological safety could provide greater freedom for improvisation. Stoverink et al. (2020) argue that a key distinction of team-level resilience from individual- or organizational-level resilience is the greater emphasis on interdependence; that is, the performance of individuals within the team is much more dependent on others. Consequently, the setbacks described in the adversity stage reflect process losses or breakdown in interdependence, and the reactive phase places emphasis on how teams cooperate in response to adversity. This may be contextual because the kind of work performed may indicate what resources and actions are needed to achieve positive outcomes. For example, emotionally demanding work may demand particular team-level resources (such as emotional support). Similarly, inter-dependence is likely to be crucial for safety critical work (e.g., prison officers).

Taken together, these models highlight the need to identify traits, capacities, and other resources possessed by entities, examine responses to adversity in terms of both adaptation and absorption, and consider outcomes. With the exception of Stoverink et al. (2020), these models do not explicitly consider interactions between the levels of analysis; for example, how organizations influence individual resilience, and how individuals may influence organizational resilience, for better or worse. Thus, to develop the process models further, there is a need to consider resilience as a multi-level process, which we explore in the next section.

Links between the levels

In parts of the resilience literature, there are assumptions—for example, grounded in a psychological approach—which assume that "resilient organizations" must be comprised of "resilient individuals" (Gover & Duxbury, 2018). For example, this is reflected in a text (Strycharczyk & Elvin, 2014) on organizational resilience in which the content focuses primarily on resilience as a mindset, as opposed to alternative conceptualisations; for example, resources-related definitions common to ecological approaches (Gover & Duxbury, 2018). However, some scholars argue that a team is not necessarily resilient if it is comprised of resilient individuals (Gucciardi et al., 2018; Stoverink et al., 2020), and nor is an organization resilient if it is comprised of resilient teams (Stoverink et al., 2020). In addition to the fact that different levels of resilience may call for different resources or actions (Thibodeaux, 2021), the actions of an entity at one level may actually be detrimental to the welfare of others at the same or different levels (Gucciardi et al., 2018; Stoverink et al., 2020). For example, an individual in a team may take actions that advantage themselves at the expense of their team, as in the case of individuals who may engage in social loafing while enjoying a share of team rewards (Pearsall et al., 2010). Similarly, a team may engage in competitive action to benefit itself above other teams within the same organization (Stoverink et al., 2020), and indeed some organizational cultures may encourage this.

There has been relatively little attention to relations between the different levels of resilience (Thibodeaux, 2021), but theoretical work is emerging that helps to elucidate them and their implications for resilience. Kahn et al. (2018) developed the theory of "geographies of strain," observing that organizations are not often affected by strain in their entirety; instead, specific parts may experience pressure (e.g., frontline workers or particular teams). The relationship between parts of an organization may influence how strain spreads; for example, as one part of an organization is overwhelmed, or managed, other parts of the organization provide support and, in turn, may be depleted. Kahn and colleagues note that groups may be nested in an organization (e.g., teams within departments within the organization), adjacent (e.g., departments at the same level), and hierarchical. Drawing on social identity theory (Tajfel & Turner, 1979; Turner, 1985), they argue that intergroup relations involving competition or cooperation are likely to shape the dynamics of strain (Kahn et al., 2018). In social identity theory, the salience of identities shapes subsequent behaviour (Ho & Yeung, 2019; Kuppens et al., 2013). Kahn and colleagues identify three patterns of response amongst network pathways: integration, in which adjoining parts of the organization cooperate and synchronise (e.g., where a team under pressure receives support with workload from other teams); disavowal, in which adjoining parts of the organization isolate the parts experiencing strain (e.g., if managers reject calls for support from frontline workers); and reclamation, in which adjoining parts of the organization initially engage in disavowal, before subsequently providing support (e.g., as a consequence of deepening crisis). When organizational identity is salient, integration may be more likely, compared to when subordinate identities are more salient (e.g., team or departmental identities), which may occur when there are threats to resources (Kahn et al., 2018).

Another model considering the network of relationships between parts of an organization and the external environment is offered by Tasic et al. (2019). Consistent with the approach taken by Conz and Magnani (2020), they treat resilience as a property that could emerge at and across each level (individual, unit, and organizational), associated with flexibility of approach, adaptability to circumstances, and redundancy of resources. Tasic et al. (2019) focus upon interdependencies, which they identified as comprising formal and informal exchanges taking place within levels (e.g., between individuals, between teams, and between organizations) and across levels. These interdependencies were considered to have important implications for organizational resilience. To illustrate with an example, a unit in which only one individual can perform an important task is more vulnerable to disruption than one in which multiple members can perform that task. However, a team lacking crucial skills among its members might be able to solicit aid from elsewhere within the organization. In contrast to Stoverink et al. (2020), these interdependencies are recognised at multiple levels of analysis.

While Kahn et al. (2018) and Tasic et al. (2019) have considered networks of support (or conflict) within organizations, Hartwig et al. (2020) developed a multi-level model of team resilience, drawing on contributions from different levels. Drawing on input-process-outcome (IPO) models of teams (Campion et al., 1993), they identify individual (e.g., adaptability, individual resilience, expertise), team (e.g., collective resources, group structure, task design), and organization (e.g., culture, strategy, support) level inputs. "Resilient" team processes include planning for adverse events, coping behaviour, and debriefing. Similar to Stoverink et al.'s (2020) model, several team states were proposed as facilitating the emergence of resilient team processes, including team trust, shared mental models, cohesion, and psychological safety. Finally, resilient team outcomes were proposed to reflect performance, team functioning, and team health. Both Stoverink et al. and Hartwig et al. draw on conservation of resources theory (Hobfoll, 1989; Hobfoll & Lilly, 1993), which proposes the existence of resource gain and loss spirals (Alarcon, 2011; Bakker & de Vries, 2021; Chen et al., 2018). In essence, individuals are motivated to gain resources and to protect the resources they already possess, but threats to resources are more salient than opportunities to gain resources. Thus, when resources are threatened, entities may be trapped in a spiral of defending what they already have, which at best results in stagnation and at worst results in decline or death for entities. For example, a business may focus on protecting a declining market share rather than seeking out new opportunities. By contrast, those already possessing good levels of resources are in a better position to acquire further resources.

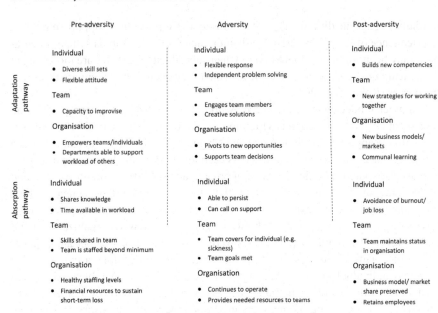

	Pre-adversity	Adversity	Post-adversity

Adaptation pathway

Pre-adversity	Adversity	Post-adversity
Individual • Diverse skill sets • Flexible attitude	**Individual** • Flexible response • Independent problem solving	**Individual** • Builds new competencies
Team • Capacity to improvise	**Team** • Engages team members • Creative solutions	**Team** • New strategies for working together
Organisation • Empowers teams/individuals • Departments able to support workload of others	**Organisation** • Pivots to new opportunities • Supports team decisions	**Organisation** • New business models/ markets • Communal learning

Absorption pathway

Pre-adversity	Adversity	Post-adversity
Individual • Shares knowledge • Time available in workload	**Individual** • Able to persist • Can call on support	**Individual** • Avoidance of burnout/ job loss
Team • Skills shared in team • Team is staffed beyond minimum	**Team** • Team covers for individual (e.g. sickness) • Team goals met	**Team** • Team maintains status in organisation
Organisation • Healthy staffing levels • Financial resources to sustain short-term loss	**Organisation** • Continues to operate • Provides needed resources to teams	**Organisation** • Business model/ market share preserved • Retains employees

FIGURE 2.2   Individual, team, and organizational processes across the adversity process

Taken together, these models highlight both the nature of social relations between entities and the sharing of resources. Drawing on the work of Kahn et al. (2018), we suggest that demands can be exerted through these channels; for example, managers imposing change initiatives on teams to help the organization respond to adversity. Developing the model illustrated in Figure 2.1, we aim to show how linkages between levels may occur across the process of adversity (see Figure 2.2).

While there has been relatively little empirical attention to multi-level resilience, research that have developed multi-level frameworks has begun to emerge.

Two studies examined the role of organizational practices on individual-level resilience. Cooper et al. (2019) reported a multilevel study gathering data across 16 Chinese banks, with data collected at the branch level (from 62 managers) and at the individual level (from 561 employees who were matched to branch managers). Human resource management (HRM) practices, such as the quality of relationships with managers, information sharing, and job security, social climate, and resilience, were measured through surveying employees, while branch managers provided ratings of their subordinates' performance. The findings suggested that HRM practices were associated with a more positive social climate, and thereby linked to individual resilience (Cooper et al., 2019). They also found a weak but positive association between employees' self-rated resilience and their manager's ratings of employee performance. Cooper and colleagues suggested that the HRM practices were associated with individual resilience via positive collective climate conducive to trust and cooperation, which was found to fully mediate the relationship. However, while common method bias was avoided in examining the link between resilience and performance, the measurement of HR practices was based on employee perception only. Similarly, in a study of 1,167 employees across 194 teams in 38 companies, team-level resilience was reported to be influenced by organizational practices relating primarily to wellbeing and development, team work, transformational leadership, and collective efficacy (Vera et al., 2017). As with Cooper et al. (2019), although some variables were conceptualised at the organizational level or team level, this data were still based upon the report of individual employees. The measure of resilience used by Vera et al., (2017) drew on a definition of team resilience incorporating efficacy beliefs (Carmeli et al., 2013), which may confound trait resilience with self-reported efficacy (if these are distinct constructs).

By contrast, Fan et al. (2020) reported a dyadic study, in which followers (N = 309) were matched with their leaders (N = 87). Both leaders and followers completed measures of trait resilience at Time 1, while at Time 2 followers completed a measure of burnout and leaders rated their followers' performance of organizational citizenship behaviours. A moderate positive association was found between the self-rated resilience of leaders and followers, and follower resilience at Time 1 mediated a relationship between leader resilience and follower burnout. The authors interpreted the association between leader and follower resilience as potentially resulting from emotional contagion, followers adopting leader coping strategies, or drawing on social resources from the leader. These proposed mechanisms would benefit should be examined in future research. While the dyad-based approach avoided common method bias, as noted by the authors, they did not adopt a full panel design, which could have enabled the testing of reciprocal relationships (e.g., followers contributing to leader resilience). It is also important to note that associations between resilience at the different levels might reflect the impact of working in the same environment (i.e., with pressures exerted on both leaders and followers).

Gover and Duxbury (2018) conceptualised organizational resilience as the capacity to cope with change. In a qualitative study drawing on interviews with 39 employees, they reported that factors such as management style, flexibility and commitment of staff, pace of change, and budgets contributed to the capacity for change. However, given the qualitative nature of this study, the factors identified may reflect how participants made sense of the change, or elements that were salient during change, rather than representing "objective" features of the process. Nevertheless, the study offers some insight into pathways from individual attributes and behaviours to organizational resilience, in addition to organizational-level features, which could be tested quantitatively in future.

Two studies of organizational resilience are of interest in that they considered organizational-level performance (Kunz & Sonnenholzner, 2022; Sajko et al., 2021). Sajko et al. (2021) drew on publicly available information about a sample of 301 CEOs in the United States who served prior to the global financial crash of 2008. They reported that CEO "greed," operationalised as extraordinarily high payment levels, was associated with lower levels of investment in corporate social responsibility (CSR), particularly when more of the CEO rewards were based on short-term bonuses. The authors also reported that lower levels of CEO greed were associated with better organizational recovery following the 2008 financial crisis, which they attributed to longer-term thinking and greater inter-dependencies with stakeholders. However, they did note that CEO greed and CSR investments did not result in differential stock price drops. In contrast to much of the resilience literature, a recovery period (of 36 months following the financial crisis) was explicitly included in the statistical model. Nonetheless, it should be noted that the CEO characteristic was inferred from organizational level data and might therefore reflect the influence of the environment (e.g., organizational or sector cultures) rather than individual differences.

Kunz and Sonnenholzner (2022) conducted a review of studies examining the impact of managerial (including CEO) overconfidence on resilience. Most of the studies included operationalised overconfidence as investment behaviours or options; as with Sajko et al. (2021), the research has largely inferred an individual characteristic from organizational data. Kunz and Sonnenholzner (2022) treated resources as the foundation of an organization's capacity for resilience (in the form of robustness and adaptability). They considered three resources: social resources based on member interactions (e.g., collegial support), material resources in the sense of available "slack" (i.e., financial resources beyond current requirements), and procedural resources (i.e., routines that reduce complexity, and flexible decision-making, absorbing complexity). They reported a mixed impact on material resources, a positive impact on social resources (reflected in supplier networks and employee commitment), and a negative impact on procedural resources (e.g., accounting and auditing and error management). They observe that overconfident managers can have both positive impacts (through greater willingness to take risks) and negative impacts (by undermining procedures) on innovation. Thus, they argue that overconfident managers may foster innovation under particular conditions, namely in environment characterised by competition in which risk taking is required. As with Sajko et al. (2021), what is described as overconfidence may reflect the organizational environment.

While these studies have aimed to investigate relationships across levels (e.g., individual, team, and/or organizational), it seems notable that the measures used to operationalise these constructs remain at single levels of analysis—for example, survey studies incorporating individual perceptions of organizational practices (Fan et al., 2020) and studies examining organizational performance that infer manager characteristics from existing data (Sajko et al., 2021). However, given that theorisation has only recently considered multiple levels explicitly (e.g., Stoverink et al. 2020), it is likely to be some years before formal tests of these models emerge.

Future directions and conclusions

Drawing on the work that has been reviewed in this chapter, we suggest that it will be useful to identify specific linkages between organizational (or societal and other) levels of analysis to test specific propositions. Given that factors required for resilient outcomes at individual, team, and organizational levels are likely to be context driven (Gucciardi et al., 2018), specific adversities emerging from these different contexts could influence the selection of constructs, as well as the predicted outcomes. However, we broadly suggest that drawing on models influenced by the conservation of resources model (e.g., Hartwig et al., 2020) will help consider exchanges of resources between levels (Tasic et al., 2019). Measures will need to be selected at multiple levels (e.g., individual, team, and organizational) and subjected to multi-level analysis. Multi-level research drawing on multiple organizations in similar contexts (to control for variation in key characteristics) could make a significant contribution to the literature. Where scholars focus on individual level resilience, we encourage them to also measure environmental factors that may shape resilience processes, drawing on both observations and other available sources of data. More specifically, what are the characteristics of individuals and teams in certain organizational contexts that enable them to thrive and what resources can help them do so?

It has been argued that more attention is needed to the "dark side" of resilience processes (e.g., exploitation, Stoverink et al., [2020]) because organizational adaptive processes may, for example, impair the performance of teams (Maynard et al., 2015). For example, an organization experiencing short staffing during a health crisis may place onus on teams to "do more with less," leading to intensification of work that, in turn, will increase the risk of burnout. Similarly, there should be consideration of how individual adaptative strategies may cause problems for teams and organizations to which they belong. Therefore, we suggest that in taking a resources based view, and considering Kahn et al.'s (2018) "geographies of strain," it is useful to examine not only how individuals and organizations may mutually reinforce each other (e.g., organizations providing appropriate resources to individuals, and individuals providing their abilities to organizations), but also how an entity might thrive at the expense of its constituents, or how constituents might thrive at the expense of the superordinate entity.

Such an approach could usefully draw upon the temporal approach highlighted in models such as Raetze et al. (2022), Conz and Magnani (2020), and others, that have been discussed in this chapter. This might explore the outcomes that emerge over various timescales. For example, an organization might achieve flexibility or "greater resilience" by imposing new shift patterns or contracts (e.g., "zero hours") on employees. This flexibility may enable the organization to adapt to changing levels of demand and "thrive," but impact individuals negatively in terms of work-life conflict and poor recovery, potentially resulting from changes to shift patterns (Albertsen et al., 2014), or job insecurity, potentially resulting from precarious work (Smith & McBride, 2022). These practices may or may not be sustainable over longer periods of time and lead to health breakdown, absenteeism, and attrition, depending on context (e.g., availability of alternative employment to workers). Conversely, there could be attention to individual attributes and behaviours—for example, counterproductive work behaviours (Fox et al., 2001; Penney & Spector, 2005)—such as sabotage and social loafing (Karau & Williams, 1993), which may impair team functioning and thereby influence organizational resilience. Thus, there is a need to consider how different components of systems (e.g., organizations, teams, and individuals) act upon each other and are acted upon, in turn, over different timescales.

To achieve multi-level designs, it will be useful to gather data across multiple organizations in similar contexts (e.g., shared sector), with nested statistical models, as have been used in some studies (Fan et al., 2020). In future, more organizational-level data could be obtained that would enable testing of boundary conditions; for example, under which conditions particular resources or processes are required. Particular contexts could be selected, permitting a specification of what resilience means in context. However, such designs are likely to be challenging given the number of organizations that would be required as a sample. Another strategy that may help develop our understanding would be more use of longitudinal case study designs, which permit a more in-depth exploration of context (Dittfeld et al., 2022). These might centre on specific organizations and sectors, encountering specific adversities. For example, research on healthcare organizations (such as the National Health Service) during the COVID-19 pandemic might collect organizational level data, such as staffing levels and the number of patients admitted with COVID-19, team level data (e.g., communication practices and team climate), and individual level data (e.g., trait resilience, perceived workload, fear of infection) to test nested models. Data from managers (e.g., leadership style) might also be collected. Whilst challenging, such designs might enable tests of the impact of staffing levels on resilience, whether leadership and team practices moderate these effects, and the consequences for outcomes such as employee turnover and burnout. Given that organizations may be undertaking adaptive processes, alternative research designs such as action research may be appropriate for capturing the dynamic nature of resilience during adversity. This could include research co-created by employees, allowing a bottom-up approach to examining organizations undergoing adversity.

While much of the literature has focused on a resource-based approach to resilience in individuals and organizations, a recent approach has emerged that focuses on resilience through organizational learning (Do et al., 2022; Nava, 2022). Some of the resilience models previously discussed have suggested learning may occur during or as a result of the recovery process (Duchek, 2020; Stoverink et al., 2020). Nava (2022) proposes that organizations can learn from disasters (e.g., how to avoid or prepare for similar instances) and through disasters (e.g., by positively transforming as a result, or reshaping the organizational mission in light of the crisis). Therefore, it might be appropriate to consider how organizational learning unfolds during adversity, and to what extent this learning transfers across different adverse scenarios. Drawing on the temporal approach (e.g., Raetze et al., 2022), capacity for organizational learning prior to crisis could be incorporated into models. Sensemaking at various levels of the organization may form an important part of the process in which learning influences resilience. For example, at the team level, Talat & Riaz (2020) reported that team bricolage, the act of making do by recombining available resources, mediated the relationship between sensemaking activities and resilience. Crucially, however, there currently appears to be a lack of multi-level approaches to the links between organizational learning and resilience. Nevertheless, given that there are multi-level learning approaches (Senge, 2006), this seems to be an area with potential for development. For example, drawing on the work of Kahn et al. (2018), it may be useful to consider how (or if) what is learned in one part of the organization under strain is disseminated under particular circumstances, and how this might be institutionalised across organizational levels.

In this chapter, we have argued that there are advantages to treating resilience as a process. However, as we have demonstrated, there is considerable variation in how it is currently conceptualised. Research varies in whether it appears to: (1) examine factors that are assumed to produce resilience (Cooper et al., 2019; Kunz & Sonnenholzner, 2022), (2) test a recovery outcome (Sajko et al., 2021), or (3) identify factors that may influence resilience as a capacity (Fan et al., 2020; Oshio et al., 2018). As with similarly amorphous concepts such as stress, when testing process models, it will be important for scholars to show which models of resilience they draw upon, and how they are operationalising resilience. Key questions for scholars will include "What do we mean by resilience?" and "How will we recognise resilience if we see it?" This is important because not all resilience literature may include a formal measure of resilience; for example, where resilience in terms of recovery or success has been inferred by the observation of a particular pattern. For example, the studies outlined above have inferred resilience from several different factors. One meta-analysis (Bui et al., 2019) conceptualised this as uncertainty from "volatility" in team performance, and did not identify a construct to represent resilience, instead analysing the association between diversity and communication under uncertainty. While adopting a flexible approach may enable consideration of factors relevant to specific kinds of adversity, there remains a potential for confusion in the literature. It may be necessary to only draw on specific sections of the literature relevant to a specific problem, which may reinforce the existence of silos, or to identify criteria that may mark some studies as not being "true" examinations of resilience. The latter assumes that a precise agreed upon definition is even possible (or desirable). However, a risk is that the resilience literature will remain too broad to be helpful, due to the jingle-jangle effect mentioned earlier in this chapter. Resilience may instead serve as a rubric for approaches to examining responses to adversity, much as "stress" in organizational life is conceptualised and investigated in various ways using a transactional approach (Lazarus & Folkman, 1984).

In conclusion, the resilience literature faces challenges resulting from the proliferation of concepts and theorisation with little unity. There has been emerging work that theorises resilience as a process and/or a multi-level phenomenon. Operationalising multi-level theories in research is likely to present methodological challenges; for example, in gaining data from multiple sources over time and establishing statistical linkages. Multilevel theoretical developments, however, offer opportunities for bridging silos, but consensus—if it is to emerge—will likely require some bold decisions; for example, regarding what circumstances a study may be regarded as relevant to resilience. Treating resilience as a process incorporating both capacities (e.g., individual trait resilience) and outcomes as resilience (e.g., recovery trajectories) may be possible provided these are described and measured with precision and consistency across studies. We call for more research exploring specific pathways by which individuals, teams, and organizations may influence each other's resilience, and which accounts for both "positive" and "negative" processes and outcomes. We encourage attention not only to resilience, but also to the systems that give rise to adversity—which include systems and discourses of resilience themselves. It will be important to recognise that the concept of resilience is value-laden (e.g., by allocating responsibility for employee wellbeing) and can serve political functions (e.g., by offering a scientific cover for organizational decisions). By engaging in critical work, we may call attention to the ways in which entities are interconnected, both across and within levels of analysis. This would lead to a literature better placed to inform organizations and societies on how to become resilient while minimising the costs that adaptations have for employees and community members.

Note

1 Andrew would like to dedicate this chapter to the memory of Ruth Miners. Ruth was a fellow student of psychology and a wonderful human. My thoughts are with Ruth's husband Aaron and their daughters.

References

Alarcon, G. M. (2011). A meta-analysis of burnout with job demands, resources, and attitudes. *Journal of Vocational Behavior*, *79*(2), 549–562. https://doi.org/10.1016/j.jvb.2011.03.007

Albertsen, K., Garde, A. H., Nabe-Nielsen, K., Hansen, Å. M., Lund, H., & Hvid, H. (2014). Work-life balance among shift workers: Results from an intervention study about self-rostering. *International Archives of Occupational and Environmental Health*, *87*, 265–274. https://doi.org/10.1007/s00420-013-0857-x

Amiri, H., Nakhaee, N., Nagyova, I., Timkova, V., Okhovati, M., Nekoei-Moghadam, M., & Zahedi, R. (2021). Posttraumatic growth after earthquake: A systematic review and meta-analysis. *International Journal of Social Psychiatry*, *67*(7), 867–877. https://doi.org/10.1177/0020764021995856

Bakker, A. B., & de Vries, J. D. (2021). Job Demands–Resources theory and self-regulation: New explanations and remedies for job burnout. *Anxiety, Stress and Coping*, *34*(1), 1–21. https://doi.org/10.1080/10615806.2020.1797695

Bal, M., Kordowicz, M., & Brookes, A. (2020). A workplace dignity perspective on resilience: Moving beyond individualized instrumentalization to dignified resilience. *Advances in Developing Human Resources*, *22*(4), 453–466. https://doi.org/10.1177/1523422320946115

Bui, H., Chau, V. S., Degl'Innocenti, M., Leone, L., & Vicentini, F. (2019). The resilient organisation: A meta-analysis of the effect of communication on team diversity and team performance. *Applied Psychology*, *68*(4), 621–657. https://doi.org/10.1111/apps.12203

Campion, M. A., Medsker, G. J., & Higgs, A. C. (1993). Relations between work group characteristics and effectiveness: Implications for designing effective work groups. *Personnel Psychology*, *46*, 823–850.

Carmeli, A., Friedman, Y., & Tishler, A. (2013). Cultivating a resilient top management team: The importance of relational connections and strategic decision comprehensiveness. *Safety Science*, *51*(1), 148–159. https://doi.org/10.1016/j.ssci.2012.06.002

Chapman, M. T., Lines, R. L. J., Crane, M., Ducker, K. J., Ntoumanis, N., Peeling, P., Parker, S. K., Quested, E., Temby, P., Thøgersen-Ntoumani, C., & Gucciardi, D. F. (2020). Team resilience: A scoping review of conceptual and empirical work. *Work and Stress*, *34*(1), 57–81. https://doi.org/10.1080/02678373.2018.1529064

Chen, S. L., Shih, C. T., & Chi, N. W. (2018). A multilevel job demands–resources model of work engagement: Antecedents, consequences, and boundary conditions. *Human Performance*, *31*(5), 282–304. https://doi.org/10.1080/08959285.2018.1531867

Conolly, A., Abrams, R., Rowland, E., Harris, R., Couper, K., Kelly, D., Kent, B., & Maben, J. (2022). "What is the matter with me?" or a "badge of honor": Nurses' constructions of resilience during Covid-19. *Global Qualitative Nursing Research*, *9*. https://doi.org/10.1177/23333936221094862

Conz, E., & Magnani, G. (2020). A dynamic perspective on the resilience of firms: A systematic literature review and a framework for future research. *European Management Journal*, *38*(3), 400–412. https://doi.org/10.1016/j.emj.2019.12.004

Cooper, B., Wang, J., Bartram, T., & Cooke, F. L. (2019). Well-being-oriented human resource management practices and employee performance in the Chinese banking sector: The role of social climate and resilience. *Human Resource Management*, *58*(1), 85–97. https://doi.org/10.1002/hrm.21934

Davis, O. (2016). Resiling from "resilience." *Studies in Gender and Sexuality*, *17*(2), 135–138. https://doi.org/10.1080/15240657.2016.1172921

Denyer, D. (2017). *Organizational resilience: A summary of academic evidence, business insights and new thinking*. BSI and Cranfield School of Management.

Dittfeld, H., van Donk, D. P., & van Huet, S. (2022). The effect of production system characteristics on resilience capabilities: A multiple case study. *International Journal of Operations & Production Management*, *42*(13), 103–127. https://doi.org/10.1108/ijopm-12-2021-0789

Do, H., Budhwar, P., Shipton, H., Nguyen, H. D., & Nguyen, B. (2022). Building organizational resilience, innovation through resource-based management initiatives, organizational learning and environmental dynamism. *Journal of Business Research*, *141*, 808–821. https://doi.org/10.1016/j.jbusres.2021.11.090

Duchek, S. (2020). Organizational resilience: A capability-based conceptualization. *Business Research*, *13*(1), 215–246. https://doi.org/10.1007/s40685-019-0085-7

Fan, W., Luo, Y., Cai, Y., & Meng, H. (2020). Crossover effects of leader's resilience: A multilevel mediation approach. *Journal of Managerial Psychology, 35*(5), 375–389. https://doi.org/10.1108/JMP-02-2019-0109

Ferris, G. (2021). Undermining resilience: How the modern UK university manufactures heightened vulnerability in legal academics and what is to be done. *Law Teacher, 55*(1), 24–41. https://doi.org/10.1080/03069400.2021.1872865

Fox, S., Spector, P. E., & Miles, D. (2001). Counterproductive work behavior (CWB) in response to job stressors and organizational justice: Some mediator and moderator tests for autonomy and emotions. *Journal of Vocational Behavior, 309*, 291–309. https://doi.org/10.1006/jvbe.2001.1803

Gill, R., & Orgad, S. (2018). The amazing bounce-backable woman: Resilience and the psychological turn in neoliberalism. *Sociological Research Online, 23*(2), 477–495. https://doi.org/10.1177/1360780418769673

Giuffre, M. (1997). Designing research: Ex post facto designs. *Journal of Perianesthesia Nursing, 12*(3), 191–195.

Gover, L., & Duxbury, L. (2018). Inside the onion: Understanding what enhances and inhibits organizational resilience. *Journal of Applied Behavioral Science, 54*(4), 477–501. https://doi.org/10.1177/0021886318797597

Gucciardi, D. F., Crane, M., Ntoumanis, N., Parker, S. K., Thøgersen-Ntoumani, C., Ducker, K. J., Peeling, P., Chapman, M. T., Quested, E., & Temby, P. (2018). The emergence of team resilience: A multilevel conceptual model of facilitating factors. *Journal of Occupational and Organizational Psychology, 91*(4), 729–768. https://doi.org/10.1111/joop.12237

Hartmann, S., Weiss, M., Newman, A., & Hoegl, M. (2020). Resilience in the workplace: A multilevel review and synthesis. *Applied Psychology, 69*(3), 913–959. https://doi.org/10.1111/apps.12191

Hartwig, A., Clarke, S., Johnson, S., & Willis, S. (2020). Workplace team resilience: A systematic review and conceptual development. *Organizational Psychology Review, 10*(3–4), 169–200. https://doi.org/10.1177/2041386620919476

Hillmann, J. (2021). Disciplines of organizational resilience: Contributions, critiques, and future research avenues. *Review of Managerial Science, 15*(4), 879–936. https://doi.org/10.1007/s11846-020-00384-2

Ho, H. C. Y., & Yeung, D. Y. (2019). Effects of social identity salience on motivational orientation and conflict strategies in intergenerational conflict. *International Journal of Psychology, 54*(1), 108–116. https://doi.org/10.1002/ijop.12435

Hobfoll, S. E. (1989). Conservation of resources: A new attempt at conceptualizing stress. *American Psychologist, 44*, 513–524.

Hobfoll, S. E., & Lilly, R. S. (1993). Resource conservation as a strategy for community psychology. *Journal of Community Psychology, 21*, 128–148.

Home, J. F., & Orr, J. E. (1998). Assessing behaviors that create resilient organizations. *Employment Relations Today, 24*, 29–39.

Hu, T., Zhang, D., & Wang, J. (2015). A meta-analysis of the trait resilience and mental health. *Personality and Individual Differences, 76*, 18–27. https://doi.org/10.1016/j.paid.2014.11.039

Ion, A., Mindu, A., & Gorbănescu, A. (2017). Grit in the workplace: Hype or ripe? *Personality and Individual Differences, 111*, 163–168. http://dx.doi.org/10.1016/j.paid.2017.02.012

Kahn, W. A., Barton, M. A., Fisher, C. M., Heaphy, E. D., Reid, E. M., & Rouse, E. D. (2018). The geography of strain: Organizational resilience as a function of intergroup relations. *Academy of Management Review, 43*(3), 509–529. https://doi.org/10.5465/amr.2016.0004

Karau, S. J., & Williams, K. D. (1993). Social loafing: A meta-analytic review and theoretical integration. *Journal of Personality and Social Psychology, 65*(4), 681–706.

King, D. D., Lyons, B., & Phetmisy, C. N. (2021). Perceived resiliency: The influence of resilience narratives on attribution processes in selection. *Journal of Vocational Behavior, 131.* https://doi.org/10.1016/j.jvb.2021.103653

Kinman, G., & Grant, L. (2017). Building resilience in early-career social workers: Evaluating a multi-modal intervention. *British Journal of Social Work, 47*(7), 1979–1998. https://doi.org/10.1093/bjsw/bcw164

Krishnan, C. S. N., Ganesh, L. S., & Rajendran, C. (2022). Entrepreneurial interventions for crisis management: Lessons from the Covid-19 pandemic's impact on entrepreneurial ventures. *International Journal of Disaster Risk Reduction, 72.* https://doi.org/10.1016/j.ijdrr.2022.102830

Kuldas, S., & Foody, M. (2021). Neither resiliency-trait nor resilience-state: Transactional resiliency/e. *Youth and Society, 54*(8), 1352–1376. https://doi.org/10.1177/0044118X211029309

Kunz, J., & Sonnenholzner, L. (2022). Managerial overconfidence: Promoter of or obstacle to organizational resilience? *Review of Managerial Science, 17,* 67–128. https://doi.org/10.1007/s11846-022-00530-y

Kuppens, T., Yzerbyt, V. Y., Dandache, S., Fischer, A. H., Kuppens, T., Yzerbyt, V. Y., Dandache, S., & Fischer, A. H. (2013). Social identity salience shapes group-based emotions through group-based appraisals. *Cognition and Emotion, 27*(8), 1359–1377.

Lazarus, R. S., & Folkman, S. (1984). *Stress, appraisal, and coping.* Springer.

Lin, Y., Mutz, J., Clough, P. J., & Papageorgiou, K. A. (2017). Mental toughness and individual differences in learning, educational and work performance, psychological well-being, and personality: A systematic review. *Frontiers in Psychology, 8,* 1–15. https://doi.org/10.3389/fpsyg.2017.01345

Liu, J. J. W., Ein, N., Gervasio, J., Battaion, M., Reed, M., & Vickers, K. (2020). Comprehensive meta-analysis of resilience interventions. *Clinical Psychology Review, 82.* https://doi.org/10.1016/j.cpr.2020.101919

Maynard, M. T., Kennedy, D. M., & Sommer, S. A. (2015). Team adaptation: A fifteen-year synthesis (1998–2013) and framework for how this literature needs to "adapt" going forward. *European Journal of Work and Organizational Psychology, 24*(5), 652–677. https://doi.org/10.1080/1359432X.2014.1001376

Mithani, M. A. (2020). Adaptation in the face of the new normal. *Academy of Management Perspectives, 34*(4), 508–530. https://doi.org/10.5465/AMP.2019.0054

Munoz, A., Billsberry, J., & Ambrosini, V. (2022). Resilience, robustness, and antifragility: Towards an appreciation of distinct organizational responses to adversity. *International Journal of Management Reviews, 24*(2), 181–187. https://doi.org/10.1111/ijmr.12289

Nava, L. (2022). Rise from ashes: A dynamic framework of organizational learning and resilience in disaster response. *Business and Society Review, 127*(S1), 299–318. https://doi.org/10.1111/basr.12261

Oshio, A., Taku, K., Hirano, M., & Saeed, G. (2018). Resilience and Big Five personality traits: A meta-analysis. *Personality and Individual Differences, 127,* 54–60. https://doi.org/10.1016/j.paid.2018.01.048

Pangallo, A., Zibarras, L., Lewis, R., & Flaxman, P. (2015). Resilience through the lens of interactionism: A systematic review. *Psychological Assessment, 27*(1), 1–20. https://doi.org/10.1037/pas0000024

Pearsall, M. J., Christian, M. S., & Ellis, A. P. J. (2010). Motivating interdependent teams: Individual rewards, shared rewards, or something in between? *Journal of Applied Psychology*, *95*(1), 183–191. https://doi.org/10.1037/a0017593

Penney, L. M., & Spector, P. E. (2005). Job stress, incivility, and counterproductive work behavior (CWB): The moderating role of negative affectivity. *Journal of Organizational Behavior*, *796*(May), 777–796. https://doi.org/10.1002/job.336

Price, A., Mansfield, C., & McConney, A. (2012). Considering 'teacher resilience' from critical discourse and labour process theory perspectives. *British Journal of Sociology of Education*, *33*(1), 81–95. https://doi.org/10.1080/01425692.2011.614748

Raetze, S., Duchek, S., Maynard, M. T., & Wohlgemuth, M. (2022). Resilience in organization-related research: An integrative conceptual review across disciplines and levels of analysis. *Journal of Applied Psychology*, *107*(6), 867–897. https://doi.org/10.1037/apl0000952.supp

Rice, V., & Liu, B. (2016). Personal resilience and coping with implications for work. Part I: A review. *Work*, *54*(2), 325–333. https://doi.org/10.3233/WOR-162300

Sajko, M., Boone, C., & Buyl, T. (2021). CEO greed, corporate social responsibility, and organizational resilience to systemic shocks. *Journal of Management*, *47*(4), 957–992. https://doi.org/10.1177/0149206320902528

Senge, P. M. (2006). *The fifth discipline: The art and practice of the learning organization*. Random House Business.

Shaw, J., McLean, K. C., Taylor, B., Swartout, K., & Querna, K. (2016). Beyond resilience: Why we need to look at systems too. *Psychology of Violence*, *6*(1), 34–41. https://doi.org/10.1037/vio0000020

Smith, A., & McBride, J. (2022). 'It was doing my head in': Low-paid multiple employment and zero hours work. *British Journal of Industrial Relations*, *61*(1), 3–23. https://doi.org/10.1111/bjir.12689

Srivastava, S., & Dey, B. (2020). Workplace bullying and job burnout: A moderated mediation model of emotional intelligence and hardiness. *International Journal of Organizational Analysis*, *28*(1), 183–204. https://doi.org/10.1108/IJOA-02-2019-1664

Stoverink, A. C., Kirkman, B. L., Mistry, S., & Rosen, B. (2020). Bouncing back together: Toward a theoretical model of work team resilience. *Academy of Management Review*, *45*(2), 395–422. https://doi.org/10.5465/amr.2017.0005

Strycharczyk, D., & Elvin, C. (2014). *Developing resilient organizations: How to create an adaptive, high-performance and engaged organization*. Kogan.

Tajfel, H., & Turner, J. C. (1979). An integrative theory of intergroup conflict. In W. G. Austin, & S. Worchel (Eds.), *The social psychology of intergroup relations* (pp. 33–48). Brooks Cole.

Talat, A., & Riaz, Z. (2020). An integrated model of team resilience: Exploring the roles of team sensemaking, team bricolage and task interdependence. *Personnel Review*, *49*(9), 2007–2033. https://doi.org/10.1108/PR-01-2018-0029

Tasic, J., Tantri, F., & Amir, S. (2019). Modelling multilevel interdependencies for resilience in complex organisation. *Complexity*, *2019*. https://doi.org/10.1155/2019/3946356

Thibodeaux, J. (2021). Conceptualizing multilevel research designs of resilience. *Journal of Community Psychology*, *49*(5), 1418–1435. https://doi.org/10.1002/jcop.22598

Tisch, D., & Galbreath, J. (2018). Building organizational resilience through sensemaking: The case of climate change and extreme weather events. *Business Strategy and the Environment*, *27*(8), 1197–1208. https://doi.org/10.1002/bse.2062

Turner, J. C. (1985). Social categorization and the self-concept: A social cognitive theory of group behaviour. In E. J. Lawler (Ed.), *Advances in group processes: Theory and research* (Vol. 2, pp. 77–122). JAI Press.

Vanhove, A. J., Herian, M. N., Perez, A. L. U., Harms, P. D., & Lester, P. B. (2016). Can resilience be developed at work? A meta-analytic review of resilience-building programme effectiveness. *Journal of Occupational and Organizational Psychology, 89*(2), 278–307. https://doi.org/10.1111/joop.12123

Vera, M., Rodríguez-Sánchez, A. M., & Salanova, M. (2017). May the force be with you: Looking for resources that build team resilience. *Journal of Workplace Behavioral Health, 32*(2), 119–138. https://doi.org/10.1080/15555240.2017.1329629

Webster, D., & Rivers, N. (2019). Resisting resilience: Disrupting discourses of self-efficacy. *Pedagogy, Culture and Society, 27*(4), 523–535. https://doi.org/10.1080/14681 366.2018.1534261

Weick, K. E. (1993). The collapse of sensemaking in organizations: The Mann Gulch disaster. *Administrative Science Quarterly, 38*, 628–652.

3
CONFIGURING TEAM BOUNDARY SPANNING FOR RESILIENCE[1]

Thomas A. de Vries, Gerben S. van der Vegt, and Nevena Ivanovic

Introduction

Companies are inevitably confronted with disruptive events that, if left unattended, may have serious negative implications for their organization-wide performance or personnel wellbeing (van der Vegt et al., 2015). Such events may be large and have an abrupt impact on organizational processes and employees (e.g., pandemics, natural disasters, large strikes; Meyer et al., 1990), or they may start small as anomalies in the production or service process that escalate into larger impact disruptions (e.g., machine breakdowns, delayed deliveries of raw materials; Ivanovic et al., 2021; van den Adel et al., 2022). Whenever disruptions emerge, organizations must analyse the event, identify root causes, determine consequences, and develop countermeasures to minimise the event's negative implications for the company (de Vries et al., 2022a). Resilient organizations are effective in managing disruptions. This is reflected in their ability to maintain or even improve performance levels when facing disruptions to their production or service processes (van den Adel et al., 2022).

Minimizing the adverse consequences of disruptions is typically beyond the capacity of single individuals or teams within the organization (de Vries et al., 2016). Indeed, the teams tasked with managing disruptions on behalf of their organizations inevitably need to span their team boundaries and collaborate with other teams inside and outside their organization to develop effective and well-integrated countermeasures that ensure resilience. Such boundary spanning is vital for resilience because it enables teams to gather information about the nature of and potential solutions for the disruption, getting assistance from other teams inside or outside the organization (suppliers, customer firms, competitor firms), and coordinating responses to disruptions (Fan & Stevenson, 2018; Quick & Feldman, 2014).

DOI: 10.4324/9781003287858-5

Unfortunately, however, teams often struggle to work effectively across boundaries and realise the benefits of boundary spanning for resilience (de Vries et al., 2016; DeChurch & Zaccaro, 2010; Donahue & Tuohy, 2006).

Extant research suggests that teams may circumvent problems in boundary spanning by simply interacting more frequently with other teams (Joshi et al., 2009; Marrone, 2010). This research generally assumes that the higher the frequency of boundary spanning, the better teams will collaborate with each other, and the more successful they will be (Davison & Hollenbeck, 2012; DeChurch & Zaccaro, 2010; Faraj & Yan, 2009; Marks et al., 2005). However, most of this research has examined boundary spanning in ordinary work situations and the findings from this research may not directly translate to teams tasked with ensuring organizational resilience. Indeed, initial research suggest that this "more is better" perspective may become problematic when teams work in demanding situations. Davison et al. (2012), for example, illustrate that a high amount of uncoordinated boundary spanning between members working in so-called "multi-team systems" may decrease system performance. Other research also suggests that teams engaging in frequent boundary spanning may become buried under a storm of requests for support and coordination (de Vries et al., 2022a). Increasing the frequency of boundary spanning may, thus, unwittingly cause "collaborative overload" (Cross et al., 2016) and hinder effective disruption management.

This chapter therefore challenges the traditional "more is better" perspective on boundary spanning. We introduce a conceptual framework that specifies how specific boundary spanning configurations may facilitate inter-team collaboration during disruptions without producing collaborative overload. Drawing from research on boundary spanning and resilience, we also suggest that the effectiveness of different configurations is contingent on the characteristics of the disruption situation that teams face.

Theoretical background

Organizational resilience

In line with Britt (1988) and van den Adel et al. (2022), we define organizational resilience as an organization's effectiveness in minimizing the magnitude of disruptions' impact on its performance levels. The magnitude of a disruption's impact is reflected in (1) the overall reduction in organizational performance that a disruption induces, and (2) the duration of such a performance reduction (see Figure 3.1). Adopting a temporal perspective, we distinguish between different phases in disruption management during which an organization may reduce the magnitude of a disruption (de Vries et al., 2022a; Lettieri et al., 2009). In the "mitigation phase," an organization aims to minimise the initial drop in performance as it first encounters the disruption. Mitigation is completed when the immediate performance decline following a disruption is stabilised ("a" in Figure 3.1). Disruption mitigation

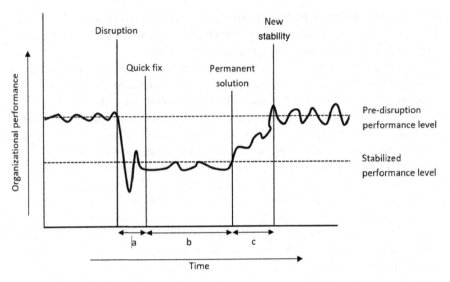

FIGURE 3.1 Organizational resilience

involves devising quick fixes to minimise immediate negative consequences for organizational performance. In the subsequent "response phase," the organization develops more permanent solutions that minimise the duration of the reduced performance levels ("b" in Figure 3.1), while it restores performance levels to pre-disruption levels or even beyond in the "recovery" phase ("c" in Figure 3.1). The recovery phase ends when organizational performance is restored to a new stable level, following the temporary reduction in performance levels due to the disruption.

Organizational resilience can, therefore, be determined by assessing an organization's performance over time, prior to, during, and after a disruption. A resilient organization quickly stabilises its performance level after a disruption and minimises the time that its performance level is below the pre-disruption level. A resilient organization may even improve its post-disruptions performance levels beyond the pre-disruption level by implementing permanent improvements in its processes (Britt, 1988; van den Adel et al., 2022). Figure 3.2 depicts the performance trend of a resilient firm. This figure shows a short and minimal decline in performance after a disruption emerges, illustrating the organization's ability to quickly stabilise the impact of the disruption through quick fixes. Moreover, the duration of the reduced performance period is relatively short, further showing the organization's resilience. An organization lacking resilience, however, struggles to stabilise performance levels after encountering a disruption, resulting in a steep and enduring drop in its performance. Figure 3.3 depicts the performance trend of an organization with lower resilience. This figure reveals a large, enduring drop in organizational performance after a disruption.

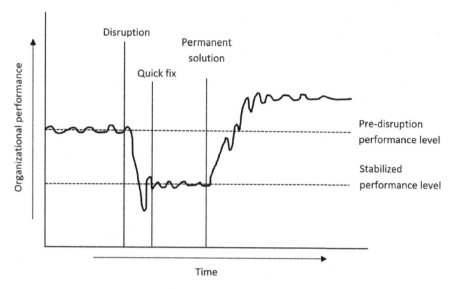

FIGURE 3.2 Performance trend line of a resilient organization

Teams, boundary spanning, and organizational resilience

Organizations often use one or a few designated teams to minimise the disruption's adverse effects and ensure resilience. Examples include the cross-functional teams studied in van den Adel et al. (2023) and the multiteam system studied in Goodwin et al. (2012) and de Vries et al. (2022a). Such teams receive a mandate to

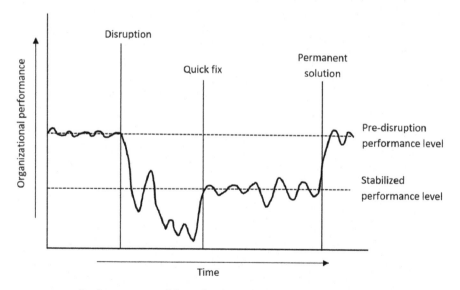

FIGURE 3.3 Performance trend line of an organization with lower resilience

analyse the disruption and develop countermeasures on behalf of the organization as a whole. These designated teams are typically also in charge of overseeing the implementation of countermeasures in the wider organization. Organizations typically rely on such teams for their excellent problem-solving capacities and ability to deal with complex tasks. Indeed, such teams facilitate open discussions between diverse members and enable the exchange of knowledge by allowing members to work alongside each other in an interdependent manner towards joint (team) goals.

Importantly, however, teams' ability to deal with complex problems largely depends on their access to complete information about the problem at hand, as well as the expertise needed to deal with it (de Vries et al., 2022a; van den Adel et al., 2023). Research suggests that without such information and expertise, teams may struggle to deal with disruptions (de Vries et al., 2022a). In almost all cases, not all of the required information and expertise is available within the team, and teams must reach out to other teams both inside and outside their organization (van den Adel et al., 2022). Teams' ability to deal with disruptions therefore greatly depends on their ability to engage in boundary spanning (de Vries et al., 2022a; van den Adel et al., 2023).

Team boundary spanning facilitates organizational resilience in different ways. First, engaging in boundary spanning with a diverse range of outside team members makes it more likely that teams receive early warning signals for upcoming disruptions (de Vries et al., 2022b). Relatedly, teams within an organization could engage in boundary spanning to quickly alert other teams of malfunctioning equipment that may have implications for these teams' functioning. This exchange of information may enable teams to start developing countermeasures for the disruption quicker, thereby potentially reducing the initial drop in performance after the emergence of a disruption. Second, research has shown that boundary spanning is essential for developing joint practices (Levina & Vaast, 2005). Boundary spanning may thus facilitate the access to and distribution of effective countermeasures within the organization, thereby reducing the duration of the reduction in organizational performance. Third, teams' boundary spanning may inspire the development of out-of-the-box solutions for novel and complex problems. Research indicates that interactions between different groups, departments, and expertise fields enables cross-pollination and exchange of ideas, and result in innovation (Chatenier et al., 2009; Laursen & Salter, 2006; West et al., 2014). Coming up with improvements may enable teams to restore the organizational performance level up to or even beyond pre-disruption levels.

Configuring boundary spanning for resilience

Despite boundary spanning's importance for resilience, engaging in such activities is difficult and needs to be carefully managed. Boundary spanning typically involves interactions with unfamiliar outside team members who have different (and sometimes conflicting) goals, interests, and working methods (Ancona &

Caldwell, 1992; de Vries et al., 2014). Thus, teams need to spend considerable time on explaining their actions to other teams' members, as well as on clarifying their requests for information and expertise. Without carefully managing boundary spanning, such activities may consume a disproportionate amount of team members' time and distract them from other important team activities, such as working on their teams' primary tasks (Gibson & Dibble, 2013). Therefore, it is important for teams to find ways to optimise their boundary spanning, such that these activities continue to provide them with the information, expertise, and assistance needed for dealing with disruptions, but also do not overly strain their members.

To realise that goal, we propose a configural approach that considers how team members divide boundary spanning tasks among each other, who they target with such activities, and for what purposes they engage in boundary spanning. Prior research has suggested that any team activity, such as boundary spanning, requires the investment of resources (time, attention) and that such resources are limited (Kudaravalli et al., 2017; Porter et al., 2010). Correspondingly, the key premise of our configural perspective is that boundary spanning is most beneficial when it is designed to require minimal resource investments while yielding maximal returns (Crawford & LePine, 2013; Leicht-Deobald et al., 2020). Specifically, for a more complete understanding of the boundary spanning–resilience link, we propose it is important to consider the investments as well as the potential returns associated with specific configurations of a team's boundary spanning. This is in line with prior research conceptualising boundary spanning as a configural team construct (Marrone, 2010).

Conceptual model

Building on conceptual team research (Crawford & LePine, 2013; Humphrey & Aime, 2014; Leenders et al., 2016) and our own observations (de Vries et al., 2022a; Leicht-Deobald et al., 2020), we focus on the structures and patterns of boundary spanning interactions during disruptions, rather than on the frequency of boundary spanning. To develop this configural approach, we reviewed existing literature and identified potentially important configurations of boundary spanning, characteristics of disruptions, and developed propositions on how such disruption characteristics may affect the effectiveness of different boundary spanning configurations for ensuring resilience. Drawing from boundary spanning literature, we identified the "Distribution of boundary spanning among teams' members," "Target of boundary spanning efforts," and "Purpose for which teams engage in boundary spanning" as important dimensions. Moreover, to understand the effectiveness of boundary spanning configurations, we tie together micro-level insights on boundary spanning with those from macro-level organization theory. Organization theory suggests that the design of an organization should match the environmental complexity and novelty it faces (de Vries et al., 2022b). Integrating this macro-level theoretical rationale with our micro-level insights on boundary spanning, we argue

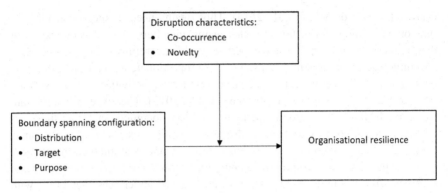

FIGURE 3.4 Conceptual model

that effective teams match how they configure boundary spanning to the novelty and co-occurrence of the disruptions they face (see Figure 3.4).

Configural dimensions of boundary spanning

Distribution of boundary spanning tasks

We identified three approaches to distribute boundary spanning tasks among teams' members. First, teams may choose to "differentiate" boundary spanning tasks among members by appointing one or a few members to execute the bulk of all boundary spanning activities. In such structures, the one or few members tasked with boundary spanning are called boundary spanners, brokers, liaisons, or coordinators and they are responsible for building and maintaining external relationships with other teams (inside or outside the organization) on behalf of the team as whole (Davison et al., 2012; de Vries et al., 2022a). These boundary spanners thus specialise in representing the team to external members, thereby allowing other team members to focus on internal team tasks. These team members depend on the central boundary spanning member for obtaining insights from external members. Such a differentiated structure creates oversight by limiting the number of members involved in boundary spanning, but it also requires sufficient knowledge exchange between the boundary spanner and the remaining team members (de Vries et al., 2016; van den Adel et al., 2023).

Second, teams may spread boundary spanning tasks thinly among members and involve all or most of their members. In such a "generic" structure, every team member builds and maintains work-related connections with external members without having to check or work with a central intermediary in the team; team members engage in boundary spanning alongside their other internal team activities. The key advantage of such a generic boundary spanning structure is that it can enable open and unmediated collaboration among teams, because there are no central boundary spanners that can distort or delay team members' external interactions. Research has shown the importance of generic boundary spanning configurations for cross-functional teams in business contexts characterised by risks and disruptions, suggesting that teams utilizing a generic boundary spanning structure can get access to large amounts of relevant information on the causes and consequences of disruptions (van den Adel et al., 2023).

Third, teams may use a "dynamic" configuration that combines differentiated and generic structures. Teams using dynamic configurations typically switch between differentiated and generic structures when demands in the disruption environment change. Only a handful of studies have examined how teams may dynamically combine such different boundary spanning structures (Mathieu et al., 2018). One key example is the study by de Vries et al. (2022a), who introduced the concept "provisional hierarchy" to explain how teams change their boundary spanning configuration as disruption-response efforts evolved. This study illustrates how teams first used differentiated structures to develop a strategic response, after which they shifted to generic boundary spanning structures to allow different teams' members to work out the details and implement solutions.

Target of boundary spanning

Recent meta-analytical research has identified that teams' boundary spanning may target external members *inside* or *outside* their organization, labelled "intra-organizational" and "extra-organizational" boundary spanning, respectively (Leicht-Deobald et al., 2020). Intra-organizational boundary spanning may take place either between or within hierarchical layers (e.g., Davison et al., 2012; de Vries et al., 2016; Firth et al., 2015). Boundary spanning between members from different hierarchical layers is called "vertical" boundary spanning (Davison et al., 2012). This type of boundary spanning enables higher-level leaders to assist specialist team members by developing and then providing a big-picture understanding of developments and actions in the organization (Davison et al., 2012; de Vries et al., 2016), which can be vital when dealing with disruption situations.

Boundary spanning *within* a hierarchical layer is called "horizontal" boundary spanning (de Vries et al., 2016) and can take place at the operational level (e.g., between specialists members) or at the managerial level (between leaders). Horizontal boundary spanning facilitates the coordination of detailed operational tasks (de Vries et al., 2022a). Team members may discuss what type of information they need from each other's teams to be able to contribute to collective efforts. When teams' leaders engage in horizontal boundary spanning, they exchange information, discuss, and align general countermeasures on a more strategic level.

Besides intra-organizational boundary spanning, teams may also interact with teams outside their organization. Although most prior research has examined intra-organizational boundary spanning, the few studies that have studied extra-organizational boundary spanning hint at its importance for resilience. These studies suggest that extra-organizational boundary spanning may help teams to align efforts with partner organizations (e.g., suppliers, customers), and obtain insights on disruptions that are unavailable within the organization. For example, research has shown how teams from different organizations may use boundary spanning to deal with disruptions to a shared railway system, such as blockages or delays in the railway infrastructure due to broken-down trains, collisions, or bad weather conditions (de Vries et al., 2022a; van den Adel et al., 2022). These teams used extra-organizational boundary spanning to coordinate how they can combine their resources (towing locomotives, mechanics, and support staff) to resolve disruptions, as well as to discuss how to quickly "bounce back" (restart interdependent train schedules after a disruption). Other research has shown that teams may use extra-organizational boundary spanning to obtain insights from competitors on how to deal with a disruption to their supply chain (van den Adel et al., 2023).

Purpose of boundary spanning

Our final dimension of boundary spanning configurations considers the purpose of teams' external interactions. Research suggests that boundary spanning can serve the purpose of coordinating work, representing team interests, and scouting external information and knowhow (Ancona & Caldwell, 1992; de Vries et al., 2014). Of these purposes, *coordination activities* represent the most intense form of boundary spanning. It requires members from different teams to discuss and agree on who will do what at what point in time, in order to avoid duplicate, redundant, or conflicting responses to disruptions. Coordination types of boundary spanning are by nature reciprocal. Only when teams' members engage in active discussions and joint decision-making will they be able to align the content and schedules of their activities when dealing with a disruption. As such, this type of boundary spanning is labour-intensive in terms of required investment of time and effort. Members from different teams will need to be deeply acquainted with each other's working methods, goals, and activities to engage in meaningful coordinative boundary spanning. At the same time, the intensity and reciprocity of coordinative boundary spanning enables exchange of rich information and it can motivate active support and assistance from outside team members (de Vries et al., 2014, 2016, 2022a).

Teams' boundary spanning may also serve the purpose of representing and connecting the team to higher-level management (ambassadorial activities). This type of boundary spanning emerges mostly between members of different hierarchical layers within the same organization (e.g., between lower-level team members or leaders and higher-level executives; Ancona & Caldwell, 1992; Marrone, 2010). In the context of resilience, teams may use ambassadorial activities to secure managerial support and financial resources. Although such activities have obvious relevance for resilience, the importance of ambassadorial boundary spanning in disruption contexts remains relatively unexplored in prior empirical research.

Finally, teams' boundary spanning may serve the purpose of finding information from other teams and stakeholders inside and outside the organization (information scouting; Ancona & Caldwell, 1992; van den Adel et al., 2023). Scouted information can provide insights on the causes, consequences, and potential solutions of a disruption, but does not include teams discussing how to use such insights for managing the disruption, as in boundary spanning aimed at coordination. As such, this type of boundary spanning requires the least amount of investment of team members' time and attention, but is also the least likely to result in strong external relationships that have been shown to enable the exchange of rich knowledge and active support. As such, information scouting seems particularly useful for teams that can benefit from exchanging information with each other but have little need or incentive to coordinate work, such as between competing teams (Ivanovic et al., 2022; van den Adel et al., 2023).

Disruption characteristics

Macro-level organizational theory highlights the need to look at contextual factors, such as complexity and novelty of the work environment, when considering the effectiveness of organizational collaboration processes (de Vries et al., 2022a; de Vries et al., 2022b; van den Adel et al., 2022, 2023). Against this theoretical backdrop, we consider both the *co-occurrence* and the *novelty* of the disruption as contextual factors that may influence the effectiveness of specific boundary spanning configurations.

Disruption co-occurrence

Research indicates that the complexity of a disruption is primarily determined by the timing of the disruption relative to other disruptions that may affect the organization (de Vries et al., 2022a,b; Rudolph & Repenning, 2002; van den Adel et al., 2023). A disruption is particularly complex when it emerges at a time when many other disruptions are already affecting the organization (Ivanovic et al., 2021). When facing such co-occurring disruptions, team members must focus their attention on resolving the focal disruption without neglecting the other adverse events or tasks unrelated to disruptions that may also affect the organization's performance (Comfort et al., 2012; Roux-Dufort, 2007). Moreover, implications of co-occurring disruptions may interact with the potential consequences of the focal disruption, and teams must thus consider scenarios that are more complex. This means that team members must obtain, share, and process larger amounts of information about the disruption before they can develop effective, well-coordinated responses.

Accordingly, and based on the work of Rudolph and Repenning (2002), de Vries et al. (2022a,b) and van den Adel et al. (2023) argued that situations with larger numbers of co-occurring disruptions are more likely to lead to information overload, which may cause team members to overlook critical information and hinder the development of effective countermeasures. Based on the task-switching literature, other researchers have come to similar conclusions (e.g., Ivanovic et al., 2021).

These scholars note that team members typically go back and forth between different activities when facing co-occurring disruptions, which consumes valuable time and attentional resources. As such, co-occurring disruptions may require different insights and place different demands on a team's boundary spanning.

Disruption novelty

Disruption novelty refers to how familiar a team is with certain disruptions. A disruption is relatively routine when a team has dealt with it before and more novel when it is unprecedented on some important dimension (van den Adel et al., 2022). In their study of the Dutch railway system, for example, van den Adel et al. (2022) considered rail disruptions (e.g., broken-down trains, failed rail infrastructure) more or less novel depending on how often a similar type of disruption had occurred in the same part of the railway system in the past year (see also, de Vries et al., 2022a). The exact location of a rail disruption was important, because it influenced what kind of solutions were possible. Teams that had dealt with a disruption at certain locations before were better aware of possible solutions and could rely on existing knowledge to develop countermeasures.

A configural framework

Combining micro insights on the role of boundary spanning with those from organization theory about the importance of organizations' macro-level environments, we argue that the effectiveness of boundary spanning configurations depends on their alignment with the co-occurrence and novelty of the disruption faced by the team. Co-occurrence and novelty represent orthogonal disruption characteristics, meaning that higher levels of co-occurrence do not necessitate higher levels of novelty, nor vice versa. Correspondingly, we offer propositions regarding how teams might effectively configure boundary spanning while facing disruptions that differ on those dimensions. Table 3.1 summarises our propositions.

Isolated, routine disruptions

Routine disruptions that emerge in isolation represent anomalies that teams may face on a daily basis when organizational processes otherwise run relatively smoothly. Although such situations may not seem severe, they do require immediate attention from teams to ensure that they will not escalate into larger, more complex disruptive situations (Rudolph & Repenning, 2002). Given the limited complexity and novelty of these disruptions, teams usually do not need external insights or assistance for ensuring resilience. Moreover, when such a disruption emerges in isolation (i.e., other processes are running smoothly and are not disrupted), it is relatively easy for a team to keep oversight of the situation and to develop countermeasures that do not duplicate or interfere with other teams' efforts (de Vries et al., 2022a).

TABLE 3.1 Proposed boundary spanning configurations

Disruption characteristics	Effective boundary spanning configuration	Rationale
Isolated, routine disruptions	Differentiated, intra-organizational, and focused on ambassadorial activities	Teams must efficiently inform management of their actions within the organization
Co-occurring, routine disruptions	Differentiated, intra-organizational, focused on coordination	Teams must create oversight and coordinate efforts inside the organization
Isolated, novel disruptions	Generic, extra-organizational, focused on information scouting	Teams must obtain innovative insights from other organizations
Co-occurring, novel disruptions	Dynamically shifting from differentiated, extra- and intra-organizational boundary spanning towards generic, intra-organizational boundary spanning. Focused on coordination and information scouting.	Teams must both create oversight and enable open problem-solving between their members and other organizations.

While teams do not need much support or assistance from external team members in these situations, boundary spanning may still be valuable because it helps the team to inform other important stakeholders inside the organization about the disruption and what was done to manage the situation. It is, however, important that teams do not invest too much of their time and effort in such activities. Teams may benefit the most when only one or a few members target hierarchical leadership inside the organization (differentiated vertical boundary spanning). Such key team members keep hierarchical leadership up-to-date of the disruptive situation, enabling the leadership to step in if needed, while enabling their fellow team members to focus most of their time and attention on within-team tasks. Furthermore, by exclusively focusing on intra-organizational boundary spanning with management (ambassadorial activities), teams ensure that one or a few team members can execute boundary spanning without running risks of becoming overloaded.

Co-occurring, routine disruptions

If several routine disruptions co-occur, teams must figure out how these multiple disruptions may affect the team and organization, and they must manage relationships with all involved stakeholders (de Vries et al., 2022a). To do so, a team may need to engage in substantial boundary spanning and acquire up-to-date information from other teams in the organization on how disruptions may interact with each other (Ivanovic et al., 2021; van den Adel et al., 2023). These insights are needed to develop effective countermeasures. Moreover, boundary spanning is instrumental for the team in aligning the team's responses with other teams to avoid conflicts or redundancies with responses to co-occurring disruptions (Choi, 2002; Fan & Stevenson, 2018).

We propose that teams will be more effective in ensuring resilience in these situations when they differentiate their boundary spanning. By using a differentiated structure, a central team member can maintain oversight of all between-team interactions, which is important when dealing with multiple co-occurring disruptions. Moreover, the central member can make sure that different team members do not collect redundant information and that important external members are properly involved in the team's response actions. Due to the low novelty of this type of disruption, we further expect that this differentiated boundary spanning is most effective when targeted at other teams and leaders *inside the organization*. Solutions for routine disruptions are often already present inside the organization, and therefore do not require more labour-intensive extra-organizational boundary spanning. Moreover, due to the high complexity resulting from disruption co-occurrence, we expect that intra-organizational boundary spanning is primarily needed for determining how disruptions' consequences may interact. We expect that boundary spanning is most likely to generate such insights when initiated in a vertical manner by higher-level leaders. Higher-level leaders are in a prime position to generate a broad overview of disruptions in the organization, and vertical boundary spanning may enable teams to obtain such insights from leaders in a cost-effective manner (Davison et al., 2012).

We further expect that teams' boundary spanning should focus on coordination. A key challenge for teams facing multiple co-occurring routine disruptions is developing integrated and well-coordinated countermeasures. When boundary spanning focuses on coordination, it allows teams to align and synchronise their disruption responses. Although coordination with other teams typically requires team members to engage in intense discussions, which can consume significant amounts of time, the synchronization and alignment of countermeasures may prevent that different teams develop ineffective, redundant, or conflicting countermeasures to coinciding disruptions.

Isolated, novel disruptions

For isolated but novel disruptions, the need for managing activities with external stakeholders and aligning responses among teams are relatively low. Due to the novelty of these disruptions, however, boundary spanning may be useful for providing team members with novel insights, information, and expertise from other teams that are not available within the team. This boundary spanning will likely be more effective when it is generic. With a generic boundary spanning structure, all team members can directly approach external team members without checking or coordinating with a central boundary spanner. Generic boundary spanning enables quick and spontaneous linkages between the team and external members, which are more likely to provide access to unfamiliar insights and information, as well as enable open problem solving between the team and external members. Such open problem-solving and access to external resources can help the team to develop innovative solutions for isolated disruptions.

Since isolated and novel disruptions are, by definition, unprecedented for the organization, we further argue that a team may be most effective if it targets its boundary spanning activities at members outside of its organization. Specifically, the team may approach partners within its supply chain (customers, suppliers) or even competitors to gauge whether these entities have dealt with similar disruptions and, if so, to obtain information on effective countermeasures. Although such boundary spanning may require team members to spend significant time in overcoming inter-organizational differences (e.g., working methods, goals, and interests), such efforts may still be worthwhile in terms of the input received in return. Moreover, the team does not have to spend significant time on internally developing creative solutions from scratch. This timesaving will compensate for the time that teams need to invest in extra-organizational boundary spanning.

Boundary spanning's key purpose during isolated and novel disruptions is to enable a team to scout information (from outside organizational members) on how to deal with the situation. Due to the unprecedented nature of the disruption, teams need to reach out beyond their organization to obtain valuable insights on how to minimise the disruptions consequences. Team members engage less in coordinating efforts with other teams, as the disruption represents an isolated event. Correspondingly, we expect boundary spanning to be most cost-effective when it is oriented towards information scouting.

Co-occurring, novel disruptions

For co-occurring and novel disruptions, teams need to generate oversight of the consequences of co-occurring disruptions, as well as external insights to develop creative countermeasures. Generating oversight and enabling creative solutions require dynamic boundary spanning configurations. Differentiated boundary spanning activities are likely most useful during the early phases of the disruption-response effort. The early phases of co-occurring and novel disruptions usually have the potential to lead to collaborative overload because team members receive more external requests for information and support than they can handle efficiently (Cross et al., 2016). This may prevent teams from developing quick fixes that minimise the immediate consequences of disruptions. A differentiated boundary spanning structure avoids such problems in the early mitigation phases of the disruption-response effort. By appointing a few central boundary spanners, the remaining members can focus on tasks related to the disruption-response effort. This ensures that teams exchange information and develop oversight of the situation (through key boundary spanners), while also preserving their team members' time and capacity for translating such insights in quick fixes during mitigation (de Vries et al., 2022a).

Once the mitigation phase is completed, teams may need to restructure and use more generic boundary spanning in the response and recovery phase to develop and implement countermeasures that are more permanent. After central boundary spanners have helped to develop a common understanding of the situation and put temporary measures in place, there is less need for team members to seek clarification or information from other teams (Davison et al., 2012). The amount of boundary spanning may thus reduce, rendering generic boundary spanning feasible and cost-effective (de Vries et al., 2022a). By engaging in generic boundary spanning, members from different teams can combine ideas into permanent solutions for the disruption.

It further seems important that teams use a combination of extra- and intra-organizational boundary spanning. Extra-organizational boundary spanning allows teams to obtain best practices from other organizations on how to deal with the unprecedented nature of the disruption. Intra-organizational boundary spanning may be vital to integrate (externally acquired) information and coordinate countermeasures. Inside the organization, we suggest that teams should use a combination of horizontal and vertical boundary spanning during mitigation. Through horizontal boundary spanning, central boundary spanners are capable of developing a complete and common understanding of the disruption situation that can facilitate its containment (Davison et al., 2012; Firth et al., 2015). To develop and distribute this oversight, it is important that the central person is well integrated in the team and can go back-and-forth between sharing information between team members and other teams' boundary spanners (de Vries et al., 2016). Vertical boundary spanning is needed for this purpose, as it enables the central boundary spanner to share the insights and information from other boundary spanners within the team, as well as to collect internal insights from the team.

During subsequent response and recovery phases, it is most effective if teams focus on intra-organizational boundary spanning to combine existing expertise and information into permanent solutions for the disruption. Specifically, teams might use horizontal boundary spanning to bring different teams' specialist members together so that they can combine their first-hand insights to refine and implement countermeasures. The common understanding developed and distributed by central boundary spanners during the mitigation phase facilitates team members to engage efficiently in such horizontal boundary spanning (de Vries et al., 2016). When the disruption situation changes and the common understanding becomes outdated, horizontal boundary spanning may become too labour-intensive. It might then be more efficient for team members to use vertical boundary spanning to delegate boundary spanning to teams' central boundary spanners (Davison et al., 2012). Central boundary spanners can update the common understanding through horizontal boundary spanning with other boundary spanners, which can then enable teams to return to horizontal boundary spanning between team members (de Vries et al., 2016).

In terms of configuring boundary spanning purpose, it seems particularly important that teams use boundary spanning for a combination of coordination and information scouting. During mitigation, central boundary spanners benefit from scouting information from other organizations and their home teams when developing a common understanding of the disruption situation. Central boundary spanners may also align their temporary solutions to co-occurring disruptions, thereby ensuring compatibility between teams' separate responses and preventing redundant or even conflicting countermeasures (de Vries et al., 2022a). Coordinating work and scouting external information through boundary spanning is equally important during response and recovery phases of co-occurring and novel disruptions, but serves different goals and transpires mostly between teams' members (through horizontal boundary spanning). During response and recovery, information exchange will help teams' members to obtain additional details on the nature of co-occurring disruptions from peers in other teams. Team members are directly involved in the execution of their team's tasks and therefore well equipped to gauge what additional external information the team needs to finalise countermeasures that can reduce the long-term consequences of novel and co-occurring disruptions. Coordination boundary spanning, on the other hand, is needed between teams' specialist members to align their subsequent implementation actions.

Conclusion

This chapter builds on existing research to conceptualise how teams might configure boundary spanning for resilience. We suggest that teams can "differentiate" boundary spanning tasks among members, use "generic" structures that spread boundary spanning tasks thinly among more members, or dynamically combine both structures. Furthermore, we distinguish between intra-organizational and extra-organizational boundary spanning, as well between boundary spanning aimed at coordinating activities, representing the team, and scouting information. We posit that teams may be most effective at ensuring resilience when they match their boundary spanning configurations with the co-occurrence and novelty of the disruptions they face.

Future research directions

Our configural model is conceptual in nature and therefore awaits empirical validation. Using large data sets detailing how teams have used different boundary spanning approaches to deal with different disruptions may be particularly useful in this respect. Some previous studies on resilience, teams, and boundary spanning, for example, have used a multi-round supply-chain simulation in which cross-functional teams represented different companies that could engage in boundary spanning to deal with varying numbers of supply chain disruptions and warnings (de Vries et al., 2022b; van den Adel et al., 2023). Other research used combinations of log-files from inter-organizational communication systems, phone records, and archival records on disruptions to examine how and when organizational teams successfully used boundary spanning to deal with disruptions to infrastructure networks (de Vries et al., 2022a; Ivanovic et al., 2021; van den Adel et al., 2022). Future research might use these methods to examine our configural model empirically, preferably within a sample of diverse organizations.

Future research should also investigate the mechanisms behind the emergence of the boundary spanning configurations we introduced, their temporal change, and time-dependent association with resilience. A promising new approach in this regard is the use of so-called relational event models (Klonek et al., 2019; Leenders et al., 2016; Pilny et al., 2016; Schecter et al., 2018). These models allow us to identify behavioural patterns responsible for the emergence of boundary spanning configurations. Relational event approaches avoid aggregation of measurement by capturing team processes in a fine-grained manner through intensive data collection (Klonek et al., 2019). They make it possible to model temporal dependence between team members' behaviour across time. As such, relational event models can unravel how team members actually switch between different boundary spanning configurations (Ivanovic et al., 2022; Quintane et al., 2022).

Additionally, research examining intra- and extra-organizational boundary spanning has developed in isolation from each other. (Davison et al., 2012; de Vries et al., 2014, 2016; van den Adel et al., 2022). As such, it remains unclear when intra-organizational or extra-organizational boundary spanning may be more effective, as well as when teams need to engage in intra-organizational and extra-organizational boundary spanning in parallel. Drawing from our configural model, we predict that extra-organizational boundary spanning will be particularly effective when teams face novel disruptions, while intra-organizational boundary spanning may be uniquely important when teams face co-occurring disruptions. Further research may expand on these ideas and integrate research on intra-organizational and extra-organizational boundary spanning by testing our prediction that disruption characteristics moderate the implications of intra-organizational and extra-organizational boundary spanning for resilience.

Finally, additional research is needed on boundary spanning purposes. Although there is research examining boundary spanning aimed at coordination (de Vries et al., 2022a) and information scouting (van den Adel et al., 2023), we could not find a single study examining how and when ambassadorial boundary spanning may support resilience. This is an importance omission because ambassadorial activities may allow teams to obtain support from management that can provide legitimacy for their countermeasures. Based on our configural model, we expect such benefits of ambassadorial activities to be particularly salient when teams face isolated, routine disruptions. By engaging in ambassadorial activities in such situations, teams can keep management updated on their progress and secure the support for resolving these straightforward disruptions in an efficient and autonomous manner. Subsequent research could test these predictions and examine if disruption novelty and co-occurrence indeed moderate the relationship between ambassadorial boundary spanning and a team's ability to ensure resilience.

Note

1 The authors acknowledge the financial support provided by The Dutch Research Council (NWO) [Grant 016.Veni.195.257].

References

Ancona, D. G., & Caldwell, D. F. (1992). Bridging the boundary: External activity and performance in organizational teams. *Administrative Science Quarterly, 37*(4), 634–665.

Britt, D. W. (1988). Analyzing the shape of organizational adaptability in response to environmental jolts. *Clinical Sociology Review, 6*(1), 59–78.

Chatenier, E. D., Verstegen, J. A. A. M., Biemans, H. J. A., Mulder, M., & Omta, O. (2009). The challenges of collaborative knowledge creation in open innovation teams. *Human Resource Development Review, 8*(3), 350–381.

Choi, J. N. (2002). External activities and team effectiveness: Review and theoretical development. *Small Group Research, 33*(2), 181–208.

Comfort, L. K., Waugh, W. L., & Cigler, B. A. (2012). Emergency management research and practice in public administration: Emergence, evolution, expansion, and future directions. *Public Administration Review, 72*(4), 539–548.

Crawford, E. R., & LePine, J. A. (2013). A configural theory of team processes: Accounting for the structure of taskwork and teamwork. *Academy of Management Review, 38*(1), 32–48.

Cross, R., Rebele, R., & Grant, A. (2016). Collaborative overload. *Harvard Business Review, 2016* (January-February).

Davison, R. B., & Hollenbeck, J. R. (2012). Boundary spanning in the domain of multi-team systems. In S. J. Zaccaro, M. A. Marks, & L. A. DeChurch (Eds.), *Multi-team systems: An organization form for dynamic and complex environments* (pp. 323–362). Routledge.

Davison, R. B., Hollenbeck, J. R., Barnes, C. M., Sleesman, D. J., & Ilgen, D. R. (2012). Coordinated action in multiteam systems. *Journal of Applied Psychology, 97*(4), 808–824.

de Vries, T. A., Hollenbeck, J. R., Davison, R. B., Walter, F., & van der Vegt, G. S. (2016). Managing coordination within multiteam systems: Integrating micro and macro perspectives. *Academy of Management Journal, 59*(5), 1823–1844.

de Vries, T. A., van der Vegt, G. S., Bunderson, J. S., Walter, F., & Essens, P. J. M. D. (2022a). Managing boundaries in multiteam structures: From parochialism to integrated pluralism. *Organization Science, 33*(1), 311–331.

de Vries, T. A., van der Vegt, G. S., Scholten, K., & van Donk, D. P. (2022b). Heeding supply chain disruption warnings: When and how do cross-functional teams ensure firm robustness? *Journal of Supply Chain Management, 58*(1), 31–50.

de Vries, T. A., Walter, F., van der Vegt, G. S., & Essens, P. J. M. D. (2014). Antecedents of individuals' interteam coordination: Broad functional experiences as a mixed blessing. *Academy of Management Journal, 57*(5), 1334–1359.

DeChurch, L. A., & Zaccaro, S. J. (2010). Perspective: Teams won't solve this problem. *Human Factors, 52*(2), 329–334.

Donahue, A. K., & Tuohy, R. V. (2006). Lessons we don't learn: A study of the lessons of disasters, why we repeat them, and how we can learn them. *Homeland Security Affairs, 2*(2), 1–28.

Fan, Y., & Stevenson, M. (2018). Reading on and between the lines: Risk identification in collaborative and adversarial buyer–supplier relationships. *Supply Chain Management: An International Journal, 23*(4), 351–376.

Faraj, S., & Yan, A. (2009). Boundary work in knowledge teams. *Journal of Applied Psychology, 94*(3), 604–617.

Firth, B., Hollenbeck, J. R., Miles, J., Ilgen, D. R., & Barnes, C. M. (2015). Same page, different books: Extending representational gaps theory to enhance performance in multiteam systems. *Academy of Management Journal, 58*(3), 813–835.

Gibson, C. B., & Dibble, R. (2013). Excess may do harm: Investigating the effect of team external environment on external activities in teams. *Organization Science, 24*(3), 697–715.

Goodwin, G. F., Essens, P. J. M. D., & Smith, D. (2012). Multi-team systems in the public sector. In S. J. Zaccaro, M. A. Marks, & L. A. DeChurch (Eds.), *Multi-team systems: An organization form for dynamic and complex environments* (pp. 53–78). Routledge.

Humphrey, S. E., & Aime, F. (2014). Team microdynamics: Toward an organizing approach to teamwork. *Academy of Management Annals, 8*(1), 443–503.

Ivanovic, N., de Vries, T. A., & van der Vegt, G. S. (2021). Heeding small-scale disruptions: The benefits of network fragmentation. *Academy of Management Proceedings*, 12560.

Ivanovic, N., de Vries, T. A., & van der Vegt, G. S. (2022). Managing attention in virtual hackathons: Effective configurations of team external communication. *Academy of Management Proceedings*, 14794.

Joshi, A., Pandey, N., & Han, G. (2009). Bracketing team boundary spanning: An examination of task-based, team-level, and contextual antecedents. *Journal of Organizational Behavior, 30*, 731–759.

Klonek, F., Gerpott, F. H., Lehmann-Willenbrock, N., & Parker, S. K. (2019). Time to go wild: How to conceptualize and measure process dynamics in real teams with high-resolution. *Organizational Psychology Review, 9*(4), 245–275.

Kudaravalli, S., Faraj, S., & Johnson, S. L. (2017). A configurational approach to coordinating expertise in software development teams. *MIS Quarterly, 41*(1), 43–64.

Laursen, K., & Salter, A. (2006). Open for innovation: The role of openness in explaining innovation performance among U.K. manufacturing firms. *Strategic Management Journal, 27*(2), 131–150.

Leenders, R. T. A. J., Contractor, N. S., & DeChurch, L. A. (2016). Once upon a time: Understanding team processes as relational event networks. *Organizational Psychology Review, 6*(1), 92–115.

Leicht-Deobald, U., Backmann, J., de Vries, T. A., Weiss, M., Hohmann, S., Walter, F., & van der Vegt, G. S. (2020). How team boundary spanning is most effective. *Academy of Management Annual Meeting Proceedings*.

Lettieri, E., Masella, C., & Radaelli, G. (2009). Disaster management: Findings from a systematic review. *Disaster Prevention and Management: An International Journal, 18*(2), 117–136.

Levina, N., & Vaast, E. (2005). The emergence of boundary spanning competence in practice: Implications for implementation and use of information systems. *Management Information Systems Quarterly, 29*(2), 335–363.

Marks, M. A., DeChurch, L. A., Mathieu, J. E., Panzer, F. J., & Alonso, A. (2005). Teamwork in multiteam systems. *Journal of Applied Psychology, 90*(5), 964–971.

Marrone, J. A. (2010). Team boundary spanning: A multilevel review of past research and proposals for the future. *Journal of Management, 36*(4), 911–940.

Mathieu, J. E., Luciano, M. M., & DeChurch, L. A. (2018). Multiteam systems: The next chapter. In *The SAGE handbook of industrial, work & organizational psychology* (pp. 333–353). SAGE.

Meyer, A. D., Brooks, G. R., & Goes, J. B. (1990). Environmental jolts and industry revolutions: Organizational responses to discontinuous change. *Strategic Management Journal, 11*, 93–110.

Pilny, A., Schecter, A., Poole, M. S., & Contractor, N. (2016). An illustration of the relational event model to analyze group interaction processes. *Group Dynamics, 20*(3), 181–195.

Porter, C. O. L. H., Gogus, C. I., & Yu, R. C. F. (2010). When does teamwork translate into improved team performance? A resource allocation perspective. *Small Group Research, 41*(2), 221–248.

Quick, K. S., & Feldman, M. S. (2014). Boundaries as junctures: Collaborative boundary work for building efficient resilience. *Journal of Public Administration Research and Theory, 24*(3), 673–695.

Quintane, E., Wood, M., Dunn, J., & Falzon, L. (2022). Temporal brokering: A measure of brokerage as a behavioral process. *Organizational Research Methods, 25*(3), 459–489.

Roux-Dufort, C. (2007). Is crisis management (only) a management of exceptions? *Journal of Contingencies and Crisis Management, 15*(2), 105–114.

Rudolph, J. W., & Repenning, N. P. (2002). Disaster dynamics: Understanding the role of quantity in organizational collapse. *Administrative Science Quarterly, 47*(1), 1–30.

Schecter, A., Pilny, A., Leung, A., Poole, M. S., & Contractor, N. (2018). Step by step: Capturing the dynamics of work team process through relational event sequences. *Journal of Organizational Behavior, 39*(9), 1163–1181.

van den Adel, M. J., de Vries, T. A., & van Donk, D. P. (2022). Resilience in interorganizational networks: Dealing with day-to-day disruptions in critical infrastructures. *Supply Chain Management: An International Journal, 27*(7), 64–78.

van den Adel, M. J., de Vries, T. A., & van Donk, D. P. (2023). Improving cross-functional teams' effectiveness during supply chain disruptions: The importance of information scouting and internal integration. *Supply Chain Management, 28*(4), 773–786.

van der Vegt, G. S., Essens, P., Wahlstrohm, M., & George, G. (2015). From the editors – managing risk and resilience. *Academy of Management Journal, 58*(4), 971–980.

West, J., Salter, A., Vanhaverbeke, W., & Chesbrough, H. (2014). Open innovation: The next decade. *Research Policy, 43*(5), 805–811.

4

CAREER ADAPTABILITY AND CAREER RESILIENCE IN THE WORKPLACE

Nikos Drosos and Alexander-Stamatios G. Antoniou

Introduction

The present chapter aims at investigating the concepts of career adaptability and career resilience in the workplace. Nonetheless, to understand their importance, it is essential to understand the contemporary world of work and its effects on people. Today's labour market is characterised by rapid technology advancements, non-linear careers, and demand for life-long learning and training.

Jeremy Rifkin published a study with the title "The end of work," highlighting the anticipated impact of information technology and automation on various occupations (Rifkin, 1995). Trying to conceptualise these changes, several researchers refer to the severe increase of technological unemployment (unemployment caused by technological advancements), and possibly a "world without work" (Susskind, 2020). Automation and artificial intelligence will substitute people in several occupations, whereas new occupations will emerge. Moreover, technological changes contribute to a discrepancy between the skills sought by employers and those that worker or work-seekers have. To address these challenges, there is a great emphasis put on the necessity of up-skilling and reskilling current employees and unemployed people. The main reasoning for this approach is simple: when we observe a mismatch between (1) the skills and training required in various vacant job positions and (2) the skills and training of people looking for a job, the obvious answer is the training and the acquisition of new skills that correspond to the skills that are necessary for the vacant job positions (Puckett et al., 2020). Nonetheless, this kind of approach is rather simplistic because it does not take into account that career and work are crucial aspects of people's identities.

It is very difficult for someone who has developed a certain career identity to simply accept that they have to be trained in new skills and subjects and change

DOI: 10.4324/9781003287858-6

career because the labour market has need of different skills. The emphasis should be put on assisting people to understand today's challenges; identify their own interests, work values, and skills; develop a new career plan; determine the new skills they want to learn; understand how these new skills will help them advance their career; and give new meaning to their careers. The demand for career counselling has increased drastically in the last few years as people try to find meaning in their careers (and life) within the contemporary socio-economic reality. The necessity for psychosocial resources such as career adaptability and career resilience that help people address the challenges that they face has become evident.

Today's development of more sophisticated artificial intelligence and machine learning techniques has led us to the on-going "Fourth Industrial Revolution" (Schwab, 2016), which includes not only technology-related development but changes in social patterns as well. As Schwab (2016) states, there is a "blurring [in] the lines between the physical, digital, and biological spheres," and we would add between the personal and professional spheres as well. The COVID-19 pandemic and subsequent lockdowns have been an accelerator to many technology-related changes that we expected to occur within the next few decades, but came much earlier and people were forced to adjust. Due to lockdowns and social isolation measures, many businesses were forced to have their employees working from home. In some countries, the rate of employees that worked from home surpassed 45%, and in some industries (e.g., financial, scientific, and technical services) it surpassed 50% (OECD, 2021). This was made possible because information and communication technologies (ICT) have advanced enough to allow meetings via online platforms and, in many occupations, the vast majority of activities can be performed from home. Nonetheless, the technology may have been available, but people were not ready for such a drastic change in such a small amount of time.

Teleworking during the pandemic is negatively associated with wellbeing in general (Elbaz et al., 2022) because teleworkers tend to feel increased stress and anxiety and/or depression symptoms. As the pandemic fades out, many businesses are considering keeping telework—at least for some days of the week—because it is considered "no longer a temporary pandemic response but an enduring feature of the modern working world" (McKinsey & Company, 2022). Job performance (in contrast to wellbeing) seems not to have been negatively affected by telework, but in some cases it has been improved (Elbaz et al., 2022). Working from home in the post–COVID-19 era may contribute heavily to the further blurring between personal and professional life—especially in the case where someone has family and children. To ensure a better work–life balance, in some countries, employers are not allowed to send work-related emails or texts to employees outside of work hours (EurWORK, 2021). Work–life balance in this new socio-economic reality is a challenge that individuals have to address, and both adaptability and resilience can have a hand in this.

Contemporary and future workers will have to craft their careers in a labour market that is characterised by uncertainty and decreased job stability. Linear careers where somebody enters a job and advances in the same job throughout their career as described in Super's traditional career development model (Super, 1957, 1990) are becoming more and more rare, whereas new concepts have emerged to describe newly emerged career patterns. "Protean" career is a label aimed to describe the increasing trend of careers characterised by transitions between organizations, work settings, and/or job content (Hall, 2004), whereas "boundaryless" career refers to the increasing trend of workers who move across boundaries among different employers or work settings. In this post-modern world of work, workers are expected to have to change jobs or careers in a much greater extent than in previous years. Career issues and life issues have become interconnected as career decisions have heavy impact on our life. Therefore, career design should be considered as life design (Savickas et al., 2009). Career adaptability and resilience's role is crucial in this new era of uncertainty.

To all the aforementioned challenges for today's workers, we have to add the impact of the pandemic because many people felt threatened of losing their job and experienced a high level of social isolation (Ouwerkerk & Bartels, 2022). Several studies show increased stress, burnout, and fatigue symptoms among workers (Mockaitis et al., 2022). Nonetheless, workers' experience and reaction to the disruptions caused by COVID-19 varied significantly. Some workers can cope or recover from this situation better and faster than others, and, although external support system contributes heavily, internal psychosocial resources are also very important (Mockaitis et al., 2022).

In this chapter, we aim to discuss two psychosocial constructs that have been introduced to describe characteristics and skills that we use to successfully cope with the various unexpected events that may occur in our careers: career adaptability and career resilience. We will try to conceptualise these terms and discuss their importance for people and businesses highlighting their practical applications.

Career adaptability

Career adaptability can be conceptualised as the person's readiness to address both the predictable tasks that arise in a person's career and the unpredictable changes and transitions that occur in their work life (Savickas, 1997). It is a psychosocial construct because it is not a stable personal trait but it consists of resources that occur from the interaction of the individual and their environment. In other words, career adaptability refers to the individual's resources for coping with current and future career-related tasks, transitions and work traumas, and describes their readiness to engage in exploration activities to successfully address career tasks and unforeseen career challenges. In career construction theory, career adaptability is operationalised as a multi-dimensional construct (Savickas, 2013; Savickas &

Porfeli, 2012) consisting of four dimensions: (1) concern, (2) control, (3) curiosity, and (4) confidence.

- Career concern refers primarily to the importance that the individual attributes to the preparation for future career tasks and challenges. In simple words, it is the feeling that preparing for the future is important. This career adaptability dimension is very important because planful attitudes lead the individual to engage in activities and experiences that facilitate the development of competencies and skills that are useful in addressing future challenges, and in that sense it has a very proactive role.
- Career control refers to self-regulation and the intra-personal self-discipline that is necessary for coping with career tasks, transitions, and challenges. It is also a very important career adaptability dimension because it fosters engagement with career tasks and challenges rather than avoidance.
- Career curiosity refers to exploration attitudes and behaviours. To make informed decisions, the individual has to explore both themselves and the work environment. Career curiosity leads to better knowledge of both the individual's self and the world of work and, consequently, to more realistic choices that fit both the self and the situation.
- Career confidence refers to self-efficacy feeling and beliefs regarding the individual's ability to successfully make all the necessary steps and actions needed to make career choices, address anticipated or unexpected career challenges, and pursue their career goals.

Nye et al. (2018) suggested that a fifth dimension of career adaptability should be added to the aforementioned four dimensions: cooperation. Cooperation refers to the individual's ability to work with other people and successfully interact with them when facing career tasks and challenges. When individuals with high levels of career adaptability face career developmental tasks, transitions, challenges, or traumas, they tend to exhibit concern for their career future, they have a sense of control over it, they engage in exploration activities to gather the necessary information to make career choices, and they feel confident that they can overcome the current difficulties, plan their career future, and achieve their goals. Nonetheless, some people may experience disharmony in the development rate of the different career adaptability dimensions (Savickas, 2013).

Career resilience

When facing stressful and adverse career-related challenges, some people manage to successfully overcome them while others fail to do so. In today's uncertain world of work where people are expected to make career transitions and encounter many challenges in their career, it is essential to better understand the mechanism that contributes to effectively coping with them and the concept of "career resilience" is increasingly gaining popularity by both policy makers and researchers. Nonetheless, the literature review shows a lack of consensus regarding its definition.

Resilience in general refers to exhibiting adaptive functioning despite adverse circumstances (Luthar, 2006). Some scholars define it as the ability to cope effectively and successfully with changes and instability (Luthans et al., 2006) or as a positive adaptation despite adversity (Kirmani et al., 2015). According to some researchers, it is a dynamic process (as opposed to a stable trait) that occurs when an individual faces a significant adversity and exhibits positive adaptation (Luthar et al., 2000). The person's successful coping with adversities is based on both individual and environmental characteristics. Rochat et al. (2017) conceptualise resilience as the "effective functioning under disabling circumstances," acknowledging that in this "effective functioning" contribute multiple factors, such as the person's social support resources, their skills and competences, and their motivations.

Career resilience was identified as a separate construct by London (1983), who described it as "a person's resistance to career disruption in a less than optimal environment" (p. 621). London considered career resilience as a component of career motivation. According to this early trial to conceptualise career resilience, a resilient person is characterised by high self-efficacy beliefs, is willing to take risks, and does not seek other people's approval for their decisions. Other scholars have defined career resilience as the ability to recover from career disruptions or traumas (e.g., Abu-Tineh, 2011), while others view it as a process (Mansfield et al., 2012) or as desirable outcome (Van Vuuren & Fourie, 2000). Van Vuuren and Furie regarded career resilience as a three-dimensional construct consisting of self-sufficiency, lack of concern for traditional perspectives regarding success, and openness to change. Luthans (2002) defined resilience in the workplace as the capacity to "rebound or bounce back from adversity, conflict, and failure or even positive events, progress, and increased responsibility" (p. 702).

Two more recent definitions of career resilience derive from the works of Mishra and McDonald (2017) and Rochat et al. (2017). Mishra and McDonald (2017) attempted to provide an updated definition of career resilience conceptualising it as "a developmental process of persisting, adapting, and/or flourishing in one's career despite challenges, changing events, and disruptions over time" (p. 10). In their view, career resilience is a developmental process that transpires over the individual's career and it is exhibited when people face career related setbacks that may occur from challenges and disruptions in their work or personal life. Rochat et al. (2017) consider career resilience as an interactive process between the person and the context, defining it as "the effective vocational functioning under disabling career-related circumstances" (p. 131). In their definition, they highlight the existence of a career-related challenge, risk and protective factors, and an adaptive outcome.

Despite the different definitions, all scholars agree that career-resilient people manage to "bounce back," effectively cope, and recover from the disruptions, setbacks, and challenges that occur in their work life. Developing a career-resilient workforce that will be able to handle the uncertainty of the post-modern world of work has been stated from policy makers. As we move to careers that are non-linear, multi-faceted, and transitional, people will have to cope with disruptions, setbacks, and traumas, and adapt to new circumstances.

Career adaptability and career resilience

There is no doubt that both concepts (career adaptability and career resilience) share some common characteristics. They have both derived as a response to the fact that individuals engage in career transitions and face career challenges, which they have to address effectively (Bimrose & Hearne, 2012). Nonetheless, they are fundamentally different constructs (Rochat et al., 2017) because career adaptability refers to the readiness to address predictable or unexpected career-related tasks, challenges, and transitions, while career resiliency refers to effective functioning despite stressful and disabling career-related challenges, disruptions, and transitions. Therefore, career adaptability has a more proactive character, while career resilience relates to effectively coping with challenges when they occur and, therefore, it has a more reactive dimension (Bimrose & Hearne, 2012).

Both career adaptability and career resilience are positively correlated with each other and with various other career-related aspects. Career adaptability predicts positively workers' wellbeing, happiness, and quality of life, and negatively perceived career barriers and occupational stress (Maggiori et al., 2013; Rochat et al., 2017). In a 2015 study in university students' career self-efficacy, career adaptability and career resilience were found to be interrelated, indicating that these constructs share common characteristics (Sidiropoulou-Dimakakou et al., 2015). The strong relationships between the career adaptability dimensions of control, curiosity, and confidence and career resilience may indicate that exhibiting career-related resilient behaviours require a sense of self-regulation, exploratory behaviour, and self-efficacy.

In line with the aforementioned findings, a recent study among hospitality students (Rivera et al., 2021) showed that career adaptability is a positive predictor of resilience with hope as a mediator. Rivera et al. hypothesised the mediating role of hope as various studies have shown that hope is an important predecessor of life satisfaction (e.g., Karaman et al., 2020); and career adaptability, on the other hand, has been found to be a precursor of hope (Santilli et al. 2014, 2017). Moreover, career adaptability in various studies using different population (hospitality students: Rivera et al. [2021]; adults with substance use disorder: Di Maggio et al. [2019]; and middle school students: Santilli et al. [2020]) predicted people's life satisfaction through the indirect relationship of hope and resilience.

Discussion

In the post-modern world of work, people will face several difficulties, setbacks, challenges, and transitions in their work life. The goal of both career counselling practitioners and organizational psychologists would be to help individuals to successfully cope with these challenges. As we are moving towards a world of work without linear careers and job stability throughout people's lives, our goal would be to foster the development of career adaptability and career resilience (Maree, 2017). These concepts refer to constructs that the individual uses to get employed, maintain their job, make transitions when/if needed, and ultimately live a satisfied life (Tien & Wang, 2017).

In this chapter, we tried to present both constructs of career adaptability and resilience and to make clear that they are not stable personal traits, but they can be developed through career interventions. Our role as career practitioners is to design the appropriate and effective interventions to facilitate the development of career adaptability and resilience and as a result to promote and enhance their employ-ability (Glavin et al., 2017).

Given the strong relationship between career adaptability, career resilience and career self-efficacy, Sidiropoulou-Dimakakou et al. (2015) argue that career interventions focusing on the development of a sole skill may foster many other relevant skills. In this line of thinking, Sidiropoulou-Dimakakou et al. (2013) had already developed a comprehensive career intervention aiming at enhancing career adaptability in university students and future employees. The intervention consists of seven 1-hour sessions, in which special designed experiential activities are used to enhance the corresponding skill, while participants work in small groups.

The aforementioned career intervention is based on career construction theory, which emphasises the importance of career adaptability for addressing career challenges. The life design paradigm for career counselling also has its root in career construction theory and advocates a holistic approach that acknowledges that career is an essential part of people's lives and that career planning is in fact life planning. According to Maree (2017), life design interventions promote both career adaptability and career resilience in a labour market characterised by uncertainty and, at the same time, they enable people to make meaning and find purpose in their careers.

According to career construction theory, each individual constructs a subjective career and imposes meaning and direction to their vocational behaviour. The construction of a subjective career is actually the construction of the story about their working life. This subjective career story accompanies individuals in their career transitions and changes and, therefore, career interventions should aim at assisting individuals to develop a narrative regarding their career where they assume an active agent role being simultaneously authors and actors of their career story (Savickas, 2015). By fostering agency, individuals take charge of their careers and find meaning in their career. Life design interventions help people see that even work-related situations that seem threatening can be converted into opportunities, and when somebody is in charge of their career, they can lead it in the direction that they want.

Rossier et al. (2017) argue that the life design paradigm highlights that various personal and environmental barriers as well as resources may influence individual's career stories and development. They consider career adaptability and career resilience as crucial personal resources for individuals to design their career. Rochat et al. (2017) describe that via life design interventions, counsellors can contribute to develop the individual's "resilience self-efficacy." This can be achieved by the ways that self-efficacy beliefs are developed, namely: (1) by helping the person to identify past challenging situations with positive vocational outcome and recognise that they exhibited resilience (verbal persuasion), (2) by introducing them to career stories of persons exhibiting resilience (e.g., in movies or books) and helping them to examine the similarities between these career stories and their own (vicarious learning), and (3) by facilitating positive emotions regarding current challenges and developing empowering scenarios for their career stories (physiological arousal).

In the same line of thinking, Glavin et al. (2017) suggest the use of several techniques derived from the life design intervention model such as the Career Construction Interview (Savickas, 2015) or My Career Story Workbook (Savickas & Hartung, 2012), which facilitate both the development of career adaptability and career resilience. Watson and McMahon (2017) suggest the use of the Integrative Structured Interview Process (ISI), an approach that motivates individuals to assume an active and energetic agent role by examining and reflecting on the multiple stories regarding their careers and transitions, and though to develop and explore both career adaptability and resilience.

Finally, we should emphasise that despite the fact that career adaptability and resilience are crucial in overcoming the barriers and challenges of today's world of work, they are still not receiving the necessary attention in the policy discourse that mostly examines other work-related aspects, such as work stress and job burnout or employability, neglecting the importance of wellbeing and mental health in the workplace. Following the COVID-19 pandemic, which maximised mental health issues at work, both the International Labor Organization and the World Health Organization (WHO, 2022; WHO/ILO, 2022) published guidelines regarding fostering mental health at the workplace. Nonetheless, there is little-to-no mention on career adaptability or career resilience.

A very interesting initiative in this area comes from Greece, with the launching of four day-centres for workers that operate in the metropolitan area of Athens and Thessaloniki aiming at psychosocial support of workers. The target groups include public employees, private employees, freelancers, and people working in NGOs or social businesses. It is an initiative aiming to mitigate the psychosocial impact of the pandemic and the economic crisis in Greece. The day-centres are staffed with psychologists, career counsellors, social workers, psychiatrists, and lawyers offering a wide range of services. Among their services, there is individual and group counselling aiming at fostering career adaptability and career resilience of workers. Career services will have a holistic approach based on the paradigm developed by Drosos et al. (2021), career counselling long-term unemployed people.

References

Abu-Tineh, A. M. (2011). Exploring the relationship between organizational learning and career resilience among faculty members at Qatar University. *International Journal of Educational Management, 25*, 635–650.

Bimrose, J., & Hearne, L. (2012). Resilience and career adaptability: Qualitative studies of adult career counseling. *Journal of Vocational Behavior, 81*, 338–344.

Di Maggio, I., Shogren, K. A., Wehmeyer, M. L., Nota, L., & Sgaramella, T. M. (2019). Career adaptability, self-determination, and life satisfaction: A meditational analysis with people with substance use disorder. *Journal of Career Development, 48*(3), 213–228. https://doi.org/10.1177/0894845319847006

Drosos, N., Theodoroulakis, M., Antoniou, A.-S., & Cernja Rajter, I. (2021). Career services in the post-COVID-19 era: A paradigm for career counseling unemployed individuals. *Journal of Employment Counseling, 58*(1), 36–48. https://doi.org/10.1002/joec.12156

Elbaz, S., Richards, J. B., & Provost Savard, Y. (2022). Teleworking and work–life balance during the COVID-19 pandemic: A scoping review. *Canadian Psychology/Psychologie canadienne*. Advance online publication. https://doi.org/10.1037/cap0000330.

EurWORK (2021, Dec 01). Right to disconnect. Retrieved from: https://www.eurofound. europa.eu/observatories/eurwork/industrial-relations-dictionary/right-to-disconnect

Glavin, K. W., Haag, R. A., & Forbes, L. K. (2017). Fostering career adaptability and resilience and promoting employability using life design counseling. In K. Maree (Ed.), *Psychology of career adaptability, employability and resilience* (pp. 433–445). Springer. https://doi.org/10.1007/978-3-319-66954-0_25

Hall, D. T. (2004). The protean career: A quarter-century journey. *Journal of Vocational Behavior, 65*(1), 1–13. https://doi.org/10.1016/j.jvb.2003.10.006

Karaman, M. A., Vela, J. C., & Garcia, C. (2020). Do hope and meaning of life mediate resilience and life satisfaction among Latinx students? *British Journal of Guidance and Counselling, 48*(5), 685–696. https://doi.org/10.1080/03069885.2020.1760206

Kirmani, M. N., Sharma, P., Anas, M., & Sanam, R. (2015). Hope, resilience and subjective wellbeing among college going adolescent girls. *International Journal of Humanities & Social Science Studies, 2*(1), 262–270.

London, M. (1983). Toward a theory of career motivation. *Academy of Management Review, 8*, 620–630. doi: 10.5465/AMR.1983.4284664

Luthans, F. (2002). The need for and meaning of positive organizational behavior. *Journal of Organizational Behavior, 23*, 695–706. doi: 10.1002/job.165

Luthans, F., Vogelgesang, G. R., & Lester, P. B. (2006). Developing the psychological capital of resiliency. *Human Resource Development Review, 5*(1), 25–44.

Luthar, S. S. (2006). Resilience in development: A synthesis for research across five decades. In D. Cicchetti & D. J. Cohen (Eds.), *Developmental psychopathology: Risk, disorder, and adaptation* (2nd ed., Vol. 3, pp. 739–795). Wiley Publications.

Luthar, S. S., Cicchetti, D., & Becker, B. (2000). The construct of resilience: A critical evaluation and guidelines for future work. *Child Development, 71*, 543–562. doi: 10.1111/1467-8624.00164

Maggiori, C., Johnston, C. S., Krings, F., Massoudi, K., & Rossier, J. (2013). The role of career adaptability and work conditions on general and professional wellbeing. *Journal of Vocational Behavior, 83*(3), 437–449. https://doi.org/10.1016/j.jvb.2013.07.001

Mansfield, C. F., Beltman, S., Price, A., & McConney, A. (2012). "Don't sweat the small stuff:" Understanding teacher resilience at the chalkface. *Teaching and Teacher Education: An International Journal of Research and Studies, 28*, 357–367.

Maree, K. (2017). The psychology of career adaptability, career resilience, and employability: A broad overview. In K. Maree (Ed.), *Psychology of career adaptability, employability and resilience* (pp. 3–11). Springer. https://doi.org/10.1007/978-3-319-66954-0_1

McKinsey & Company (2022, Jun 23). Americans are embracing flexible work—and they want more of it. Retrieved from: https://www.mckinsey.com/industries/real-estate/our-insights/americans-are-embracing-flexible-work-and-they-want-more-of-it

Mishra, P., & McDonald, K. (2017). Career resilience: An integrated review of the empirical literature. *Human Resource Development Review*, *16*(3), 1–28. https://doi.org/10.1177/1534484317719622

Mockaitis, A. I., Butler, C. L., & Ojo, A. (2022). COVID-19 pandemic disruptions to working lives: A multilevel examination of impacts across career stages. *Journal of Vocational Behavior*, *138*, 103768. https://doi.org/10.1016/j.jvb.2022.103768

Nye, C. D., Leong, F., Prasad, J., Gardner, D., & Shelley Tien, H.-L. (2018). Examining the structure of the Career Adapt-Abilities Scale: The cooperation dimension and a Five-Factor Model. *Journal of Career Assessment*, *26*(3), 549–562. doi: 10.1177/1069072717722767

OECD (2021, Sept 21). Teleworking in the COVID-19 pandemic: Trends and prospects. Retrieved from: https://www.oecd.org/coronavirus/policy-responses/teleworking-in-the-covid-19-pandemic-trends-and-prospects-72a416b6/

Ouwerkerk, J. W., & Bartels, J. (2022). Is anyone else feeling completely nonessential? Meaningful work, identification, job insecurity, and online organizational behavior during a lockdown in the Netherlands. *International Journal of Environmental Research and Public Health*, *19*(3), 1514. https://doi.org/10.3390/ijerph19031514

Puckett, J., Hoteit, L., Perapechka, S., Loshkareva, E., & Bikkulova, G. (2020, Jan 15). *Fixing the global skills mismatch*. Boston Consulting Group. Retrieved from: https://www.bcg.com/publications/2020/fixing-global-skills-mismatch

Rifkin, J. (1995). *The end of work: The decline of the global labor force and the dawn of the post-market era*. Putnam Publishing Group.

Rivera, M., Shapoval, V., & Medeiros, M. (2021). The relationship between career adaptability, hope, resilience, and life satisfaction for hospitality students in times of covid-19. *Journal of Hospitality, Leisure, Sport & Tourism Education*, *29*, 100344. https://doi.org/10.1016/j.jhlste.2021.100344

Rochat, S., Masdonati, J., & Dauwalder, J. P. (2017). Determining career resilience. In K. Maree (Ed.), *Psychology of career adaptability, employability and resilience* (pp. 125–141). Springer. https://doi.org/10.1007/978-3-319-66954-0_8

Rossier, J., Ginevra, M. C., Bollmann, G., & Nota, L. (2017). The importance of career adaptability, career resilience, and employability in designing a successful life. In K. Maree (Ed.), *Psychology of career adaptability, employability and resilience* (pp. 65–82). Springer. https://doi.org/10.5167/uzh-159320

Santilli, S., Nota, L., Ginevra, M. C., & Soresi, S. (2014). Career adaptability, hope and life satisfaction in workers with intellectual disability. *Journal of Vocational Behavior*, *85*, 67–74. doi:10.1016/j.jvb.2014.02.011

Santilli, S., Marcionetti, J., Rochat, S., Rossier, J., & Nota, L. (2017). Career adaptability, hope, optimism, and life satisfaction in Italian and Swiss adolescents. *Journal of Career Development*, *44*(1), 62–76. https://doi.org/10.1177/0894845316633793

Santilli, S., Grossen, S., & Nota, L. (2020). Career adaptability, resilience, and life satisfaction among Italian and Belgian middle school students. *The Career Development Quarterly*, *68*(3), 194–207. https://doi.org/10.1002/cdq.12231

Savickas, M. L. (1997). Career adaptability: An integrative construct for life-span, life-space theory. *The Career Development Quarterly, 45*(3), 247–259.

Savickas, M. L. (2013). Career construction theory and practice. In R. W. Lent & S. D. Brown (Eds.), *Career development and counseling: Putting theory and research to work* (2nd ed., pp. 144–180). Wiley Publications.

Savickas, M. L. (2015). Life-design counseling manual. Retrieved from http://www.vocopher.com/.

Savickas, M. L., Nota, L., Rossier, J., Dauwalder, J.-P., Duarte, M. E., Guichard, J., Soresi, S., Van Esbroeck, R., & van Vianen, A. E. M. (2009). Life designing: A paradigm for career construction in the 21st century. *Journal of Vocational Behavior, 75*(3), 239–250. https://doi.org/10.1016/j.jvb.2009.04.004

Savickas, M. L., & Porfeli, E. J. (2012). The career adapt-abilities scale: Construction, reliability, and measurement equivalence across 13 countries. *Journal of Vocational Behavior, 80*(3), 661–673.

Savickas, M. L., & Hartung, P. J. (2012). My career story workbook. Retrieved from http://www.vocopher.com/.

Schwab, K. (2016, Jan 14). *The fourth industrial revolution: What it means, how to respond.* The World Economic Forum. Retrieved from: https://www.weforum.org/agenda/2016/01/the-fourth-industrial-revolution-what-it-means-and-how-to-respond/

Sidiropoulou-Dimakakou, D., Argyropoulou, K., Drosos, N., Mikedaki, K., & Tsakanika, R. (2013, September). *Leaving job stability behind and moving towards career adaptability. A career guidance program for a successful future career.* Poster presented at the IAEVG international conference: Career counseling: a human or a citizen's right? International Association for Educational and Vocational Guidance (IAEVG), Montpellier (24-27/9).

Sidiropoulou-Dimakakou, D., Argyropoulou, K., Drosos, N., Kaliris, A., & Mikedaki, K. (2015). Exploring career management skills in higher education: Perceived self-efficacy in career, career adaptability and career resilience in Greek university students. *International Journal of Learning, Teaching and Educational Research, 14*(2), 36–52.

Super, D. E. (1957). *The psychology of careers.* Harper & Row.

Super, D. E. (1990). A life-span, life-space approach to career development. In D. Brown & L. Brooks (Eds.), *Career choice and development: Applying contemporary theories to practice* (2nd ed., pp. 197–261). Jossey-Bass.

Susskind, D. (2020). *A world without work: Technology, automation and how we should respond.* Allen Lane.

Tien, H.-L. S., & Wang, Y.-C. (2017). Career adaptability, employability and career resilience of Asian people. In K. Maree (Ed.), *Psychology of career adaptability, employability and resilience* (pp. 299–314). Springer. doi: 10.1007/978-3-319-66954-0_18

Van Vuuren, L., & Fourie, C. (2000). Career anchors and career resilience: Supplementary constructs? *SA Journal of Industrial Psychology, 26*, 15–20.

Watson, M., & McMahon, M. (2017). Adult career counselling: Narratives of adaptability and resilience. In K. Maree (Ed.), *Psychology of career adaptability, employability and resilience* (pp. 189–204). Springer. https://doi.org/10.1007/978-3-319-66954-0_12

WHO (2022). Guidelines on mental health at work. Retrieved from: https://www.who.int/publications/i/item/9789240053052

WHO/ILO (2022). Mental health at work: policy brief. Retrieved from: https://www.ilo.org/wcmsp5/groups/public/—ed_protect/—protrav/—safework/documents/publication/wcms_856976.pdf

5

UNPICKING ORGANIZATIONAL RESILIENCE

A Systems Perspective on Uncertainty, Information, and the Potential for Crisis

Denis Fischbacher-Smith

Introduction

> Resilience is everywhere; it is the idea and the encounter. It is the root and the branch. It is a travelling concept, a conceptual "rhizome" that has risen to prominence in debates about how we seek to understand, manage and solve the wicked riddle of uncertain times.
>
> *Rogers (2017, p. 13)*

There is little doubt that organizational resilience has, to paraphrase Rogers, taken root across a range of policy and practice domains. In some respects, the concept is akin to an invasive species because it has supplanted other established concepts such as emergency and contingency planning, crisis management, and business continuity to become, perhaps, the dominant descriptor for that collection of activities at both local and national levels that are concerned with systems failures. Governments, for example, have established resilience divisions whose role it is to address the problems associated with adverse events caused by both geo-physical and socio-technical triggers. In addition, commercial organizations and their supporting networks are increasingly lauding resilience as a core management concept (World Economic Forum & McKinsey & Company, 2022, 2023). Put another way, resilience has become a shorthand for attempts to deal with events that have the potential to generate crises for a range of organizations across the public–private sectors. As Rogers alludes, resilience also attempts to deal with a range of seemingly wicked problems and, through its relationships with crisis management, one might argue organizational messes (Ackoff, 1981; Mitroff et al., 2004). At the same time, attempts to implement the practices around resilience can also be seen to be something of challenge due to its ambiguous nature and chimeric characteristics,

DOI: 10.4324/9781003287858-7

which are exacerbated further by drawing on several academic disciplines in terms of its definition and core elements. Some of the elements that are seen to underpin resilient organizations have been identified across a range of theoretical perspectives such as those around high reliability theory (Roberts et al., 2001; Sutcliffe, 2011). However, there have also been debates regarding the universal applicability of such perspectives (Leveson et al., 2009; Shrivastava et al., 2009). At present, much of the debates about the effectiveness of organizational performance under conditions of threat and uncertainty can be seen to fall under the broad umbrella of resilience.

Despite its shortcomings, resilience has become firmly established in the policy and practice discourse as a shorthand for organizational responses to significant perturbations that have the potential to generate a crisis. However, that shorthand is not always clearly understood in term of the precise meaning of the term in practice. As a consequence, Rogers argues that resilience is a complex process in that each adaption to the shocks impacting upon the system will lead to "embedding diverse, and sometimes contradictory, logics into the practices it informs" (Rogers, 2017, p. 13). Achieving and maintaining resilience will become a dynamic process in which management practices may, over time, serve to embed vulnerabilities within the system that will run counter to achieving resilience unless such adaptations are carefully managed.

This polysemic nature of the term, in which it can have several meanings depending on its situational context, has the potential for resilience to be multi-layered and confusing for both practitioners and members of those communities and organizations who are called upon to enact the processes of becoming resilient. However, as Herrera (2017) observes, the flexibility that is inherent in the term generates problems for its operationalisation in practice and the different perspectives that stakeholders have of the term as a consequence. Resilience is used in a variety of contexts from engineering, through psychology, to systems biology/ecology and each academic discipline will emphasise different facets of the term's core characteristics, thereby adding to the potential ambiguities around its use (Angeler et al., 2018; Mamouni Limnios et al., 2014).

Perhaps one of the most useful shorthand descriptions of resilience comes from Hollnagel (2006), who describes it in terms of the "challenge of the unstable" and it is in the ways that organizations respond to unstable conditions, which typifies the process of resilience. Hollnagel (2012) also offers another important insight into the ways that organization's manage unstable systems. He argues that success and failure have the same root cause and so we shouldn't consider the failure process to be abnormal per se but, echoing Perrow (1984), seen as part of normal organizational processes. In addition, he also observes that people within organizations will adapt ways of working to meet the task demands associated with any emergent conditions that arise within the system. Woods (2006) observes that resilience can have both top-down and bottom-up implications. From a top-down perspective, managers may introduce goals that cause problems at lower levels within the organization whilst from a bottom-up perspective, those goals may be resisted or local adaptations may occur (see Reason, 1997). The result is that boundary conditions are often the spaces within the system where resilience can become degraded (Woods, 2006; Woods & Cook, 2006). These processes around adaptation will generate resonance, which may be identified as early warnings of possible unstable elements within the system (Hollnagel, 2012) assuming that the organization has effective processes for weak signal detection in place. The result is that the information processing aspects of organizational controls become core to the development of effective resilience practices.

When considering resilience as a practice, we are immediately faced with confronting issues of uncertainty, ambiguity, and vulnerability and these are issues, along with information processing and early warning detection, that managers need to address. These can be considered as part of the problems associated with those complex, often poorly structured messes that confront organizations and are one of the key elements of managerial task demands that require anticipation as well as response. That response will involve the development of effective adaptive capabilities and robust contingency plans to address the potential for a crisis that many of these messes bring with them, but will also require managers to seek out the fundamental flaws in their own processes and practices that can "incubate" the potential for failure (Turner, 1976, 1994). This also requires the organization to develop effective information processes to identify and act upon any such weak signals if it is to become resilient and adapt to emergent conditions. The relationships between unstable conditions, adaptation to those perturbations, the associated incubation of vulnerabilities, and the generation of information (as weak signals and early warnings) around systems failures can be seen as other elements within organizational resilience that also need to be addressed.

The aim of this chapter is to examine the nature of these issues in shaping resilience and the focus here is on organizational and managerial responses to those unstable conditions that have the potential to escalate to generate a crisis. It is the anticipatory aspects associated with organizational messes that challenge organizations due to primarily the difficulties in addressing the cultural elements that inhibit managers from recognising that they may themselves be part of the problem (Fischbacher-Smith, 2016). One such element relates to the ways that uncertainty is managed and the reliance on a range of calculative practices within risk analysis in situations where the predictive validity associated with those approaches is potentially weak. This can generate a sense of complacency within organizations and result in the development of a culture than can become crisis prone (Mitroff & Mason, 1983; Mitroff et al., 1989). The boundaries of organizational resilience can be explored as a means of contextualising the issues raised above within the wider landscape.

The approach taken here is based on a systems thinking perspective that sees the issues in a holistic way and contextualises the processes of resilience within organizations as socio-technical systems. In order to explore these issues further, we can use an approach from the soft systems methodology of Check-land (1999) and Checkland & Scholes (1990) as a means of identifying some of the key parameters about resilience. The chapter sets out elements of the or-ganizational resilience landscape by using work taken from the World Economic Forum and McKinsey & Company before considering the nature of resilience from a systems perspective. It then considers the nature of the threat landscape and its relationships with the asset base that the organization is trying to protect. It is here that organizational defences, which are key to developing resilience at a baseline level, are subject to perturbations and challenges that can bypass those controls and allow for an escalation in the task demands facing the organi-zation. A key element here concerns the use of calculative practices to determine the uncertainty within the system and to seek out any vulnerabilities that may become embedded in systems controls. Again, the provision of information is key to this process.

Framing the problem space

Leaders are now discussing resilience as the essential condition. How can pub-lic- and private-sector organizations arrive at a resilient stance, alert to what is over the horizon, ready to withstand shocks and accelerate into the next reality? Resilience has been described as the ability to recover quickly but recovery alone is not an adequate goal. Truly resilient organizations bounce back better and even thrive.

World Economic Forum & McKinsey & Company (2022, p. 5)

The quote from the World Economic Forum & McKinsey report highlights a range of the issues around the "practice" of resilience, along with some of the ambigui-ties that exist in the common usage of the term. By unpicking the elements of this particular framing of resilience as a form of practice, we can begin to sketch out some of the principal components of the term and the associated issues that they generate.

First, there is a recognition that resilience should be seen as an "essential condi-tion" for organizations and those who lead them. As such, there is an expectation that resilience should be a central attribute of management and organizational be-haviours. Whilst this is clearly a laudable goal, it has implications for the ways in which managers and leaders are developed, both within organizations and across the range of supporting business schools (Fischbacher-Smith & Fischbacher-Smith, 2013; Lalonde & Roux-Dufort, 2013). However, it could be argued that both avenues for leadership development are lacking in that regard, as evidenced by the consequences of several organizational problems, a number of which are long-standing and that could also be seen to have considerable ethical implications (Shantz et al., 2023; Shrivastava et al., 2013; Tombs & Smith, 1995). Recent ex-amples include the profits made by some companies as a result of the 2022–2023 energy crisis and some of the actions taken during the COVID-19 pandemic, especially in terms of claims around vaccine effectiveness (see, for example, Boytchev, 2021; Yamey & Gonsalves, 2020). What allows a producing organization to remain resilient in the face of environmental complexity may not always benefit other elements of society who bear the costs associated with meeting those challenges. Similar issues can be found in the actions or inactions of several national governments who have also been found wanting in terms of their leadership actions, especially those governments of a more populist nature (Lasco, 2020; Ortega & Orsini, 2020; Rutschman, 2021). Thus, whilst resilience might prove to be an essential condition for one part of a system, it may have differential impacts elsewhere (Woods, 2006).

Second, the opening quote also speaks to the question of what threats and associated impacts the organization is going to be resilient to and over what time-period. It also highlights the question of what "bouncing back better" looks like, especially in the face of a catastrophic failure where considerable damage has been caused and where some parts of the system may not recover at all. The 2007–2008 financial crisis serves as a case in point here (Appelbaum et al., 2012; Lu & Whidbee, 2013). Whilst the origins of the term "crisis" imply both a negative and a positive outcome and is seen as denoting "a turning point, a point of crucial differentiation" (Zimmermann, 1996, p. 162), there is an issue about the scale of the perturbation/shock that the organization or system faces and the capabilities needed to respond to it. An inability to deal with the task demands associated with a significant perturbation will have the potential to generate a crisis from which the notion of bouncing back may prove to be problematic because organizations may simply fail to recover despite their best efforts (Sipika & Smith, 1993; Smith & Sipika, 1993). In addition, organizations will have to function across different and dynamic environmental states that can be seen to range from ordered, through complex, to chaotic (Kauffman, 1993) and this will impact on their abilities to respond to the task demands and uncertainties that each system state will generate.

Third, to be an "essential condition" for organizations, resilience must be defined in terms of the parameters of what it means for the organization in question at a point in both time and space, both in terms of its theoretical underpinnings and practice implications. The World Economic Forum/McKinsey report, highlights some of these elements of the resilience agenda as a central condition. These include the links between resilience and organizational crises, the recognition that crises evolve across categories of threat as well as organizations, the need for situational awareness around the threat landscape, and the fact that networks can hide some of the interdependencies within and between organizations (World Economic Forum & McKinsey & Company, 2022). Additional work by the group has also highlighted the importance of organizational leadership in shaping and sustaining these resilience capabilities and practices (World Economic Forum & McKinsey & Company, 2023). In particular, the point about being alert to potential threats is clearly a core element in the anticipatory capabilities of an organization, as is the notion of a resilience stance. The former implies an agile organization, whilst the latter could be seen to emphasise robustness in the face of environmental shocks and this issue of definition is often seen as a key factor in the confusion that the use of the term generates. Mamouni Limnios et al. (2014), for example, define resilience as "the magnitude of disturbance the system can tolerate and still persist" (p. 104), but later highlight the processes of adaptive change as a core attribute.

Angeler et al. (2018) argue that there are two main perspectives on resilience that place a different emphasis on the nature of stability in the face of perturbations. In the first, they argue that the focus is on "a single equilibrium regime (*basin of attraction*)" in which the focus is on "*resistance, persistence, variability*" (p. 544) and is generally associated with the engineering model of resilience (Angeler et al., 2018). For Holling & Gunderson (2002), the "engineering" approach to resilience is seen as having a core focus on the issues of "efficiency, control, constancy, and predictability—all attributes at the core of desires for fail-safe design and optimal performance. Those desires are appropriate for systems where uncertainty is low" (p. 27).

Within that context, it could be argued that such a perspective on resilience has validity for those systems in which the environment is stable and the degree of (technical) uncertainty is sufficiently low as to allow for the development of a considerable degree of control over the main parameters of systems performance. This does, of course, make the use of the bounce-back approach in socio-technical systems somewhat problematic due to the often-unpredictable nature of human actors and this adds to the ambiguities surrounding the term in a practical sense. In contrast, the second approach sees resilience in terms of complex adaptive behaviours in which it is seen as "the magnitude of disturbance that can be absorbed (adaptive capacity) before the system passes a threshold, which leads to a substantial reorganization of its structure and functions and stabilization in an alternative regime" (Angeler et al., 2018, p. 544).

In discussing this approach to resilience, Holling and Gunderson argue that it is typified by issues of "persistence, adaptiveness, variability, and unpredictability—all attributes embraced and celebrated by those with an evolutionary or developmental perspective" (Holling & Gunderson, 2002, p. 27). This approach has a focus on resilience operating in a system that is far from an "equilibrium steady state" (p. 27) in which the unstable nature of the system has the potential to move it to a new systems state. Put another way, it recognises that systems can be framed in terms of the uncertainty that has to be addressed. Resilience in such a context is seen in terms of the scale and duration of the perturbation that can be absorbed before it requires a new, adaptive, change in the control functions (Holling & Gunderson, 2002).

Angeler et al., (2018) observe that the two approaches are not necessarily mutually exclusive and that the engineering approach can be seen to exist within the wider context of an ecosystem. In organizational terms, this could result in a division or operating site being subject to a perturbation in which the unit effectively bounces back, but the wider organization adapts to take account of the lessons learned from that process. Thus, multiple stable system regimes can exist within an organization but within the context of ecological resilience, the equilibrium state in which the perturbation occurred cannot be returned to because the organization has adapted to a new systems state. Thus, the notion of a resilience stance needs to take account of both perspectives on resilience. The point made in the World Economic Forum/McKinsey report about being alert to potential threats is clearly a core element in the development of the anticipatory capabilities of an organization and will impact on the resilience stance adopted. The processes associated with managing information in such a context is, therefore, key to developing resilience.

Fourth, the notion of an anticipatory stance highlights the need for managers to develop both foresight and the required "requisite imagination" (Westrum, 1993) needed to anticipate the potential threats that their organizations face, but also to recognise and respond to the vulnerabilities that exist within the control systems that they have in place, especially in the face of emergent conditions that arise out of the interactions between elements of a socio-technical system (Fischbacher-Smith, 2016; Tenner, 1996). This raises the role of knowledge and expertise within the decision-making processes and the challenges generated by emergence within the failures of socio-technical systems. It highlights what Turner (1976, 1978) termed a failure of foresight and later framed as "sloppy management" practices (Turner, 1994). In this regard, managers can become authors of their own misfortune because of the actions that they take which can generate vulnerabilities within the systems that they manage. This anticipatory stance also highlights the importance of information processing within the organization, the ways in which that information is codified, and the challenges that can arise where information flows are constrained (Boisot, 1995; Boisot et al., 2007; Fischbacher-Smith & Fischbacher-Smith, 2014). Increasingly, organizations need to address the challenges associated with mis/disinformation about their activities, which again requires an anticipatory stance to be adopted. This was particularly evident in the COVID-19 pandemic where healthcare organizations were forced to address issues around vaccine hesitancy arising out of misinformation and conspiracy theories and attacks on expert judgements (Fischbacher-Smith, 2021; Gottlieb & Dyer, 2020). The fact that COVID-19 was an emergent virus added to the problems around information processing, trust, and the burden of proof and, in some cases, led to attacks on those deemed to be expert in the field (Dyer, 2020; Rutledge, 2020). The issue of information-processing has also been a core element in the crisis management literature in which the distinction is made between routine and exceptional information processing requirements (Egelhoff & Sen, 1992). For Galbraith (1973), the gap in the information required to deal with the task demands of an event and the information that is available, points to the extent of the uncertainty that the organization is attempting to manage. Under conditions of crisis, this uncertainty is dynamic in that information is constantly changing (due primarily to the turbulence that is generated by the crisis event) and requires a degree of verification that is not always achievable given the intensity and pace of the event.

The issue of responding to uncertainty highlights the fifth issue from the opening quote, and there is an argument that we need to use the term "risk" when dealing with "measurable uncertainty" (Knight, 1957) where the probabilities and consequences of particular hazards can be calculated with a high degree of predictive validity. If this is not achievable, then we are dealing with uncertainty rather than risk and it is this that has led Dowie (1999) to claim that the term is a conceptual pollutant. This highlights a paradox within resilience as the risk analysis processes used within socio-technical systems are best suited for failures that are random in their nature. As the behaviours of human actors are invariably difficult to predict across both errors (slips, lapses, and mistakes) as well as intentional acts (violations) then attempts to quantify those behaviours will not generate the required predictive validity that is required in decision-making. The result is that the demand for effective risk analysis will invariably always outstrip the capabilities of the range of calculative practices used to determine both the probabilities and consequences associated with a hazard and where the failures within the system are the result of human agency and, therefore, not random (Fischbacher-Smith, 2023). This highlights the problem that risk as a construct is seen by some as a "conceptual pollutant" (Dowie, 1999) due to the ambiguities in the way that "risk" is defined and used in practice.

Finally, the acceleration into the next reality can be seen to relate to the aforementioned "basins of attraction" (Angeler et al., 2018) and builds upon the notion of an anticipatory capability, pointing also to the ability to manage uncertainty effectively in the process. This is particularly important in relation to the rate of change that is required to deal with the scale and intensity of the perturbation which can shape the process of accelerating into the "next reality." This also highlights the challenges around failures of foresight (Turner, 1976, 1978), especially when combined with a high pace of change. This has been highlighted within the crisis management literature as being potentially problematic for organizations (Reason, 1997; Tenner, 1996) and especially where the systems involved are "interactively complex" (Perrow, 1984) such that the complex interactions between elements of the system allow for emergence to occur and for failures to cascade across those connected elements to generate consequences that were unforeseen or deemed highly unlikely (Erikson, 1994; Smith, 2005). Again, this highlights the importance of uncertainty and information processing within the resilience process.

Figure 5.1 highlights these elements arising out of the quote from the World Economic Forum/McKinsey report as a means of illustrating the complex, and multi-layered nature of the issues that resilience as a construct needs to address. Ultimately, organizational resilience has a core function around making decisions under conditions of uncertainty for systems that are unstable or close to instability and to do so without allowing the issues to escalate to the point of a crisis. In making those decisions, managers will have to operate across environmental conditions that can move from an ordered state, through complex, to chaotic and this will generate challenges around the ways that the organization processes information and

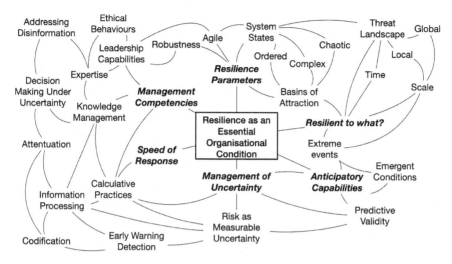

FIGURE 5.1   An initial exposition of the elements of organizational resilience

utilises knowledge and expertise in the process. Inevitably, the balance between risk (as measurable uncertainty) and uncertainty will shift as the environment moves towards a chaotic state and any managerial interventions to contain the instability will have the potential to generate emergent conditions that will heighten that already unstable systems state. The issues highlighted in Figure 5.1 also underpin the relationships that exist between resilience and theories around crisis management. A failure to maintain resilience in the face of perturbations will have the potential to generate a crisis in which the task demands exceed the organization's abilities to address them. In particular, it requires managers to reflect on the role that they play in the generation of vulnerabilities within the organization in what has been termed a "crisis of management" (Smith, 1990, 2006).

The perspective on resilience provided by the World Economic Forum/ McKinsey report assumes that the organization can anticipate and respond to a range of potential shock events that have the potential to generate a crisis and to effectively learn from that experience so as to become stronger post-recovery than before. There are, however, a series of barriers to organizational learning that impact an organizations' abilities to make such changes in the aftermath of a crisis (Smith, 1995; Smith & Elliott, 2007). This generates a potential paradox at the core of resilience because managers have to learn to be anticipatory whilst, at the same time, overcoming the barriers to effective learning that might exist within the organization as a function of the collective "paradigm blindness" that shapes their worldviews (Fischbacher-Smith, 2012). This will necessitate overcoming their own assumptions and core beliefs that have been seen to sit at the core of a crisis-prone culture (Mitroff et al., 1989). This paradox relates to the ways in which organizations manage the inherent uncertainty that exists around the management of extreme, shock events, in which the surprising nature of the hazards reflect the inherent uncertainties associated with their management and the non-linear nature of the threats arising out of emergence within complex socio-technical systems. The more traditional contingency planning process does not alleviate the potential for a crisis because the underlying causal factors that incubate vulnerability are often not considered in the process (Shrivastava et al., 1988; Smith, 1990). Similarly, the calculative practices associated with risk analysis are also problematic, especially for low probability high consequence (extreme) events.

Such extreme events are challenging because of both the role played by emergent conditions in their generation and the role of human agency in responding to such emergence. Neither emergence nor human agency lend themselves to analysis through calculative practices that generate the predictive validity required. Put simply, this paradox relates to the fact that resilience is inherently dependent on the provision of information (especially in terms of early warnings and near-miss events) around the totality of the threat landscape facing the organization. Inevitably, that information will always be incomplete and, therefore, organizations will always struggle to manage the risk (that is, measurable uncertainty) that resilience seeks to address. The ambiguities inherent in the term "resilience" itself can also be seen to contribute to that uncertainty, thereby reinforcing the core paradox around information availability and management. At the core of many of these issues is the process of intelligence/knowledge management and the communication of information, especially concerning near-miss events and early warning detection. Taken together, these issues provide a starting point at which to consider some of the significant challenges associated with resilience from a practice-based perspective.

A systems perspective on resilience

> "When I use a word," Humpty Dumpty said in a rather scornful tone, "it means what I choose it to mean – neither more nor less."
> *Lewis Carroll (1872),* Through the Looking Glass

The question of what resilience sets out to achieve is key to defining the parameters of the term and the range of challenges associated with its practice. As a starting point in that "definition," there are three core questions that need to be asked which are drawn from the work of Checkland (1985, 1999) and Checkland & Scholes, (1990) around soft systems methodology (SSM). These questions are: why do it (what are the underlying drivers), what will the system do, and how will it achieve its goals. These, and additional questions that emerge from them, are shown in Figure 5.2 and this procedure, qualifications, and records (PQR) process provides a means of further examining what resilience means in an organizational setting.

Starting with the question of "Why do organizations engage in the processes of becoming resilient?" we can argue that there is an obvious requirement to deal with the potential for adverse consequences arising from the organization's core

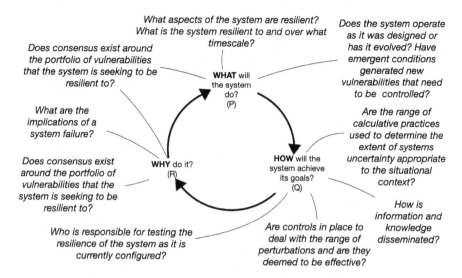

FIGURE 5.2   Core questions within Checkland's soft systems methodology (PQR process)

activities. Again, this will vary according to the organization and there is a need to effectively map the assets that the organization is seeking to protect set against the consequences of a loss of those assets (VERIS Community, nd). Those assets can be both tangible and intangible (Hall, 1991, 1992, 1993) and both should be included in an organization's strategies for developing resilience. However, it is likely that there will be different perceptions about the relative importance of those assets as well as the threats that the organization faces and the effectiveness of the controls that are in place. In essence, this can be seen to sit at the core of Checkland's SSM because it seeks to consider the transformations that exist within the system, the role of organizational actors (both operators and managers) in designing and operating that system, and those people who will be affected by the consequences of the system's activities. Inevitably, each of these groups will have a different worldview on the system and its consequences and this can have implications for the development of resilience as a practice.

The transformations that take place as part of the normal activities within the organization can also deviate from those that are planned and generate harmful outcomes as a result (Perrow, 1984; Reason, 1997; Turner, 1994). It is here that the calculative practices associated with risk analysis will start to shape the assumptions around uncertainty and the steps taken to manage it. Such analyses need, however, to be dynamic as the system evolves to take account of changes in the operating environment and the adjustments made by operators to ensure that core tasks are achieved. This process of risk analysis will also serve to inform, and be informed by, the intelligence (environmental scanning) processes within the organization (Beer, 1984, 1985).The focus here will invariably be in terms of identifying the main elements in the organization's threat landscape and on judging the potential impacts associated with changes in the operating environment. These activities place knowledge management and expert judgement into the practices around developing resilience and moves us into a consideration of how the system goals will be achived. The issue of why should organizations seek to become resilient can be seen, therefore, as a core function of management itself.

There is also a question here in terms of *resilience to what* and this will shape the controls used around core functions in terms of what the system will do relative to its threat landscape. Managing uncertainty is a key element in developing a resilient organization. If, as Hollnagel (2006) suggests, resilience is about managing the unstable, then a critical element in achieving that goal will revolve around managing the uncertainty generated within the organization and from changes in the external environment. Managing that "threat landscape" (VERIS Community, nd) will be a key task, as will making sense of the often contradictory fragments of information which emerge. Here, the organization will rely heavily on formal processes for information capture and analysis. Inevitably, however, the amount of information needed about systems performance will invariably exceed that captured though formal processes (Fischbacher-Smith & Fischbacher-Smith, 2014). A resilient organization will seek to reduce that gap and will also recognise the impact of deficiencies in the knowledge base of the organization in making decisions.

This information deficit also impacts on the role played by risk analysis within a resilient organization. The calculative practices associated with measuring uncertainty are more effective when dealing with failures that are random in nature as this allows probabilities associated with failure modes and effects to be calculated with a reasonable degree of predictive validity. Its effectiveness breaks down when dealing with human actors in socio-technical systems due to the often-unpredictable nature of human behaviours when confronted with emergent conditions for which they have no prior experience.

For Knight (1957), risk is defined as measurable uncertainty and is based on three core assessments. The first are a priori–based, in which the determination of that uncertainty is based on general principles—that is, some activities are clearly hazardous and need to be designed out of the system. The second group are based on statistical assessments using data around failure modes and their associated effects. This allows for a robust degree of predictive validity when dealing with random failures. Both a priori and statistically based assessments allow for uncertainty to be measured and they are normally based on a robust knowledge base or in those areas where research would allow that knowledge to be generated. There is also the issue of the unknown knowns (Rumsfeld, 2011), those things that are known and understood by some within the system (tacit knowledge) but which runs counter to the accepted understanding of those who manage and control the system (see, for example, Wynne, 1989, 1996). It is here that weak signals associated with problems can be situated.

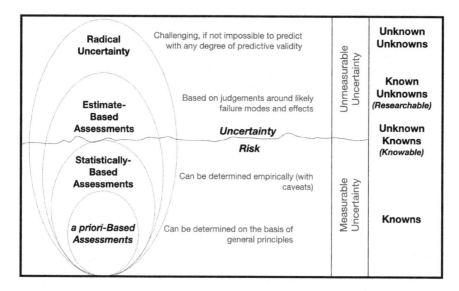

FIGURE 5.3   Risk, uncertainty, and the nature of knowledge

Source: Fischbacher-Smith (2023, p. 418).

Problems begin to arise when dealing with estimates of uncertainty based on expert judgements or where the extent of the uncertainty is deemed to be so high as to be considered radical uncertainty (Kay & King, 2020). Here, the judgements are likely to be made on an incomplete knowledge base—what Rumsfeld (2002, 2011) termed the known unknowns and the unknown unknowns. Whilst the known unknowns allow for the issues to be researched, this can be problematic when dealing with emergent conditions and especially so in a time-sensitive, high-hazard environment. Taken together, this represents the unmeasurable uncertainty within the organization which, at best, is subject to expert judgements and often has weak predictive validity (see Figure 5.3). In some cases, this should require the organization to take a more precautionary approach towards dealing with those potential hazards, although such an approach can also be problematic as a function of managerial resistance (Calman & Smith, 2001; Fischbacher-Smith & Calman, 2010). The available knowledge base will be critical in generating a resilient organization because it will shape the effectiveness of controls that are put in place and which will be set against what is known about the threat landscape. It will also be dependent on the capabilities of the organization to capture and communicate that information.

If we consider resilience as a means of responding to a range of threats (as perturbations to the system) that the organization faces, then the determination of those potential perturbations will be a function of the worldviews that are held by key actors within the system. The question of what the organization is *seeking to be resilient to* will differ across sectors and, for the individual organization, over time. If the organization operates in an international setting, then the threat landscape will also differ in spatial terms as will the vulnerabilities in that system. The result is the generation of what can be seen as "spaces of destruction" within that extended network as vulnerable pathways are generated due to differences in both the operating landscape and the threat profile (Fischbacher-Smith & Smith, 2015). If we add to this the three environmental systems states as outlined by Kauffman (1993)—namely, ordered, complex, and chaotic—then an extended organizational network may also have to contend with elements of that network operating in each of the three systems states with the attendant vulnerabilities that can generate. Each of these systems states may generate task demands that can bypass existing organizational controls and do so in a way that would allow vulnerabilities to be incubated in a system, especially were sequential control arrangements are in place (Hollnagel, 2006). These issues can be exacerbated if threat actors, who can be financially or ideologically/theologically motivated to cause harm to the organization, are able to identify and exploit weaknesses in organizational controls because of the threats generated by the environmental conditions in which the organization is operating.

Figure 5.4 shows the relationship between the various elements of the threat landscape and the elements of the organization that would be addressed by a resilience approach. As the environment moves from an ordered to a complex state, there are likely to be increasing perturbations in the operating environment that will, in turn, lead to the exposure of gaps in organizational defences that can be exploited by external threat actors, subject to them having the capabilities to exploit

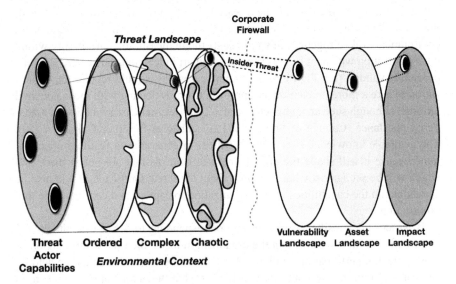

FIGURE 5.4 The threat landscape and the core elements of organizational resilience

them. Those defences are in place to protect the organization's asset base and will become vulnerable as holes appear within defences in what Reason (1995, 1997) sets out as a Swiss cheese model. If those gaps align, then vulnerabilities will be generated within the organization in what Reason (1993) terms latent conditions. The remaining elements of the resilience landscape—assets and the impacts associated with their loss—represent a modified version of the Veris framework in which risk is seen to lie at the intersection between the threat, asset, vulnerability, and impact landscapes (VERIS Community, nd). Resilience can be seen to be centred around the assets that the organization is seeking to protect and the consequences of a loss (permanently or temporarily) of those assets, along with an assessment of the vulnerabilities that exist within the system relative to the potential threats that exist, both now and in the future. The assets and the controls that are in place to protect them sit behind the corporate firewall, which is designed to minimise the threat from external actors. However, insider threat actors can bypass many of the controls that are in place within the organization and may be coerced by external actors to provide access. Insider threat actors have the advantage of often knowing where the vulnerabilities lie within the organization and can more easily expose those vulnerabilities. Examples of insiders exploiting vulnerabilities can be found across a range of organizational types, including those that are deemed to be the most secure (Adams, 1995; Greewald, 2014). Changes in the operating environment can serve to increase the potential for threat actors to exploit existing and emergent vulnerabilities. The matching of the range of potential threat actors and their associated capabilities with the opportunities provided by vulnerabilities within the system becomes, therefore, a significant element of the resilience landscape for many organizations.

Within this context, information flows are important, especially in terms of deviations from normal operating practices that might serve to generate vulnerabilities or where the organization's operating environment leads to violations of control protocols as part of an adaptive process that is not reported to managers. The result is that the system can be operating far from its designed-for state and in a new emergent equilibrium state. It is here that perturbations to the system will have the potential to escalate beyond control limits and generate the potential for crisis.

Under normal contingency planning arrangements, organizations will plan for a portfolio of potential threats and these will represent the boundaries of accepted knowledge about systems performance. However, success and failure are seen to have the same root within systems (Hollnagel, 2012). Organizations may also incubate the potential for failure within a relatively stable environmental context (Turner, 1976, 1978) which can result from management practices and assumptions about managers' capabilities to manage uncertainty (Fischbacher-Smith, 2016; Turner, 1994). In such cases, organizations become crisis prone (Mitroff et al., 1989; Pauchant & Mitroff, 1992; Pearson & Mitroff, 2019) where perturbations within a stable operating environment can expose vulnerabilities in organizational assumptions and controls around systems performance (Smith, 2005).

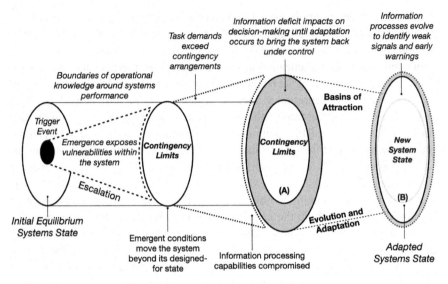

FIGURE 5.5 Escalation beyond the systems contingency limits

Figure 5.5 sets out the initial development of these shocks to the system (as a trigger event) that exposes the vulnerabilities that have been embedded in systems controls. Emergence can occur as a function of local adaptations to the system as the environment moves away from an ordered state and pushes the organization to a new "basin of attraction" in which additional vulnerabilities may incubate until a trigger event exposes them (Turner, 1976, 1978). Within this context, information can be seen to be central to resilience. It shapes our abilities to adapt and to anticipate future scenarios (and associated planning processes) and, when evolving to a new basin of attraction, it can allow for a consideration of the uncertainty within that new systems state to be considered and mapped. It also highlights two additional issues that are central to the development of organizational resilience, which were outlined earlier.

The first of these is the ability to manage those complex problems that are ill-defined and complex—what Ackoff (1979) termed "messes." Organizational crises have been framed as "ill-structured messes" (Mitroff et al., 2004) in which the complexities of interactions between systems elements and the speed at which they occur can overwhelm the abilities of decision-makers to address the messes that they face. The "tight coupling" of systems and the "interactive complexities" (Perrow, 1984) within them can be seen to be key components of these messy problems. As the organization's operating environment shifts from an ordered state, through a complex one, and into a chaotic systems state (see, Kauffman, 1993) then the abilities to adapt to these changes (where the messy nature of the problem space will increase) and the speed at which adaptation will be required will be essential to being resilient.

Authors of their own misfortune? Resilience and management practices

From a management perspective, resilience can be seen to be heavily dependent on the ability of management processes and practices to deal with the uncertainty that is generated by shock events/perturbations to the system. However, as Gunderson et al. (2002) argue, resilience can also be seen in terms of the absorptive capacity of the system to deal with the task demands generated by management actions because of the uncertainty that is inherent in their decision-making processes and the challenges of working in a dynamic environment. Thus, Gunderson et al. (2002) go on to argue that "Resilience allows a system to withstand the failure of management actions. Management is necessarily based upon incomplete understanding, and therefore ecological resilience allows people in resource systems the opportunity to learn and change" (pp. 6–7). Organizational learning can be seen, by extension, to be a critical component of a resilient system. This has much in common with the arguments set out within the crisis management field by Turner (1976, 1978, 1994), who argued that effective organizational learning was a key component in addressing failures of both foresight and hindsight.

In addition to the informational aspects of resilience, the quote from Gunderson et al. also highlights a set of critical elements associated with the resilience construct, namely: the management of the uncertainty that exists in the decisions that are taken by management, the processes that exist around adaption within that uncertain setting, the need for effective organizational learning in response to that uncertainty, and the implied role played by calculative practices within those management processes. A key aspect of the information requirements within an organization that seeks to be resilient concerns the ways in which it deals with the variety (that is, the complexity) of the information that is available to it. Ashby's Law of Requisite Variety states that this variety should be managed by variety within the mechanisms used to control that information. However, the scale of information flows within the organization inevitably leads to it being attenuated as it is communicated (Beer, 1985; Boisot, 1995; Fischbacher-Smith & Fischbacher-Smith, 2014). The management of that attenuation process serves to shape the organization's abilities to identify, and respond to, weak signals and early warnings of potential problems (Ansoff, 1975; Ilmola & Kuusi, 2006).

One of the dominant themes within the crisis management literature has been the role played by managers within the processes of incubating the potential for failure in operating process and practices (Reason, 2000; Turner, 1994) in what can be seen as a "crisis of management" (Smith, 1995). Here, a range of factors serve to shape the embedding of vulnerabilities within the organization that effectively serve as a pre-cursor for the escalation of a perturbation into a crisis (Fischbacher-Smith, 2016). For an organization to develop a resilience-based culture, managers need to consider their own potential role in ensuring resilience at multiple levels and, in particular, to recognise how the generation of policies and practices may well erode resilience by generating resistance and adaptation at the local level that isn't identified due to a lack of weak signal detection capabilities.

Clearly, resilience must be contextualised against the organization's threat landscape but there is a need to recognise that should include a consideration of how colleagues within the organization can become threats because of their treatment by managers. The generation of such insider threats has proved to be particularly problematic in some supposedly highly secure organizations where the individual has felt that their moral code has been violated by organizational actions (Greewald, 2014; Ring, 2015). In some cases, the threats from insiders can come from those managers who lead the organization and who are responsible for developing resilience. In those cases, the actions of leaders can generate the very perturbation which can propel the organization into a state of crisis and erode the resilience that the organization is seeking to develop (Milosevic et al., 2020). The problems around insider threats highlights the challenges that organizations face in terms of recruitment and selection practices as well as the ongoing monitoring of colleagues' performance at multiple levels within the organization (Fischbacher-Smith, 2015).

Conclusions

Given the complex nature of the organizational resilience construct, the discussion here has simply scratched the surface of the issues. The aim was to set out some of the elements associated with resilience and to highlight the challenges around information processing as a key aspect of the process. If resilience is to truly become an "essential condition" as advocated by the World Economic Forum, then organizations will need to actively address many of the issues highlighted here.

A key problem remains in regard to the definition of resilience as an operational construct. Whilst resilience might well be a "travelling concept" (Rogers, 2017) it is only likely to become relevant to practice once it is contextualised in the local threat environment. Resilience is not, and probably cannot be, a ubiquitous concept that can be universally applied—it is only meaningful when set within its situational context and the issues of what, when, and how the organization is to become resilient. Resilience is, as Hollnagel (2006) points out, a process of trying to manage the unstable. However, this instability also refers to the role played by management practices in generating that instability and which may well contribute the erosion of resilience through the embedding of vulnerability within the system. Instability will inevitably require organizations to be agile but that also needs to recognise that being agile also brings with it some uncertainty, especially when operating in a complex or chaotic environment where the pace of change required is high. Like the processes around hazard identification and management, resilience is not a static phenomenon, and the dynamic nature of the threat environment will ensure that it does not easily lend itself to the calculative practices that prevail within risk analysis. This has implications for the training of managers and the ways in which they address that uncertainty and recognise their own role in generating it. Taken to its ultimate conclusion, if we make resilience a central function within management practice, then there will need to be a rethinking of the ways in which managers are trained and developed and this will involve a fundamental shift in management education. By making resilience the "essential condition" for management, we will need to radically reassess its fundamental implications—developing resilience within organizations is not simply a matter of bolting on a series of concepts and practices, but rather a re-alignment of what the organization does and how it operates.

References

Ackoff, R. L. (1979). The future of operational research is past. *Journal of the Operational Research Society*, *30*(2), 93–104.

Ackoff, R. L. (1981). The art and science of mess management. *Interfaces*, *11*(1), 20–26.

Adams, J. (1995). *Sell out. Aldrich Ames, the spy who broke the CIA* (2017 ed.). Endeavour Press (Printed eBook).

Angeler, D. G., Allen, C. R., Garmestani, A., Pope, K. L., Twidwell, D., & Bundschuh, M. (2018). Resilience in environmental risk and impact assessment: Concepts and measurement. *Bulletin of Environmental Contamination and Toxicology*, *101*(5), 543–548.

Ansoff, H. I. (1975). Managing strategic surprise by response to weak signals. *California Management Review*, *18*(2), 21–33.

Appelbaum, S. H., Keller, S., Alvarez, H., & Bédard, C. (2012). Organizational crisis: Lessons from Lehman Brothers and Paulson & Company. *International Journal of Commerce and Management*, *22*(4), 286–305.

Beer, S. (1984). The viable system model: Its provenance, development, methodology and pathology. *Journal of the Operational Research Society*, *35*(1), 7–25.

Beer, S. (1985). *Diagnosing the system for organisations*. John Wiley & Sons.

Boisot, M. H. (1995). *Information space. A framework for learning in organizations, institutions and culture*. Thompson Business Press.

Boisot, M. H., MacMillan, I. C., & Han, K. S. (2007). *Explorations in information space: Knowledge, agents, and organization*. Oxford University Press.

Boytchev, H. 2021. Why did a German newspaper insist the Oxford AstraZeneca vaccine was inefficacious for older people—without evidence? *BMJ: British Medical Journal (Online)*, 372.

Calman, K., & Smith, D. (2001). Works in theory but not in practice? Some notes on the precautionary principle. *Public Administration*, *79*(1), 185–204.

Checkland, P. (1985). Achieving 'desirable and feasible' change: An application of soft systems methodology. *The Journal of the Operational Research Society*, *36*(9), 821–831.

Checkland, P. (1999). *Soft systems methodology: A 30 year retrospective*. John Wiley & Sons.

Checkland, P. B., & Scholes, J. (1990). *Soft systems methodology in action*. Wiley.

Dowie, J. (1999). Communication for better decisions: Not about 'risk'. *Health, Risk & Society*, *1*(1), 41–53.

Dyer, O. (2020). Covid-19: Trump sidelines "lying" CDC from collecting mortality data. *BMJ*, *370*, m2855.

Egelhoff, W. G., & Sen, F. (1992). An information-processing model of crisis management. *Management Communication Quarterly*, *5*(4), 443–484.

Erikson, K. (1994). *A new species of trouble. Explorations in disaster, trauma, and community*. W. W. Norton and Company.

Fischbacher-Smith, D. (2012). Getting pandas to breed: Paradigm blindness and the policy space for risk prevention, mitigation and management. *Risk Management, 14*(3), 177–201.

Fischbacher-Smith, D. (2015). The enemy has passed through the gate. Insider threats, the dark triad, and the challenges around security. *Journal of Organizational Effectiveness: People and Performance, 2*(2), 134–156.

Fischbacher-Smith, D. (2016). Leadership and crises: Incubation, emergence, and transitions. In J. Storey (Ed.), *Leadership in organizations: Current issues and key trends* (3rd ed., pp. 70–95). Routledge.

Fischbacher-Smith, D. (2021). Suppressing the 'seeker of truth' in the Covid-19 pandemic: Medical populism, radical uncertainty, and the assault on expertise. In A. Waring (Ed.), *The new authoritarianism. Volume 3: A risk analysis of the corporate/radical-right axis* (pp. 301–346). ibidem.

Fischbacher-Smith, D. (2023). Addressing the risk paradox: Exploring the demand challenges around risk and uncertainty and the supply side of calculative practices. In G. Eyal, & T. Medvetz (Eds.), *Oxford handbook of expertise and democratic politics*. Oxford University Press.

Fischbacher-Smith, D., & Calman, K. (2010). A precautionary tale–The role of the precautionary principle in policy making for public health. In P. Bennett, K. Calman, S. Curtis, & D. Fischbacher-Smith (Eds.), *Risk communication and public health* (pp. 172–212). Oxford University Press.

Fischbacher-Smith, D., & Fischbacher-Smith, M. (2013). Tales of the unexpected: Issues around the development of a crisis management module for the MBA program. *Journal of Management Education, 37*(1), 51–78.

Fischbacher-Smith, D., & Fischbacher-Smith, M. (2014). What lies beneath? The role of informal and hidden networks in the management of crises. *Financial Accountability & Management, 30*(3), 259–278.

Fischbacher-Smith, D., & Smith, L. (2015). Navigating the "dark waters of globalisation": Global markets, inequalities and the spatial dynamics of risk. *Risk Management, 17*(3), 179–203.

Galbraith, J. (1973). *Designing complex organizations*. Addison-Wesley.

Gottlieb, M., & Dyer, S. (2020). Information and disinformation: Social media in the COVID-19 crisis. *Academic Emergency Medicine, 27*(7), 640–641.

Greewald, G. (2014). *No place to hide. Edward Snowden, the NSA and the surveillance state*. Hamish Hamilton (Penguin Group).

Gunderson, L. H., Holling, C. S., Pritchard Jr, L., & Peterson, G. D. (2002). Understanding resilience: Theory, metaphors, and frameworks. In L. H. Gunderson, & L. Pritchard Jr. (Eds.), *Resilience and the behavior of large-scale systems* (pp. 3–20). Washington DC: Island Press (SCOPE 60).

Hall, R. (1991). The contribution of intangible resources to business success. *Journal of General Management, 16*(4), 41–52.

Hall, R. (1992). The strategic analysis of intangible resources. *Strategic Management Journal, 13*(2), 135–144.

Hall, R. (1993). A framework linking intangible resources and capabilities to sustainable competitive advantage. *Strategic Management Journal, 14*(8), 607–618.

Herrera, H. (2017). Resilience for whom? The problem structuring process of the resilience analysis. *Sustainability, 9*(7), 1196.

Holling, C. S., & Gunderson, L. H. (2002). Resilience and adaptive cycles. In L. H. Gunderson, & C. S. Holling (Eds.), *Panarchy. Understanding transformations in human and natural systems* (pp. 25–62). Island Press.

Hollnagel, E. (2006). Resilience: The challenge of the unstable. In E. Hollnagel, D. D. Woods, & N. Leveson (Eds.), *Resilience engineering. Concepts and precepts* (pp. 9–17). Ashgate.

Hollnagel, E. (2012). *FRAM, the functional resonance analysis method: Modelling complex socio-technical systems*. CRC Press.

Ilmola, L., & Kuusi, O. (2006). Filters of weak signals hinder foresight: Monitoring weak signals efficiently in corporate decision-making. *Futures, 38*(8), 908–924.

Kauffman, S. A. (1993). *The origins of order. Self organization and selection in evolution*. Oxford University Press.

Kay, J., & King, M. (2020). *Radical uncertainty. Decision-making for an unknowable future*. The Bridge Street Press.

Knight, F. H. 1957. *Risk, uncertainty and profit* (2006 imprint ed.). Dover Publications.

Lalonde, C., & Roux-Dufort, C. (2013). Challenges in teaching crisis management: Connecting theories, skills, and reflexivity. *Journal of Management Education, 37*(1), 21–50.

Lasco, G. (2020). Medical populism and the COVID-19 pandemic. *Global Public Health, 15*(10), 1417–1429.

Leveson, N., Dulac, N., Marais, K., & Carroll, J. (2009). Moving beyond normal accidents and high reliability organizations: A systems approach to safety in complex systems. *Organization Studies, 30*(2–3), 227–249.

Lu, W., & Whidbee, D. A. (2013). Bank structure and failure during the financial crisis. *Journal of Financial Economic Policy, 5*(3), 281–299.

Mamouni Limnios, E. A., Mazzarol, T., Ghadouani, A., & Schilizzi, S. G. (2014). The resilience architecture framework: Four organizational archetypes. *European Management Journal, 32*(1), 104–116.

Milosevic, I., Maric, S., & Lončar, D. (2020). Defeating the toxic boss: The nature of toxic leadership and the role of followers. *Journal of Leadership & Organizational Studies, 27*(2), 117–137.

Mitroff, I. I., Alpaslan, M. C., & Green, S. E. (2004). Crises as ill-structured messes. *International Studies Review, 6*(1), 175–182.

Mitroff, I. I., & Mason, R. O. (1983). Can we design systems for managing messes? Or, why so many management information systems are uniformative. *Accounting, Organizations and Society, 8*(2–3), 195–203.

Mitroff, I. I., Pauchant, T. C., Finney, M., & Pearson, C. (1989). Do (some) organizations cause their own crises? Culture profiles of crisis prone versus crisis prepared organizations. *Industrial Crisis Quarterly, 3*, 269–283.

Ortega, F., & Orsini, M. (2020). Governing COVID-19 without government in Brazil: Ignorance, neoliberal authoritarianism, and the collapse of public health leadership. *Global Public Health, 15*(9), 1257–1277.

Pauchant, T. C., & Mitroff, I. I. (1992). *Transforming the crisis-prone organization. Preventing individual organizational and environmental tragedies*. Jossey-Bass.

Pearson, C. M., & Mitroff, I. I. (2019). From crisis prone to crisis prepared: A framework for crisis management, *Risk management* (pp. 185–196). Routledge.

Perrow, C. (1984). *Normal accidents*. Basic Books.

Reason, J. (1995). A systems approach to organizational error. *Ergonomics, 38*(8), 1708–1721.

Reason, J. (2000). Safety paradoxes and safety culture. *Injury Control and Safety Promotion, 7*(1), 3–14.

Reason, J. T. (1993). The identification of latent organizational failures in complex systems. In J. A. Wise, V. D. Hopkin, & P. Stager (Eds.), *Verification and validation of complex systems: Human factors issues* (vol. 110, pp. 223–237). Springer.

Reason, J. (1997). *Managing the risks of organizational accidents*. Ashgate.

Ring, T. (2015). The enemy within. *Computer Fraud & Security, 2015*(12), 9–14.

Roberts, K. H., Bea, R., & Bartles, D. L. (2001). Must accidents happen? Lessons from high-reliability organizations. *The Academy of Management Executive, 15*(3), 70–78.

Rogers, P. (2017). The etymology and genealogy of a contested concept. In D. Chandler, & J. Coaffee (Eds.), *The Routledge handbook of international resilience* (pp. 13–25). Routledge.

Rumsfeld, D. 2002. DoD News Briefing - Secretary Rumsfeld and Gen. Myers. News Transcript. *US Department of Defense, Office of the Assistant Secretary of Defense (Public Affairs)*, http://www.defense.gov/Transcripts/Transcript.aspx?TranscriptID=2636.

Rumsfeld, D. (2011). *Known and unknown. A memoir*. Sentinel.

Rutledge, P. E. (2020). Trump, COVID-19, and the war on expertise. *The American Review of Public Administration, 50*(6–7), 505–511.

Rutschman, A. S. (2021). Is there a cure for vaccine nationalism? *Current History, 120*(822), 9–14.

Shantz, A., Sayer, M., Byrne, J., & Dempsey-Brench, K. 2023. Grand challenges and the MBA. *Journal of Management Education, 47*(3), 292–323. https://doi.org/10.1177/10525629231154891

Shrivastava, P., Mitroff, I., & Alpaslan, C. M. (2013). Imagining an education in crisis management. *Journal of Management Education, 37*(1), 6–20.

Shrivastava, P., Mitroff, I. I., Miller, D., & Miclani, A. (1988). Understanding Industrial Crises. *Journal of Management Studies, 25*(4), 285–303.

Shrivastava, S., Sonpar, K., & Pazzaglia, F. (2009). Normal accident theory versus high reliability theory: A Resolution and call for an open systems view of accidents. *Human Relations, 62*(9), 1357–1390.

Sipika, C., & Smith, D. (1993). From disaster to crisis: The failed turnaround of Pan American airlines. *Journal of Contingencies and Crisis Management, 1*(3), 138–151.

Smith, D. (1990). Beyond contingency planning – towards a model of crisis management. *Industrial Crisis Quarterly, 4*(4), 263–275.

Smith, D. (1995). The dark side of excellence: Managing strategic failures. In J. Thompson (Ed.), *Handbook of strategic management* (pp. 161–191). Butterworth-Heinemann.

Smith, D. (2005). Dancing with the mysterious forces of chaos: Issues around complexity, knowledge and the management of uncertainty. *Clinician in Management, 13*(3/4), 115–123.

Smith, D. (2006). The crisis of management: Managing ahead of the curve. In D. Smith, & D. Elliott (Eds.), *Key readings in crisis management. Systems and structures for prevention and recovery* (pp. 301–317). Routledge.

Smith, D., & Elliott, D. (2007). Exploring the barriers to learning from crisis: Organizational learning and crisis. *Management Learning, 38*(5), 519–538.

Smith, D., & Sipika, C. (1993). Back from the brink – post crisis management. *Long Range Planning, 26*(1), 28–38.

Sutcliffe, K. M. (2011). High reliability organizations (HROs). *Best Practice & Research Clinical Anaesthesiology, 25*(2), 133–144.

Tenner, E. (1996). *Why things bite back. Technology and the revenge effect.* Fourth Estate.

Tombs, S., & Smith, D. (1995). Corporate social responsibility and crisis management: The democratic organisation and crisis prevention. *Journal of Contingencies and Crisis Management, 3*(3), 135–148.

Turner, B. A. (1976). The organizational and interorganizational development of disasters. *Administrative Science Quarterly, 21,* 378–397.

Turner, B. A. (1978). *Man-made disasters.* Wykeham.

Turner, B. A. (1994). The causes of disaster: Sloppy management. *British Journal of Management, 5,* 215–219.

VERIS Community. (nd). VERIS Overview. *veriscommunity.net,* http://veriscommunity. net/veris-overview.html.

Westrum, R. (1993). Cultures with requisite imagination. In J. A. Wise, V. D. Hopkin, & P. Stager (Eds.), *Verification and validation of complex systems: Human factors issues.* NATO ASI Series (Series F: Computer and Systems Sciences, Vol. 110, pp. 401–416). Springer.

Woods, D. D. (2006). Essential characteristics of resilience. In E. Hollnagel, D. D. Woods, & N. Leveson (Eds.), *Resilience engineering. Concepts and precepts* (pp. 21–34). Ashgate.

Woods, D. D., & Cook, R. I. (2006). Incidents – Markers of resilience or brittleness? In E. Hollnagel, D. D. Woods, & N. Leveson (Eds.), *Resilience engineering. Concepts and precepts* (pp. 69–76). Ashgate.

World Economic Forum, & McKinsey & Company (2022). Resilience for sustainable, inclusive growth. White Paper: World Economic Forum with McKinsey & Company.

World Economic Forum, & McKinsey & Company (2023). Seizing the momentum to build resilience for a future of sustainable inclusive growth. White Paper: World Economic Forum with McKinsey & Company.

Wynne, B. (1989). Sheep farming after Chernobyl: A case study in communicating scientific information. *Environment: Science and Policy for Sustainable Development, 31*(2), 10–39.

Wynne, B. (1996). May the sheep safely graze? A reflexive view of the expert-lay knowledge divide. In S. Lash, B. Szerszynski, & B. Wynne (Eds.), *Risk, environment and modernity. Towards a new ecology* (pp. 44–83). SAGE.

Yamey, G., & Gonsalves, G. (2020). Donald Trump: A political determinant of covid-19. *BMJ, 369,* m1643.

Zimmermann, E. (1996). Crises, opportunities and moments of surprise: Allusions, illusions and disillusions. *Journal of Contingencies and Crisis Management, 4*(3), 162–168.

Resilience Under Examination

Occupational and Contextual Issues of Concern

PART II

Resilience Under
Exploitation

Experimental and Contextual
Issues of Saturation

6

STRESS AND RESILIENCE IN THE HUMAN SERVICES

The Importance of Radical Social-Ecological Systems Perspectives

Kate van Heugten

Introduction

There is longstanding worldwide recognition that working in the human services is frequently stressful. Causes of workplace stress include high workloads, client trauma, lack of resources, and lack of public respect, which ultimately result in depleted workers and organizations and high turnover rates. There are concerns over an ageing workforce, due to a lack of recruits coupled with low retention rates (Collins, 2008; Dollard et al., 2003; Gibson et al., 1989; Jayaratne & Chess, 1984; Kinman & Grant, 2011; van Heugten, 2011). Professional social work organizations, including in the United Kingdom, the United States, and New Zealand, have expressed concerns over high workloads and underfunding leading to a lack of resources, whilst simultaneously emphasising that competent workers are professionally responsible for practicing "self-care" and showing "resilience" in the face of these challenges (Aotearoa New Zealand Association of Social Workers, 2019; Ballantyne et al., 2019, pp. 13–14; National Association of Social Workers, 2021; Newell, 2020; Social Workers Registration Board, 2021).

Internationally, community social welfare and wellbeing are frequently given low, residual priority. The public image of human service workers is tied to the image of the welfare beneficiary population and, at least in part due to this association, they are relatively poorly regarded. When social workers are in the news, it is often in relation to failures or perceived failures in service delivery to vulnerable client groups, in particular children who have been neglected or abused. This publicity negatively impacts perceptions of the entire workforce which is often mistakenly associated purely with child services. When a broader scope of human services work is recognised, workers are typecast as underpaid soft-skilled female helpmates to other professions (Akesson et al., 2021). In the health sector, lack of

DOI: 10.4324/9781003287858-9

clarity about the social work role on the part of other professionals is particularly stressful as the tasks of social workers are often considered secondary, or not requiring specialist skills and therefore able to be carried out by other disciplines (Rose & Palattiyil, 2020). Feelings of neglect pervade the sector, which have been overtly expressed in the context of the coronavirus disease (COVID-19) pandemic, during which, for example, the efforts of health social workers have rated far fewer positive mentions in the media by contrast with nurses and other health professions (Alston et al., 2021; Kranke et al., 2021).

Whilst social work is stressful, it is also evident that stress does not preclude job satisfaction; many social workers express high levels of job satisfaction and are pleased to have chosen to pursue their occupation. In particular older workers frequently appear to evidence a robustness or resilience, and attention has turned to a search for factors that contribute to job satisfaction and how these can be enhanced (Collins, 2008, 2017; Rose & Palattiyil, 2020; Senreich et al., 2020).

Detailed characteristics and measurements of resilience are heavily debated in the social sciences and it is beyond the scope of this chapter to delve extensively into that debate. However, resilience does have a special relationship with the human services and with social work, often expressed through an emphasis on "strengths perspectives," and social work involvement in resilience related research and theorising dates back to the late 1980s (van Breda, 2018). The strengths perspective emerged in mental health social work, building on a realisation that a persistent emphasis on problems and on expert solutions led to service users (including individuals and communities) being disenfranchised and disengaged from their capabilities (Weick et al., 1989). Identifying, fostering, and building on personal and community capacities was recognised as a valuable alternative to a focus that concentrated on treating professionally identified problems with top-down solutions. Although strengths-based education became the norm, lack of resources and risk aversion limited implementation of this more positive orientation. As the concept of resilience gained prominence in the social sciences, the idea that people may adapt, bounce back, or even bounce forward and thrive amid adversity, seemed well aligned with the already familiar strength-based perspective, which holds that everyone has within them the potential for growth if they are provided with an environment that is sufficiently resourced. There was perhaps a somewhat naïve early enthusiasm for this more broadly adopted interdisciplinary concept of resilience, without an immediate apprehension of how it might be used to overly emphasise personal responsibility.

Following this earlier enthusiasm, concern has grown, at least in the context of workplace stress in human services, that the idea of resilience tends to emphasise micro-level responsibilities for staff wellbeing. An increasingly common concern reported in the social work literature is that the idea of professional resilience is too often equated with an ability to pragmatically accept negative conditions of work and the ongoing lack of availability of resources to help human service users as if they are inevitabilities. Those who are distressed at these conditions may be accused of lacking personal resilience and hence be considered professionally unfit (Rose & Palattiyil, 2020; van Heugten, 2014). In the face of such concerns, questions have arisen over the ongoing utility of the concept of resilience. In particular, Garrett (2016) has suggested that the concept is too deeply imbued with individualistic and neoliberal anti-welfare ideology for it to be able to be rehabilitated. Others, however, reason that the misuse of a concept for neoliberal ends should not lead to the discarding of a useful and well-researched body of knowledge for practice (Collins, 2017; van Breda, 2019) and that the challenges that have been voiced can help push thinking about resilience beyond an individualistic focus to more holistic and structural considerations.

Social work theorists now typically hasten to express that they conceive of resilience from a bio-psychosocial systems perspective whereby person and environmental factors are seen to interact (Adamson et al., 2014). Nevertheless, in relation to workplace stress, the social work literature still frequently revolves around a focus on how individual social workers can cope. When organizational factors are raised, these typically include the provision of supervision and education, but those interventions are ultimately aimed at building workers' coping skills, rather than bringing about whole of workplace culture change, or achieving changes in broader socio-economic and political conditions for human services.

This chapter considers long-standing stressors in human services and more recent issues brought into focus during the COVID-19 pandemic. It discusses how the concept of resilience has been conceptualised and applied in human services. The chapter concludes with a review of recent attempts to reframe workplace resilience from social-ecological perspectives that attend to the relevance of organizational cultures and macro-level socio-political contexts.

Workplace stress in human services

The reasons for high stress levels in social work and, more broadly speaking, social services or human services work, are multiple and complex. Commonly identified causes include the consequences of working with traumatised client groups who face complex challenges that are difficult to overcome without substantial social and economic support (Harker et al., 2016; van Breda, 2016) and who may at times act aggressively towards workers (Harker et al., 2016; Molakeng et al., 2021). At an organizational level, well-established pressures include unsustainably high workloads (including administrative workloads), lack of resources, and lack of consistent high-quality professional support and supervision (Rose & Palattiyil, 2020; van Heugten, 2011).

These stressors are exacerbated, and at least in part caused, by public and political lack of willingness to adequate invest in staffing and resourcing of human services (Akesson et al., 2021; Molakeng et al., 2021; van Breda, 2016). Whilst pay rates for those working in human services are frequently lower relative to other professions with similar levels of education and responsibilities, improved pay-rates alone are unlikely to overcome the disillusionment that arises for workers when there appear to be no realistic avenues available to help people overcome structurally embedded obstacles which prevent them from improving their lives (van Heugten, 2011). Macro-level factors that negatively impact the resourcing of the human services are associated with a global neoliberal market focussed ethos that has persisted since the 1980s. This resulted in a more restrictive and bureaucratic approach to the delivery of welfare. Human service organizations in the third sector took over the delivery of many previously publicly provided services under contract. They became required to respond to relentless auditing expectations, which many have suggested overly emphasise quantitative outputs at the expense of quality engagements with people in need (Mueller & Morley, 2020; Rose & Palattiyil, 2020; Valenzuela, 2021; van Breda, 2016). When social workers know what needs to be done to assist clients but are unable to deliver, due to lack of freedom to apply a holistic approach that attends to structural injustices rather than merely offering case based support, or due to lack of permission to depart from a proscribed task list, lack of resources, and lack of time, this can lead to a particular kind of stress, termed ethical or moral distress (Mueller & Morley, 2020; van Heugten, 2011, 2014). Moral distress also arises in the health sector when the overriding focus of the organization is on physical health related wellbeing without regard for emotional, social, cultural, or spiritual wellbeing. In that context, an additional significant stressor relates to the lack of clarity amongst other professionals and health service users about the role and purpose of social work (Akesson et al., 2021).

Human services in disaster contexts: COVID-19

Widespread public and professional confusion about the social work role, coupled with lack of regard for non-technological responses, may in part explain why human service workers appear somewhat overlooked as first responders to community disasters (Alston et al., 2021; Kranke et al., 2021). This is the case despite social workers typically being enlisted to provide essential services on the frontlines. Already understaffed in ordinary times, they are asked to extend themselves, potentially beyond the limits of their training, risking their own and their loved ones' psychological and physical wellbeing (Kranke et al., 2021; Tosone et al., 2012; van Heugten, 2014). During the recent COVID-19 pandemic, authors have again commented that contributions from social work and social services have been marginalised by comparison to those of other professions, such as nurses and medical practitioners, teachers, hospitality workers, and food retail workers (Alston et al., 2021; Kranke et al., 2021; Mueller & Morley, 2020).

When many countries went into lockdown for much of 2020 and 2021, this led to major changes in how social work was carried out, and reports identified specific professional adversities related to working in this disaster. During lockdowns, much human service work was moved online but many service users lacked access or adaptability to online technologies. Furthermore, less comprehensive online assessments may lead to a failure to identify complex needs (Alston et al., 2021; Seng et al., 2021). Social workers participating in a survey conducted in Australia and New Zealand noted electronic communications could also give rise to problems with safeguarding client privacy and confidentiality (Alston et al., 2021). Internationally, researchers reported workloads increased because service users experienced more health concerns, higher levels of violence, and socio-economic deprivation including homelessness (Alston et al., 2021; Aykanian, 2022). Whilst workloads increased, fewer workers were available and yet bureaucratic expectations continued unabated (Seng et al., 2021). Added to pressures at work were increased pressures at home. Human services work is gendered, carried out mostly by women, especially on the frontlines, and during lockdowns, many women held additional responsibilities for educating children at home as schools closed and for supporting at risk older family members. This reflects how, globally, caring roles still tend to fall on female shoulders and, far from challenging gender norms, the pandemic only served to exacerbate this situation (Alston et al., 2021; Stevano et al., 2021). When face-to-face work was able to be carried out, this furthermore gave rise to worries over becoming infected with COVID-19 and potentially taking the illness home to vulnerable family members (Alston et al., 2021; Aykanian, 2022; Seng et al., 2021).

In the main, where human service workers have been surveyed on this topic, most have confirmed they have been reasonably well provisioned with protective devices and reasonably well informed regarding the transmissibility and health impacts of COVID-19 (Alston et al., 2021). However, this has not been universally the case. For example, Aykanian (2022) reported on a survey with 132 frontline homeless shelter workers undertaken in Texas, United States, from April to June of 2021, between peaks in COVID-19 cases. Workers expressed high levels of concern over contracting the virus in the shelters. Despite such shelters being recognised as high-risk work settings, the participants reported they lacked personal protective equipment (PPE) and had received little guidance in relation to how to avoid infection. Worker satisfaction went down for more than a quarter of participants. Less satisfaction correlated with higher stress levels, higher levels of burnout, and lower compassion satisfaction. In research by Seng et al. (2021), undertaken in Singapore, human service workers employed outside the health sector felt less well prepared with information about COVID-19 than health sector workers who received information through their membership of the health sector workforce.

In addition to human service workers in some sectors feeling less supported and prepared than in other sectors, they may also be more stressed by comparison to other workers in the same sector. This finding predates the pandemic and there is some evidence that it holds true also in the pandemic context. For example, in the United States, Holmes et al. (2021) noted higher than national averages of post-traumatic stress disorder amongst social workers who comprised 181 of 808 participants in a survey of pandemic first responders, essential service workers, and members of the general public. More than a quarter of the social workers appeared to meet the diagnosis based on self-reported information. This was despite coexisting high levels of compassion satisfaction amongst the social workers (in excess of 99%). The authors pointed to the applicability of concepts such as "collective trauma," originally coined by Tosone (2011) after the September 11 attacks on the Twin Towers in 2001, and "wounded healers." The latter concept was introduced by Carl Jung and is used to suggest that social workers may be particularly attuned to, as well as challenged by, the suffering of others as a result of having been drawn to the profession after experiencing personal difficulties (Buchbinder, 2007; Newcomb et al., 2015; Stevens & Higgins, 2002). Holmes et al. (2021) pointed to a potential for post-traumatic growth but also the need for careful workload management, not only in terms of numbers but types and mixtures of work assignments, to ensure workers do not become over-burdened. And in relation to resilience, not only self-care but the promotion of an organizational culture of staff support was considered critical.

Meaningful work, opportunities for development, quality social interactions, and a sense of being able to have a level of control and choice (autonomy) over how to negotiate challenges are well established as important factors in achieving wellbeing in personal and professional lives (Hesketh et al., 2019, p. 58). Unfortunately, all these factors are negatively affected for many human service workers (Molakeng et al., 2021). The adequate management of resources and demands frequently falters and even more so in the wake of disasters when work becomes more demanding and complex, management expectations increase, and supervisory support becomes less rather than more available (Mueller & Morley, 2020; van Heugten, 2014). Peer support is also reduced, which was especially problematic during the COVID-19 lockdowns and may have especially impacted less experienced workers (Seng et al., 2021). Under such circumstances, the initial satisfaction derived from being able to help others at a critical time, which is a core component of meaningful work in the human services, often turns into fatigue and disillusionment and eventually wears human service workers down, emotionally and physically (van Heugten, 2011, 2014).

In addition to reports of workplace stress amongst qualified workers, student social workers have also reported distress during the COVID-19 pandemic. Evans et al. (2021) found social work students expressed high levels of stress over studies, less joy, feelings of isolation, and concerns over access to food, housing, and mental health services. Internships were also more difficult to source. Impacts on education may result in a worsening of pre-existing workforce sustainability problems.

Mitigating stress

The consequences of the various types of stressful working conditions discussed above include psychological distress, burnout, and secondary traumatic stress (van Heugten, 2011, 2014). In many countries, social work turnover is higher than turnover for professionals working in the same sectors, for example, by comparison to nurses and doctors (Rose & Palattiyil, 2020). This includes not only movement horizontally into other social work roles, but movement out of social work altogether.

Several themes are discernible in the social work workplace stress literature on efforts to mitigate stress overload and to stem the movement of workers out of the profession. These are discussed in the remainder of this chapter. Amongst recommendations are basic exhortations to practise healthy eating, undertake exercise, and ensure enough sleep; all of which are things that stressed workers can find difficult to achieve. Training and continuing professional development offered by educational institutions and workplaces are also frequently mentioned in the literature where they are often incorporated under organizational approaches, although these interventions are in fact still directed at helping the worker to change, rather than changing the conditions in which work takes place. This has led to accusations that building social workers' resilience to stress has, at least to some extent, been seized upon as a possible means of "developing 'better' workers who can accommodate the ever-increasing demands of casework" (Valenzuela, 2021, p. 1477). However, more emphasis is being directed to the concept of organizational resilience, at least in the peer reviewed literature and in research and education (van Breda, 2016). Organizational-level recommendations include making professional supervision accessible, encouraging collegiality and peer support as an aspect of workplace culture, and the importance of workload management resulting in an appropriately sized and balanced workload. Even more recently, the appropriateness of encouraging resilience without addressing a need for macro-level changes in public and governmental support for the human services sector has also begun to be scrutinised. In response, some efforts have emerged to reconceptualise professional resilience as the capacity to resist neoliberalisation despite pressures to the contrary (Fenton, 2020; Mueller & Morley, 2020).

Interventions aimed at individual resilience

Kunzler et al. (2020) noted there is still, at least at the present time, scant evidence for lasting efficacy of resilience training for social workers. Beyond recommendations such as general healthcare and seeking social support, some research has been done to fill this gap by identifying the efficacy of some specific resilience promoting approaches.

When faced with stressful work circumstances, workers may approach this through problem focussed or emotion focussed coping (Lazarus & Folkman, 1984). When problems such as lack of resources seem unsolvable, emotion-focussed coping becomes the more likely approach. Therefore, it has been suggested that, during their education, social workers and human service workers need to be better prepared for the inevitability that they will encounter unsolvable hardships and witness extreme trauma and they should be taught emotion focussed coping skills to help them handle those encounters (Kalliath & Kalliath, 2014; Newell, 2020). Methods directed at increasing emotional coping and improving emotional regulation include cognitive behavioural methods such as challenging cognitive "distortions" and positive reappraisal techniques, and mindfulness-based techniques, where mindfulness has been defined as "paying attention in a particular way: on purpose, in the present moment, and non-judgmentally" (Kabat-Zinn, 1994, p. 4, cited in Crowder & Sears, 2017, p. 18).

In association with exploring methods aimed at improving emotion-based coping, theorists and researchers have also considered the place of empathy in human services work, and have questioned whether the use of empathy, which is considered a core practice skill, predisposes workers to emotional distress and depletion (van Heugten, 2011). A practical implication of this idea suggests that negative consequences of empathy might be mitigated through, for example, learning to set healthy boundaries around professional labour encroaching on personal lives (Grant & Kinman, 2014; Kinman & Grant, 2011).

Recently, some social work researchers have explored whether mindfulness-based practices might assist social workers to improve their resilience by learning to empathise without dwelling on and becoming overwhelmed by the emotions of another person or persons. For example, Harker et al. (2016) surveyed 133 human service professionals and found that mindfulness appeared to shield workers from emotional distress and helped them balance their emotional responses. However, whilst finding a positive correlation, the research was unable to ascertain a cause-and-effect relationship. Crowder and Sears (2017) undertook qualitative research with 14 social workers in Canada to explore if mindfulness-based meditation practices might be helpful to social workers pursuing improved resilience. They noted that they did not want to suggest that social workers should adapt to oppressive conditions but that they hoped social workers might "build their individual resilience in order to respond to and resist oppressive structures with more cognitive and emotional clarity" (p. 18). They found that participants' perceptions of stress were reduced and workers were better able to de-identify with negative thoughts and emotions. They showed more compassion towards themselves and were more inclined to seek out work–life balance, and they were more satisfied with their work role.

In the context of the COVID-19 pandemic, Kranke et al. (2021) developed 11 guidelines in response to concerns over high rates of turnover of social workers in healthcare organizations, and a worldwide shortage of social workers. The guidelines focussed on how social workers could be emotionally better prepared for such community events and accompanying distressing workplace situations such as encountering clients unable to attend the bedside of dying loved ones, lack of guidance from leaders, difficulties experienced in relation to the use of technology for sensitive interactions, and lack of resources for supporting families and service users including in order to be able to work with them by distance. Despite the nature of these stressors being contextual, the 11 guidelines offered by the authors (whilst not specifically mentioning the word "resilience") were overwhelmingly focussed on the emotional preparedness of individual social workers, rather than a more holistic approach. For example, "(1) Being aware of triggers related to their own trauma that could be impacted by the event." And "(3) Considering how the range of social worker's emotions may alter before, during and after the event, and in the short-term and long-term recovery." Being "mindful" and aware were emphasised in the guidelines, and workers were encouraged to minimise their "fear of contracting the virus by wearing appropriate PPE when conducting home visits in an uncontrolled environment." Where there are gaps in services or where social workers might notice "stigmatized groups" are differently affected during the pandemic, they should be "prepared" (Kranke et al., 2021, pp. 254–255).

Such emphasis on individual resilience and on methods derived from positive psychology is meeting with considerable concern and critique (Considine, 2019). Rose and Palattiyil (2020) cautioned that "there is a fine line between positive appraisal and uncritical acceptance … of unrealistic and demanding work environments" (p. 38). Garrett (2016) warned against uncritical adoption of resilience discourses, pointing to an overwhelming tendency of these discourses to individualise problems and solutions. Garrett opined that social work has adopted the concept of resilience as if it is a common-sense notion that does not require critical analysis and that resilience is thematically linked to neoliberalism in the social work literature. Such authors caution that there has been a subtle shift in emphasis from encouraging social workers' resistance to adversity, to encouraging social workers' resilient acceptance of adversity as a hallmark of professionalism. This shift in emphasis diverts attention away from employers, policy makers, governments, and others who have the power to do something about a situation (Garrett, 2016; Molakeng et al., 2021).

This concern, that there may in effect be a negative outcome of emphases on resilience training, cognitive reappraisal, or mindfulness-based interventions, in the form of lessening emotional responsiveness towards clients' distress coupled with an acceptance of inequities as inevitable, combines with concerns over a more general neoliberal turn in the human services. The trajectory towards the neoliberalisation of the human services, including the social work profession, is a complex phenomenon. As part of this shift, it has been noted that from the 1980s onwards, younger generations, in particular, have inculcated neoliberal economic ideas and have moved away from the ideals of redistributive economics adhered to by earlier generations (Grasso et al., 2019). Fenton (2020) suggested that more recent generations of students and qualified social workers who are "less politically engaged had more disparate views and … [might hold] traditionally left wing socially liberal views (for example, promotion of diversity) … alongside economically right-wing views and support for more punitive measures towards those who break the law" (p. 8).

Fenton (2020) noted that some of these younger workers who hold more right of centre political views on welfare and criminal justice may take a pragmatic position towards lack of resources. If workers do not see beyond the individualistic neoliberal approach to managing human services' clients and outcomes, then they are unlikely to experience moral distress from a clash in values and they will be more inclined to pursue behavioural change in clients. Practitioners may see work prioritised by the agency or the agency's contractee as taking precedence. If there is no time available for more community or socio-politically oriented work then this will be considered a practical problem rather than an ethical dilemma by some practitioners (Fenton, 2020). The underlying concern here is that social work professional practices and perspectives may be undergoing a major value shift in this regard. This values shift is further supported by an emphasis on "self-care" in professional associations' conceptualisations of what is "professional" practice behaviour (Fenton, 2020; Garrett, 2016; Mueller & Morley, 2020).

Organizational resilience

To move away from problematic individualistic conceptualisations of resilience, attempts have been made to more clearly articulate the idea of organizational resilience. Van Breda (2016) drew on systems theory and ideas about family resilience to propose that

> organizational resilience can be thought of as the processes that organizations (including the individual members of the organization and the organization as a community or collective) engage in, in the face of significant adversity (which may emerge through individual members, the organization itself, or the social environment around the organization), to maintain the well-being and functioning of the system and to recover efficiently from disruption.
>
> *van Breda (2016, p. 63)*

Van Breda (2016) identified that there were four organizational resilience factors that help organizations to withstand stressors and achieve goals, including the goal of sustaining worker wellbeing: "supportive networks, problem solving, appraisal, and harmony" (p. 64).

Brown et al. (2019) argued that organizational environments are powerful factors in terms of social worker satisfaction. Social workers are not necessarily deterred by challenging work, large workloads, and difficult to solve social problems. It is when their employers are unsupportive and lack genuine concern that they become disenchanted and may decide to leave. Support for this view also emerged in Rose and Palattiyil's (2020) social constructionist qualitative study with 13 social workers in Scotland in which they explored how participants achieved resilience and thriving despite stress levels in social work. Participants in the research clarified that they found organizational change and issues relating to organizational structures and functioning more stressful than working with service users. Work with service users is expected to be challenging but workers look to their workplaces and managers for support, and it is not surprising that they become distressed when that support is unavailable. The authors identified "emotional intelligence" on the part of managers and the alignment of organizational and professional values as being of critical importance (p. 28). They noted that "The insights from the study exhort us to re-examine the scope of social work organizations to enhance the resilience of their workers" (p. 23).

A similar finding arose in a larger scale, quantitative survey by Senreich et al. (2020). In this study the researchers undertook an online survey with 6,112 licensed social workers in 13 U.S. states. Despite over half of the participants not feeling their profession was publicly appreciated, a majority of 83% were still glad to have chosen social work as their profession. And despite work with service users posing many challenges, "Feeling valued as a professional in the workplace had by far the largest beta value of all the variables in this study in regard to impact on compassion satisfaction" (p. 104). Valuing workers is expressed through organizational responsibility taking for factors that are within the organization's control, which may include such things as ensuring workers have access to supervision, are protected from overload, and are kept safe from bullying and harassment through appropriate workplace policies and approaches (Kinman & Grant, 2017; Senreich et al., 2020; van Heugten, 2013). Attention to worker wellness and work–life balance is beneficial, provided it is an expression of an organizational culture of genuine regard for workers' perspectives and needs rather than a token gesture (Brown et al., 2019; Newell, 2020).

The role of leaders in promoting organizational resilience and valuing workers was recognised in an intervention-based study undertaken with healthcare leaders, including social service providers, in Italy in the context of the COVID-19 pandemic. Giordano et al. (2022) studied the outcomes of a 10-session resilience programme for healthcare leaders. The programme took a social-ecological multi-system approach and as such addressed leaders' stress and coping skills, how to provide effective responses to individual workers' concerns, the building of intra-organizational resources to support workers, how to network with external resources for worker support, the need to actively address problematic organizational policies, and the importance of listening and providing feedback having regard to downward as well as upward accountability. The researchers found the programme benefitted both direct participants and workers in the leaders' teams.

Politicised resilience

Even this more organizational perspective on resilience does little, however, to overcome the impacts of the internationally common lowly status of human services work and lack of resourcing for the welfare of human service clients (Akesson et al., 2021). Akesson et al. (2021) used a mixed methods Delphi technique to consult with 43 experts across international social services. While the qualifications and roles of social workers differ from country to country, frontline social work is almost always carried out by women and poorly resourced, both for clients and for workers who carry heavy workloads and receive low pay. When the participating experts were asked what might be done to improve working conditions, they stressed that "improving working conditions is highly dependent upon elevating public understanding and perceptions of the profession across the globe" (p. 808).

In response to concerns about the individualistic emphasis of social work writing and research on resilience and calls for a more political perspective, van Breda (2019) countered by pointing to a long history of social work writing on resilience that views the concept from social-ecological/person-in-environment perspectives, moving beyond individual and intra-organizational levels to consider socio-political concerns (see also Kinman & Grant, 2011). Without denying that resilience theory is vulnerable to capture by neoliberal agendas, social work theorists and researchers who continue to engage with the idea of resilience make worthy efforts to disassociate from those agendas. Consider, for example, Hart et al.'s (2016) redefinition of "resilience as 'overcoming adversity, while also potentially changing, even dramatically transforming, (aspects of) that adversity'" (Hart et al., 2016, p. 3, cited in van Breda, 2019, p. 274). And Considine (2019) suggested that "resilience can [be reconsidered from a more social communitarian perspective and] be reconceptualised around the metaphor of gaining strength through supportive networks" (p. 143). Considine (2019) found at least some social work students seek a radical reconsideration of the concept so that is comes to stand for a capacity for questioning, rather than for adapting and fitting in.

Fenton (2020), however, suggested that, rather than rehabilitating the concept of resilience, it is the concept of stress, in particular moral distress, that should be liberated and reconsidered as a positive and "a hopeful concept for social work and should be embraced by social workers as a marker that something may not be 'right.' It should lead to an examination of that feeling to inspire moral courage to take action and address what does not feel 'right'" (p. 17).

Educators can teach students to value moral discomfort and analyse the reasons for its existence from a more radical social work position. Fenton (2020) recommended they should "explicitly encourage the deconstruction of neoliberal assumptions and highlight the real necessity and benefit of allowing social workers to experience, and act on, ethical stress, rather than 'cope with' and suppress it in the name of 'resilience'" (p. 16). Mueller and Morley (2020) suggested that such more radical approaches, whereby workers are encouraged and supported to act in solidarity to counter neoliberal anti-welfare dictates, may be effective at overcoming burnout in the human services.

Conclusion

Considerations of strengths and resilience have a long history in the human services in relation to work with clients. Workers themselves experience stress and distress when undertaking challenging work in difficult circumstances and more recently efforts have been made to explore how their resilience can be enhanced. There is some research evidence to support the benefits of resilience-based methods to assist individual social workers in relation to their self-care. Individualised approaches to resilience have, however, been criticised for potentially encouraging adaptation to, rather than resistance against, the resource deprivations which impact the occupation and its clients. Since efforts to overcome social injustice and inequities are at the core of the human service endeavour, this criticism must be heeded. It has been responded to by theorists who note that the concept of resilience does not inherently preclude holistic approaches that consider and address organizational and socio-political concerns. An interesting alternative proposal suggests that distress, and in particular moral distress, should be embraced as a marker or warning that conditions are deleterious and require resistance and change. This warning can then be used to encourage solidarity to counter injustices and inequities, and such united efforts may restore meaning and pride in the profession. These debates contribute to the development of an emerging socio-political angle to resilience related theorising.

References

Adamson, C., Beddoe, L., & Davys, A. (2014). Building resilient practitioners: Definitions and practitioner understandings. *The British Journal of Social Work, 44*(3), 522–541. https://doi.org/10.1093/bjsw/bcs142

Akesson, B., Milne, L., Canavera, M., Meyer, E., & Reinke, C. (2021). Changing public perceptions and supporting improved working conditions for the social service workforce: Expert perspectives from a global Delphi study. *Journal of Social Service Research, 47*(6), 808–822. https://doi.org/10.1080/01488376.2021.1926399

Alston, M., Irons, K., Adamson, C., Boddy, J., Fronek, P., Briggs, L., Hay, K., Howard, A., Rowlands, A., Hazeleger, T., & Foote, W. (2021). Australian and New Zealand social workers adjusting to the COVID-19 pandemic. *The British Journal of Social Work, 52*(4), 1859–1877. https://doi.org/10.1093/bjsw/bcab163

Aotearoa New Zealand Association of Social Workers. (2019). *Code of ethics 2019*. Author. https://www.anzasw.nz/code-of-ethics/

Aykanian, A. (2022). The effects of COVID-19 on the mental health and job stress of frontline homelessness services workers in Texas (U.S.). *Health & Social Care in the Community, 30*(5), e2793–e2804. https://doi.org/10.1111/hsc.13723

Ballantyne, N., Beddoe, L., Hay, K., Maidment, J., Walker, S., & Merriman, C. (2019). *Enhancing the readiness to practise of newly qualified social workers in Aotearoa New Zealand (Enhance R2P) -Report on phase three: The professional capabilities framework*. https://ako.ac.nz/knowledge-centre/enhancing-the-readiness-to-practise-of-newly-qualified-social-workers/report-on-phase-three-the-professional-capabilities-framework/

Brown, A. R., Walters, J. E., & Jones, A. E. (2019). Pathways to retention: Job satisfaction, burnout, & organizational commitment among social workers. *Journal of Evidence-Based Social Work, 16*(6), 577–594. https://doi.org/10.1080/26408066.2019.1658006

Buchbinder, E. (2007). Being a social worker as an existential commitment: From vulnerability to meaningful purpose. *The Humanistic Psychologist, 35*(2), 161–174. https://doi.org/10.1080/08873260701273894

Collins, S. (2008). Statutory social workers: Stress, job satisfaction, coping, social support and individual differences. *The British Journal of Social Work, 38*(6), 1173–1193. https://doi.org/10.1093/bjsw/bcm047

Collins, S. (2017). Social workers and resilience revisited. *Practice (Birmingham, England)*, *29*(2), 85–105. https://doi.org/10.1080/09503153.2016.1229763

Considine, T. P. (2019). *How do social work students perceive the meaning of resilience in their practice?* [ProQuest Dissertations Publishing]. https://go.exlibris.link/NGCcLqSp

Crowder, R., & Sears, A. (2017). Building resilience in social workers: An exploratory study on the impacts of a mindfulness-based intervention. *Australian Social Work*, *70*(1), 17–29. https://doi.org/10.1080/0312407X.2016.1203965

Dollard, M. F., Dormann, C., Boyd, C. M., Winefield, H. R., & Winefield, A. H. (2003). Unique aspects of stress in human service work. *Australian Psychologist*, *38*(2), 84–91. https://doi.org/10.1080/0005006031001707087

Evans, E. J., Nam, K., Noureddine, N., & Curry, S. R. (2021). COVID-19 impacts on social work and nursing now and into the future: National administration plans. *Health & Social Work*, *46*(3), 152–157. https://doi.org/10.1093/hsw/hlab020

Fenton, J. (2020). 'Four's a crowd'? Making sense of neoliberalism, ethical stress, moral courage and resilience. *Ethics and Social Welfare*, *14*(1), 6–20. https://doi.org/10.1080/17496535.2019.1675738

Garrett, P. M. (2016). Questioning tales of 'ordinary magic': 'Resilience' and neo-liberal reasoning. *The British Journal of Social Work*, *46*(7), 1909–1925. https://doi.org/10.1093/bjsw/bcv017

Gibson, F., McGrath, A., & Reid, N. (1989). Occupational stress in social work. *The British Journal of Social Work*, *19*(1), 1–18. https://doi.org/10.1093/oxfordjournals.bjsw.a055517

Giordano, F., Cipolla, A., & Ungar, M. (2022). Building resilience for healthcare professionals working in an Italian red zone during the COVID-19 outbreak: A pilot study. *Stress and Health*, *38*(2), 234–248. https://doi.org/10.1002/smi.3085

Grant, L., & Kinman, G. (2014). Emotional resilience in the helping professions and how it can be enhanced. *Health and Social Care Education*, *3*(1), 23–34. https://doi.org/10.11120/hsce.2014.00040

Grasso, M. T., Farrall, S., Gray, E., Hay, C., & Jennings, W. (2019). Thatcher's children, Blair's babies, political socialization and trickle-down value change: An age, period and cohort analysis. *British Journal of Political Science*, *49*(1), 17–36. https://doi.org/10.1017/S0007123416000375

Harker, R., Pidgeon, A. M., Klaassen, F., & King, S. (2016). Exploring resilience and mindfulness as preventative factors for psychological distress burnout and secondary traumatic stress among human service professionals. *Work (Reading, Mass.)*, *54*(3), 631–637. https://doi.org/10.3233/WOR-162311

Hesketh, I., Cooper, C., & Ivy, J. (2019). Leading the asset: Resilience training efficacy in UK policing. *Police Journal (Chichester)*, *92*(1), 56–71. https://doi.org/10.1177/0032258X18763101

Holmes, M. R., Rentrope, C. R., Korsch-Williams, A., & King, J. A. (2021). Impact of COVID-19 pandemic on posttraumatic stress, grief, burnout, and secondary trauma of social workers in the United States. *Clinical Social Work Journal*, *49*(4), 495–504. https://doi.org/10.1007/s10615-021-00795-y

Jayaratne, S., & Chess, W. A. (1984). Job satisfaction, burnout, and turnover: A national study. *Social Work*, *29*(5), 448–453. https://doi.org/10.1093/sw/29.5.448

Kalliath, P., & Kalliath, T. (2014). Work-family conflict: Coping strategies adopted by social workers. *Journal of Social Work Practice*, *28*(1), 111–126. https://doi.org/10.1080/02650533.2013.828278

Kinman, G., & Grant, L. (2011). Exploring stress resilience in trainee social workers: The role of emotional and social competencies. *The British Journal of Social Work*, *41*(2), 261–275. https://doi.org/10.1093/bjsw/bcq088

Kinman, G., & Grant, L. (2017). Building resilience in early-career social workers: Evaluating a multi-modal intervention. *The British Journal of Social Work*, *47*(7), 1979–1998. https://doi.org/10.1093/bjsw/bcw164

Kranke, D., Mudoh, Y., Milligan, S., Gioia, D., & Dobalian, A. (2021). Emotional preparedness as a mechanism to improve provider morale during the pandemic. *Social Work in Mental Health*, *19*(3), 248–257. https://doi.org/10.1080/15332985.2021.1904090

Kunzler, A. M., Kunzler, A. M., Helmreich, I., Chmitorz, A., König, J., Binder, H., Wessa, M., & Lieb, K. (2020). Psychological interventions to foster resilience in healthcare professionals. *Cochrane Database of Systematic Reviews*, *2020*(7), CD012527. https://doi.org/10.1002/14651858.CD012527.pub2

Lazarus, R. S., & Folkman, S. (1984). *Stress, appraisal, and coping*. Springer.

Molakeng, M. H., Truter, E., & Fouché, A. (2021). Resilience of child protection social workers: A scoping review. *European Journal of Social Work*, *24*(6), 1028–1050. https://doi.org/10.1080/13691457.2021.1901660

Mueller, V., & Morley, C. (2020). Blaming individuals for burnout: Developing critical practice responses to workplace stress. *Social Alternatives*, *39*(3), 20–28. https://doi.org/10.3316/informit.767920662624987

National Association of Social Workers. (2021). *NASW code of ethics*. Author. https://www.socialworkers.org/About/Ethics/Code-of-Ethics/Code-of-Ethics-English

Newcomb, M., Burton, J., Edwards, N., & Hazelwood, Z. (2015). How Jung's concept of the wounded healer can guide learning and teaching in social work and human services. *Advances in Social Work and Welfare Education*, *17*(2), 55–69. https://doi.org/10.3316/aeipt.212510

Newell, J. M. (2020). An ecological systems framework for professional resilience in social work practice. *Social Work*, *65*(1), 65–73. https://doi.org/10.1093/sw/swz044

Rose, S., & Palattiyil, G. (2020). Surviving or thriving? Enhancing the emotional resilience of social workers in their organisational settings. *Journal of Social Work*, *20*(1), 23–42. https://doi.org/10.1177/1468017318793614

Seng, B. K., Subramaniam, M., Chung, Y. J., Syed Ahmad, S. A. M., & Chong, S. A. (2021). Resilience and stress in frontline social workers during the COVID-19 pandemic in Singapore. *Asian Social Work and Policy Review*, *15*(3), 234–243. https://doi.org/10.1111/aswp.12237

Senreich, E., Straussner, S. L. A., & Steen, J. (2020). The work experiences of social workers: Factors impacting compassion satisfaction and workplace stress. *Journal of Social Service Research*, *46*(1), 93–109. https://doi.org/10.1080/01488376.2018.1528491

Social Workers Registration Board (2021). *Ngā Paerewa Kaiakatanga Matua Core Competence Standards*. Social Workers Registration Board, New Zealand Government. https://swrb.govt.nz/practice/core-competence-standards/

Stevano, S., Mezzadri, A., Lombardozzi, L., & Bargawi, H. (2021). Hidden abodes in plain sight: The social reproduction of households and labor in the COVID-19 pandemic. *Feminist Economics*, *27*(1-2), 271–287. https://doi.org/10.1080/13545701.2020.1854478

Stevens, M., & Higgins, D. J. (2002). The influence of risk and protective factors on burnout experienced by those who work with maltreated children. *Child Abuse Review*, *11*(5), 313–331. https://doi.org/10.1002/car.754

Tosone, C. (2011). The legacy of September 11: Shared trauma, therapeutic intimacy, and professional posttraumatic growth. *Traumatology (Tallahassee, Fla.)*, *17*(3), 25–29. https://doi.org/10.1177/1534765611421963

Tosone, C., Nuttman-Shwartz, O., & Stephens, T. (2012). Shared trauma: When the professional is personal. *Clinical Social Work Journal*, *40*(2), 231–239. https://doi.org/10.1007/s10615-012-0395-0

Valenzuela, R. (2021). Audit culture, accountability, and care: A phenomenological anthropology of child welfare. *Qualitative Social Work*, *20*(6), 1477–1495. https://doi.org/10.1177/14733250211039512

van Breda, A. (2018). A critical review of resilience theory and its relevance for social work. *Social Work*, *54*(1), 1–18. https://doi.org/10.15270/54-1-611

van Breda, A. D. (2016). Building resilient human service organizations. *Human Service Organizations, Management, Leadership & Governance*, *40*(1), 62–73. https://doi.org/10.1080/23303131.2015.1093571

van Breda, A. D. (2019). Reclaiming resilience for social work: A reply to Garrett. *The British Journal of Social Work*, *49*(1), 272–276. https://doi.org/10.1093/bjsw/bcy010

van Heugten, K. (2011). *Social work under pressure: How to overcome stress, fatigue and burnout in the workplace*. Jessica Kingsley Publishers. https://go.exlibris.link/2vNmtk1w

van Heugten, K. (2013). Resilience as an underexplored outcome of workplace bullying. *Qualitative Health Research*, *23*(3), 291–301. https://doi.org/10.1177/1049732312468251

van Heugten, K. (2014). *Human service organizations in the disaster context*. Palgrave Macmillan. https://doi.org/10.1057/9781137387424

Weick, A., Rapp, C., Sullivan, W. P., & Kisthardt, W. (1989). A strengths perspective for social work practice. *Social Work*, *34*(4), 350–354. https://doi.org/10.1093/sw/34.4.350

7

APPLYING A PSYCHOLOGICALLY INFORMED APPROACH TO RESILIENCE IN HEALTH AND SOCIAL CARE ORGANIZATIONS

Felicity R. L. Baker, Kevin L. Baker, and Jo Burrell

There have been multiple definitions of organizational resilience, variously described as a capacity to manage threat, a dynamic process of adaptation to threat, and an outcome of successful navigation of threat. The concept has been explored in a wide range of contexts, including individual, social, economic, ecological, incident management, computing, and engineering sciences, to name a few (Gaillard, 2007; Gibson & Tarrant, 2010; Holling, 2001; Rutter, 2006). This wide array of definitions and applications has produced many attempts to capture a complex and multi-dimensional concept in ways that can be applied to organizations, but which often include some simplistic and mechanistic approaches to resilience and are difficult to apply in practice (Gibson & Tarrant, 2010).

Interest in resilience for health and social care organizations has grown following health crises such as the Ebola epidemic and the COVID-19 pandemic. This interest has been further stimulated by the increased economic and financial pressures placed on nations and governments to manage complex care systems. In a relatively short period of time, several theoretical frameworks or models of resilience for care organizations have been developed (e.g., Biddle et al., 2020; Turenne et al., 2019). However, explorations about how to apply these frameworks have not yet been widely reported (Forsgren et al., 2022), and the development of resilience for care organizations continues to be a difficult and complex problem.

Initially, resilience for care organizations was generally described in terms that relate to how an organization bounces back following a health crisis or a natural disaster like an earthquake, tsunami, or flood. However, care organizations have often struggled to implement changes following a crisis for a range of reasons and so "bouncing back" is perhaps a poor metaphor. Health and social care organizations are usually large, complex, and adaptive systems providing essential services to society and, as such, they are rarely permitted to completely "fail." Consequently,

DOI: 10.4324/9781003287858-10

while there may be multiple barriers to change and improvements, they will eventually be pressurised into absorbing and adapting in response to threats and stress (Blanchet & James, 2013). For example, following the SARS outbreak, research identified that staff who experienced distress at work were more likely to experience burnout, physical and mental ill-health, and take more time off work (Chan & Huak, 2004; Maunder et al., 2006). Despite this research leading to calls for more support for health workers, few changes were made until the COVID-19 pandemic forced organizations to look more closely at staff stress.

In their review of the literature on resilience in health systems, Barasa et al. (2018) described a tendency of researchers to focus on the organizational characteristics that are thought to be important for responding to crises and threats. These include preparedness and planning, information management, collateral pathways and resource redundancy, material resources, and processes that focus on improved governance. However, they pointed out that there is a need to also recognise how an organization responds to chronic, everyday challenges in addition to acute crises. These challenges are more clearly reflected in the ways in which staff react and function day-to-day. The tendency of organizations to ignore everyday threats to functioning is most often associated with a culture in which an economic model of service delivery blinds them to wider models and approaches that could deliver improved outcomes for patients and staff. They noted that although organizational procedures and processes are generally prioritised by theorists and researchers, the more human or "soft" interpersonal structures and processes are equally important when responding to organizational threats and challenges. These include leadership practices, organizational culture, human capital, social networks and collaboration. Biddle et al. (2020) described this distinction as representing two sides of the same coin, asserting that creating resilience in organizations involves understanding both the "top-down" influence of organizational processes and the "bottom-up" processes of the individuals working in the organization.

Implementing strategies for developing resilience—the challenges

Evidence that many health and social care organizations struggle to understand and implement the changes needed for improved resilience suggests that this is a challenging endeavour. Implementation science for health services has been heavily influenced by a focus on knowledge translation and transfer (Grieg et al., 2012). In this approach, the emphasis is placed on identifying strategies and processes that appear to contribute to improvements in an organization. These are then transferred or applied across organizations, translating "best practice" into different, but related contexts (Nutley et al., 2007). However, there is a clear recognition that operationalising knowledge transfer is difficult, and especially so in care organizations (Grieg et al., 2012).

It is possible to survey organizations to explore the range of strategies that help build organizational resilience. However, this must be done in ways which do not restrict the findings to generalisations that are so broad such that they cannot be translated to the contexts of individual organizations. Attempts to understand the complexity and dynamic nature of care organizations often lead to a tendency to conceptualise policy making, staff management, and clinical activity as largely separate and discrete activities (Walshe & Rundall, 2001). Unfortunately, this conceptualisation actually works to inhibit knowledge transfer because it fails to expand on why and how various strategies can contribute to building resilience in both individuals in the organization and the organization as a whole (Forsgren et al., 2022; Grieg et al., 2012). We argue that any investigation into organizational resilience is limited if it ignores the interpersonal dynamics of the individuals within the organization and their experience of chronic, everyday stress (Barasa et al., 2018, Biddle et al., 2020).

A psychologically informed approach

As clinical psychologists, we are interested in applying what we know from our clinical work with individuals and systems to our work with organizations. We have found that progress can be made through taking a psychologically informed approach to the problem of developing and implementing changes that are not solely focused on knowledge transfer but also address the complexities of interpersonal and process factors (Baker et al., 2021). Beginning with an assessment of the threats to an organization's resilience with an analysis of the factors involved in responding to threats, this then informs a strategy of implementation that is unique to the particular threat, system, and individuals concerned.

This approach is not new or unique, and neither is it specific to a health and social care context. The aircraft industry has responded to threats to safety and efficiency by using feedback systems to drive improvements. These systems rely on collecting information about threats and recommending changes that eliminate or diminish those threats. Each plane has a "black box" flight-recorder, which can be used in an investigation to securely supply a range of data, even after a plane has crashed. Investigations following any incident or near-miss will use this information to provide learning points and recommend changes to help improve aircraft design, protocols for staff, and other processes that ultimately improve air safety and make travel more accessible and profitable.

An example of how this process of analysis and learning has been applied can be seen in the case of the United Airlines Flight 173 crash in 1978. This was a scheduled routine passenger flight from New York to Portland with experienced pilots and crew on board. The plane crashed during its approach to Portland, with 10 people losing their lives out of the 189 people on board. The disaster was due to the plane running out of fuel while the pilot and crew were trying to resolve a landing gear problem. Remarkably, the highly experienced crew failed to monitor the fuel effectively, despite warnings from the flight engineer. The subsequent investigation included data from the black box and interviews with the cabin crew. Its findings focused on the psychological and relational aspects of the crews' interactions with the pilot and found that the hierarchy within the cabin prioritised the decisions of the pilots over the engineers with catastrophic consequences.

The investigation's recommendations were influential in changing the way that pilots and crews are trained, by focusing on reducing or modifying the effect of hierarchy and how they communicate with each other. The report recommended that the pilots were trained in "participative management" and that crews were trained in assertive communication (National Transportation Safety Board, 2022, p. 30). This was named "Crew Resource Management" training, adopted by United Airlines in 1981, and then later by the global airline industry, leading to increased efficiency in flight crew communication and collaboration and hence fewer errors.

This example shows that it is not only the technical data that are important for making essential changes to improve safety and efficiency, but also a contextual understanding of the data. Relationships and their impact on interactions are crucial features of this context. Many organizations rely on a form of hierarchy to ensure efficiency. These hierarchies influence the social relationships between all staff throughout an organization, impacting the thoughts and behaviours of those staff. Understanding how these interpersonal factors play out in work situations is essential to understanding how people respond to the challenges involved in their work.

With a core purpose to protect health and life, the consequences of failure within health and social care organizations are potentially just as catastrophic as in the aircraft industry. But the nature of the work, focused as it is on the provision of care, adds another layer of complexity in which intra- and interpersonal psychological processes have the potential to undermine resilience and create barriers to good care that act as further sources of threat to organizational functioning.

Intra- and inter-personal factors

The mental health impact of being in a caring role, whether professional or unpaid, has long been recognised (e.g. Happell et al., 2013; Hussain et al., 2016). In order to function effectively, care staff need to maintain an empathic approach alongside a degree of professional detachment so that they do not become overwhelmed by their own emotions (Ballatt & Campling, 2011). Many student nurses, care workers, and doctors report that they chose their profession because of a desire to help others. Their professional training often involves the development of skills to contain their emotional responses, allowing them to act professionally and effectively. However, as a result of this detachment, professional healthcare workers can gradually become distanced from patients, losing a degree of empathy and compassion (Neumann et al., 2011; Nolan et al., 2014; Richardson et al., 2015). Care can also become problematic when the care worker is overwhelmed by stress, either chronically or acutely, leading to burnout, which can negatively impact the quality and safety of care (Arnetz et al., 2019; Johnson et al., 2017).

It is important that these complex intra- and interpersonal processes are recognised and managed by the system in which care workers are employed, to maintain good quality care and to protect both individual and organizational resilience. This points to the complexity evident in care organizations which, when understood in psychological terms, can contribute to clarifying how organizational resilience can be improved. Although not an exclusive or exhaustive list, the following four areas of research are perhaps the most relevant in supporting our approach.

Staff resilience and wellbeing

Extensive research in healthcare settings has highlighted the importance of staff mental health and wellbeing for patient care. Staff working in healthcare settings, and particularly in mental health, typically experience higher levels of work-related stress than the general UK population (O'Connor et al., 2018). When staff are struggling to maintain a reasonable level of wellbeing, this affects their ability to remain in work, to relate to clients, and to offer the care and support that is central to their role (e.g., Delgadillo et al., 2018; Volpe et al., 2014). Recent estimates from the 2020/2021 Labour Force Survey in the United Kingdom show that stress, anxiety, and depression accounted for 50% of all work-related ill-health (HSE, 2021). In 2020/2021, 822,000 workers experienced work-related stress, anxiety, and depression leading to the loss of 12.8 million working days across all sectors. Contributing factors identified by the HSE (2021) include staff feeling unable to cope with the demands of their jobs, unable to control the way they do their work, having insufficient information and support, being unclear about their role, conflict, relationship difficulties, and organizational change. "Human health and social work" was one of the hardest hit sectors. This makes the poor mental health of staff a major threat to organizational functioning and a barrier to resilience.

Understanding and responding to threats to staff functioning is a key factor in promoting organizational resilience. The capacity of employees to draw on their skills and knowledge is fundamental to their ability to "do the job" and personal attributes of hope, self-efficacy, optimism, and resilience are now seen as playing a key role in "positive organizational behaviour" (Eliot, 2020; Luthans et al., 2004). Fundamentally, if staff do not have the skills and support to manage their work demands and to ensure their own wellbeing and resilience, they present a threat to the resilience of the whole organization.

Trust, belonging, and inclusion

In care organizations, promoting a sense of belonging and collaboration builds trust and improves quality of care and patient-centredness (Campling, 2015). Creating and sustaining a caring culture requires honesty and realism and an awareness of the barriers and threats that can undermine it. It requires a reliance on positive values that are supported and embedded across the whole organization. When training, support, and teamwork are openly and actively supported by organizational structures, staff are better able to actively balance their empathy and compassion for the people they are caring for with an appropriate level of professional detachment, allowing them to continue functioning effectively.

Cited in the report of the UK Government Health and Social Care Committee (House of Commons, 2021), Professor Jeremy Dawson of Sheffield University said "We have evidence that shows that organisations where there is more opportunity for staff to take part in making decisions and influence how things are decided are the trusts that have lower mortality rates. They have better outcomes generally for patients and better outcomes generally for staff." This requires psychological safety.

Psychological safety in individuals and teams

Psychological safety has been defined as "feeling able to show and employ oneself without fear of negative consequences to self-image, status, or career" (Kahn, 1990). It allows staff to feel able to speak up about mistakes and errors and to voice concerns about potential threats to the work of the organization (Clark, 2020). As such, when individuals experience psychological safety in their workplace, they are more likely to learn and innovate than they are in blaming cultures where the fear of reprisal can inhibit and prevent learning (Edmondson & Lei, 2014). Arnetz et al. (2019) found that work environments in which nurses reported higher levels of psychological safety and competence development were linked to physiological markers associated with better wellbeing.

A well-developed organizational culture of psychological safety and openness is associated with high levels of trust and feelings of belonging that lead to improved team cooperation, innovation, and collaboration, and inter-team working (West, 2012; Malik et al., 2021). Employees experience greater control and autonomy over how they do their work and feel valued, respected, and supported in their contribution (West & Coia, 2019; West et al., 2020). Furthermore, a culture of psychological safety underpins resilience in teams, allowing them to reflect on setbacks and failures, to identify threat at an early stage and to develop new skills and strengths to overcome challenge. Team resilience is associated with a sense of belonging, team learning, understanding, and coordination in dealing with pressure, and greater wellbeing through challenging situations (Morgan et al., 2013).

In contrast, when a team is perceived as unsafe, team members behave cautiously, develop an anxious watchfulness in their work, keep innovative ideas and suggestions to themselves, and are less likely to report errors. A study of safety in teams focusing on intensive care nursing found that learning from errors was only possible where there was a culture of safety and trust (Edmondson, 1996). Such "team reflexivity" in healthcare settings has further been linked with higher levels of team effectiveness, quality of patient care and ongoing improvement in care (Widmer et al., 2009).

Leadership

Leaders who promote psychological safety, creating a positive socio-emotional climate within their teams, are experienced as genuinely open to conversations about set-backs and failures. Consequently, they have greater awareness of potential threats to team and organizational functioning and are in a better position to manage their own responses and to offer support to their teams. The resultant culture of openness allows resilient leaders to prepare for threat, to foster strong relationships and networks, and build resilience capacity in advance of acute crises (Hobfoll et al., 2015).

In an evaluation of culture and leadership in the National Health Service in England, five key cultural factors were found to contribute to improved employee wellbeing, flourishing, and work engagement. These were later extended to provide a culture and leadership programme that focused on developing high quality care through:

- shared vision/narrative around delivering high quality care
- clear goals across the whole system 'from ward to Whitehall' to unite the agencies involved
- opportunities for learning and innovation through flatter hierarchical structures to provided freedom and resources for staff to make improvements in their areas of work
- support through compassionate, open and authentic leadership
- high levels of trust and inclusion and low levels of discrimination
- highly developed team and inter team working where teams had clear objectives, met regularly to review performance and consider ways to improve it

(Dixon-Woods et al., 2014)

Leaders are central to the promotion of these cultural factors, providing a facilitative environment in which staff are supported to rise to new challenges when faced with threat and change (Fletcher & Sarkar, 2016).

Process factors

We are aware that developing organizational resilience does not rest simply on providing training for individual staff and making changes to organizational processes and procedures. We argue that while it is necessary to incorporate an awareness of the intra- and interpersonal factors, some of which are outlined above, this will not be sufficient for successful implementation of any intervention strategies. We have found that the process of assessing an organization has to be done carefully and thoughtfully.

Similar to working psychologically with individuals, engaging with an organization's threats and challenges requires an understanding of its internal world, what it stands for, its beliefs and values that ultimately make up its "culture." Flamholtz and Randle (2012) defined organizational culture as a kind of "corporate personality" consisting of the values, beliefs, and norms that influence employee thoughts, emotions, and behaviour. They proposed that organizational culture exists at multiple levels including:

- observable in everyday behaviour
- beliefs and assumptions underlying the behavioural norms
- attitudes to risk, ethics, professionalism or hierarchy
- bureaucracy

As such, organizational culture will influence the policies and procedures needed to maintain the smooth running of the organization, to understand and manage everyday threats and acute crises and will inform its approach to governance and to staff wellbeing.

Furthermore, understanding an organization's culture will be an important part of the process of understanding its barriers to resilience and how it may struggle to learn from failures in response to acute crises and/or everyday challenges. For example, in healthcare organizations Edmondson (2004) has shown that many hospital staff feel restricted by hierarchical management structures and that some cultural practices arising out of medical training can inhibit staff from challenging decisions about patient care and discourage them from admitting to errors. When these practices are unchecked, the concerns of the care system can become prioritised over patient-centred care, and feedback from patient-facing staff is discouraged or ignored. This has been described as a "closed culture" (CQC, 2022), which can seriously threaten the work of the organization. Errors can go unnoticed and are consequently not managed effectively. In turn, this can impact patient care and diminishes the resilience of the organization.

There is evidence that staff members and teams operating in a closed culture can be encouraged to lose their focus on patient-centred care, become neglectful or even abusive. In the United Kingdom, over the past decade alone, the list of public inquiries into poor and abusive care include the Mid-Staffordshire Hospitals (Francis, 2013), Winterbourne View (Department of Health, 2012), Liverpool Care Pathway (Neuberger, 2013), Whorlton Hall (BBC, 2019), and, most recently, the Edenfield Centre in Prestwich, Manchester (BBC, 2022). Unfortunately, such scandals are not new, with inquiries dating back to at least the 1960s. Responses to the investigation reports have typically focused on audit-based initiatives to improve quality of care, with calls for increased inspections and regular reporting. Despite this, it seems that regulatory inspections focused on improved governance often fail to uncover or prevent poor and abusive care in some instances (e.g., BBC, 2022).

What is noticeable is that this form of response fails to address the individual or interpersonal factors that are involved in neglectful and abusive care. Additionally, it cannot account for the differences between those staff teams that provide good care and those that do not. The Francis report on the Mid-Staffordshire Hospitals scandal, for example, noted that despite clear organizational failings, some staff teams had continued to provide good quality care, while others allowed neglect and abuse to proliferate. This indicates that understanding the complex mix of individual, systemic, and cultural factors is required for good quality care to be delivered and maintained. It follows from this that any assessment of organizational culture needs to include a consideration of a wide range of influences.

Organizational culture can impact the very analysis of threats and challenges that consequently affect the implementation of interventions to develop resilience. Tucker and Edmonson (2003) pointed out that most care organizations respond to problems and difficulties by implementing "quick fixes" and "workarounds," rather than the type of robust root cause analysis and systematic problem solving employed following the UA173 disaster. This type of reactive response too often focuses on systems and procedures whilst ignoring the roles of culture, hierarchy, and interpersonal factors, and their relative contributions to both the risk and resolution of problems. It is unlikely to lead to implementing strategies for resilience, but instead leads to a state of "survival with impairment," where functioning is impaired in comparison to that before the adverse event and, consequently the organization remains vulnerable to future threats and challenges (O'Leary, 1998; O'Leary & Ickovics, 1995).

There are no black box recorders in operating theatres, inpatient wards, or social care services. Obtaining clear accounts from doctors, nurses, and social workers about mistakes and near misses is likely to be difficult when they are under high levels of stress within an organization that may be experiencing a series of adverse events. Any investigation needs to take into account the full variety of psychological and systemic factors involved, including the impact of culture and hierarchy. It is this complexity that makes the analysis of an organization difficult, but not impossible. When done well, it can contribute to the development of strategies that address not only *what* is needed to manage the threat but also *how* this can be implemented so that greater organizational resilience can be developed.

The interpersonal process model of organizational resilience

We have developed the interpersonal process model of organizational resilience to address the points made above. The model encourages a consideration of the intra- and interpersonal factors relevant to an organization's context, prioritising the dynamics of the people in the organization, especially leaders, so that all staff are supported effectively in the process of implementation. The key to building organizational resilience is a commitment at all levels of the organization to processes that support the analysis of threats and barriers to resilience, and the implementation of targeted measures that allow organizations and staff to manage present and future threat effectively.

The barriers to implementation of any approach aimed at improving organizational resilience are mostly located at the interpersonal level, associated with the interactions between leaders tasked with implementing new strategies and the staff being encouraged to change or adapt the way they work. Understanding how groups of staff will respond to new strategies and supporting leaders to implement change effectively can be informed by the psychological literature on learning and behaviour change in human systems (e.g., Bateson, 1973; Mason, 1993; Tramonti, 2018). Drawing on this literature provides useful insights that can inform a process of assessment and formulation, which indicates how strategies can be introduced and will facilitate the design of interventions to support this. Additionally, we recommend that the introduction of strategies is evaluated so that learning can be embedded within the system. A diagrammatic description of the process is laid out in Figure 7.1.

Assessment

The process begins with a clear assessment of the organization and the specific threats it is experiencing. Implementing a plan to successfully improve organizational resilience first requires a deep understanding of the threats and challenges faced (Tucker & Edmonson, 2003). These challenges may be internal or external to the organization, associated with acute crisis or everyday pressure and demand. The phase of assessment should address the perceived threats to the organization, the culture of the organization, the individual resilience skills and wellbeing of all staff, as well as the resources available to develop them, and finally the skills of those in leadership roles. This framework of assessment can be conceived as a triangle rather than simply a list, inspired by the fire triangle model (heat + fuel + oxygen = fire). In this framework, if any of the three elements are removed, the resilience will "go out" (see Figure 7.2).

This framework necessitates that all aspects of the organization are included in the analysis and understood in the context of the psychological processes of the staff involved. This will ensure that both the internal barriers to change and the external threats are understood. Additionally, it will be important to understand the organization's stage of change, its readiness to adapt systems and processes, and the barriers to doing so (Prochaska et al., 2001; Tyler & Tyler, 2006).

Formulation

Drawing all these components together can be done through a process known as a "formulation." In mental health contexts, formulations are used to help care staff make sense of the complexities of psychological and psychiatric distress and to identify appropriate interventions (Johnstone & Dallos, 2014). Likewise, in the context of organizational threats and challenges, a well-constructed and informed formulation will not only describe the organization's functions, dysfunctions, and dynamics but will also point towards appropriate interventions. The interventions

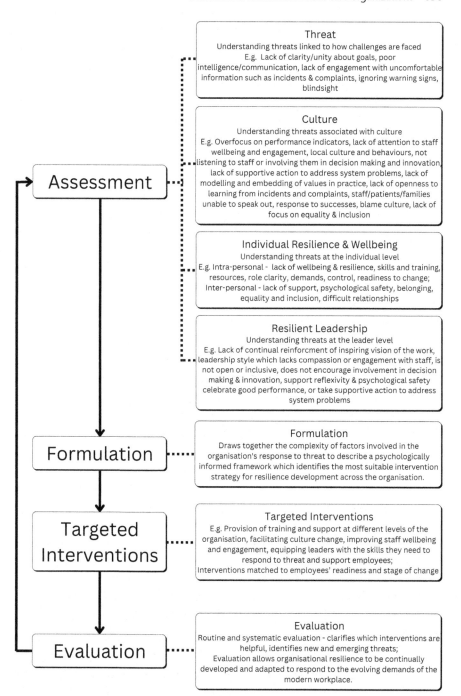

FIGURE 7.1   The interpersonal process model of organizational resilience

FIGURE 7.2   The assessment framework of the interpersonal process model of organizational resilience

are consequently targeted directly to the identified needs and are designed to achieve the desired organizational resilience outcomes.

The literature on change in human systems indicates that context and relationships are of prime importance when considering how to develop interventions to support psychological wellbeing (Hayes et al., 2006; Stolorow & Atwood, 1992; Tramonti, 2018). Through the process of formulation, these insights can be applied to inform how to introduce positive changes that contribute to the organization's resilience. For example, in relation to context, leaders should understand how staff will perceive the intended changes, ensuring that everybody "is on the same page" and then consider how changes can be implemented. Changes which introduce too much "difference" will produce uncertainties and anxieties in some staff (Bateson, 1973; Mason, 1993) and threaten their successful implementation.

Similarly, strong supportive relationships have long been known to be central to psychological wellbeing and thriving (e.g. Feeney & Collins, 2015; Gilbert, 2009;

Ozbay et al., 2007; Sorce et al., 1985; Southwick et al., 2016) and in the work context, it is the connections and dynamics between people and the presence of psychological safety that are essential to the successful implementation of policies, procedures, and strategies.

Targeted interventions

The formulation can be used to inform interventions that may be put in place by Human Resource Management (HRM) and Human Resource Development (HRD) teams. Interventions aimed at improving organizational resilience will be varied and wide ranging but should be targeted at managing the unique sources of threat and barriers to change identified in the assessment and formulation. Examples may include provision of training and support at different levels of the organization, facilitating culture change, or equipping leaders with the skills needed to respond to threat and support employees. The psychological factors identified in the formulation phase will provide detail about any barriers to implementation and how to overcome them. HRM is central to developing the strategies and policies needed to integrate any new initiatives into everyday practice. HRD ensures that training is based on the identified staff needs and their perceived stage of change, so that support and skill development respond to the unique challenges faced by staff and facilitate change.

Interventions that are tailored to employees' readiness for and stage of change have been shown to increase engagement and participation and are more likely to overcome resistance (Levesque et al., 2001; Prochaska et al., 2001). Leader buy-in is key to the success of stage-matched interventions, requiring that leaders have been through the process of change themselves and are able to recognise that employees need time to do the same.

Evaluation

Resilience is a dynamic process and an emergent property of the organization that is dependent on the history of successful navigation of threat. For this reason, routine and systematic evaluation is essential, not only to clarify which interventions have been helpful but also to identify new and emerging threats. Through a process of ongoing monitoring and evaluation, organizational resilience skills and strategies can be continually developed and adapted to respond to the evolving demands of the modern workplace.

Practice-based evidence

The Interpersonal Process Model of Organisational Resilience was developed in response to the need for a psychologically informed approach to organizations looking to address their resilience. Whilst the approach is evidence-based, drawing its content from the academic literature, it is also drawn from practice-based evidence. Practice-based evidence is that which is collected through engagement with real world scenarios and as such reflects and responds to the complexities and limitations that exist for many services. This makes the process more applicable and generalisable to the experience of actual organizations. Taking this approach has allowed us to engage with organizations through a bespoke understanding of their cultural practices, styles of leadership, and what is important to their staff. The model highlights the importance of analysing threats, recognising barriers to resilience, and the implementation of targeted strategies that allow organizations and staff to manage present and future threat effectively.

The model's assessment framework is supported by accounts of organizations that have successfully improved their response to adverse events through better management of threats and improvements to their functioning. This is evident in the organizations described in the "Driving Improvement" reports, published by the Care Quality Commission (CQC, 2017, 2018a 2018b, 2018c, 2019). All of the organizations had experienced some significant threats and their inspection failure had additionally impacted staff morale, raising anxieties for service users, their carers, and families. Each organization developed strategies based on the factors which contributed to their failed inspections. These can be grouped into the three broad categories of our assessment framework: organizational culture, staff wellbeing and resilience, and leadership.

Measures relating to "organizational culture" focused on encouraging staff and leaders to be more curious and open to the views of service users and the public. These measures were also aimed at removing blame cultures. Themes included promoting staff health and wellbeing, listening to staff and encouraging involvement in decision-making, problem-solving and innovation, providing helpful feedback, celebrating good performance, and taking supportive action to address system problems.

Strategies that focused on improving staff wellbeing and resilience were based on a recognition that staff at all levels had a part to play in contributing to organizational responses to threat. These strategies were aimed at reducing staff stress but also engaged and empowered staff, indicating that they were listened to and valued.

The case studies also show that effective leadership was important in influencing change at all levels of an organization, including strengthening processes and governance to improve learning from incidents and better identification and responsiveness to risks. These strategies supported leaders in developing the confidence and skills to motivate and inspire staff and to create an open and transparent culture in which they felt supported.

When a threat or adverse event leads to markedly lower functioning, the organization can be said to have succumbed (Carver, 1998). This outcome is not reasonable or viable for care organizations on whom people's health and welfare rely. Thriving, on the other hand, is associated with new skills and strategies that are brought into play, leaving the individual or organization strengthened and improved in their functioning (O'Leary & Ickovics, 1995; Rutter, 2013). The reports describe how these organizations moved from potentially "succumbing" to adverse events, to "thriving," setting out the strategies used to manage threat and initiate improvements in functioning.

While the "Driving Improvement" reports describe the strategies used by failing care organizations to significantly improve functioning and performance, similar strategies can be seen in consistently resilient or thriving care organizations. The Northumbria Healthcare NHS Trust responded to the stresses and threats posed by the COVID-19 pandemic in ways that did not significantly disrupt its functioning. Before the pandemic, the Trust had the highest scores in the 2019 NHS Staff Survey for health and wellbeing, morale, equality, diversity and inclusion (The Kings Fund, 2022). The organizational culture, processes, and procedures that contributed to these high scores allowed the Trust to respond agilely and flexibly from the outset of the pandemic. Recognising the threat of the pandemic to staff wellbeing and the need for a supportive workplace, the Trust adapted their staff engagement platform to quickly implement a short web-based survey allowing staff to raise issues, voice concerns, and share their experiences. The survey asked staff to rate their motivation for work on a weekly basis. This data was then used to inform an evolving action plan that could readily adapt to the unique physical, social, and emotional wellbeing needs of staff as they changed and developed through the various challenges of the pandemic. The success of this intervention was largely due to a recognition of the importance of everyday resilience within the organization, the presence of compassionate leadership, and a culture in which staff were encouraged to speak up and voice concerns (The Kings Fund, 2022). These factors meant that the Trust already had the systems in place to analyse and respond to threat effectively, allowing them to recover and improve functioning quickly.

Summary and conclusion

In this chapter, we have attempted to illustrate what is needed for organizational resilience and also how this can be implemented. We have argued that, for lasting change and improvement to occur, it is essential to fully understand the problem (threat), identify the unique barriers to resilience, and develop strategies to respond effectively. Solutions must be tailored to the needs of the organization and target the psychological dynamics of the people involved.

Our experience of working as clinical psychologists within care organizations has naturally led us to focus on the intra- and interpersonal aspects of how staff, leaders, and organizational systems interact to promote resilient responses to threat. In doing so, and by supporting our observations with evidence from the literature, we have been able to respond to the question of both *what* is needed for the growth of resilience in modern organizations and *how* this can be achieved. Further, drawing on our clinical knowledge of processes involved in psychological and behavioural change, we have identified the need for robust assessment, formulation, targeted intervention, and evaluation in order to successfully and resiliently respond to threat. Linked to the development of greater awareness of the unique intra- and interpersonal dynamics involved, this process provides direction to organizations on the actions required to build and improve their resilience.

References

Arnetz, J., Sudan, S., Goetz, C., Counts, S., & Arnetz, B. (2019). Nurse work environment and stress biomarkers. *Journal of Occupational and Environmental Medicine, 61*(8), 676–681. https://doi:10.1097/JOM.0000000000001642

Baker, F. R., Baker, K. L., & Burrell, J. (2021). Introducing the skills-based model of personal resilience: Drawing on content and process factors to build resilience in the workplace. *Journal of Occupational and Organizational Psychology, 94*, 458–481. https://doi.org/10.1111/joop.12340

Ballatt, J., & Campling, P. (2011). *Intelligent kindness: Reforming the culture of healthcare* (pp. 53). Royal College of Psychiatrists.

Barasa, E., Mbau, R., & Gilson, L. (2018). What is resilience and how can it be nurtured? A systematic review of empirical literature on organizational resilience. *International Journal of Health Policy and Management, 7*, 491–503.

Bateson, G. (1973). *Steps to an ecology of mind*. Palladin.

BBC. (2022, 4 October). Edenfield Centre: Car Watchdog Praises Bosses at Abuse Hospital. BBC News. https://www.bbc.co.uk/news/uk-63095331

BBC. (2019, 22 May). Whorlton Hall: Hospital 'Abused' Vulnerable Patients. BBC News. https://www.bbc.co.uk/news/health-48367071

Biddle, L., Wahedi, K., & Bozorgmehr, K. (2020). Health system resilience: A literature review of empirical research. *Health Policy and Planning, 35*, 1084–1109. doi: 10.1093/heapol/czaa032

Blanchet, K., & James, P. (2013). The role of social networks in the governance of health systems: The case of eye care systems in Ghana. *Health Policy and Planning, 28*(2), 143–156. https://doi.org/10.1093/heapol/czs031

Campling, P. (2015). Reforming the culture of healthcare: The case for intelligent kindness. *BJPsych Bulletin, 39*(1), 1–5. doi: 10.1192/pb.bp.114.047449

Care Quality Commission (CQC). (2017). Driving improvement: Case studies from NHS Trusts. https://www.cqc.org.uk/publications/evaluation/driving-improvement-case-studies-nhs-trusts.

Care Quality Commission (CQC). (2018a). Driving improvement: Case studies from nine adult social care services. https://www.cqc.org.uk/publications/evaluation/driving-improvement-case-studies-nine-adult-social-care-services.

Care Quality Commission (CQC). (2018b). Driving improvement: Case studies from seven mental health NHS Trusts. https://www.cqc.org.uk/publications/evaluation/driving-improvement-case-studies-seven-mental-health-nhs-trusts.

Care Quality Commission (CQC). (2018c). Driving improvement: Case studies from 10 GP Practices. https://www.cqc.org.uk/publications/evaluation/driving-improvement-case-studies-10-gp-practices.

Care Quality Commission (CQC). (2019). Driving improvement: Case studies from eight independent hospitals. https://www.cqc.org.uk/publications/evaluation/driving-improvement-case-studies-eight-independent-hospitals.

Care Quality Commission (CQC). (2022). How CQC identifies and responds to closed cultures. https://www.cqc.org.uk/guidance-providers/all-services/how-cqc-identifies-responds-closed-cultures.

Carver, C. S. (1998). Resilience and thriving: Issues, models, and linkages. *Journal of Social Issues*, *54*(2), 245–266.

Chan, A. O., & Huak, C. Y. (2004). Psychological impact of the 2003 severe acute respiratory syndrome outbreak on health care workers in a medium sized regional general hospital in Singapore. *Occupational Medicine*, *54*, 190–196.

Clark, T. R. (2020). *The 4 stages of psychological safety: Defining the path to inclusion and innovation* (pp. 2). Berrett-Koehler.

Delgadillo, J., Saxon, D., & Barkham, M. (2018). Associations between therapists' occupational burnout and their patients' depression and anxiety treatment outcomes. *Depression and Anxiety*, *35*, 844–850. https://doi.org/10.1002/da.22766

Department of Health. (2012). Transforming Care: A National Response to Winterbourne View Hospital. Department of Health Review: Final Report. Department of Health.

Dixon-Woods, M., Baker, R., Charles, K., Dawson, J., Jerzembek, G., Martin, G., McCarthy, I., McKee, L., Minion, J., Ozieranski, P., Willars, J., Wilkie, P., & West, M. (2014). Culture and behaviour in the English national health service: Overview of lessons from a large multimethod study. *BMJ Quality & Safety*, *23*(2), 106–15. doi: 10.1136/bmjqs-2013-001947

Edmondson, A. C. (1996). Learning from mistakes is easier said than done: Group and organisational influences on the detection and correction of human error. *Journal of Applied Behavioural Science*, *32*, 5–28.

Edmondson, A. C., & Lei, Z. (2014). Psychological safety: The history, renaissance and future of an interpersonal construct. *Annual Review of Organizational Psychology and Organizational Behavior*, *1*(1), 23–43. https://doi.org/10.1146/annurev-orgpsych-031413-091305

Edmondson, A. (2004). Learning from failure in health care: Frequent opportunities, pervasive barriers. *Quality Safety in Health Care*, *13*(Suppl II), ii3–9. doi: 10.1136/qshc.2003.009597

Eliot, J. L. (2020). Resilient leadership: The impact of a servant leader on the resilience of their followers. *Advances in Developing Human Resources*, *22*(4), 404–418. https://doi.org/10.1177/1523422320945237

Feeney, B. C., & Collins, N. L. (2015). A new look at social support: A theoretical perspective on thriving through relationships. *Personality and Social Psychology Review*, *9*, 113–147.

Flamholtz, E. G., & Randle, Y. (2012). Corporate culture, business models, competitive advantage, strategic assets and the bottom line: Theoretical and measurement issues. *Journal of Human Resource Costing & Accounting*, *16*(2), 76–94. https://doi.org/10.1108/14013381211284227

Fletcher, D., & Sarkar, M. (2016). Mental fortitude training: An evidence-based approach to developing psychological resilience for sustained success. *Journal of Sport Psychology in Action*, *7*(3), 135–157. doi: 10.1080/21520704.2016.1255496

Forsgren, L., Tediosi, F., Blanchet, K., & Saulnier, D. D. (2022). Health systems resilience in practice: A scoping review to identify strategies for building resilience. *BMC Health Services Research*, *22*, 1173. https://doi.org/10.1186/s12913-022-08544-8

Francis, R. (2013). *Report of the Mid Staffordshire NHS Foundation Trust Public Inquiry*. The Stationary Office.

Gaillard, J.-C. (2007). Resilience of traditional societies in facing natural hazards. *Disaster Prevention and Management*, *16*(4), 522–544.

Gibson, C. A., & Tarrant, M. (2010). A "conceptual models" approach to organisational resilience. *The Australian Journal of Emergency Management 25*(2), 6–12. https://search.informit.org/doi/10.3316/informit.084520139241216

Gilbert, P. (2009). Introducing compassion-focused therapy. *Advances in Psychiatric Treatment, 15*, 199–208. doi: 10.1192/apt.bp.107.005264

Grieg, G., Entwistle, V. A., & Beech, N. (2012). Addressing complex healthcare problems in diverse settings: Insights from activity theory. *Social Science and Medicine, 74*, 305–312. https://doi.org/10.1016/j.socscimed.2011.02.006

Happell, B., Dwyer, T., Reid-Searl, K., Burke, K. J., Caperchione, C. M., & Gaskin, C. J. (2013). Nurses and stress: Recognizing causes and seeking solutions. *Journal of Nursing Management, 21*(4), 638–647. https://doi.org/10.1111/jonm.12037

Hayes, S. C., Luoma, J. B., Bond, F. W., Masuda, A., & Lillis, J. (2006). Acceptance and commitment therapy: Model, processes and outcomes. *Behaviour Research and Therapy, 44*, 1–25.

Health and Safety Executive. (2021). Work-related stress, anxiety or depression statistics in Great Britain. http://www.hse.gov.uk/statistics/lfs/index.htm

Hobfoll, S. E., Stevens, N. R., & Zalta, A. K. (2015). Expanding the science of resilience: Conserving resources in the aid of adaptation. *Psychological Inquiry, 26*(2), 174–180.

Holling, C. S. (2001). Understanding the complexity of economic, ecological and social systems. *Ecosystems, 4*, 390–405.

House of Commons Committees. (2021, June 8). Workforce burnout and resilience in the NHS and social care. https://publications.parliament.uk/pa/cm5802/cmselect/cmhealth/22/2202.htm

Hussain, R., Wark, S., Dillon, G., & Ryan, P. (2016). Self-reported physical and mental health of Australian carers: A cross-sectional study. *BMJ Open, 6*(9), e011417. https://doi.org/10.1136/bmjopen-2016-011417

Johnson, J., Hall, L. H., Berzins, K., Baker, J., Melling, K., & Thompson, C. (2017), Mental healthcare staff well-being and burnout: A narrative review of trends, causes, implications, and recommendations for future interventions. *International Journal of Mental Health Nursing, 27*, 20–32. https://doi.org/10.1111/inm.12416

Johnstone, L., & Dallos, R. (Eds.) (2014). *Formulation in psychology and psychotherapy: Making sense of people's problems* (2nd ed.). Routledge.

Kahn, W. A. (1990). Psychological conditions of personal engagement and dis-engagement at work. *Academy of Management Journal, 33*, 692–724. https://doi.org/10.5465/256287

Levesque, D. A., Prochaska, J. M., Prochaska, J. O., Dewart, S. R., Hamby, L. S., & Weeks, W. B. (2001). Organizational stages and processes of change for continuous quality improvement in health care. *Consulting Psychology Journal: Practice and Research, 53*(3), 139–153. https://doi.org/10.1037/1061-4087.53.3.139.

Luthans, F., Luthans, K. W., & Luthans, B. C. (2004). Positive psychological capital: Beyond human and social capital. *Business Horizons, 47*(1), 45–50. doi: 10.1016/j.bushor.2003.11.007.

Malik, R. F., Buljac-Samardžić, M., Amajjar, I., Hilders, C. G. J. M., & Scheele, F. (2021). Open organisational culture: What does it entail? Healthcare stakeholders reaching consensus by means of a Delphi technique. *BMJ Open, 11*, e045515. doi: 10.1136/bmjopen-2020-045515

Mason, B. (1993). Towards positions of safe uncertainty. *Human Systems, 4*(3-4), 189–200.

Maunder, R. G., Lancee, W. J., Balderson, K. E., & Bennett, J. P., et al. (2006). Long term psychological and occupational effects of providing hospital healthcare during SARS outbreak. *Emerging Infectious Diseases, 12*, 1924.

Morgan, P. B. C., Fletcher, D., & Sarkar, M. (2013). Defining and characterizing team resilience in elite sport. *Psychology of Sport and Exercise, 14*(4), 549–559. https://doi.org/10.1016/j.psychsport.2013.01.004.

National Transportation Safety Board. (2022). AAR-79-07. https://www.ntsb.gov/investigations/AccidentReports/Reports/AAR7907.pdf

Neuberger, J. (2013). *More care, less pathway: A review of the Liverpool care pathway.* Department of Health.

Neumann, M., Edelhauser, F., Tauschel, D., Fischer, M. R., Wirtz, M., & Woopen, C., et al. (2011). Empathy decline and its reasons: A systematic review of studies with medical students and residents. *Academic Medicine, 86*(8), 996–1009. https://doi.org/10.1097/ACM.0b013e318221e615

Nolan, M., Oliver, F., McIntosh, L., & Lee, J. (2014). Examining compassion and resilience through various lenses. *Practice Midwife, 17*(8), 20–23.

Nutley, S., Walter, I., & Davies, H. T. O. (2007). *Using evidence: How research can inform public services.* Policy Press.

O'Connor, K., Neff, D. M., & Pitman, S. (2018). Burnout in mental health professionals: A systematic review and meta-analysis of prevalence and determinants. *European Psychiatry, 53,* 74–99. http://dx.doi.org/10.1016/j.eurpsy.2018.06.003

O'Leary, V. E. (1998). Strength in the face of adversity: Individual and social thriving. *Journal of Social Issues, 54*(2), 425–446.

O'Leary, V. E., & Ickovics, J. R. (1995). Resilience And thriving in response to challenge: An opportunity for a paradigm shift in women's health. *Women's Health, 1*(2), 121–142.

Ozbay, F., Johnson, D. C., Dimoulas, E., Morgan, C. A., Charney, D., & Southwick, S. (2007). Social support and resilience to stress: From neurobiology to clinical practice. *Psychiatry, 4,* 35–40.

Prochaska, J. M., Prochaska, J. O., & Levesque, D. A. (2001). A transtheoretical approach to changing organizations. *Administration and Policy in Mental Health, 28,* 247–261. https://doi.org/10.1023/A:1011155212811

Richardson, C., Percy, M., & Hughes, J. (2015). Nursing therapeutics: Teaching student nurses care, compassion and empathy. *Nurse Education Today, 35*(5), e1–5. doi: 10.1016/j.nedt.2015.01.016

Rutter, M. (2006). Implications of resilience concepts for scientific understanding. *Annals of the New York Academy of Sciences, 1094*(1), 1–12.

Rutter, M. (2013), Annual research review: Resilience–clinical implications. *Journal of Child Psychology and Psychiatry, 54,* 474–487. https://doi.org/10.1111/j.1469-7610.2012.02615.x

Sorce, J. F., Emde, R. N., Campos, J. J., & Klinnert, M. D. (1985). Maternal emotional signalling: It's effect on the visual cliff behaviour of 1-year-olds. *Developmental Psychology, 21,* 195–200. doi:10.1037/0012-1649.21.1.195

Southwick, S., Sippel, L., Krystal, J., Charney, D., Mayes, L., & Pietrzak, R. (2016). Why are some individuals more resilient than others: The role of social support. *World Psychiatry, 15,* 77–79. doi:10.1002/wps.20282

Stolorow, R. D., & Atwood, G. E. (1992). *Contexts of being: The intersubjective foundations of psychological life.* The Analytic Press.

The Kings Fund. (2022). *Listening to staff during Covid-19: Northumbria Healthcare NHS Foundation Trust.* https://www.kingsfund.org.uk/publications/what-is-compassionate-leadership.

Tramonti, F. (2018). Steps to an ecology of psychotherapy: The legacy of Gregory Bateson. *Systems Research and Behavioral Science, 36*(1), 128–139. doi: 10.1002/sres.2549

Tucker, A., & Edmonson, A. (2003). Managing routine exceptions: A model of nurse problem solving behavior. *Advances in Health Care Management, 3*, 87–113.

Turenne, C. P., Gautier, L., & Degroote, S. et al. 2019. Conceptual analysis of health systems resilience: A scoping review. *Social Science & Medicine*, 232, 168–180.

Tyler, C. L., & Tyler, J. M. (2006). Applying the transtheoretical model of change to the sequencing of ethics instruction in business education. *Journal of Management Education, 30*(45), 45–64. doi: https://doi.org/10.1177/1052562905280845

Volpe, U., Luciano, M., Palumbo, C., Sampogna, G., Del Vecchio, V., & Fiorillo, A. (2014). Risk of burnout among early career mental health professionals. *Journal of Psychiatric and Mental Health Nursing, 21*, 774–781. https://doi.org/10.1111/jpm.12137

Walshe, K., & Rundall, T. G. (2001). Evidence-based management: From theory to practice in health care. *The Milbank Quarterly, 79(3)*, 429–457.

West, M., & Coia, D. (2019). *Caring for doctors, caring for patients: How to transform UK healthcare environments to support doctors and medical students to care for patients.* General Medical Council. https://www.rcpath.org/uploads/assets/e10a530c-1875-4336-94fc91d0124e974c/Caring-for-Doctors-Caring-for-Patientspdf-80706341.pdf

West, M., Bailey, S., & Williams, E. (2020). *The courage of compassion: Supporting nurses and midwives to deliver high-quality care.* The Kings Fund. https://www.kingsfund.org.uk/publications/courage-compassion-supporting-nurses-midwives

West, M. A. (2012). *Effective teamwork: Practical lessons from organisational research* (pp. 7–8). John Wiley & Sons Ltd.

Widmer, P., Schippers, M., & West, M. A. (2009). Recent developments in reflexivity research: A review. *Psychology of Everyday Activity, 2*(2), 2–11.

8

BUILDING RESILIENCE IN SOCIAL WORK

A Multi-Level Approach

Gail Kinman and Louise Grant

Introduction

A social worker's role is multi-faceted but, ultimately, they aim to improve people's lives in order to enhance their individual and collective wellbeing and seek to protect children and adults from harm. Research findings show that, for the most part, social work practitioners find their work meaningful and satisfying, feel valued by service users and are proud of their profession (Grant & Kinman, 2014; YouGov, 2020). Nonetheless, the job is challenging and emotionally demanding. For several years, the annual Labour Force Survey (Health and Safety Executive, 2022) in the United Kingdom has found that social work practitioners have a higher risk of work-related stress, depression, and anxiety than most other occupational groups.

Social workers are particularly susceptible to burnout, a syndrome resulting from excessive and prolonged workplace stress that is characterised by emotional exhaustion, depersonalization, and reduced personal accomplishment (Maslach et al., 1996). A survey of 1,359 UK social workers found that the mean level of burnout exceeded normative scores from the health and caring professions, with almost three-quarters of the sample (73%) scoring in the "high" category for emotional exhaustion (McFadden, 2015). Particular risk factors for practitioner burnout are working in child protection, in mental health, with refugees and homeless people, and with adults with physical disabilities (McFadden, 2015; Waegemakers Schiff & Lane, 2019; Wirth et al., 2019).

Work-related stress and burnout have serious implications for the wellbeing of social workers, increasing the risk of mental health problems such as depression (Hakanen & Schaufeli, 2012) and physical illness (Kim et al., 2011) over

DOI: 10.4324/9781003287858-11

time. Social workers are also particularly vulnerable to work–life conflict, where the high workload and emotional demands of the job can threaten the quality of personal life and impair recovery processes (Kalliath et al., 2012; Kinman & McDowall, 2014). The highly pressured working environment can also diminish the professional effectiveness of social workers, impairing their ability to make meaningful connections with service users. Supporting people in distress requires emotional effort that can, over time, deplete the practitioner's emotional resources. Without appropriate intervention, emotional exhaustion can promote negative, cynical, and depersonalising attitudes towards service users and engender compassion fatigue, characterised by feelings of indifference to other people's suffering (Radley & Figley, 2007). It should be emphasised, however, that clear links between burnout and adverse outcomes for service users are not always found because practitioners strive to ensure that their performance is not compromised (Kinman & Teoh, 2018; Montgomery et al., 2019). Nonetheless, this additional pressure is, over time, likely to exacerbate burnout and other mental health problems (Rogers et al., 2014).

As well as risks for their own wellbeing and professional effectiveness, work-related stress and burnout are common causes of sickness absence and presenteeism among social workers (Ravalier, 2019) that are costly for individuals and organizations. The UK social care sector is currently experiencing a staffing crisis, with high workload, stress, and poor work–life balance being common reasons for leaving (GovUK, 2022; Ravalier et al., 2022). A recent survey of almost 3,000 UK social workers (UNISON, 2022) reported that more than half (53%) had considered leaving the sector. Although leaving intentions do not necessarily result in actual turnover, recent UK workforce statistics report turnover rates for children and family social workers of 15%, with one-third of those having been in their post for less than two years (GovUK, 2022). This is a serious concern, given that it takes an average of two years post qualification for practitioners to work independently and effectively (Csiernik et al., 2010). As well as the costs of recruiting and training new staff, high turnover among social workers will compromise the continuity and quality of service provision and increase caseloads for the staff that remain.

Social work: The risk factors for work-related stress and burnout

Social work in the United Kingdom has been described as a profession that is "on the brink of burnout" (Bunce et al., 2019; Unison, 2016). The research discussed above provides evidence for the emotionally demanding and stressful nature of the work and its implications for employee wellbeing and performance. A range of factors has been associated with an increased risk of stress and burnout, including the following:

- Workload pressure; high and complex caseloads; working across multiple agencies; heavy administrative burden; long working hours.
- Limited resources; low staffing levels; lack of cover.
- Lack of autonomy and influence; little input into decision-making.
- Insufficient support from managers or colleagues, experiences of bullying, harassment and aggression.
- Excessive and poorly managed change; frequent reorganizations and regular revision of policies and procedures.
- Pressure to meet targets; value conflicts and inability to provide the standard of care required.
- Lack of reward and recognition; practitioners' achievements and efforts being undervalued.
- Poor psychological safety climate; limited opportunities for emotional support; stigmatisation of help seeking; physical or cultural barriers to accessing support.
- Emotional labour demands; supporting distressed and traumatised service users; working with angry service users.
- Public scrutiny and mistrust exacerbated by a 'blame' culture; negative perceptions of the profession promoted by the media.

(Grant & Kinman, 2014; Kinman & Grant, 2020; McFadden et al. 2019; Ravalier, 2019; Ravalier et al., 2021; UNISON, 2022; YouGov, 2020)

In addition to organizational level hazards, some individual difference factors have been associated with a greater risk of stress and burnout for social workers. These include attitudes towards the job (e.g., over-involvement with service users and a "rescuing" orientation), personal characteristics (e.g., low psychological capital, lack of confidence in one's abilities, inflexibility and an insecure and avoidant attachment style), and boundary management issues (e.g., affective rumination and poor work–life balance) (Grant & Kinman, 2014; Jia & Fu, 2022; Kalliath et al., 2012; Virga et al., 2020; West, 2015). Similar to other helping professions (Kinman & Teoh, 2018), organizational factors (such as work overload and low support) tend to be stronger predictors of distress among social workers than occupational factors (such as supporting service users) (Grant & Kinman, 2014). Nonetheless, although few studies have used models of work stress, it is likely that a combination of factors increase a practitioner's vulnerability, for example, if high job demands are accompanied by a lack of control, support or other resources; if they perceive an imbalance between the effort they put into their work and the rewards they receive (especially if they are highly committed to the job) and if maladaptive habits acquired during training are reinforced by working in a highly pressured environment with a "self-sacrificing" culture (Grant & Kinman, 2014).

The COVID-19 pandemic compounded the demands experienced by social workers in a sector already widely considered in crisis. In general, practitioners reported a general deterioration in their quality of working life and an increased risk of burnout and trauma (McFadden et al., 2022). Many of the organizational hazards highlighted above (such as heavy workloads, poor support, and change) were found to intensify during this time (Ravalier et al., 2022; UNISON, 2022). Other threats experienced by social workers were related more directly to the pandemic, such as lack of personal contact with service users and the need to use "creative and improvisatory" modes of engagement with technology to interact with them (Dima et al., 2021; Pink et al., 2022). The unprecedented challenges of the pandemic also increased the potential for moral injury—a strong cognitive and emotional response resulting from actions (or inactions) that violate a person's moral or ethical code (Williamson et al., 2020). Feelings of shame and guilt are common responses to moral injury and people are at increased risk of traumatic stress, depression, and suicidality (Hagerty & Williams, 2022; Williamson et al., 2018).

What is resilience and why is it important?

It is widely recognised that social workers need to develop the psychological resources required to help them cope effectively with the challenges they face (Collins, 2008). Resilience, in particular, is a quality that can support positive adaptation to adversity and can be a key resource for people working in emotionally demanding occupations (Grant & Kinman, 2015). The protective effects of resilience have been demonstrated, with strong links found with mental and physical health, enhanced job performance (self-rated and supervisor-rated), organizational citizenship behaviours, openness to change, and job satisfaction and engagement (Finstad et al., 2021; Hartmann et al., 2020; Robertson et al., 2015; Yu et al., 2022). Resilience has also been found to mediate the relationship between individual and organizational-level factors and various wellbeing and performance outcomes and moderate the harmful effects of key hazards such as job demands, interpersonal conflict, and job insecurity (Hartmann et al., 2020).

While resilience appears to have many benefits for wellbeing, it is a complex and multi-faceted construct and, therefore, difficult to define. While resilience is used to refer to a trait, a process, and an outcome, it is typically viewed as a quality of the individual—a stable personality trait, or a "bundle" of strengths, resources, attitudes, and mindsets, that facilitate positive adaptation to adversity (Fletcher & Sarkar, 2013; Hartmann et al., 2020). An alternative approach, however, sees resilience as a *process* whereby a combination of individual qualities and environmental contingencies predicts a person's ability to respond successfully to environmental challenges (Fraser et al., 1999). This perspective supports the view that what is considered "resilience" will vary according to the type of demands people experience and the environment within which they operate (Ungar & Liebenberg, 2011).

Resilience is frequently conceptualised as the ability to maintain (or return to) normal functioning following difficulties and setbacks, but it is recognised that negative experiences can enhance coping capacity via the development of skills, knowledge, and confidence (Carver, 1998; Jackson et al., 2007). For example, a review conducted by Finstad et al. (2021) identified the potential for resilience to not only protect workers from depression, anxiety, and burnout during the COVID-19 pandemic, but to also facilitate personal growth from traumatic experiences during this time via enhanced self-efficacy, cognitive flexibility, and coping skills.

Resilience and social workers

An analysis of the resilience needs of different occupations (Kossek & Perrigino, 2016) identified its key importance for social workers, due to the sustained emotional and cognitive demands that they face. This is recognised by resilience having been incorporated into "the official discourse" of social work (Collins, 2017) and acknowledged as a key professional capacity (Grant & Kinman, 2014; Health and Care Professions Council, n.d.). Studies of social workers support its role in enabling positive adaptation to stressful situations and protecting against psychological distress and burnout (Collins, 2017; Grant & Kinman, 2014; Kinman & Grant, 2011). The findings of a survey of child protection social workers conducted by McFadden et al. (2019) highlighted the benefits of resilience in reducing the risk of burnout, as it not only offered direct protection against emotional exhaustion but also mediated the negative effects of low control and lack of value congruence. Potential benefits for social work practice, both direct and indirect, have also been identified with positive associations found between resilience and feelings of personal accomplishment, empathy and compassion satisfaction, enhanced professional capacity, and sustainability and increased retention (Frost, 2017; Grant & Kinman, 2013, 2014; McFadden et al., 2019).

Although resilience can have benefits for social workers' wellbeing and practice, the concept is subject to growing criticism, mainly due to its focus on the employee and failure to acknowledge the structural, political and organizational causes of distress. Considine et al. (2015) argue that an emphasis on building individual resilience in social work education and practice can promote the view that a "failure to cope" is a personal weakness not a reaction to intolerable circumstances. Such views were also expressed in a study that explored social work educators' views of resilience in the profession (Grant et al., 2014b). We maintain that practitioners need to be sufficiently resilient to manage the demands they face without burning out, but individually focused initiatives will not in themselves be sufficient to support wellbeing in a high-pressured working environment. Organizations therefore have a duty of care to support the wellbeing of their employees by reducing psychosocial hazards at source wherever possible, as well as ensuring that the working environment builds their capacity for resilience.

While some of the factors that protect and promote resilience will be similar across different contexts, the risks in generalising findings from situation to another are recognised (Gucciardi et al., 2018). Resilience is shaped by many factors such as the occupational context and climate, the type of stressors experienced and their intensity, and the individual qualities required to recover from difficulties and build capacity in particular working environments (Collins, 2007; Kossek & Perrigino, 2016). For example, for teachers, "resilience" may be characterised by effective classroom management skills, for faculty, it may require the ability to reframe rejection for faculty, and for prison officers, it may be demonstrated by the capacity to manage threats to their physical safety. The features of the organization that can foster resilience will also depend on the characteristics of the job and the working environment. Therefore, it is crucial to identify the factors that support resilience at the organizational as well as the individual level in specific settings. A more contextualised approach to protecting and promoting resilience will inform interventions that are more congruent with the workplace environment. The next sections draw on research that has identified some of the characteristics that underpin resilience at individual, team, and organizational levels, with particular focus on the implications for social workers. Some examples of interventions at each level that take account of the workplace context are also provided.

Developing resilient social workers

To enhance resilience at an individual level, we need insight into the underlying qualities of resilient people. At a management level, workers are considered more "resilient" when they are able to sustain their "usual" level of performance and engagement under pressure, are less vulnerable to stress and burnout, and can overcome negative experiences such as discrimination (Kossek & Perrigino, 2016). Regarding personal qualities, Pooley and Cohen (2010) consider resilience to be synonymous with resourcefulness, emphasising the ability to utilise internal and external resources to respond to challenges positively and flexibly, adjust to change effectively, and maintain a sense of control. Although adaptability, commitment, and control are commonly identified as qualities of resilient people, a wider range of attitudes, traits and behavioural tendencies, social skills, and cognitive abilities has been highlighted. Other personal characteristics linked with resilience include a sense of mastery and purpose, positive attitudes towards the self, well-developed problem-solving and planning skills, emotional literacy, the ability to maintain perspective, and an optimistic explanatory style (Grant & Kinman, 2014a).

Some insight has been gained into social workers' understandings of the concept of resilience and the personal characteristics that can help them manage the demands of the job effectively. While some qualities, such as effective coping skills, self-care and the maintenance of work–life boundaries, are likely to be effective in any working environment, others are more relevant to the social work role. Reflecting the multifaceted nature of resilience discussed above, some variation was found in practitioners' views regarding the meaning of resilience and how it can be enhanced (see Box 8.1). The lack of clarity found, particularly among social work trainees, supports previous calls for additional training to support resilience and wellbeing from an early stage and an enhanced understanding of the organization's key roles and responsibilities in sustaining it (Beddoe et al., 2013; Collins, 2017; Grant et al., 2014b).

BOX 8.1   SOCIAL WORKERS' VIEWS: WHAT IS RESILIENCE, WHY IS IT IMPORTANT, AND HOW CAN IT BE ENHANCED?

Grant and Kinman (2013) explored personal representations of resilience in 300 trainee and qualified social workers. The following issues were examined:

What is resilience?

This was conceptualised either in reactive terms (i.e., a quality that enhances one's capacity to cope with stressful circumstances without being unduly damaged), or more proactively (i.e., as a protective resource, or set of tools, that help people identify and alleviate stressful experiences and address future challenges). A wide range of qualities, such as adaptability, flexibility, perseverance, hardiness, self-awareness, and self-reflection, were thought to underpin resilience. Some key differences emerged; trainees typically perceived resilience as an innate, fixed quality that could not necessarily be developed via training, while experienced practitioners tended to emphasise the interaction between personal attributes and protective features of the environment.

Why is it important for social workers to be resilient?

Resilience was generally considered essential to maintain optimum physical, emotional, and cognitive functioning in this high-pressured role. Two inter-related themes were identified where: (1) resilience was thought to underpin optimum job performance by helping practitioners manage complex and challenging issues while ensuring that professional standards are maintained; and (2) resilience facilitates self-protection by helping practitioners manage the emotional demands and complexity of the job without burning out and/or leaving the profession. Also identified was the role played by resilience in sustaining perseverance, optimism, and hope in the face of obstacles—which were considered key qualities for social workers.

What can be done to enhance resilience?

Respondents emphasised the joint responsibility of the individual social worker and their employer in supporting resilience via: (1) internal strategies, such as the development of self-awareness, reflective abilities, effective coping skills, and appropriate self-care; and (2) external initiatives, such as organizational resources, stress management training, and effective support and supervision. The organization's responsibility to provide high-quality support and personal development opportunities was also emphasised, but the need for the individual practitioner to be assertive in ensuring that such initiatives were available and accessible was also recognised.

Other studies have offered insight into what is means to be a resilient social worker. The 13 practitioners interviewed by Rose and Palattiyil (2020) tended to see resilience in interactional terms, highlighting features of the organization, the individual, and their role within it. Being resilient was generally considered essential to "keep your head above water" and manage the stress of the job successfully (p. 30). Some characteristics thought to underpin resilience at the individual level were identified, such as effective emotional regulation skills, the ability to achieve a balance between showing empathy to service users and maintain protective boundaries, being realistic about what can be achieved with limited resources, and forging supportive networks. Also emphasised was the key role of organizations in building practitioner resilience via support and training, but heavy workloads and tensions between maintaining core social work values within "a managerial and consumerist culture" (p. 33), were thought to challenge even the most resilient worker.

Multi-faceted and dynamic understandings of resilience also emerged from interviews conducted with social workers in New Zealand (Adamson et al., 2014) and the importance of relational and contextual factors was recognised. The findings informed a conceptual framework with three elements: *the self* (core attributes such as identity, autonomy, optimism, personal history, and internalised moral and ethical codes); *the practice context* (features of the organizational structure and culture), and *mediating factors* between the self and the context (such as support from supervisors and colleagues, coping and problem-solving skills, effective boundary setting, and developmental learning). As in the study conducted by Rose and Palattiyil (2020), the risk of job demands, stress, and burnout destabilising individual resilience was recognised. Although based on small samples, these two studies have useful implications for practice by identifying how personal qualities of the practitioner might interact with the characteristics of their working context to predict vulnerability and protective factors.

Larger-scale quantitative studies of social workers have also identified some individual-level factors that strengthen resilience and its implications for wellbeing. The focus has largely been placed on early career practitioners as they appear to be more vulnerable to stress and burnout and, as indicated above, are at particular risk of leaving the profession (GovUK, 2022; Kinman & Grant, 2022). Findings suggest that emotional literacy (the ability to perceive and understand emotion in the self and others, appreciate the complexity of emotions, and use emotions to facilitate thought) is a particularly important personal resource for resilience and wellbeing. A study of 240 trainee social workers conducted by Kinman and Grant (2011) found that those with more highly developed emotional and social competencies, such as emotional literacy, reflective skills, coping flexibility, and "bounded" empathy (maintaining emotional boundaries), tended to report higher levels of resilience. Supporting its benefits for wellbeing, a strong relationship was found between resilience and mental health. Subsequent research by Kinman and Grant (2017) examined whether a multi-modal intervention enhanced the resources their research has previously associated with resilience among social workers over time. Following training in cognitive behavioural skills, mindfulness, goal setting, reflective supervision, and peer support, significant improvements were noted in levels of emotional literacy, reflective ability, and self-compassion compared to controls. The need for additional support for early career social workers recognised above is underlined by the finding that psychological distress and compassion fatigue reduced over time in the study group but increased among controls. This study highlighted the benefits of a "toolbox" approach, whereby trainees are exposed to a range of potential strategies that might suit their needs and preferences.

Another intervention study (Grant et al., 2014a) found that training in enhancing emotional competencies had benefits for social work trainees over time, where emotional literacy, reflective ability, and empathy (assessed by questionnaire and reflective logs) increased and psychological distress reduced. Evidence that relatively brief interventions can develop some of the capacities associated with resilience among practitioners and potentially protect wellbeing during this highly pressured period is promising. The findings of other studies of social workers can also inform training to develop the resources required to manage the demands of the job and build resilience, particularly initiatives focusing on the fulfilment of psychological needs (Bunce et al., 2019), increasing self-compassion (Kinman & Grant, 2020), and reducing maladaptive perfectionism (Kinman & Grant, 2022).

Building resilient teams in social work

As well as individual resilience, the characteristics of resilient teams have been explored. Team resilience has been defined as "a dynamic psychosocial process that protects a team from the potential negative effects of the disturbances they collectively encounter" (Morgan et al., 2013, p. 552). Disturbances can be any type of disruption, external or internal, with the potential to threaten team functioning. A more developmental perspective is provided by Flint-Taylor and Cooper (2017) who conceptualise team resilience as a process involving "…managing pressure effectively across the team as a whole, that further strengthens the capacity of the team to deal with future challenges in adversity" (p. 130). Individual resilience may form the foundation for team resilience (McEwen & Boyd, 2018), but a resilient team is not just the sum of the individual members' capacities, for example, a group of resilient individuals will not necessarily manage disruptions well at a collective level if communication skills or support are lacking (Alliger et al., 2015). We see a resilient team as one whose members use their individual and collective resources to adapt positively to the challenges they face and builds capacity to maintain wellbeing and performance and achieve common goals or outcomes in the future.

A systematic review conducted by Hartwig et al. (2020) has identified various attributes of resilient teams comprising: (1) *input factors* at the individual, team, and context levels (e.g., adaptability, social and communication skills, shared values, team learning orientation, and organizational culture; (2) *team processes* (e.g., cooperation, anticipating challenges, and providing emotional support); (3) *mediating states* (e.g., team cohesion, trust, a shared mental model of the team, psychological safety, and a sense of belonging); and (4) *outcomes* (e.g., health, performance, enhanced team functioning, and post-adversity team thriving). The authors recognise, however, that different resilient team processes—what they term "minimising, managing, and mending behaviours"—will be required at different stages of disruption, or to manage different types of challenge. We would argue that the team processes required are also dependent on the job role and characteristics of the working environment.

This framework developed by Hartwig et al. (2020) can provide a basis to help build resilient teams, but insight is needed into the characteristics required in different working contexts. Team resilience is particularly important in complex and uncertain environments such as social work, where effective collaboration within and between teams is crucial to manage collective challenges and achieve outcomes and where disruptions to team functioning can have serious consequences. In a social work context, "disturbances to functioning" might include a dramatic rise in referrals, increasingly complex cases, changes to team organization or organizational leadership, as well as day-to-day difficulties such as worker absence and turnover. The COVID-19 pandemic also had strong potential to destabilise the functioning of social work teams and the mutual support they provide. For many, working at home during the pandemic presented challenges for peer support and the functioning of the team as a secure base (see below), that could undermine their sense of psychological safety (Cook et al., 2020). Nonetheless, evidence was provided that well-established teams tended to manage the challenges more effectively than those who had been more recently formed. Many examples of creative strategies used to sustain support "virtually" between social work team members and make connections with new members were, however, identified during this time (Kinman, 2021)

Kinman and Grant (2021) have identified some of the key features of resilient social work teams. Particularly important characteristics are a collective sense of purpose and goal alignment, flexibility and resourcefulness, maintaining a solution (rather than a problem) focus, monitoring progress towards goal achievement, using networks to solve problems and gain capacity, seeking feedback to identify what works, adequate opportunities for reflection and growth, and having mechanisms to celebrate success while putting perceived "failures" in perspective. A mutual appreciation of the need for self-care and a collective sense of responsibility for supporting the wellbeing of members are also important priorities for social work teams. An open and trusting team culture is needed to enable members to identify the idiosyncratic signs and symptoms that colleagues might show if they are struggling, as well as the type of support that they would find most effective.

As recognised throughout this chapter, positive, supportive working relationships between team members provide a firm foundation for resilience, enabling practitioners to manage the challenges of social work and build individual and

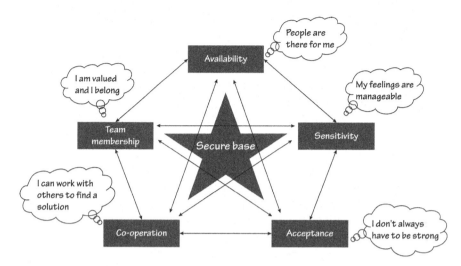

FIGURE 8.1 Key dimensions for developing the team as a secure base (Biggart et al., 2017). © University of East Anglia

team capacity (Kinman & Grant, 2021; McFadden et al., 2015). The importance of a secure base for the resilience and wellbeing of social workers is widely acknowledged; this is particularly important at a team level to help foster mutual trust and a sense of belongingness. Biggart et al. (2017) provide insight into how social work teams and organizations can create a "safe haven" where workers feel supported, psychologically safe, and are able to flourish. They identified five key dimensions for a secure base at the team level: availability, sensitivity, acceptance, co-operation, and team membership (see Figure 8.1). This provides a useful framework to help enhance team support and functioning. The importance of a secure base is discussed further below in relation to organizational resilience.

Developing resilient social work organizations

Resilient organizations are needed to support resilient individuals and teams. As discussed earlier in this chapter, organizations have a fundamental role in creating a workplace climate that builds the capacity for resilience; this will help ensure that work is not detrimental to employees' wellbeing or their effectiveness and build capacity for future challenges. Definitions of organizational resilience often refer to an organization's ability to recover and return to "normal" functioning after a disturbing or unexpected event by having appropriate strategies in place. Although, as discussed above, the ability to respond to crises is a crucial aspect of resilience for social work organizations, insight is needed into the conditions required to help individuals and teams manage the everyday challenges of practice, reduce their risk of stress and burnout, and facilitate good quality work.

Organizations have a legal, moral, and social duty of care to support the health and wellbeing of their employees and there is a sound business base to do so (Lewis et al., 2011). The UK Health and Safety Executive Management Standards approach (Health and Safety Executive, n.d.) offers a framework to help organizations monitor employee wellbeing by assessing the risk of key work-related psychosocial hazards (i.e., demands, control, support, relationship quality, and the management of change). This approach has been used in the social work sector to examine employees' perceptions of working conditions and compare the findings with national benchmarks (Ravalier et al., 2021). This risk assessment framework can also inform targeted interventions to reduce the risk of work-related stress. Clearly, processes are needed to identify and reduce structural hazards, but building a resilient organization also requires the identification of the conditions required to support wellbeing at individual and team levels. Examples of ways to enhance organizational resilience include ensuring effective leadership, improving job content and the working environment, enhancing autonomy, enriching support networks, facilitating employee input into decision-making processes, sharing good practice, and fostering a culture that prioritises self-care. It is also crucial to respond to issues that pose a serious threat to organizational stability, such as the ongoing challenges of the COVID-19 pandemic.

The findings of a longstanding research project conducted in the UK social work sector by Grant and Kinman (2021) highlight the value of conceptualising resilience as contextual, multi-dimensional, and systemic. This chapter has drawn on some of the findings of this research programme, as well as other studies, in identifying the features of resilient social workers and teams and setting out priorities for action to enhance their wellbeing and effectiveness. A key part of this work has involved identifying the characteristics of resilient social work organizations. The benefits of involving employees in shaping relevant interventions to improve their working conditions and wellbeing are widely recognised (Abildgaard et al., 2018), so our model was co-produced with diverse groups of social workers from trainees to senior leaders. We initially identified the characteristics associated with organizational resilience and, following consultation and validation with stakeholder groups, developed a framework with five dimensions:

Secure base

- The organization offers a sense of containment, protection, belonging, safety, and being cared for. It also fosters a culture of mutual support.
- The organization provides opportunities for workers to explore fears and concerns and to raise constructive challenge to practice and organizational change.
- This "safe space" provides workers with support and gives them renewed energy and resources.

Sense of appreciation

- Workers feel valued and that their individual talents and skills are appreciated.
- Leaders are open and approachable, genuinely interested in workers, and trust them to do a good job.
- Leaders understand the pressures of the work and the need to support people to prioritise self-care and ensure a healthy work–life balance.
- Leaders listen and engage with workers and provide constructive feedback.

Learning organization

- Within the organization, there is a system of shared beliefs, goals, and objectives and this is communicated clearly.
- Individuals, teams, and the organization itself are able to reflect and learn from experience.
- There is an evidence-informed approach to improving practice and managing change, with the input of individuals actively encouraged.
- Challenges provide opportunities for learning rather than blame and individual scapegoating.
- People have the freedom to speak up to raise concerns without feeling compromised, blamed, or victimised.

Mission and vision

- Leaders are committed to a clear mission and vision for the organization and use their communication skills to consult with and motivate others.
- Leaders are optimistic but realistic and focus on continuous improvement, inspiring workers to identify what good practice looks like and how it can be achieved.
- Change is managed constructively, especially during times of uncertainty.
- There is a sense of purpose and values are translated into action.

Wellbeing

- Workers perceive a deep commitment to their wellbeing; wherever possible, stress is tackled at source and working conditions improved.
- Reasonable adjustments are made to support people to work in ways that suit their preferences and circumstances.
- Workers feel able to thrive in a job that is rewarding and manageable and to make a difference to people who access services
- For these reasons, people are committed to the organization and their role within it.

Also identified in this research process were some critical "golden threads"—factors thought to be particularly influential in underpinning the conditions required for organizational resilience in social work organizations. These involve a strong commitment to maintaining values and building trust, effective management of change and uncertainty, consulting employees in decision-making and change processes, having effective communication structures, managing cultural diversity successfully, and a commitment to developing emotional literacy (Grant et al., 2022).

The findings of this research have formed the basis for a systematic approach to help leaders of social work organizations identify and enhance the conditions underpinning individual, team, and organizational resilience, with a view to improving wellbeing and professional effectiveness (Grant et al., 2022). The Social Work Organisational Resilience Diagnostic (SWORD) framework identifies the knowledge, skills, and attributes that can help those responsible for managing the workforce build sustainable resilience. The framework includes a diagnostic tool that identifies social workers' perceptions of the conditions found to underpin resilience providing leaders with targeted guidance on multi-level interventions with potential to enhance resilience in the five dimensions shown above. To date, a wide range of social work organizations across England has participated and feedback is positive, but the impact of the intervention on the factors found to underpin resilience and wellbeing at individual and team levels, as well as other outcomes such as engagement and retention, needs to be formally evaluated over time.

Conclusion

To support resilience, wellbeing, and optimal practice in social work organizations, as well as improve recruitment and retention, multi-level interventions underpinned by evidence are required. The research findings and frameworks outlined in this chapter have strong potential to guide such initiatives. The framework developed by Adamson et al. (2014) will help inform a systemic approach to building resilience in social work organizations because it highlights the dynamic relationship between attributes of the individual, the practice context, and important mediating factors.

At the organizational level, careful diagnosis of the key psychosocial hazards using validated frameworks, such as the HSE Management Standards approach, is required to monitor employee wellbeing and guide interventions to improve it. Line managers also have a critical role to play in developing the skills required to support wellbeing and ensuring that high-quality reflective supervision is available. The SWORD approach described in this chapter was developed to help organizations identify whether they have the conditions required to support resilience and provide targeted interventions on areas for improvement and growth. This chapter has also highlighted the characteristics of resilient social work teams that can also help build collective resilience, as well as protect and promote the resilience of individual members. The importance of workplace relationships in fostering resilience has been identified in this chapter; although individual social workers and teams have some responsibility for ensuring effective support networks are in place, it has been argued that employer-level interventions are also needed to promote relationship-focused initiatives (McFadden et al., 2018). The key role of a secure base in underpinning resilience and wellbeing in this context has been recognised in this chapter and the framework developed by Biggart et al. (2017) can provide a useful framework to enhance team support and functioning, as well as engender a sense of psychological safety.

Although organizations have a duty of care to support the wellbeing of their employees, individual social workers need to develop the competencies that will help them manage the demands of practice and avoid burning out. This chapter has identified some of the individual characteristics that underpin resilience and wellbeing in this context and how they might be enhanced. Initiatives to promote bounded empathy, self-compassion, and self-care are particularly important, although social workers may feel they need "permission" to prioritise their own wellbeing over other people's needs (Egan et al., 2019; Kinman et al., 2020). A toolbox approach is likely to be particularly effective in providing practitioners with a range of options to enhance resilience and wellbeing that will fit individual needs and preferences. Some examples include mindfulness, cognitive behavioural and reflective skills, emotional literacy, and time management.

Organizational-level interventions to support resilience will not, however, be successful unless they are supported by public policy initiatives, such as national workload management schemes, fair pay and other terms and conditions of service, effective recruitment and retention strategies, as well as risk assessments and "pulse checks" at the sector level to monitor wellbeing over time (see Grant et al., 2022). Moreover, although training and preparation for practice provides social workers with a strong foundation to develop their resilience and wellbeing (McFadden et al., 2015), provision across the sector is inconsistent. Calls have been made for an evidence-informed national "emotional curriculum" that offers research-informed, relevant training initiatives at all career stages (Collins, 2017; Grant & Kinman, 2014; Grant et al., 2014b). Support for early career social workers should be prioritised, in light of the evidence provided that they are particularly vulnerable to stress and may lack core protective factors.

For social workers to feel truly supported, they need to be provided with effective tools to manage stress and complexity during their initial education, early career, and as they become experts. Moreover, for resilience and wellbeing to be sustainable, they need to be nurtured within teams and organizations that provide conditions for effective social work practice to provide the best possible services when people need them most. There are a number of research priorities that will help inform support initiatives. Longitudinal studies using a range of methodologies, including daily diaries, are needed to provide insight into the development of resilience among social workers over time and the individual, team, and organizational-level factors that help support it.

References

Abildgaard, J. S., Nielsen, K., & Sverke, M. (2018). Can job insecurity be managed? Evaluating an organizational-level intervention addressing the negative effects of restructuring. *Work & Stress*, *32*(2), 105–123. https://doi-org.ezproxy.lib.bbk.ac.uk/10.1080/02678373.2017.1367735

Adamson, C., Beddoe, L., & Davys, A. (2014). Building resilient practitioners: Definitions and practitioner understandings. *British Journal of Social Work*, *44*(3), 522–541. https://doi.org/10.1093/bjsw/bcs142

Alliger, G. M., Cerasoli, C. P., Tannenbaum, S. I., & Vessey, W. B. (2015). Team resilience: How teams flourish under pressure. *Organizational Dynamics*, 44(3), 176–184. https://psycnet.apa.org/doi/10.1016/j.orgdyn.2015.05.003

Beddoe, L., Davys, A., & Adamson, C. (2013). Educating resilient practitioners. *Social Work Education*, *32*(1), 100–117. https://doi.org/10.1080/02615479.2011.644532

Biggart, L., Ward, E., Cook, L., & Schofield, G. (2017). The team as a secure base: Promoting resilience and competence in child and family social work. *Children and Youth Services Review*, *83*, 119–130. https://doi.org/10.1108/JCS-07-2020-0031

Bunce, L., Lonsdale, A. J., King, N., Childs, J., & Bennie, R. (2019). Emotional intelligence and self-determined behaviour reduce psychological distress: Interactions with resilience in social work students in the UK. *The British Journal of Social Work*, *49*(8), 2092–2111. https://doi-org.ezproxy.lib.bbk.ac.uk/10.1093/bjsw/bcz008

Carver, C. S. (1998). Resilience and thriving: Issues, models, and linkages. *Journal of Social Issues*, *54*(2), 245–266. https://doi.org/10.1111/j.1540-4560.1998.tb01217.x

Collins, S. (2007). Social workers, resilience, positive emotions and optimism. *Practice*, *19*(4), 255–269. https://doi-org.ezproxy.lib.bbk.ac.uk/10.1080/09503150701728186

Collins, S. (2008). Statutory social workers: Stress, job satisfaction, coping, social support and individual differences. *British Journal of Social Work*, *38*(6), 1173–1193. https://doi.org/10.1093/bjsw/bcm047

Collins, S. (2017). Social workers and resilience revisited. *Practice*, *29*(2), 85–105. https://doi.org/10.1080/09503153.2016.1229763

Considine, T., Hollingdale, P., & Neville, R. (2015). Social work, pastoral care and resilience. *Pastoral Care in Education*, *33*(4), 214–219. https://doi.org/10.1080/02643944.2015.1080289

Cook, L. L., Zschomler, D., Biggart, L., & Carder, S. (2020). The team as a secure base revisited: Remote working and resilience among child and family social workers during COVID-19. *Journal of Children's Services*, *15*(4), 259–266. https://doi.org/10.1108/JCS-07-2020-0031

Csiernik, R., Smith, C., Dewar, J., Dromgole, L., & O'Neill, A. (2010). Supporting new workers in a child welfare agency: An exploratory study. *Journal of Workplace Behavioral Health*, *25*(3), 218–232. https://doi.org/10.1080/15555240.2010.496333

Dima, G., Meseşan Schmitz, L., & Şimon, M. C. (2021). Job stress and burnout among social workers in the VUCA world of COVID-19 pandemic. *Sustainability*, *13*(13), 7109. https://doi.org/10.3390/su13137109

Egan, H., Keyte, R., McGowan, K., Peters, L., Lemon, N., Parsons, S., & Mantzios, M. (2019). 'You before me': A qualitative study of health care professionals' and students' understanding and experiences of compassion in the workplace, self-compassion, self-care and health behaviours. *Health Professions Education*, *5*(3), 225–236. https://doi.org/10.1016/j.hpe.2018.07.002

Finstad, G. L., Giorgi, G., Lulli, L. G., Pandolfi, C., Foti, G., León-Perez, J. M., & Mucci, N. (2021). Resilience, coping strategies and posttraumatic growth in the workplace following COVID-19: A narrative review on the positive aspects of trauma. *International Journal of Environmental Research and Public Health, 18*(18), 9453. https://doi.org/10.3390/ijerph18189453

Fletcher, D., & Sarkar, M. (2013). Psychological resilience. *European Psychologist, 18*(1), 12–23. https://doi.org/10.1027/1016-9040/a000124

Flint-Taylor, J., & Cooper, C. L. (2017). Team resilience: Shaping up for the challenges ahead. In M. Crane (Ed.), *Managing for resilience* (pp. 129–149). Routledge.

Fraser, M. W., Galinsky, M. J., & Richman, J. M. (1999). Risk, protection, and resilience: Toward a conceptual framework for social work practice. *Social Work Research, 23*(3), 131–143. https://doi.org/10.1093/swr/23.3.131

Frost, N. (2017). From "silo" to "network" profession–a multi-professional future for social work. *Journal of Children's Services, 12*(2-3), 174–183. https://doi.org/10.1108/JCS-05-2017-0019

GovUK (2022). *Children's Social Work Workforce.* https://explore-education-statistics.service.gov.uk/find-statistics/children-s-social-work-workforce

Grant, L., & Kinman, G. (2013). 'Bouncing back?' Personal representations of resilience of student and experienced social workers. *Practice, 25*(5), 349–366. https://doi.org/10.1080/09503153.2013.860092

Grant, L., & Kinman, G. (Eds.). (2014). *Developing resilience for social work practice.* Bloomsbury Publishing.

Grant, L., & Kinman, G. (2015). Emotional resilience in the helping professions and how it can be enhanced. *Health and Social Care Education, 3*(1), 23–34. https://doi.org/10.11120/hsce.2014.00040

Grant, L., Kinman, G., & Alexander, K. (2014a). What's all this talk about emotion? Developing emotional intelligence in social work students. *Social Work Education, 33*(7), 874–889. https://doi.org/10.1093/bjsw/bcw164

Grant, L., Kinman, G., & Alexander, K. (2022). *Social work research diagnostic. Research in practice.* SWORD. http://www.sword.researchinpractice.org.uk/

Grant, L., Kinman, G., & Baker, S. (2014b). 'Put on your own oxygen mask before assisting others: Social work educators' perspectives on an 'emotional curriculum.' *The British Journal of Social Work, 45*(8), 2351–2367. https://doi.org/10.1093/bjsw/bcu066

Gucciardi, D. F., Crane, M., Ntoumanis, N., Parker, S. K., Thøgersen-Ntoumani, C., Ducker, K. J., ... & Temby, P. (2018). The emergence of team resilience: A multilevel conceptual model of facilitating factors. *Journal of Occupational and Organizational Psychology, 91*(4), 729–768. https://doi.org/10.1111/joop.12237

Hagerty, S. L., & Williams, L. M. (2022). Moral injury, traumatic stress, and threats to core human needs in health-care workers: The COVID-19 pandemic as a dehumanizing experience. *Clinical Psychological Science, 10*(6), 1060–1082. https://doi.org/10.1177/21677026211057554

Hakanen, J. J., & Schaufeli, W. B. (2012). Do burnout and work engagement predict depressive symptoms and life satisfaction? A three-wave seven-year prospective study. *Journal of Affective Disorders, 141*(2-3), 415–424. https://doi.org/10.1016/j.jad.2012.02.043

Hartmann, S., Weiss, M., Newman, A., & Hoegl, M. (2020). Resilience in the workplace: A multilevel review and synthesis. *Applied Psychology, 69*(3), 913–959. https://doi.org/10.1111/apps.12191

Hartwig, A., Clarke, S., Johnson, S., & Willis, S. (2020). Workplace team resilience: A systematic review and conceptual development. *Organizational Psychology Review, 10*(3-4), 169–200. https://doi.org/10.1177/2041386620919476

Health and Care Professions Council (n.d.). Developing resilience. https://www.hcpc-uk.org/covid-19/advice/applying-our-standards/developing-resilience/

Health and Safety Executive (2022). *Work-related Stress, Anxiety or Depression Statistics in Great Britain.* https://www.hse.gov.uk/statistics/causdis/stress.pdf

Health and Safety Executive (n.d.). *Notes on HSE Management Standards Indicator Tool.* https://www.hse.gov.uk/stress/standards/notesindicatortool.htm

Jackson, D., Firtko, A., & Edenborough, M. (2007). Personal resilience as a strategy for surviving and thriving in the face of workplace adversity: A literature review. *Journal of Advanced Nursing, 60*(1), 1–9. https://doi.org/10.1111/j.1365-2648.2007.04412.x

Jia, C. X., & Fu, C. (2022). The influence of work-family conflict on social worker job satisfaction. *Journal of Social Work, 22*(4), 970–991. https://doi.org/10.1177/14680173211051977

Kalliath, P., Hughes, M., & Newcombe, P. (2012). When work and family are in conflict: Impact on psychological strain experienced by social workers in Australia. *Australian Social Work, 65*(3), 355–371. https://doi.org/10.1080/0312407X.2011.625035

Kim, H., Ji, J., & Kao, D. (2011). Burnout and physical health among social workers: A three-year longitudinal study. *Social Work, 56*(3) 258–268. https://www.jstor.org/stable/23719205

Kinman, G. (2021). *Supporting Wellbeing Remotely.* Research in Practice. https://www.researchinpractice.org.uk/media/5687/supporting_wellbeing_remotely_lb_web.pdf

Kinman, G., & Grant, L. (2011). Exploring stress resilience in trainee social workers: The role of emotional and social competencies. *The British Journal of Social Work, 41*(2), 261–275. https://doi.org/10.1093/bjsw/bcq088

Kinman, G., & Grant, L. (2017). Building resilience in early-career social workers: Evaluating a multi-modal intervention. *British Journal of Social Work, 47*(7), 1979–1998. https://doi.org/10.1093/bjsw/bcw164

Kinman, G., & Grant, L. (2020). Emotional demands, compassion and mental health in social workers. *Occupational Medicine, 70*(2), 89–94. https://doi.org/10.1093/occmed/kqz144

Kinman, G., & Grant, L. (2022). Being 'good enough': Perfectionism and well-being in social workers. *The British Journal of Social Work, 52*(7), 4171–4188. https://doi.org/10.1093/bjsw/bcz073

Kinman, G., Grant, L., & Kelly, S. (2020). 'It's my secret space': The benefits of mindfulness for social workers. *The British Journal of Social Work, 50*(3), 758–777. https://doi.org/10.1093/bjsw/bcz073

Kinman, G., & McDowall, A. (2014). The work-home interface: Building effective boundaries. In L. Grant, & G. Kinman (Eds.), *Developing resilience for social work practice* (pp. 33–53). Bloomsbury Publishing.

Kinman, G., & Teoh, K. (2018). What could make a difference to the mental health of UK doctors? A review of the research evidence. Society of Occupational Medicine and Louise Tebboth Foundation. https://www.som.org.uk/sites/som.org.uk/files/What_could_make_a_difference_to_the_mental_health_of_UK_doctors_LTF_SOM.pdf

Kossek, E. E., & Perrigino, M. B. (2016). Resilience: A review using a grounded integrated occupational approach. *Academy of Management Annals, 10*(1), https://doi.org/10.5465/19416520.2016.1159878

Lewis, R., Yarker, J., & Donaldson-Feilder, E. (2011). *Preventing stress in organizations: How to develop positive managers.* John Wiley & Sons.

Maslach, C., Jackson, S., & Leiter, M. (1996) *Maslach burnout inventory manual* (3rd ed.). John Wiley & Sons.

McEwen, K., & Boyd, C. M. (2018). A measure of team resilience: Developing the resilience at work team scale. *Journal of Occupational and Environmental Medicine, 60*(3), 258–272. https://doi.org/10.1097/JOM.0000000000001223

McFadden, P. (2015). Measuring Burnout among UK Social Workers. Community Care https://pure.qub.ac.uk/en/publications/measuring-burnout-among-uk-social-workers-a-community-care-study

McFadden, P., Campbell, A., & Taylor, B. (2015). Resilience and burnout in child protection social work: Individual and organisational themes from a systematic literature review. *The British Journal of Social Work, 45*(5), 1546–1563. https://doi.org/10.1093/bjsw/bct210

McFadden, P., Mallett, J., Campbell, A., & Taylor, B. (2019). Explaining self-reported resilience in child-protection social work: The role of organisational factors, demographic information and job characteristics. *The British Journal of Social Work, 49*(1), 198–216. https://doi.org/10.1093/bjsw/bcy015

McFadden, P., Manthorpe, G., & Mallett, J. (2018). Commonalities and differences in social work with learning disability and child protection: Findings from a UK 'burnout' national survey. *British Journal of Social Work, 48*(5), 1199–1219. https://doi.org/10.1093/bjsw/bcx070

McFadden, P., Neill, R. D., Mallett, J., Manthorpe, J., Gillen, P., Moriarty, J., & Ross, J. (2022). Mental well-being and quality of working life in UK social workers before and during the COVID-19 pandemic: A propensity score matching study. *The British Journal of Social Work, 52*(5), 2814–2833. https://doi.org/10.1093/bjsw/bcab198

Montgomery, A., Panagopoulou, E., Esmail, A., Richards, T., & Maslach, C. (2019). Burnout in healthcare: The case for organisational change. *British Medical Journal, 366.* https://doi.org/10.1136/bmj.l4774

Morgan, P. B., Fletcher, D., & Sarkar, M. (2013). Defining and characterizing team resilience in elite sport. *Psychology of Sport and Exercise, 14*(4), 549–559. https://doi.org/10.1016/j.psychsport.2013.01.004

Pink, S., Ferguson, H., & Kelly, L. (2022). Digital social work: Conceptualising a hybrid anticipatory practice. *Qualitative Social Work, 21*(2), 413–430. https://doi.org/10.1177/14733250211003647

Pooley, J. A., & Cohen, L. (2010). Resilience: A definition in context. *Australian Community Psychologist, 22*(1), 30–37. https://psychology.org.au/aps/media/acp/pooley.pdf

Radley, M., & Figley, C. (2007). The social psychology of compassion. *Clinical Social Work Journal, 35,* 207–214.

Ravalier, J. M. (2019). Psycho-social working conditions and stress in UK social workers. *The British Journal of Social Work, 49*(2), 371–390. https://doi.org/10.1093/bjsw/bcy023

Ravalier, J. M., McFadden, P., Boichat, C., Clabburn, O., & Moriarty, J. (2021). Social worker well-being: A large mixed-methods study. *The British Journal of Social Work, 51*(1), 297–317. https://doi.org/10.1093/bjsw/bcaa078

Ravalier, J., McFadden, P., Gillen, P., Mallett, J., Nicholl, P., Neill, R., & Curry, D. (2022). Working conditions and well-being in UK social care and social work during COVID-19. *Journal of Social Work, 23*(2), 165–188. https://doi.org/10.1177/14680173221109483

Robertson, I. T., Cooper, C. L., Sarkar, M., & Curran, T. (2015). Resilience training in the workplace from 2003 to 2014: A systematic review. *Journal of Occupational and Organizational Psychology, 88*(3), 533–562. https://doi.org/10.1111/joop.12120

Rogers, M. E., Creed, P. A., & Searle, J. (2014). Emotional labour, training stress, burnout, and depressive symptoms in junior doctors. *Journal of Vocational Education & Training, 66*(2), 232–248. https://doi.org/10.1080/13636820.2014.884155

Rose, S., & Palattiyil, G. (2020). Surviving or thriving? Enhancing the emotional resilience of social workers in their organisational settings. *Journal of Social Work, 20*(1), 23–42. https://journals.sagepub.com/doi/pdf/10.1177/1468017318793614

Ungar, M., & Liebenberg, L. (2011). Assessing resilience across cultures using mixed methods: Construction of the child and youth resilience measure. *Journal of Mixed Methods Research, 5*(2), 126–149. https://doi.org/10.1177/1558689811400607

UNISON. (2016). *A day in the life of social work.* UNISON. https://www.unison.org.uk/content/uploads/2017/03/CC-SocialWorkWatch_report_web.pdf

UNISON. (2022). *Social work and the impact of the COVID pandemic.* UNISON. https://www.unison.org.uk/content/uploads/2022/06/26799-social-work-survey-FULL-final.pdf

Virga, D., Baciu, E., Lazar, T., & Lupsa, D. (2020). Psychological capital protects social workers from burnout and secondary traumatic stress. *Sustainability, 12*(6), 2246. https://doi.org/10.3390/su12062246

Waegemakers Schiff, J., & Lane, A. M. (2019). PTSD symptoms, vicarious traumatization, and burnout in front line workers in the homeless sector. *Community Mental Health Journal, 55*(3), 454–462. doi: 10.1007/s10597-018-00364-7

West, A. L. (2015). Associations among attachment style, burnout, and compassion fatigue in health and human service workers: A systematic review. *Journal of Human Behavior in the Social Environment, 25*(6), 571–590. https://doi.org/10.1080/10911359.2014.988321

Williamson, V., Murphy, D., & Greenberg, N. (2020). COVID-19 and experiences of moral injury in front-line key workers. *Occupational Medicine, 70*(5), 317–319. https://doi.org/10.1093/occmed/kqaa052

Williamson, V., Stevelink, S. A., & Greenberg, N. (2018). Occupational moral injury and mental health: Systematic review and meta-analysis. *The British Journal of Psychiatry, 212*(6), 339–346. https://doi.org/10.1192/bjp.2018.55

Wirth, T., Mette, J., Prill, J., Harth, V., & Nienhaus, A. (2019). Working conditions, mental health and coping of staff in social work with refugees and homeless individuals: A scoping review. *Health & Social Care in the Community, 27*(4), e257–e269. https://doi.org/10.1111/hsc.12730

YouGov. (2020). *A Report on the Social Work Profession.* https://www.socialworkengland.org.uk/media/3326/yougov-the-social-work-profession.pdf

Yu, M., Wen, J., Smith, S. M., & Stokes, P. (2022). Building-up resilience and being effective leaders in the workplace: A systematic review and synthesis model. *Leadership & Organization Development Journal, 43*(7), 2098–1117. https://doi.org/10.1108/LODJ-09-2021-0437

9

RESILIENCE AS A LEADERSHIP TRAIT IN MODERN ORGANIZATIONS

Alexander-Stamatios G. Antoniou, Evangelia Markopoulou, and Virginia-Eirini Angelou

Introduction

The notion of resilience

The Latin word "resilire," which refers to the action of springing back or recoiling, is where the word resilience gets its etymological root (Giustiniano et al., 2020). The term "resilience" was originally used in material science as "the capacity of a strained body to recover its size and shape after compressive stress deformation" (Campbell et al., 2008, p. 61). According to relevant studies in other fields (e.g., psychology), resilience appears to be a complex concept; although, researchers tend to agree that it contains certain specific aspects. As a result, resilience has been associated with the following characteristics: an ability to restore balance after being exposed to extreme conditions; a constant, dynamic psychological procedure that entails being adaptive and successful in an adverse environment; a trait, outcome, or capacity that includes surviving, recovering, and thriving through any misfortune; an ability to find or make meaning despite suffering, hardship, and disaster; and a predisposition that enables resilient people to see how they might move past their current difficulties and into a better, predictable future (Campbell et al., 2008; Everly et al., 2020; Foerster & Duchek, 2017; Ledesma, 2014; Qiao et al., 2022; Sommer et al., 2016; Southwick et al., 2017).

Resilience can be different for every person. Resilience is the capacity to adapt to and evolve with essential change, not merely the capacity to be ready for challenge, endure, and to do so with vigour (Van Wart et al., 2021). Regardless of the definition that is chosen, Martin (2017) argues that resilience is a strong notion that spans multiple dimensions and has three main parts: emotional intelligence, authenticity, and meaning in life. In a study by Chance (2022) about Black women

DOI: 10.4324/9781003287858-12

in higher education, the participants stated that in the face of trauma, adversity, and the stresses of life, developing and maintaining resilience has helped them get through difficult experiences and promote personal and professional growth. People who are resilient make the most out of the resources they have at their disposal, they discover connections and imagine possibilities in circumstances where less resilient people could become blocked and disheartened (Campbell et al., 2008). Resilience does not imply that a person will not experience adversity, trauma, or distress; on the contrary, Chance (2022) found that resilience referred to those protective factors and positive adaptations a person makes in light of those situations. According to Baykal (2018), more than a conventional adaptation is implied by resilience. In actuality, resilience functions as a reservoir to raise the likelihood of adaptability. Although there is a strong likelihood, there's no guarantee that resilience will emerge (Baykal, 2018).

Steadfastness is the capacity to persist over the long run with courage and in spite of obstacles (Van Wart et al., 2021). People who maintain this characteristic are frequently praised for their capacity to "rebound" from difficulties. Many people consider this to be the most important component of resilience (Van Wart et al., 2021). Resilience is sometimes regarded or characterised as resolving issues or as something that is readily attainable, a definition that appears to be insufficient according to Chance (2022). The power, privilege, and oppression structures that have an everyday influence on the lives of marginalised people are not taken into account here. In Chance's (2022) study, Black women in leadership positions reported to resort to adopting the conventional role of the Black superwoman, by preserving an absurd and extreme work ethic, and adhering to the adage that they must work harder and more diligently than their White counterparts to even achieve half their accomplishments (or receive half the recognition). Resilient people have a very realistic grasp on their reality and its adversities. The ability to effectively assess challenges and issues while retaining a fierce sense of resolve to succeed is what resilience entails (Campbell et al., 2008).

The concept of resilience can also be applied on an organizational level. In this concept, resilience can be characterised as the ability to ensure positive adjustment under stressful circumstances, as a result of which an organization, for example, develops stronger, more resourceful structures (Baykal, 2018). According to Giustiniano et al. (2020), businesses and other organizations need to turn stressors, crises, and shocks into innovative, long-lasting solutions in order to survive and prosper. To integrate the reactive and adaptive components of resilience, the process calls for experimenting with the unlearning–learning balance. Unlearning is the capacity to transition to a different mental model rather than forgetting anything. As part of this "learning to unlearn and learn," one must embrace experimentation and get through any resistance that stands in the way of trying something new. Leaders must respond and adapt while avoiding partial answers and getting rid of habits of ingrained cognitive prejudice if they want to foster resilience (Giustiniano et al., 2020).

The notion of leadership

Leadership, however, is the process through which an individual influences other team members to achieve defined goals and a leader is a person in a group or organization who exerts the greatest influence on others (Greenberg & Baron, 2013). Leadership focuses on efforts of social influence, which are manifested in the long course of human existence (Antoniou, 2021). Leadership involves complex interpersonal processes and is not just about the leader telling others what to do. The true leader of a group may not be the person who is typically designated for this role (Arnold & Randall, 2020). The main approaches to leadership refer to transactional, transformational, and charismatic forms of leadership.

Transactional leadership is based on rewards or exchanges for desired behaviours by the followers (Arnold & Randall, 2020). In transactional leadership, each side in the transaction-based relationship is consciously aware of the strengths of the other, and their communication is analogous to the forms of transaction envisaged. The relationship between the leader and the subordinates remains at transactional levels and does not evolve (Antoniou, 2008, 2021). There are tasks that must be completed and the leader prepares the plan and controls the behaviours (Antoniou et al., 2019). In transactional leadership, employees are ensured the freedom to take initiatives, accurate and truthful information about the opportunities for the company or the problems and risks it is about to face, and finally, the fair distribution of positive or negative feedback (Athinaiou & Antoniou, 2008). The strength of transactional leadership, which involves concomitant rewards and punishments, is based on the fact that it motivates subordinates by utilizing passive and active management. Exceptions are cases where the leader/manager simply observes the actions of subordinates before proceeding to provide rewards on a case-by-case basis for specific behaviours or instead chooses to let subordinates act at will (laissez-faire) without providing any guidance. The transactional leader aims to achieve the obedience of their subordinates in any way possible without taking into account their ideals and values (Antoniou, 2008, 2021).

In transformational leadership, leaders use their charisma in order to transform and revitalise their organizations (Greenberg & Baron, 2013). Transformational leaders inspire and challenge subordinates to act by providing a dominant goal and setting a personal example (Arnold & Randall, 2020). This type of leadership is considered more inclusive than the others because it has a decisive influence on the productivity of teams and the decision-making within systems (Antoniou, 2021). More specifically, transformational leadership contributes significantly to employee performance and long-term customer satisfaction, causes high employee engagement with the organization, enhances employees' trust in employers, increases employee job satisfaction, and reduces work stress and contributes to wellbeing (Antoniou & Galaktidou, 2010). Bass (1985), as cited in Arar and Oplatka (2022), argued that in this type of leadership, the leaders' relationships with followers are based on four factors: (1) *idealised influence* in which the leader provides vision and a sense of purpose while at the same time is totally committed, (2) *inspirational motivation* that requires leaders to enthusiastically communicate high-performance expectations, (3) *individualised consideration* that entails coaching and mentoring the followers in order to fulfil each follower's needs, and (4) *intellectual stimulation* that challenges followers to embrace new and critical ways of thinking and doing. The transformational leader encourages followers to present new ideas and is tolerant when they make mistakes.

Charismatic leaders are the ones who powerfully influence followers, judging by their performance. They are characterised by great self-confidence, present a clearly expressed vision, behave in surprising ways, are recognised as agents of change and are sensitive to the environmental constraints they face (Greenberg & Baron, 2013). This type of leadership has been associated with behaviours that express confidence by providing vision for the future, showing counter-conformist behaviours and the ability to inspire others (Antoniou, 2021). House (1977), as cited in Mhatre and Riggio (2014), argued that by promoting a compelling and perhaps radical future vision, charismatic leaders can inspire their followers. The emotional relationships that charismatic leaders' followers frequently form with them lay the groundwork for their desire to be obedient and dedicated to their causes. People who perceive charismatic leaders as having extraordinary qualities and strengths tend to believe that these qualities will enable them to realise the radical vision that they have articulated. Transactional and charismatic leadership have been associated with high level performance by followers, teams, and organizations, probably because of a variety of mechanisms such as motivation, commitment, and self-sacrifice (Arnold & Randall, 2020).

Nowadays, leadership is volatile because of the high rate of change, the illusion of control, and the high expectations of followers (Arnold & Randall, 2020). Transactional, transformational, and charismatic leadership are the three main pillars of leadership. However, over the years, a plethora of different leadership styles have emerged and been described, varying in their context, philosophy, sociocultural influences, and goals (Antoniou, 2021; Yukl, 2009). For example: *distributed leadership*, which refers to a form of coordinated action in which individuals work together and interact in order to create a final product (Spillane, 2006); *postmodern leadership,* which is based on the philosophical stream of postmodernism according to which reality is not one and there are multiple subjective truths (Keough & Tobin, 2001); *ethical leadership,* which assumes that the focus of leadership should be on the values, beliefs, and ethics of the leader who ought to be a role model actively shaping the ethical dimension in the organization (Arar & Oplatka, 2022; Bush, 2020) and which depends on the value system espoused or disapproved by those who choose to follow the leadership figures (Antoniou, 2016); *adaptive leadership,* which emphasises the organization's ability to adapt to unstable environments (Hickman, 2012); *invisible leadership* in which the key organizers and leaders are unknown to the others, so their motivations, contributions, and personal effort remain invisible (Hickman, 2004); and *positive leadership* in which multiple positive practices are implemented (Cameron, 2013). Moreover, over the years, new leadership styles have emerged based on different cultural backgrounds such as *Tao leadership*, which is based on the teachings of Tao Te Ching (Dreher, 2002) and *Ubuntu leadership* based on Ubuntu, which is a cultural worldview that is common among the Bantu tribes of Africa and emphasises the interconnectedness of the self within society (Brubaker, 2013).

Resilience and leadership: Managing crises

In general, resilience as a concept in an organizational environment appears to be the subject of a significant amount of research. The resilience-promoting organizational culture is more than just having a team spirit; it creates a setting where human resilience is not only encouraged but also woven into the very fabric of the company as a whole. Unity, cooperation, pride in belonging, and an organizational atmosphere where development is encouraged, support is plentiful, crisis is considered as a potential for improvement, and creativity is not a result but rather an essential continuing process are the traits that characterise the culture (Everly et al., 2020). Resilience was cited by Ledesma (2014) as a crucial quality of good leaders and was defined as the capacity to overcome difficulty, frustration, and bad luck. Foerster and Duchek (2017) claim that cultivating leaders' resilience requires many factors that affect the individual, their behaviour, and the situations they might find themselves into. These factors include the leaders' skills on a social or cognitive level, the environment they share with their families, friends, and co-workers and their behaviour in general, for example whether they are comfortable communicating in an honest way or if they display a pattern of analytical and reflective thinking. Under the most trying circumstances, effective leadership prioritises the growth of faith, trust, and resilience as well as an upbeat mission-focused vision in an environment that is centred around ethics. These types of leaders must practice putting their followers before themselves in order to lead them in a thorough, respectful manner and complete the task (Everly et al., 2020).

Grote (2019) proposed three main leadership requirements in order to cultivate resilience in an organizational environment. The first is the capacity of the leaders to change their own roles and actions in accordance with the needs for stability and flexibility that their teams must meet. Their range of action must include everything, from creating order through rules and personal guidance to sharing leadership responsibilities and ceding control when extreme flexibility is required, to merging into the background during impromptu processes of learning exchange. In addition, they must be able to recognise changes in customer needs and set themselves and their team up for the proper transitions between modes of operation. Designing organizational structures that encourage both individual and team adaptability is the second prerequisite. This mostly relates to established institutions and norms, which are often intended to provide stability. However, it must be carefully ensured that the stability produced does not result in stiffness. For example, while creating rules, one should think about including flexible rules. The third criterion is concerned with the part that leaders play in creating corporate culture. This goes beyond creating the mindful or informed culture that is typically considered a foundation for resilience (Grote, 2019).

The ability of an organization's members to continue working hard in the face of challenges is essential for the organization to survive in conditions of extreme stress and ambiguity. In other words, employees must also exhibit resilience, a quality that is currently receiving more attention in literature as a critical component of not just surviving a crisis but really benefiting from it (Sommer et al., 2016). An organization that is resilient not only survives but also flourishes in a changing and unpredictable environment (Southwick et al., 2017). For example, enhancing subordinate resilience has been highlighted by researchers as a way of helping organizations to deal with difficulties that may arise (Harland et al., 2005). Extremely resilient leaders are capable of responding constructively to crises that may affect their companies, and by doing so, they are able to enhance the degree of resilience in employees around them (Eliot, 2020). To aid in the development of resilient people and resilient teams, leaders can use a variety of strategies, such as:

1 List your advantages: Explore the special talents of each team member by meeting with them in person and individually; develop a strategy for incorporating these competencies into team responsibilities.
2 Link individual talents to accomplishing group objectives: Assist the team members in recognizing each other's assets so they may collaborate productively and cohesively.
3 Strengthening current abilities: Maintain a modest communication level with the group frequently. Find out how the team may use one another's skills in areas where further help might be required. At this point, it is imperative to prioritize the accomplishments of all participants rather than one over the others.
4 Work Tasks: In order to promote a feeling of control and self-efficacy, be sure to match members' talents with project objectives. Strength-specific task assignments that promote self-efficacy provide people a sense of mastery over their workplace.
5 Appoint Mentors: Working with mentors outside the team frequently results in a fresh outlook on procedures and working styles.
6 Performance evaluations: Identify areas of excellence frequently in performance assessments; describe the year's objectives based on abilities.
7 Promote educational growth: Assist the group in pursuing educational opportunities to advance their professional abilities. Determine the programs and courses needed either inside or outside of the work environment.
8 Promote teamwork: Rather than focusing on individual performance indicators, promote a supportive atmosphere where project goals are delivered. This lessens the competition and motivates team members to assist others in making the most of their talents.

(Southwick et al., 2017)

It is now possible to provide a potentially helpful general response to the topic of how leaders might utilise their influence to foster resilience in their subordinates, teams, or units (Campbell et al., 2008). If resilience needs the capability to place meaning on suffering, the ability to innovate, and the capacity to be adaptable, then leaders may support both individual and collective resilience by exhibiting, fostering, and promoting these crucial qualities. Effective leadership may be viewed as a "resilience reservoir" that provides and nurtures resilience through the leader's own traits and attributes and serves as an example of resilience through the leader's actions and conduct (Campbell et al., 2008). Encountering crises is expected for organizations. For Faustenhammer and Gössler (2011), every crisis demands strong organizations and strong individuals. Underlying burnout syndrome prevents executives from being able to guide an organization in order to manage a crisis. Executives and workers must maintain a perspective that has a long-term effect when it comes to managing their own resources. This way, management methods can have a lasting impact. The following suggestions can boost personal resilience:

1 Clarity of the role: the understanding that one is only playing a role which doesn't characterize him as a whole person.
2 Overcoming fear: being able to "overcome" their personal worries as well as those of others.
3 Introspection and exchange of experiences: it may be quite helpful to actively reflect on personal mistakes and crises without being constrained by norms.
4 Being proactive: providing for personal stability at a specific moment is what this suggestion describes. The firms that are most likely to survive upcoming challenges are those who are currently beginning to proactively plan for this fruitful stage of their future.

(Faustenhammer & Gössler, 2011)

Resilient leadership

The research on the subject of resilient leadership can be separated into two main categories: (1) prioritising a dimension of personality or personal quality of the leader—a personal quality that tends to lead people to recover from setback or adversity, and (2) prioritising the process—a vibrant process incorporating adaptive capacity in the face of difficulties (Țiclău et al., 2021). Being resilient as a corporate leader entails being ready for both challenges and resistance to any suggested solutions (Tengblad, 2018). Before applying such ideas, successful organization leaders make the effort to reconsider and think on them. Both the skill to convince people of their ideas and the fortitude to withstand opposition to those solutions are required. This frequently necessitates exercising power by going against the interests of other players (Tengblad, 2018). A sustainable business must have competent leadership that fosters interconnected and unified teams. As management and employees uphold the organization's vision and basic values, organizational resilience develops through time (Southwick et al., 2017).

Every industry will eventually face challenges (Eliot, 2020). No matter how many other positive qualities a leader possesses, little of substantial importance is going to be done without tenacity. Taking into account the difficulties and obstacles that leaders of every level face (either being the leader of a nation or an organization), without resilience, the chances of long-term success are limited and the likelihood of failure is high (Van Wart et al., 2021). When it comes to the subject of adaptation, resilient leadership is understood to be the ability of the person to adjust in order to better meet the demands of its surroundings (Țiclău et al., 2021). When the external environment transforms, adaptation becomes more crucial; the greater the change, the more crucial the ability to adjust to the new circumstances. Components of leadership resilience in this sense relate to those elements that affect an individual's capacity to endure and adapt to adversity or shock (Țiclău et al., 2021). Nonetheless, it must be taken into account that all of the most important leadership traits have negative counterparts, according to Van Wart et al. (2021). That is to say, leaders might be egocentric, hasty, sluggish, and self-serving rather than self-assured, resolute, energetic, and in possession of a strong moral compass. When paired with other corrupted attributes, resilience may also take on a bad form. A resilient leader who possesses these negative traits attempts to avoid the moral requirements that they face, seduce people into acting against their own interests, cause issues that they may then heroically solve, and so on (Van Wart et al., 2021).

Individual, group, organizational, or community crises and tragedies necessitate leadership that fosters resilience in the presence of peril. The COVID-19 pandemic proved exactly that; it is rife with both known and unknown unknowns, and the diverse national reactions to it best illustrate the significance of resilient leadership (Giustiniano et al., 2020). Organizational leaders are re-evaluating their leadership development efforts and outcomes in light of the requirement for collaborative visioning, dynamic strategic planning, and the fostering of passion among a fully engaged and empowered workforce in these turbulent times. Being a resilient corporate leader is a difficult duty and responsibility that necessitates, among other things, continuous communication with several other players. Only the boldest, most creative, most inventive leaders can successfully integrate their resilience resources (Tengblad, 2018).

Avery and Bergsteiner (2011) use the term "sustainable leadership" after their observations in research papers and many organizations all over the world. Developing a talented, devoted, and highly engaged team, keeping a long-term perspective when making choices, encouraging systemic innovation focused at enhancing customer value, and providing top-notch goods, services, and solutions are all necessary components of sustainable leadership. On the same note, Sommer et al. (2016) provided evidence that transformational leadership can be associated with cultivating resilience in an organization. Dartey-Baah (2015) and his analysis of the relevant literature conclude that a fusion of transformational and transactional leadership can point the way towards resolving the current global problem and welcome change and function within existing systems.

Success often benefits from a little luck, while catastrophes do not. Energy is a crucial component in emerging victorious after a setback or loss (Van Wart et al., 2021). Giustiniano et al. (2020) view the problem in the context of the intriguing saying, "Some people build walls when the winds of change blow, while others create windmills." It is possible to think about resilient leadership as simultaneously offering wind protection and devising a method for harnessing its power. For there to be no harm, protection is a must. Effective protection promotes survival and prevents collapse, while processes that take advantage of a crisis can foster flourishing, which strengthens existing protection. Crises and change may cause a lot of individuals to feel quite uncomfortable, and business leaders and organizations are not exempt from the effects of these pressures. Guiding a corporation entails overcoming a variety of obstacles in a dynamic and ever-changing corporate environment (Southwick et al., 2017). In order to accomplish these aims, leadership must devise strategies that pave the way for change while simultaneously controlling its pace, always recognizing and adapting to the continual uncertainty that any change entails (Giustiniano et al., 2020)

Whereas prioritizing systems management at the top used to be enough to guarantee excellent leadership, there is now a need for innovative leadership across a business (Hacker & Washington, 2017). Up until recently, resilience as a unique and separate leadership style was hardly discussed. The difficulties of leading in a world that has become noticeably more polarised, dealing with a global pandemic, and attempting slowly to avoid a climate disaster have highlighted the necessity for leaders who can not only identify issues and propose solutions but also persevere through the agonizingly long time it may take (Van Wart et al., 2021). When observers and authorities ask for a clear direction (in politics, economics, and society), there is a constant expectation that "something needs to be said" and that this needs to be phrased by "the leader" (Giustiniano et al., 2020). When confronted with a reality that is unravelling in the middle of doubt and ambiguity, paradoxical circumstances might arise. In order for people to maintain their composure while doing so, the stressful objective of trying to achieve recovery, while cultivating mutual trust, is necessary. It might be challenging to decide how to strike a balance between offering comfort and reacting to a threat (Giustiniano et al., 2020). Lombardi et al. (2021) suggested that resilient leadership must focus on the organization and, thus, the leader must fully comprehend their specific environment (internal and external of their organization) in order to appropriately respond to a change.

To resile is to respond to or be directed by events through a process of adjustment and development in a hostile situation, as opposed to leading, which is to direct (Giustiniano et al., 2020). Resilience indicates the ability to adapt to situations that call for rapid mobilization and ad hoc action as well as the capability to react to situations in a manner that is developed with a long-term focus (Lombardi et al., 2021). There appears to be a widespread agreement that there are four main characteristics of resilient leadership: readiness, tenacity, enthusiasm, and flexibility (Van Wart et al., 2021). However, diverse researchers and practitioners do not agree on a specific list of these traits. Either leaders or followers are considerably better equipped to face, overcome, and perhaps even use serendipity in case difficulties arise when they are well-prepared. As a core management principle, effective leaders make sure that their governments and organizations are constantly prepared for normal and foreseeable issues, such as market cycle disturbances and the need for technological advances. The strongest managers and leaders will be able to identify when it is time to pass the torch to newer generations of managers and leaders (Tengblad, 2018). However, good leaders also prepare for uncommon or lengthy crises, like the COVID-19 pandemic, which the world had not seen of this magnitude in 101 years (Van Wart et al., 2021).

Resilience and educational leadership

The distinctive features of education have for many years been an obstacle to the application of the rules and principles of management in the field of education. However, the demands of society, constant changes and developments in all sectors, better management of financial resources, and the need to reduce costs have highlighted the need for an administrative organization within the educational system (Antoniou, 1999, 2021). Educational leadership is an issue that plays a crucial role in everyday educational practice. It affects and interacts with both human resources and every factor or matter that takes place in the school context (Antoniou, 2021). Educational leadership differs from educational management. According to Connolly et al. (2019), educational management comprises assigning, accepting, and carrying the responsibility for the efficient operation of a system in an educational institution. This necessitates an organizational hierarchy. Being responsible is more of a state of mind and does not always include actions, although it commonly suggests and demands them.

Educational leadership, on the other hand, refers to the process of encouraging individuals in an educational environment in order to attain objectives through action. In educational leadership, authority is required but it is not necessarily derived from organizational hierarchy. Even though the leader may have great responsibilities, in reality, it does not mean that they are accountable for the functioning of the operation inside the educational system (Connolly et al., 2019). Research has shown that the impact of educational leadership is greater in schools in which the need to learn is more pressing. Successful leadership is strongest in schools that face challenging circumstances, so the need for an effective leader is even more salient. Thus, in these cases, leadership is part of improvement and reform (Antoniou, 2021).

Challenges of educational leadership

In order to have an impact on a variety of stakeholder groups and people in the processes of school development, leaders in schools work in dynamic, often contradictory reform contexts that tend to expand and intensify both their professional and personal lives. Such varied and perhaps conflicting policy, local context, and educational value demands test leaders' adaptability, flexibility, and mental and emotional stamina on a daily basis in addition to their depth of traits, knowledge, and abilities (Day, 2014). Running a school is a particularly difficult job, and principals face numerous challenges.

According to Steward (2014), the pressures that come with each new position at school, such as building relationships, becoming familiar with routines, and comprehending others' expectations, were some of the concerns of principals who were at the start of a new headship. From the interviews of her research, it was conducted that identifying who has the necessary skills to contribute in an effective manner to the school's development, allowing for appropriate delegation, and being fully and publicly accountable for the school's performance posed additional pressures to the principals' leadership role. Inexperienced principals were potentially the most vulnerable as they encountered the same difficulties in order to integrate into a new community as new principals, but with the added pressure of being held ultimately responsible for the first time and lacking a track record of success to bolster their credibility in the eyes of others. Also, some other difficulties were the workload and emotional challenges such as dealing with personnel, safety, or child protection issues, having responsibility without full control, isolation of the role, and public accountability.

Moreover, principals have to keep up with constant change. Day (2014) argues that due to the effect of communication and information technology, even people who live and work in remote rural areas far from the centres of policy-making must now take change into consideration. Principals must now more than ever possess and use a wider range of political, intra- and inter-personal, and organizational attributes, methods, and skills if they are to achieve and maintain success in these conditions. More importantly, principals should uphold the shared educational ideologies, moral and ethical values, and goals that guide their work and the work of their colleagues in order to succeed across a variety of challenges and articulate, communicate, and maintain these values throughout the many daily interactions (Day, 2014). One other example is the COVID-19 pandemic, where schools had to adapt to public restriction measures, online/digital learning, new technologies, and new health protocols. Principals' role and leadership were proven of vital importance (Ramos-Pla et al., 2021; Reyes-Guerra et al., 2021).

Finally, principals face various forms of discrimination (Chance, 2022; Cyr et al., 2021; Kooymans et al., 2013; Moorosi, 2010; Oberfield & Incantalupo, 2021). The study of Chance (2022), investigated how Black women in leadership positions in higher education deal with the negative effects of intersectionality, stereotype threat, and tokenism. The findings showed that Black women leaders in higher education faced challenges but overcame them, which was associated with their capacity to acquire the leadership abilities required to improve their careers. In their study, the participants described their challenges as motivation to overcome them and build essential leadership qualities. Resilience fuelled their ability to persevere in the face of difficulty. For the participants in this study, resilience ranged from motivational elements like family and connections, mentors, community support, and the support of cultural identity and diversity (Chance, 2022).

The environment in which principals work is one of intense public accountability and constant striving for improvement (Steward, 2014). As a result, principals are required to be emotionally resilient and have an inner strength that will allow them to lead (Day, 2014).

Characteristics of resilient school leaders

Özmusul (2019) argued that contemporary successful school leaders appear to be mentally, emotionally, socially, ethically, and physically resilient. More specifically, in order to overcome the challenges that they encounter, *mentally resilient* school leaders concentrate on a shared vision. Focusing on the vision helps leaders think broadly, concentrate on common goals, and treat obstacles as problems that can be overcome. In the context of a school, for example, resilient principals concentrate on a "happy school" vision even though they are dealing with conflicts, a bad climate, and a lack of motivation among staff and pupils. Additionally, these leaders are also receptive to new ideas, capable of handling difficult situations, detail-oriented, and keenly aware of the implicit and covert connections among various occurrences. Also, one of the key traits of the resilient leader is constant reading and researching, which is required in order to get additional information and get rid of misinformation. Leaders may experience emotional collapse, feeling pitiful, despair, grief, or loneliness. *Emotionally resilient leaders* remain composed and believe that everything may be overcome by concentrating on problem-solving. Emotionally resilient leaders value their purpose, enjoy their work, and do not experience tiredness. They are determined, firmly convinced, and goal-oriented as well as empathetic. Obstacles in an organization can make leaders feel loneliness, act alone when making decisions, or even become authoritarian or apathetic (Özmusul, 2019).

Despite everything, *socially resilient leaders* are concerned with relationships in their organizations. They specifically emphasise maintaining relationships, they take no offense from any individuals or groups within the organization, and they care about fostering solidarity. In addition to formal duties such as holding meetings, carrying out orders from higher organizational units, budgeting, handling student affairs, and so on, socially resilient leaders are concerned about developing the school and relationships, and offering aid and support (Özmusul, 2019). Since formal regulations do not contain all of the information and the specifics for how to behave in unforeseen circumstances or in overcoming hurdles when less-than-ideal scenarios occur, ethics are a central part of leaderships. Resilient school leaders apply an ethical filter to their actions both inside and outside of the school. By using this strategy, the leaders foster an ethical environment that encourages people to behave in a moral manner within the school. Finally, leaders should also be physically resilient by using relaxation techniques, participating in sports, getting enough sleep, eating healthy, and so on. We cannot count on a school leader who is physically fatigued, insensitive, and worn out to make a meaningful attempt to address rising issues (Özmusul, 2019).

In another research, Olmo-Extremera et al. (2022) argue that "a principal who exercises resilient leadership 'knows' (cognitive), 'does' (behavioral) and 'is' (emotional)" (p. 3). A resilient principal is aware of the school's internal dynamics, including its assets and liabilities, character, aims, and ambitions and is also aware of the environment in which their school operates and has developed reasonable, pertinent, and practical responses to it. The results from their research revealed four "key resilience factors":

1 *Purpose educational improvement*: The improvement of educational goals depends on the precise and distinctive action taken by each school in light of the conditions and difficulties present at any given time. As a result, leaders must analyse, and reorient the school in order to achieve the desired progress. The schools of the study confirmed that through leadership, they sought out effective learning opportunities based on the needs of the school, tailored the curriculum to the educational needs and proficiency of students, and implemented social and human initiatives as opposed to just academic and curricular ones.
2 *Motivate/commitment*: Attitudes that a principal adopts in order to confront and successfully overcome adversity.
3 *Leader identity*: The context (a school's historical, geographical, and social background as well as an office setting that fosters a culture of education and professionalism) has an impact on a leader's identity. The leadership style adopted by the leaders was a reflection of their identities. Resilient leadership was mentioned as being demonstrated by the principals and their dedication.
4 *Service/support*: Leaders must ask for and offer assistance in order to serve the school community. A leader who has an attitude of support and service must have certain qualities that allow them to advance in dynamic circumstances.

The findings of Olmo-Extremera et al. (2022) show that in the schools that participated in their study, principals had a set of characteristics that distinguished them as leaders who valued collaboration and support. At the same time, they were leaders who could identify their own and others' emotions, maintained a positive outlook in the face of hardship or unforeseen circumstances, created possibilities for growth, and were optimistic (Olmo-Extremera et al., 2022).

In Day's (2014) research, it became apparent that effective school principals are risk-takers who actively seek out novel chances, experiences, and challenges to help their schools grow and succeed. In order to inspire resilience in others, they ought to be resilient themselves. The main resilience traits and responsibilities of effective principals, as shown by the case study, were "vulnerability and risk, academic optimism, trust, and hope and ethical purpose" (p. 652). According to Day (2014), those who receive support in managing connections—between their beliefs, educational values, and practices and those of their organizations and colleagues—through the exercise of individual, relational, and organizational resilience, are most likely to successfully manage and lead the daily uncertainties of learning and teaching, in times when organization and professional change is inevitable in order to meet new social and economic challenges. If this is the case, then everyone who prepares, trains, and supports school leaders ought to take into account that resilience combined with moral purpose may be the secret to the long-term success of authentic education and school improvement.

Recommendations

Some recommendations to sustain, promote, and strengthen successful leadership in education, according to Steward (2014), include: increase awareness of emotional resilience and keeping the discussion open; give emotional resilience more consideration in leadership development programs; employ practices like mindfulness, meditation, or awareness, and, where necessary, learned optimism; encourage governors to assist principals in developing a plan to maintain emotional resilience during times of greatest risk and in conducting regular analyses of their own emotional resilience; create new strategies for promoting wellbeing that recognise and address the difficulties that principals face; continue to advocate for principals to receive coaching so as to give them a professional, empathetic, private space where they may reflect and communicate any feelings of vulnerability; agree on a longer-term approach to education policy-making to mitigate the effects of frequent and quick policy changes brought on by changing governments. In addition, the field's researchers and professionals should have a stronger say in policymaking (Steward, 2014).

Isaacs (2012) argued that universities that train administrators, and school districts that hire school leaders, should work to develop support systems intended to boost resiliency in light of the environment's increasing demands. The reinforcement of ongoing, high-quality professional development may aid in boosting school leaders' resilience. Establishing standards and supportive institutions within school districts might help school leaders become more resilient. Enhancing the resiliency of school leaders may be achieved through paying attention to team building, effective coaching, and the development of a culture that challenges, energises and rewards leaders. Continuous professional development also seems to be important for fostering resilience (Isaacs, 2012). Finally, support from the management team to the scholar community, and vice versa, are necessary for resilience to grow (Olmo-Extremera et al., 2022).

Conclusion

In this chapter, we examined the relationship between resilience and leadership. In the light of the COVID-19 pandemic and the other major crises humanity has faced, the concept of resilience poses an important notion in psychology. Resilience though cannot be treated as something that is strictly inherited and static. It poses a constant, dynamic psychological procedure that promotes surviving, recovering, finding inner balance and meaning in face of diversity and suffering. Of course resilience cannot be examined only at an individual level as it permeates, influences, and shapes social and organizational aspects of the working environment. Businesses and organizations face adversities and crises, and they need to turn stressors and shocks into innovative, long-lasting solutions in order to survive and prosper. Leadership can play a vital role. Until recently, there has been little discussion about resilience as a unique leadership style. However, the challenges of leading in a world that is increasingly polarised, managing a global pandemic, and working towards averting a climate catastrophe have underscored the importance of leaders who can not only recognise problems and suggest solutions but also persist through extended periods of difficulty (Van Wart et., 2021). Apart from the main approaches to leadership (transactional, transformational, and charismatic forms of leadership), there is a need for innovation, adaptation, and crises management in the field of leadership. In this context, the main characteristics of resilient leadership (readiness, tenacity, enthusiasm, and flexibility) (Van Wart et al., 2021)—even though diverse researchers and practitioners do not agree on a specific list of these traits—promote adaptation and change.

References

Antoniou, A.-S. (1999). Personal traits and professional burnout in health professionals. *Archives of Hellenic Medicine, 16*(1), 20–28.

Antoniou, A.-S. (2008). Ine efikti i askisi igesias vasi ithikon kanonon? [Is it possible to exercise leadership based on code of ethics?]. *Stratiotiki Epitheorisi – Military Review, 2008*, 110–121.

Antoniou, A.-S. (2016). *Ithiki ton epixitiseon. Filosofiki - Psichologiki theorisi tou xrimatos* [Business Ethics - Philosophical - psychological consideration of money]. Gutenberg.

Antoniou, A.-S. (2021). *Sigxroni igesia ke ekpaideutiko plaisio.* [Contemporary leadership and educational context]. Gutenberg.

Antoniou, A.-S., Drosos, N., & Kourtoglou, M. (2019). Women leaders in times of economic crisis: Leadership style, careers self-efficacy, and job insecurity. In A.-S. Antoniou, C. Cooper, & C. Gatrell (Eds.), *Women, business and leadership* (pp. 41–60). Edward Elgar.

Antoniou, A.-S., & Galaktidou, A. (2010). Diereunisi askisis metasximatistikou typou igesias kai endexomenh epidrasi tou stin epaggelmatikh eksouthenosi [Investigating the exercise of transformational leadership and its potential impact on burnout]. In A.-S. Antoniou (Ed.), *Stress- Prosopiki Anaptixi ke evimeria [Stress-personal development & wellbeing]* (pp. 73–136). Ekdoseis Papazisi.

Arar, K., & Oplatka, I (2022). *Advanced theories of educational leadership. Policy implications of research in education 14*. Springer.

Arnold, J., & Randall, R. (2020). *Psychologia tis ergasias kai organosiaki simperifora* [Work psychology and organizational behavior]. A.-S. Antoniou & V. Mpellou (Greek Eds). Broken Hill Publishers.

Athinaiou, M., & Antoniou, A.-S. (2008). Prooptikes kai dinatotites askisis ithikis igesias [Perspectives and opportunities for implementing ethical leadership]. In A-S. Antoniou (Ed.), *Ithiki ton epixitiseon II – business ethics* II (pp. 285–316). Sakkoula Publications.

Avery, G. C., & Bergsteiner, H. (2011). Sustainable leadership practices for enhancing business resilience and performance. *Strategy & Leadership, 39*(3), 5–15.

Baykal, E. (2018). Promoting resilience through positive leadership during turmoil. *International Journal of Management and Administration, 2*(3), 34–48.

Brubaker, T. A. (2013). Servant leadership, Ubuntu, and leader effectiveness in Rwanda. *Emerging Leadership Journeys, 6*(1), 114–147.

Bush, T. (2020). *Theories of educational leadership and management* (5th ed.). SAGE.

Cameron, K. (2013). *Practicing positive leadership: Tools and techniques that create extraordinary results.* Berrett-Koehler.

Campbell, D., Campbell, K., & Ness, J. W. (2008). Resilience through leadership. In B. J. Lukey, & V. Tepe (Eds.), *Biobehavioral resilience to stress* (pp. 79–110). Routledge.

Chance, N. L. (2022). Resilient leadership: A phenomenological exploration into how black women in higher education leadership navigate cultural adversity. *Journal of Humanistic Psychology, 62*(1), 44–78.

Connolly, M., James, C., & Fertig, M. (2019). The difference between educational management and educational leadership and the importance of educational responsibility. *Educational Management Administration & Leadership, 47*(4), 504–519.

Cyr, D., Weiner, J., & Burton, L. (2021). "I want to speak to a white person": Daily microaggressions and resilient leadership. *Journal of Cases in Educational Leadership, 24*(4), 60–73.

Dartey-Baah, K. (2015). Resilient leadership: A transformational-transactional leadership mix. *Journal of Global Responsibility, 6*(1), 99–112.

Day, C. (2014). Resilient principals in challenging schools: The courage and costs of conviction. *Teachers and Teaching, 20*(5), 638–654.

Dreher, D. E. (2002). Leading with the Tao: The energizing power of respect. *The Learning Organization, 9*(5), 206–213.

Eliot, J. L. (2020). Resilient leadership: The impact of a servant leader on the resilience of their followers. *Advances in Developing Human Resources, 22*(4), 404–418.

Everly, G. S. Jr, Everly, A. N., & Smith, K. J. (2020). Resilient leadership: A partial replication and construct validation. *Crisis, Stress, and Human Resilience: An International Journal, 2*(1), 4–9.

Faustenhammer, A., & Gössler, M. (2011). Preparing for the next crisis: What can organizations do to prepare managers for an uncertain future? *Business Strategy Series, 12*(2), 51–55.

Foerster, C., & Duchek, S. (2017). What makes leaders resilient? An exploratory interview study. *German Journal of Human Resource Management, 31*(4), 281–306.

Giustiniano, L., Cunha, M., Simpson, A., Rego, A., & Clegg, S. (2020). Resilient leadership as paradox work: Notes from COVID-19. *Management and Organization Review, 16*(5), 971–975.

Greenberg, J., & Baron, R. A., (2013). *Organosiaki Psichologia ke Siberifora* [Organizational psychology and behavior] (A-S., Antoniou Transl.). Gutenberg.

Grote, G. (2019). Leadership in resilient organizations. In E. Marsden, C. Kamate, & F. Daniellou (Eds.), *Exploring resilience* (pp. 59–67). Springer.

Hacker, S. K., & Washington, M. (2017). Spiritual intelligence: Going beyond IQ and EQ to develop resilient leaders. *Global Business and Organizational Excellence, 36*(3), 21–28.

Harland, L., Harrison, W., Jones, J. R., & Reiter-Palmon, R. (2005). Leadership behaviors and subordinate resilience. *Journal of Leadership & Organizational Studies, 11*(2), 2–14.

Hickman, G. R. (2004). Invisible leadership. In G. R. Goethals, G. J. Sorenson, & J. M. Burns (Eds.), *Encyclopedia of leadership* (pp. 750–754). SAGE.

Hickman, G. R. (2012). Concepts of leadership in organizational change. In M. Preedy, N. Bennett, & C. Wise (Eds.), *Educational leadership: Context, strategy and collaboration* (pp. 67–82). The Open University.

Isaacs, A. J. (2012). Resiliency and the individual demographics of school leaders: Making a difference in the quality of educational leadership. *Journal of Research in Education, 22*(1), 128–162.

Keough, T., & Tobin, B. (2001). *Postmodern leadership and the policy lexicon: From theory, proxy to practice.* Paper for the Pan-Canadian Education Research Agenda Symposium, 22–23 May, Quebec.

Kooymans, R., Jakubiec, B. A., & Preston, J. P. (2013). Common challenges faced by rural principals: A review of the literature. *The Rural Educator, 35*(1), 1.

Ledesma, J. (2014). Conceptual frameworks and research models on resilience in leadership. *Sage Open, 4*(3), 1–8.

Lombardi, S., e Cunha, M. P., & Giustiniano, L. (2021). Improvising resilience: The unfolding of resilient leadership in COVID-19 times. *International Journal of Hospitality Management, 95*, 102904.

Martin, R. (2017). PsyRes: Developing a concept of the psychologically resilient leader. *International Interdisciplinary Business-Economics Advancement Journal, 2*(1), 1–9.

Mhatre, K. H., & Riggio, R. E. (2014). Charismatic and transformational leadership: Past, present, and future. In D. V. Day (Ed.), *The Oxford handbook of leadership and organizations* (pp. 221–240). Oxford University Press.

Moorosi, P. (2010). South African female principals' career paths: Understanding the gender gap in secondary school management. *Educational Management Administration & Leadership, 38*(5), 547–562.

Oberfield, Z. W., & Incantalupo, M. B. (2021). Racial discrimination and street-level managers: Performance, publicness, and group bias. *Public Administration Review, 81*(6), 1055–1070.

Olmo-Extremera, M., Townsend, A., & Domingo Segovia, J. (2022). Resilient leadership in principals: Case studies of challenged schools in Spain. *International Journal of Leadership in Education, 25*(3), 1–20.

Özmusul, M. (2019). We need resilient school leaders in the face of chaos and complexity. In Ş Erçetin, & N. Potas (Eds.), *Chaos, complexity and leadership 2017. ICCLS 2017* (pp. 179–182). Springer Proceedings in Complexity. Springer.

Qiao, P., Fung, A., Fung, H. G., & Ma, X. (2022). Resilient leadership and outward foreign direct investment: A conceptual and empirical analysis. *Journal of Business Research, 144*, 729–739.

Ramos-Pla, A., Tintoré, M., & Del Arco, I. (2021). Leadership in times of crisis. School principals facing COVID-19. *Heliyon, 7*(11), e08443.

Reyes-Guerra, D., Maslin-Ostrowski, P., Barakat, M. Y., & Stefanovic, M. A. (2021). Confronting a compound crisis: The school principal's role during initial phase of the COVID-19 pandemic. *Frontiers in Education, 6*, 617875.

Sommer, S. A., Howell, J. M., & Hadley, C. N. (2016). Keeping positive and building strength: The role of affect and team leadership in developing resilience during an organizational crisis. *Group & Organization Management, 41*(2), 172–202.

Southwick, F. S., Martini, B. L., Charney, D. S., & Southwick, S. M. (2017). Leadership and resilience. In J. Marques, & S. Dhiman (Eds.), *Leadership today* (pp. 315–333). Springer.

Spillane, J. P. (2006). *Distributed leadership.* Jossey-Bass.

Steward, J. (2014). Sustaining emotional resilience for school leadership. *School Leadership & Management, 34*(1), 52–68.

Tengblad, S. (2018). Resilient leadership: Lessons from three legendary business leaders. In S. Tengblad, & M. Oudhuis (Eds.), *The resilience framework* (pp. 89–108). Springer.

Țiclău, T., Hințea, C., & Trofin, C. (2021). Resilient leadership. Qualitative study on factors influencing organizational resilience and adaptive response to adversity. *Transylvanian Review of Administrative Sciences, 17*(SI), 127–143.

Van Wart, M., Rahman, S., & Mazumdar, T. (2021). The dark side of resilient leaders: Vampire leadership. *Transylvanian Review of Administrative Sciences, 17*(SI), 144–165.

Yukl, G. (2009). *I igesia stous organismous [Leadership in organisations]* (A.-S. Antoniou, Greek Ed. & Transl.). Kleidarithmos.

10

RESILIENCE

From the Frontlines to the Boardroom

Sakshi Bansal

In modern organizations, employers face several problems daily. These problems range from minor inconveniences to dilemmas with massive financial implications. At the crux of each problem, lies a choice. Right from the moment when an individual decides to set up a company, they are faced with multiple choices on what the company should and should not focus on, who will help the company achieve those things, what location will be good or bad for the company, which suppliers will ensure its success, and which ones will be bad for business. Each decision has a huge impact on the way that the business exists and operates and, therefore, each decision can induce a lot of stress and pressure. There is no wonder that only a handful of businesses that are set up become successful. In fact, as per the U.S. Bureau of Labor Statistics (2022), approximately 20% of new businesses fail during the first two years of being open, 45% during the first five years, and 65% during the first 10 years. Only 25% of new businesses make it to 15 years or more (Fairlie et al., 2022). As per Denyer (2017), "Organizational Resilience is the ability of an organization to anticipate, prepare for, respond and adapt to incremental change and sudden disruptions in order to survive and prosper." Therefore, business' that successfully create value, even in uncertain economic times, are called resilient organizations.

For employees, the story is no different. From finding the right job, a supportive company, a kind boss, an interesting role, and ways of collaborating with colleagues, all decisions require a high level of analysis, interpretation, and understanding. On top of this, there is no guarantee that the choices that one makes will be the right one. In fact, employees often are faced with unintended or undesirable consequences of their choices at work. Regardless of who made the choice, employees are expected to keep their chin up and continue working. Those who are able to do this are called resilient employees (Mendy, 2020).

DOI: 10.4324/9781003287858-13

None of the choices and stressors mentioned above are new. They have always existed in organizations, taking different shapes and forms as we move from one revolution to the other. With rapid technology, increasing threats on sustainability, and noticeable impact on climate change mixed with situations like a global pandemic, wars, and economic uncertainty, it is no surprise that, of late, we see organizations talking about different types of resilience, including climate resilience, technical resilience, and resilient leadership.

Nowadays, organizations rely on trainers, coaches, facilitators, and resilience-experts to come and train their employees on developing resilience. They rely on consultants, technicians, and experts to reshape, redesign, or refocus their current operating model to promote organizational resilience. And finally, they also rely on leaders and management to keep an eye on what resilience means, how it changes definition, and what is yet to come. Organizations have therefore assumed that interval-style training or one-off coaching is enough to build resilience, which is a trait that can be developed. They also assume that the level of resilience that employees currently possess is simply not enough to meet the demands placed in the world of work.

Even after years of training and millions of pounds spent on resilience related training, we are yet to see an organization that has shown 100% resilience on all fronts. In fact, the period 2019–2022 (COVID-19 pandemic, economic downturn, and change in political scenario) has shown us that very few organizations were resilient enough to stand ground. Even those who came out strong, needed help. Failing leadership, unclear policies, burnt out employees, and the rising fear and distrust in general public are just some indicators of how we failed on the resilience front globally. The growing issue of unreasonable workload, inappropriate staffing level, bullying, toxic team dynamics, and chaotic environment with unclear goals reflect that the corporate resilience trainings are not an efficient or wholesome fix. Most organizations that we have read or heard about also admit that sustainable practices that allow them to consistently build a resilient team are hard to come by, if possible at all (Biggs et al., 2015). Therefore, organizations tend to continue to rely on one-off trainings, coaching, and workshop sessions to build resilience, in the hope that this will be enough in the face of great stress. This is true for organizations across the globe, regardless of their geography. This makes the issue of resilience global and the need to develop a sustainable way to build resilience, a common agenda.

However, the news is not all gloomy. We have all heard, read, and witnessed personal stories of community resilience across the world, where hardworking and committed people came forward to do what the governments couldn't. During the pandemic itself, we saw people delivering medicines loaded in the back of their trucks, lifting oxygen tanks three flights of stairs to reach helpless families, running online groups to link volunteers to those in need, shopping for the elderly, and even walking someone's dog. Coming together of the community in the face of conflict or calamity is not new. In fact, volunteering work can be found in some of the oldest stories that are passed down in generations. This is especially true for communities and countries where events of catastrophic nature are anything but rare. These are the countries that have dealt with and continue to deal with health epidemics and natural disasters, religious and political wars, and economic fluctuations. Let us look closely at two stories of volunteering that highlight resilience. Volunteers are individuals who offer to support the community by offering time, money, or resources to the cause, often at their personal risk. From the two stories below, the first one will highlight a journey of personal resilience.

In 2015, Kerensa Clark, a young woman from New Zealand, travelled to Nepal when she heard that the beautiful country was being devasted by earthquakes and were in need of far greater support than what was available to them (Vandenberg, 2017). Upon landing in Nepal, Kerensa decided to support the local families in the region by building shelters for them. With no engineering background or experience, Kerensa worked alongside an engineer to build these shelters. With her willingness to learn, she was not only successful in building these shelters but also conducted fund-raising events during her stay to provide resources for the local families. Kerensa also recounts her experience of facing power outages in Nepal, something that she hadn't prepared for but adapted to, to fulfil her purpose. This included personal adaptation but also practical steps like using cordless power drills to build shelters for the community. She did this with the support of the local community and other volunteers who had come to Nepal with similar intentions as her.

Kerensa accounts in her interview with Sarah Vandenberg that the key learnings for her, in the face of this mammoth task, was to listen to the people. To continuously remind herself that the people she was trying to help knew their culture best and she needed to listen to their desires and wishes. And to provide them the best help possible, she must address their issues in ways that work for them instead of applying what she thinks is best.

Kerensa's efforts in Nepal demanded many things from her. She was required to adapt quickly to a new environment, and in some ways, leading many people out of a conflicting situation. It required her to come up with new and efficient ways of working, usually on a deadline and with full consideration and consent of the community. It also demanded from her to keep herself motivated and positive, even when she felt that there was a lot more to be done.

The demands placed on Kerensa are very similar in nature to the demands that are often placed on leaders in a business, albeit in most cases with far less implication on human life. Kerensa's story highlights for us the skills and experiences that volunteers develop naturally, by force of the situation, which are very lucrative and in-demand for leaders who are trying to learn them by one-day training courses.

Kerensa's story is an account of personal resilience. To understand community resilience, we take a look at the practice of Ashar. Ashar in the areas of Afghanistan is defined as a practice where community members work together on a voluntary basis to improve the community infrastructure (Qasmi & Ahmed, 2019). Ashar has been practiced by the Hazara community in Afghanistan for many years. An example of Ashar was observed by a member of the community when the physical limitations of their body did not allow them to harvest the crops on their land. Taking a note of this, the community members voluntarily offer to harvest the crop, working for days on the land to provide timely support to the farmer. The practice of Ashar has led to building of many schools, roads, and other facilities in various regions of Afghanistan. However, the practice of community support is not free of challenges for the volunteers. While they attempt to help all communities who need support with good intention, they are often faced by communal animosity that emerges especially when helping a "rival" group. This is challenging for volunteers who often must navigate political and cultural pressures to help the community, in spite of no monetary benefit to gain from this practice. Often, this evokes a fear of defamation for the volunteers. This is also on top of the fact that most people in these volunteer pools belong to communities that lack resources themselves including essential tools and equipment's. Even then, the volunteers have found ways, often creative, to build necessary tools and to navigate the challenges while they support the community. In doing so, they often have to maintain a balance between feeding their own families and supporting their community members. Finally, the volunteers are also faced with increased urbanisation and changing culture that threatens the continuity of the practice of Ashar.

As the population grows and Western influences shape the mind of new generation, it has become increasingly hard to hold onto the practice of Ashar. Observing the decline in the practice and the resultant lack of resilience in the community, the volunteers decide to work with the changing system of influence and power in the community instead of losing hope. Alongside finding ways to motivate the new generation by sharing the benefits of Ashar, they established rapport with the well-respected individuals of the community. The volunteers compelled these individuals to become the champions of Ashar. The volunteers also spent time to identify the best channels to provide quick and efficient help, one of which included seeking volunteers in closer proximity to members of the community that needed the most help. This allowed them to create a sense of support network in the smaller regions.

The practice of Ashar in the community reminds me, once again, of the demands that employees face in organizations where there are often values, code of conduct and styles of governance that dictate the boundaries within which the employees can operate. The changing nature of communities owing to Western influence is true for organizations where the exposure to international policies, styles of working and labour issues consistently change the way that organizations operate. Often, employees are tasked with maintaining the sanctity of the organization by keeping their eyes on the goal and to continue working in "business as usual" terms. Finally, the power of influence and sponsorship is a key dynamic in organizations, which can either become the reason for hope and resilience or discouragement and stress for different employees.

In both of the above examples, we see situations that lend themselves into the workplace, for example facing fast-paced and unexpected changes, lack of resources, ongoing conflict, and power dynamics at play. These situations are often complex and are typically challenging for employees to deal with. Equally, we find that employers are at a loss of how to build capability for employees to deal with such changes.

However, for some of us, both of these examples may lack key elements that characterise employees or employers of modern workplaces. There are some key differences that may cause this. One, organizations are transactional in nature. Good behaviour, in this case, show of exemplary resilience will come with an expectation of a reward. While resilient behaviour is not always rewarded but the expectation exists. In community-based volunteerism, the expectation of receiving monetary rewards or benefits does not exist. This is not to say that true altruism guides volunteerism in communities, but on the whole, volunteers in the community are not expecting a higher bonus or better benefits if they show resilience. The second key difference is that organizations continuously strive for excellence. They assume that the current level of resilience that the employees and organization display is not enough and that an excellent level of such resilience exists and must be achieved. As arbitrary the concept of this excellence is, a lot of effort is placed on achieving this. In community volunteerism, there is no excellence and what the volunteers offer and display in terms of resilience is regarded as the best they can do and is appreciated equally. Finally, resilience in organizations is often reactive. Often, founders, executives, and shareholders only think about organizational or employee resilience when one or all of them have been impacted by the lack of it. Resilience trainings occurs when the past response of the organization hasn't been sufficient to successfully sail through challenging times. In the world of volunteering, resilience is simply a survival mechanism. It is passed down from generation to generation as a mandatory practice, often becoming second nature. In fact, if you speak to people from war-torn areas, they will mention how personal resilience can often be a burden because it allows their mind to take more stress than they should. Therefore, in such communities, resilience is proactive.

We can see that the breeding ground of resilience for organizations and for volunteers is starkly different. Even then, organizations expect their employees to go "above and beyond" in the workplace, just like the volunteers. We have seen organizations looking for creative employees who can deal with stress and continue to perform under high stress. We have read about organizations that want employees to feel like a community, a family, a tribe, and to lead with resilience as if it is second nature. Organizations have also alluded to certain skills that resilient employees bring to the table, which include but are not limited to the ability to deal with change, being tolerant, showing empathy, being collaborative and a team player, having self-,confidence and being able to deliver work that has a wider impact. These are all key strengths that a volunteer develops in their work with the community.

Despite the differences in the situation of employees and volunteers, I see a growing demand of employers for their employees to show higher level of resilience.

While organizations fail to create a true sense of community (and will continue to fail as they are, after all, a business), they expect employees to show resilience that goes above and beyond. They also expect the employees and the leaders to learn the skill of resilience quickly, often online on a training course. This incongruence is key to understand as it allows the continuation of unreasonable expectation and incomplete understanding of resilience in modern workplaces. This is the first pillar where organizations fail, where one-day trainings on resilience do not deliver and where it is impossible to develop sustainable resilience practices (Robertson et al., 2015).

This means that employees and leaders in the organizations need to re-learn the ideas of resilience quickly and effectively. This also means that this learning should come from people who have excelled in showing resilience and have reaped the benefits of it: the volunteers. One way to do this is to highlight the stories and narratives of volunteers around the world. Through my work of providing skill-based training to over 150 volunteers around the world, on topics like leadership, collaboration, creativity, project management, and so on, I was able to interview 45 volunteers, between the age of 18 and 35, from countries like India, Ghana, Nigeria, New Zealand, America, and Nepal. They spoke to me about why they volunteer, the skills they have picked up on the way, and why it is that when they join the corporate world, their volunteerism makes them a better employee than their peers who have never volunteered. During the one-to-one interviews, the volunteers mentioned an array of different skills (Khasanzyanova, 2017), such as effective communication with a variety of different stakeholders (funders, sponsors, project leaders, and end beneficiaries); management of time, priorities, and projects to accomplish tasks including balancing social work, personal life, and on-going professional work. They also mentioned problem-solving skills, especially in areas that have high risk, low resources, and changing demands, and adaptability to unpredictable work environments and new situations (Bonfield, 2021). This makes them agile, open to learning, and calm during chaos. Volunteers shared that while they experience "flow" or helper's rush when they serve the community, they are also required to constantly prove their intent as authentic and kind instead of self-serving. This involves working through status-quo in the variety of relationships they hold and keeping the eye on the goal of the project. We often see leaders in similar predicament, especially those who are interested in an authentic leadership style but need to prove it to a variety of people as they navigate the challenges at work. Another nuance of volunteer skills involves consistently motivating their peers, irrespective of their place in the hierarchy. Volunteers need to manage upwards, downwards, and sideways and they do this by sharing personal stories of failure, success and sources of inspiration. This allows them to build a collective sense of resilience and empower others. They are also able to anticipate people's needs which is a key skill for people managers (Dempsey-Brench & Shantz, 2021). Volunteers also need to evidence their impact. They do this by learning powerful storytelling and keeping close to numbers and figures. They learn to work and sense-make from large data sets, often rich and complex, to simplify the message of impact for the community and often towards the Sustainable Development Goals (UN). Finally, they also mention that helping others comes naturally to them as opposed to feeling like an obligation. They are often the first responders when asked for help, making them the key nodes of building resilience in the company. This suggests that volunteers do make better employees and are, in fact, good for a company's bottom line (Binns, 2014)

Unfortunately, in many disorganised social-work sectors around the world, volunteering is seen as the most insignificant experience in one's resume to gain entry to the working world. Therefore, the social-service sector loses thousands of volunteers every day, who are discouraged by the prospects for their future if they spend too much time volunteering. This also means that fewer and fewer people with volunteering experience apply for professional roles in organizations and as a result, organizations miss the opportunity to learn from their natural skills of resilience. My interviews with the volunteers revealed further truths about the volunteering sector. Due to the disorganised nature of volunteering in majority of the economies globally, there are numerous volunteers who despite having the best intentions at heart, have a limited knowledge of how to help the society. This lack of knowledge often leads to an unintended or undesirable consequence of imparting incorrect information to the community they are trying to help. This highlights the serious lack of training and skills services offered to the volunteers at the start of their volunteering journey. Other practical issues that deter the volunteers include inability to spend money out of their pocket, every day, to use transport that was getting increasingly expensive, to get to the community centre that the volunteer wanted to help. I realised that these were the same issues I faced as a young volunteer and that solving these issues could empower many volunteers to continue their work for the society but also keep the cycle of volunteerism going for our communities. This was the spark to take Project LEAP global. Project LEAP is a social service organization that I established at the age of 17 in New Delhi, India. Project LEAP was based on a simple premise: we help volunteers to help the community. I gathered volunteers who would help me alleviate a cause that I deeply cared about: lack of equality in education for different socio-economic sections of the country. I wrote my vision in two sentences on a piece of paper and I set out to look for people who cared about this as much as I did. Within a month, I had gathered 300 volunteers who not only cared about equal education, but who felt a need for skill-based training to create a bigger impact. I then called upon professional trainers and facilitators in the city to offer free skill-based training sessions for volunteers at Project LEAP. Project LEAP educated 1,600+ families in New Delhi alone within the first year. We were able to achieve this milestone because the volunteers were given three simple guidelines: (1) find a community to help within 10 minutes of walking distance from your home, school, or place of work; (2) all resources for volunteering including school supplies will be gathered from the community or from what we already have at home—Project LEAP is a zero-cost model and works on circular economy; (3) volunteers will enjoy free skill-based training as per their career goals and ambitions and not just what is required for Project LEAP. This set us up for long-term success. Project LEAP saw 100% volunteer retention rate for four years. During this time, the volunteers who were university students when we started went on to get professional jobs across the world. The volunteers saw various changes including government changes which impacted the education laws and rights; conflict between communities due to religious reasons, dealing with issues like domestic violence, mental health, and child labour, which often came up in our work with underprivileged families. By this time, many of our volunteers were experts and were able to deliver volunteer skill-training in-house to the fresh batch of volunteers that joined us every year. During the COVID-19 pandemic, which put India at a standstill, the volunteers not only managed difficult personal crisis, but maintained the spirit of volunteering by setting up the community members for digital communication and switching to online teaching in places where most people had never owned a laptop before. In the middle of the pandemic, when it became evident that volunteers globally could benefit from our model of working, we delivered free skill-based training to other youth volunteer groups. We believed that our model of training would allow volunteers to be prepared for future crises. We trained over 50 volunteer groups across the globe including Nepal, Sri Lanka, Africa, the United States, Australia, the United Kingdom, and Europe. Today, many volunteers of project LEAP have gone on to set up their own charities while they excel in their professional jobs. Some have taken up volunteering full time and many others continue to volunteer with us.

What would happen if organizations asked their employees what they wanted from their careers? What would happen if organizations were able to offer skills to employees that would be beneficial for them, not just for their careers at the current company but beyond? What would happen if organizations actively sought people with volunteering experience to shape the world of work?

Remember that this chapter does not suggest that we employ bright people and then provide them the opportunity to volunteer on given days during the year. While this practice, often classed under the umbrella of Corporate Sustainable Responsibility (CSR), has many benefits (Rodell, 2013), what I suggest here is to hire people who have volunteered before. The suggestion here is to enhance our perception on what volunteers can offer and to then hire differently. This change in thinking will have implications on your entire hiring process, including the job description, the advertisement of the job itself, choice of job boards, and finally the attitude of hiring managers when they see CVs of candidates that mention volunteering work. The caveat remains the same: the candidate must meet the benchmark you have set and provide you sufficient evidence that they meet the skill requirement. Finally, the attempt of this chapter was to highlight the many skills that the world of volunteering and community resilience teaches us. Volunteers make the concept of resilience more relatable and tangible, their stories provide a broad understanding of resilience beyond a limited organizational context and their styles of working point towards adaptive and change-friendly strategy. While some degree of resilience may come naturally to everyone, this skill needs the right breeding ground to bloom and thrive well. This includes setting the right expectations on what resilience means, to understand that excellence in resilience is personal and not a standard, and finally to build this skill outside of short corporate seminars to ensure that we can sustain resilience skill in the longer run.

About the author

Sakshi is the recipient of the Diana Award—the highest civilian award for humanitarian work across the globe. She is also the world's first UNESCO Kindness Leader. As the founder of Project LEAP, a social service project—committed to SDG4 and an Occupational Psychologist—Sakshi spends her time consulting on a variety of topics including people and talent, sustainability, and ESG. Sakshi has a variety of published work on topics such as Humanitarian Psychology, Career Crafting, and Skin Tone–related stereotypes. She has been guesting on various podcasts and channels across the globe where she shares her insights on these topics. Currently living in the United Kingdom, she is originally from India and often uses concepts from Indian Psychology to facilitate change management sessions across the globe. She also advises multiple AI-based start-ups after three years of her own start-up experience and is a passionate traveller.

References

Biggs, R., Schlüter, M., & Schoon, M. L. (Eds.). (2015). *Principles for building resilience: sustaining ecosystem services in social-ecological systems*. Cambridge University Press https://www.cambridge.org/core/books/principles-for-building-resilience/578EBCAA6 C9A18430498982D66CFB042

Binns, C. (2014). Do volunteers make better employees? *Stanford Social Innovation Review*. DOI: 10.48558/542e-6q64

Bonfield, D. (2021). Why employers should value volunteers. *Reality HR*. https://www. realityhr.co.uk/why-employers-should-value-volunteers

Dempsey-Brench, K., & Shantz, A. (2021). Skills-based volunteering: A systematic literature review of the intersection of skills and employee volunteering. *Human Resource Management Review, 32*(4), 100874.

Denyer, D. (2017). *Organizational resilience*. BSI and Cranfield University.

Fairlie, R., Fossen, F. M., Johnsen, R., & Droboniku, G. (2022). Were small businesses more likely to permanently close in the pandemic? *Small Business Economics, 60*, 1613–1629.

Khasanzyanova, A. (2017). How volunteering helps students to develop soft skills. *International Review of Education, 63*(3), 363–379.

Mendy, J. (2020). Bouncing back from workplace stress: From HRD's individual employee's developmental focus to multi-facetted collective workforce resilience intervention. *Advances in Developing Human Resources, 22*(4), 353–369.

Qasmi, H., & Ahmed, R. (2019). The role of participatory communication in strengthening solidarity and social cohesion in Afghanistan. *Handbook of communication for development and social change*, 1st ed. https://link.springer.com/referencework/ 10.1007/978-981-15-2014-3#bibliographic-information

Robertson, I. T., Cooper, C. L., Sarkar, M., & Curran, T. (2015). Resilience training in the workplace from 2003 to 2014: A systematic review. *Journal of Occupational and Organizational Psychology, 88*(3), 533–562.

Rodell, J. B. (2013). Finding meaning through volunteering: Why do employees volunteer and what does it mean for their jobs? *Academy of Management Journal, 56*(5), 1274–1294.

U.S. Bureau of Labor Statistics. (2022). table 7. survival of private sector establishments by opening year. https://www.bls.gov/bdm/us_age_naics_00_table7.txt

Vandenberg, S. (2017). Volunteering to Rebuild after the Nepal Earthquake: Kerensa Clark's Story. https://www.volunteerforever.com/article_post/volunteering-to-rebuild-after-the-nepal-earthquake-kerensa-clarks-story/

11

ELITE HIGH-PERFORMING MILITARY LEADERS

An Evidence-Based Analysis on the Role of Resilience in Military Careers

Ingrid K. Covington, Wika Malkowska, and Vicki Elsey

Introduction

Career resilience is a resource that predicts career success, although research on this critical predictor is still in its infancy. This chapter aims to address the gap in our understanding of this concept in the modern environment by offering unique insights into the role of career resilience in the successful journeys of elite, high-performing military leaders. The authors will address current research gaps by understanding how resilience is understood and experienced in a military environment in the context of VUCA (volatility, uncertainty, complexity, and ambiguity). They will also look at how individuals and organizations might usefully leverage career resilience as a resource, what barriers exist, and what conditions enable individuals to thrive in contemporary, resilient careers. Particular attention will be paid to the utility of understanding the concept of resilience as a spectrum, exploring the role of organizations in fostering career resilience, and examining the dynamic nature of social support and its function in building and sustaining resilience.

Career context

A career is "the evolving sequence of a person's work experiences over time" (Arthur et al., 1989, p. 8). This definition suggests that individuals would have one career (although many jobs or roles) that lasts their lifespan, and careers are, therefore, a cumulative collection of experiences (Inkson, 2015). What defines a modern-day career is not only the status or hierarchical progression experienced by an individual but also how individuals feel a sense of personal satisfaction (Arthur et al., 2005), thus making careers a concept for all. At one time, the pervasive view was that career success was defined by status, salary, and progression,

DOI: 10.4324/9781003287858-14

where those earning more money at higher ranks in organizations were more successful (i.e., objective career success). More recently, however, we are beginning to understand that satisfaction with one's career is a personal matter, not always defined by money or status but by what matters to each individual (i.e., career satisfaction) (Arthur et al., 2005). Shen et al. (2015) identified several career satisfaction elements: achievement, job characteristics such as autonomy, opportunities for learning and development, making a difference, work–life balance, and recognition such as awards or receiving positive feedback. Interestingly, whilst it might be assumed that objective and subjective success are related, the research would suggest that there is typically little relationship between these constructs (see the review article by Spurk et al., 2019).

Career theories mirror the work environment and context (Savickas et al., 2009), which has changed considerably over the last century. For example, women entering the workplace on a large scale following World War II (Domenico & Jones, 2006) and the impact of lockdown, furlough, and unemployment due to COVID-19 across the world (Dang & Nguyen, 2021) have led to changes in expectations around career development and workplaces. At one time, career development was entirely the responsibility of the organization (Bridges, 1996). The industrial revolution led to this view, "fit" (between the person and their job and the person and their environment) theories dominated, with a particular interest in how to get the most out of individuals, how to match an individual skill to the needs of the organization (i.e., producing more and doing it faster). During the early 1900s, individuals were passive recipients rather than drivers of their career development. More recently, however, we see organizations and individuals taking shared responsibility for career management, or at least we see an argument for this being the case (Akkermans & Kubasch, 2017; Bernstrøm et al., 2019; Clarke & Patrickson, 2008; Fugate et al., 2004). Person–career fit, which is the alignment between an individual's needs, values, talents and abilities, career experiences, and demands and their career path (Parasuraman et al., 2000) has emerged as a more applicable concept to the current career landscape.

In recent years, we have seen the concept of employability gaining traction, although it is believed that the earliest reference to the term came from Feintuch (1955). Employability literature has also evolved in line with societal change; at one time, it was dominated by research on school graduates (e.g., Sewell & Dacre Pool, 2010). However, now we see more research and practical application of the concept to careers over the lifespan, identifying factors that can support an individual to manage their long-term employability and achieve person–career fit (Elsey et al., 2020; De Vos & Van der Heijden, 2015).

These facilitating factors are termed *career resources* (Hirschi, 2012), thus placing employability within a conservation of resources framework (Hobfoll, 1989). Resources are "those entities that are either centrally valued in their own right or act as means to obtain centrally valued ends" (Hobfoll, 2002, p. 307). Understanding career resources is crucial for individuals and practitioners because they can be enhanced to support careers and can enable learning around what an organization and an individual can do in order to maximise sustainable careers (Chin et al., 2022; De Vos et al., 2020; Elsey et al., 2022; Newman, 2011; Van der Heijden et al., 2020) defined as "The sequence of an individual's different career experiences, reflected through a variety of patterns of continuity over time, crossing several social spaces, and characterised by individual agency, herewith providing meaning to the individual" (De Vos & Van der Heijden, 2015, p. 7).

Where jobs for life no longer exist and career development is no longer viewed solely by upward progression, individuals must be able to navigate the turbulent labour market flexibly. Career resilience has been suggested as a career resource that enables individuals to do that successfully (De Vos et al., 2020; Mishra & McDonald, 2017).

Career and resilience

As career theories often mirror the external environment (Savickas et al., 2009), we would expect to see career research related to more wellbeing, which is undoubtedly the case. A focus on resilience has led career theories to include adaptability and flexibility to manage the changing world (Fugate et al., 2004; Savickas, 2005; Van Der Heijde & Van Der Heijden, 2006). Furthermore, positive psychological and personal resources help individuals maintain their wellbeing and engagement (Demerouti et al., 2001). Haenggli and Hirschi (2020) conducted a 3-wave longitudinal study with survey measurements taken one month apart on 574 employees. The findings of this study indicated that career adaptability was highly related to Hirschi et al.'s (2018) career resources (motivational, environmental, and knowledge). However, they all explained unique facets of career success. As expected, motivational and environmental resources strongly predicted subjective career success, whereas knowledge and skills were related to objective career success (salary). Interestingly, career adaptability showed a negative relationship to salary, with more adaptable individuals earning less, reinforcing the distinction between subjective and objective career success. Overall, this large, longitudinal, quantitative study supports that career resources predict objective and subjective career success over time and that different resources are essential for different outcomes.

Career resilience is another career resource that predicts career success, although research is still in its infancy. Career resilience is defined as "a developmental process of persisting, adapting, and/or flourishing in one's career despite challenges, changing events and disruptions over time" (Mishra & McDonald, 2017, p. 216).

Therefore, it closely resembles the definition of resilience but is centralised to the career domain. The term traces back to Career Motivation Theory (London, 1983), where *career resilience* was defined as one of three domains of individual characteristics, also including *career identity* and *insight*. London (1983) identified three sub-dimensions of the resilience construct, explaining that individuals with high self-efficacy, high risk-taking, and low dependency (needing others' approval) would have more career resilience. Mishra and McDonald (2017) provide a comprehensive literature review of career resilience, suggesting that it encompasses personal and contextual factors in line with the Career Sustainability Theory (De Vos et al., 2020).

Career resilience is the coping mechanism that explains why some individuals recover from a negative/unsustainable career period by learning, showing adaptive behaviour, increasing self-awareness, and searching for a person–career fit. Indeed, among managers/professionals (Lyons et al., 2015) and nurses (Wei & Taormina, 2014), self-reported career resilience cross-sectionally predicted career satisfaction. Moreover, high career resilience predicts lower intentions of career turnover cross-sectionally (Carless & Bernath, 2007) and after a one-year time lag (Kidd & Green, 2006). Furthermore, in a cross-sectional study in the banking sector, career resilience mediated the relationship between career competencies (such as career control, motivation and networking) and career satisfaction (Ahmad et al., 2019). This research implies that the attributes of career resilience—perseverance and ability to adapt to changing circumstances—aid individuals in continuing their chosen career path. Career resilience is, therefore, particularly relevant in military occupations where individuals often do not leave voluntarily but are forced to retire (early in life compared to the civilian workforce) due to health reasons (Kaur et al., 2018). Therefore, individuals must adapt and be resilient to fulfil their career ambitions. Resilience is an essential resource for many positive outcomes, and we assume that this is no different regarding careers.

Military context

It is indisputable how the current social, economic, and cultural environment is more turbulent than ever before, with technological advancements, a global pandemic, an on-going war in Ukraine, the rapid pace of change due to globalization, and the fluctuating state of the economy (Hite & McDonald, 2020). Most researchers conclude that current careers are boundaryless (Arthur & Rousseau, 1996); the typical hierarchical progression no longer constrains individuals within one organization. Instead, they move between companies, sectors, and occupations to fulfil objective and subjective career success. Although there is mixed evidence for the notion of the boundaryless career, with job mobility data not supporting a drastic increase in individuals jumping between organizations (Chudzikowski, 2012; Rodrigues & Guest, 2010), individuals increasingly value subjective over objective career success (Dries, 2011; Hall, 1976, 1996, 2002). The focus on subjective success propels researchers to investigate what makes individuals adaptable and flexible enough to successfully navigate the less predictable career paths and remain content (e.g., Haenggli & Hirschi, 2020; Haenggli et al., 2021). However, most studies focus on white-collar professionals (Chudzikowski, 2012), ignoring the military sector, which employs 153,290 individuals in the United Kingdom alone (UK Parliament, 2022). In 2019, approximately 0.27% of the worldwide population was a part of their country's military force. In 2015, at 2.3 million strong, the US military was recognised as the largest employer in the world (World Economic Forum, 2015).

Research on the military has focused on resilience due to the common mental health issues among service members. Army members are often deployed to combat zones, operating in VUCA global environments (Barber, 1992). This dangerous context predisposes individuals to experience traumatic events, increasing the risk of post-traumatic stress disorder (PTSD) and other mental health challenges (Hoge et al. 2004). Although the military culture provides individuals with social support through camaraderie, the culture has drawbacks. Organizational culture describes the core values and beliefs, norms, attitudes, and behaviours expected from all group members (Reger et al., 2008), which is particularly unique within the military (Wilson, 2008). It diminishes one's personal identity and promotes acquisition of military group identity via solid organizational structures, removing individuality through uniform, and contagion of strong cultural norms and values throughout the group (Maharajan & Subramani, 2014). Indeed, one of the main goals of core military training is to strip the service members of their civilian identities and replace them with military ones (Dindial, 2020). Although military culture attempts to evolve in the face of social change, low gender diversity and stigma around seeking mental health support still prevail, reinforcing the traditional *macho culture* (Acosta et al., 2014; Dunavin et al., 1994; Vogt, 2011). There is ample research on resilience among military members (Meredith et al., 2011) and their families (Bowen et al., 2013) to shield them from the adverse effects of deployment and combat. Indeed, resilience was found to protect service members' wellbeing via more adaptive coping strategies in the face of adverse events (Hourani et al., 2012). New service members entering the military do not show significantly higher self-reported resilience than non-service members (Campbell, 2014); military training can increase participants' resilience via interventions (Jaeschke, 2016), although no research currently explores their career resilience.

The military continues to show hierarchical progression patterns, resembling traditional rather than contemporary careers. However, career resilience is still crucial for service members, as they experience unpredictable challenges and the threat of career unsustainability. Firstly, a typical military member will experience a Permanent Change of Station (PCS) move every 2–3 years. Whilst this "personnel turbulence" is a normal part of the military personnel operating model, it is acknowledged to have monetary and non-monetary costs to the Armed Services and the soldiers and their families (Hix et al., 1998). The decline in stability and continuity from these changes hinders organizational readiness and reduces the spouses' employment opportunities, impacting attrition rates (Tong et al., 2018). Despite the lack of research in this area, career resilience is expected to allow servicemembers to navigate PCS effectively; this chapter will explore these concepts further. Secondly, achieving objective career success through advancement to the senior ranks of the military is much more complex than in the civilian sector due to high competition, physical demands, and the need for a wide breadth of soft and technical skills (Bahtic et al., 2020). Indeed, less than 1% of US military personnel progress to the rank of General Officer (Congressional Research Service, 2022). Moreover, the prestigious rank is often followed by having to start a second career in the civilian sector in a different job role (Krigbaum et al., 2020), which is also expected to be facilitated by Career resilience.

What can organizations learn from studying the military?

Historically, occupational psychology pioneered critical topics of recruitment (Ployhart et al., 2017), leadership (Day et al., 2014), and team effectiveness (Katzell & Austin, 1992) on military samples. The military has a unique culture and set of practices that can be studied as a testbed for understanding these crucial phenomena. Continuing this tradition, we explore career resilience—a novel concept in employability and career literature—on military service personnel to catalyse more research and an in-depth, contextual understanding of this important construct.

Drawing on the lived experiences of elite high-performing military leaders, this chapter aims to draw parallels between the lived experiences of high-ranking military personnel. This is done through in-depth storytelling, high-level practitioner and academic reflections, and analysis of the career resilience literature, identifying where career resilience is utilised in pursuing a military career. This book chapter will therefore explore careers through the lens of individuals who have achieved some of the highest ranks in the army. In a business context, these leaders could be responsible for ten thousand troops and budgets of up to one hundred million dollars, the possible equivalent of Fortune 500 Company CEO. Using a context-specific angle enables the authors to focus in-depth on the career stories of individuals in similar work environments (Elsey et al., 2022; Weng & Zhu, 2020). We aim to develop knowledge of specific resources and explore their understanding of career resilience in sustainable careers.

An approach to understanding career resilience in military careers

We utilised an evidence-based practice approach building on the research and principles outlined by Barends et al. (2015) by bringing together multiple sources of evidence to explore complex and multifaceted issues as they occur in real-life settings. The Centre for Evidence-Based Management (n.d.) outlines the four sources of evidence as:

  i the best available scientific evidence
 ii the best available organisational evidence
iii the best available experiential evidence, and
iv the organisational values and stakeholder concerns.

This allowed an agile approach, which is especially important when investigating the challenge of career resilience within a VUCA context.

The multiple sources of evidence included interviews with:

- international senior military personnel on lived experiences of career resilience in the military,
- an academic expert on career resilience, and
- an organisational expert on military careers, values and concerns.

Our focus was on the senior military personnel, which brings an advantage of focusing on a population who has achieved objective career success in the VUCA context. However, this sample also limits the findings' generalisability, perhaps only applicable to high organizational echelons.

These conversations were analysed in light of a literature review on career resilience, military culture, and resilience as a concept (described below). In addition to this, we incorporated practitioner observations and sector data into our analysis to build upon the principles of career resilience to develop a deeper understanding of the concept in relation to lived experiences. Our review explores the concept of career resilience from the different perspectives of the organization, the practitioner, the academic evidence, and other stakeholder views to bring together a comprehensive review of career resilience through the lens of the military.

The literature review explored contemporary research conducted on resilience within the military in the career context. Articles published in English in the field of Psychology between 2014 and 2022 were searched for the following terms on the CORE search engine database: "career" AND "adaptability" AND "resilience*" AND ("military" OR "army"). This search resulted in 4,431 papers, which were reduced to 96 articles based on titles. The inclusion criteria included empirical quantitative and qualitative studies that focused on current servicemembers and veterans of the military. In addition, studies on military families were included if they focused on the servicemember as one of the participants also. Synonyms of resilience, such as mental toughness and grit, were also included. The 96 papers were then checked based on abstracts using the same inclusion criteria, which resulted in 38 articles.

What the evidence tells us about resilience in military careers

This chapter explores the importance of resilience in developing and maintaining careers in a modern military context. From an in depth review of our multiple sources of evidence, namely conversations with senior military leaders on lived experiences of career resilience in the military; discussions with an academic expert on career resilience; consultations with an organizational expert on military careers, values, and concerns; literature reviews on career resilience, military culture and resilience, practitioner observations, and sector data, we sought to build upon the principles of career resilience to develop a deeper understanding of its use as a concept for supporting individuals to navigate an increasingly challenging world. Our aim is to stimulate interest and research around career resilience in this unique context. Our analysis supports the notion that career resilience is an important resource for individuals and organizations. The remainder of this section will unpack this concept in more detail alongside the academic literature as a source of evidence.

Research on the military career focuses on the barriers experienced by veterans when transitioning to the civilian sector (Wolfgang, 2022). However, little is known about how career resilience is drawn upon *during* military service. This chapter addressed the research gap in understanding the lived experiences of elite high-performing military leaders, perceptions of the role and importance of resilience in developing and maintaining careers (subjective and objective career success) in a military context. Our research and inquiry into the personal experiences of senior military leaders and the views of the organizational expert and an academic expert on resilience and career success indicated three significant themes:

1 The spectrum of resilience.
2 Organizational practices that foster resilience.
3 The lonely leader and resilience.

The first significant theme to emerge was the importance of understanding the "spectrum of resilience," including the positive and negative consequences of resilience. Resilience was seen as critical for succeeding and surviving in a military environment. It was perceived to be both rewarding and punishing. The second central theme was the "organizational practices that foster resilience," notably caused by a predetermined role change every 2–3 years. It was perceived as building resilience for leaders and their families. The final theme to emerge was "the lonely leader and resilience." The sources for social support, seen as a critical resource for nurturing and sustaining resilience, were dynamic and changed in response to crucial factors, including promotion to senior ranks. The sources of support that served individuals on entry to the military no longer served them well as they progressed to senior leadership positions. The findings expose the need for a more systemic and dynamic approach to understanding the multiple factors affecting resilience concerning career sustainability.

The spectrum of resilience

The research revealed a high level of resilience and adaptability by the individuals and their superiors, peers, and subordinates. Therefore, it is essential to explain the difference between resilience and adaptability. Resilience is the capacity to recover from disruptions (Herrman et al., 2011). In terms of career resilience, it is the extent to which you can carry on making progress towards your goals despite setbacks

(Mishra & McDonald, 2017). Resilience also may require a cognitive appraisal and demands a depth of capacity to create processing and reflection space. In comparison, adaptability requires reformulating goals in response to new career realities Seibert et al. (2016). Furthermore, adaptability involves behavioural change and the development of capabilities to aid adaptation, underpinned by high levels of self-belief and self-efficacy (De Vos et al., 2020).

The resilience advantage

Resilience refers to positive adaptation, or the ability to maintain or regain mental health, despite experiencing adversity (Wald et al., 2006). Indeed, participants considered resilience essential and beneficial to individuals, the team, and the organization. Furthermore, resilience and career resilience were used interchangeably and perceived as interconnected. It was strongly linked to mental health and wellbeing. Wellbeing was used as a dashboard providing indications and warning signs for when resilience was in abundance or waning. One of the military leaders described resilience as a "bucket" that needed to be regularly topped up. Our research describes resilience as something that can be seen and touched, a valuable currency that needs protecting and frequently replenished. The most frequently described activities for maintaining resilience were time with family and leisure time, such as playing golf. Time away from work offered important space for reflection and perspective-taking. These results have implications for organizations who have a responsibility to protect their leaders' time outside of work. An abundance of research has been conducted in response to the COVID-19 pandemic that has highlighted the importance of boundary management, especially the work–family boundaries, to enhance wellbeing and promote and build a resilient work environment (Jaiswal et al., 2022). According to Jaiswal et al. (2022), this is supported by the *boundary theory* that illuminates the need to maintain balance by drawing boundaries between personal and professional lives. A consistent boundary management policy and practice supported and enforced by the entire military echelons will be essential to prevent boundary violations and promote resilience.

Our research suggested that although resilience was developed, nurtured, and challenged by a military career, it stemmed from a childhood ingrained with strong self-belief, independence and confidence. In a military context, it translated into not being afraid of challenges. It was perceived as directly impacting objective career success because superiors looked for individuals that could succeed in being tasked with complex orders. A perception existed that having a good reputation for being resilient and competent within the military environment led to promotions and more opportunities. Resilience can support individuals to achieve a balance between their personal and career identity and subjective and objective career success (Ahmad et al., 2019; Elsey et al., 2022). In our research, this was evident in their overall evaluation of achieving and sustaining a successful career (subjective and objective). The military leaders chose not to retire from the military and go to the civilian sector due to their self-described high resilience, promoted by military training and reinforced by their military identity.

Resilience and emotional intelligence

Emotional intelligence (EI) is a set of abilities that allow the processing of emotion-relevant information (Salovey & Mayer, 2004). It encompasses perceiving others' emotions, accessing and generating their own emotions to allow reflection, and understanding emotions to promote growth (Salovey & Mayer, 2004). From our research, facets of EI emerged as a critical attribute that positively linked to career resilience. It was seen as a protective quality (of self and others) and a positive resource that supported self-awareness and reflection and promoted resourcefulness. Our military leaders valued EI as an essential attribute that equipped individuals with the skills necessary for leading and building teams, ensuring that peers and subordinates could be open and honest about their struggles so that they could provide and receive the necessary support. This may require the team to adapt by stepping up and taking on more duties in response to individuals within the team whose resilience was low and who needed extra support. Indeed, a study examining the relationship between EI and the stress process concluded that EI facilitates stress resilience by buffering the effects of stressful events on wellbeing via increased social support and the processing of emotions, highlighting the importance of resources and resilience (Schneider et al., 2013). This was partly explained by the stress appraisal responding in the direction of a challenge rather than a threat. Our research suggests that organizational interventions that focus on perceiving stressors as challenges rather than threats are likely to result in positive adaptation of career resilience.

Furthermore, our research identified facets of EI as vital for enabling individuals to deal with difficult situations. For example, where experiences of toxic leadership adversely impacted health and wellbeing, social support from a trusted spouse was seen as an essential resource supporting a positive outcome. This finding supports research that shows that self-reported EI is strongly related to perceived social support (Zeidner et al., 2016). A study of university students concluded that those with stronger EI and resilience experienced lower perceived stress (Sarrionandia et al., 2018). Therefore, it is recommended that interventions focused on building resilience and EI could help lower perceived stress (Sarrionandia et al., 2018). Whilst this study on students focussed on an individual level, organizational culture plays a vital role in cultivating an environment of trust and psychological safety (Edmondson et al., 2004). Indeed, Southwick et al. (2014) concluded that not only is resilience a complex construct best understood as a continuum, but its definition may also be different for individuals, families, organizations, societies, and cultures based on the context. Importantly, Southwick et al. (2014) suggest that this complex understanding of resilience had implications for individuals and organizations by moving away from a deficit model of mental health and towards a competence and strength-based model focused on prevention and strength-building. EI, or aspects of it, is a crucial mechanism in fostering career resilience. It might serve as the mechanism behind the accumulation of social support resources by allowing individuals to foster relationships that improve resilience and career success.

The resilience disadvantage

Within the military population, not being seen as resilient is linked to being perceived as "weak" and "vulnerable." Whilst this may be driven by the pursuit of reputation management, our research identified that the motivation to avoid being seen as weak or vulnerable, in some instances, may result in individuals pursuing unattainable goals in fear of being seen as "giving up". This raises a concern over the conditions and circumstances that may foster a shadow or dark side of resilience. Indeed, researchers explore both the benefits and the dark side of personality, leadership, and the role of resilience. For example, in an empirical study of ambulance personnel, resilience mediated and moderated the effect of personality and burnout (Treglown et al., 2016). The dark side of personality (such as Machiavellian traits) was found to increase the risk of burnout, especially for people with low resilience (Treglown et al., 2016).

Mental health is a strong theme concerning perceived resilience, and mental health problems are commonplace among the military population (Jaeschke, 2016). An emerging theme from the academic literature was a link between soldiers' resilience and their ability to overcome mental health problems. Indeed, this is reinforced by participants' acknowledgement of the harmful effects of the masculine-dominated culture of the military organization and how it can exacerbate mental health issues of individuals who feel like they have to put on a persona when faced with emotional turmoil. Research supports a unique organizational culture of the military (e.g., Wilson, 2008), and our research confirmed this. The military is perceived to have a masculine culture—whilst this might be the same culture, it could be experienced differently by those who identify as men and those who identify as women. Future research should explore this assumption further as the military modernises and becomes more diverse (Hall, 2012).

Experiencing adverse, traumatic events is ingrained within the military profession. Examples from our research of traumas impacting mental health and wellbeing included gender discrimination, toxic leadership/work environment, suicides of military personnel, marriage breakdown, and deployments to combat zones. An expectation emerged from the research that the military should provide high-quality mental health support to all servicemembers returning from the war zone to prevent PTSD and suicides. Although the military has changed for the better, mental health is still stigmatised in the military, preventing uptake (Vogt, 2011). Without support from the organization on top of individuals' resilience, military service members cannot achieve the "healthy" indicator of sustainable careers (De Vos et al., 2020). The organization is responsible for promoting "health." However, our research reported that this is not the reality, which puts more pressure on the individual. This finding reinforces the military organization's need to destigmatise mental health and provide appropriate channels of professional support (Acosta et al., 2014; Dunavin et al., 1994). This is confirmed by previous research (Acosta et al., 2014; Dunavin et al., 1994; Vogt, 2011) and the current study, where individuals reported improvement in mental health support across their three-decade-long careers, but it is still not on par with the level of trauma they experience on the job.

It is worth noting that resilience and effective functioning may show an inverted-U curve relationship. Too high a level of resilience may be detrimental, as it predisposes individuals to fixate on impossible goals, leading individuals to become unduly tolerant of unpleasant circumstances (Chamorro-Premuzic & Lusk, 2017). Indeed, there is preliminary qualitative evidence for this dark side of resilience in the military, as overly resilient servicemembers cannot transition back to civilian environments upon retirement, impacting their career resilience (Allen & Allen-Hampton, 2019). Recent research on the dark side of resilience explores the contexts that foster less functional responses to resilience, including masking vulnerabilities. Allen and Allen-Hampton (2019) conclude that there is a need to differentiate between functional and less functional adaptation in relation to degrees of risk, context, and the different forms of resilience shown. Furthermore, they suggest that resilience is studied on a spectrum and understood through the lens of the limits of resilience (Mahdiani & Ungar, 2021). Therefore, we recommend further research to investigate the spectrum of resilience related to career resilience.

Organizational practices that foster resilience

Work–life continuum of resilience

An organizational consideration in career resilience is work–life interaction since the military defines life and existence for the entire family (Bowen et al., 2013). Our research suggests evidence exists that families became more resilient thanks to the frequent changes of location and the additional difficulties of living with a military servicemember who is deployed continuously. Nonetheless, there was an acknowledgement that families were strained. Particularly of concern was the stress put on the spouse who had to take over domestic and parental responsibilities upon deployments. It is calculated that service personnel are not present in the home for up to 25% of their married life. Moreover, not all families displayed the same level of resilience, resulting in broken marriages and mental health challenges among spouses, especially under specific stressors such as war (Sullivan et al., 2022).

Organizations often focus on building resilience through intervention programmes at the individual level (Hornor, 2017). However, the research suggests the need for organizations to understand that stressors inside and outside the work environment will impact overall resilience. Intervention programmes and support need to consider the work–life continuum and the organizations' and individuals' role in maintaining balance.

Permanent change of duty station practice

Military officers must have a PCS every 2–3 years (Clever & Segal, 2013), meaning that families can experience over a dozen career moves. They invariably involve finding a new home and school and adapting to a new work environment. This creates many challenges and costs for the individual, their families, and the military and is a well-researched phenomenon (Clever & Segal, 2013). Indeed, the PCS practice costs billions of dollars and is deemed less necessary in response to advanced technology (Carlock, 2021). Recent research suggests a strong business case for changing this practice based on increased military readiness achieved by increased family readiness due to greater family stability (Carlock, 2021).

Our research identified how inseparable and interwoven life is from the career context. It also shows the impact of (military) careers on the family. Indeed, over 50% of the military are married, and 40% have children (Hill, 2017). Additionally, families are impacted by deployments (60% deployed at least once) and role changes PCSing, impacting the resilience and adaptability of families as they take on new roles to support these transitions. Although families may benefit from the military career, Hill (2017) argues that they require organizational support and assistance to respond positively to organizational demands.

PCS aligns with individuals who prefer variety—and personal gratitude towards the military for the ability to have various jobs, something they felt was specific to a career in the army. In addition, observed attributes of adaptability and resilience allow individuals to respond positively to the ever-changing VUCA military environment, as relocations and job changes occur frequently. Thus, our exploratory research provides evidence for the benefits of PCS for adaptable, resilient individuals and families, which ought to be explored further to provide a counter-balance to the current focus, which is on the *costs* of the PCS model.

Furthermore, the PCS practice could be viewed as a large-scale natural experiment. Conducting a longitudinal study on the impact of this practice on organizational outcomes and individuals' behaviours and attributes, including resilience, may offer researchers an opportunity to measure and understand how organizations wittingly or unwittingly shape and drive behaviours more deeply. Conversely, practices such as those employed by the Civil Service, whereby individuals may remain in the same role for decades, may inadvertently foster attributes of continuity at the expense of resilience and adaptability.

Sense of purpose

Service members stay in the military for a variety of reasons including sense of purpose, duty, or to create meaning (see Figure 11.1).

In our research, meaning and a sense of purpose contributed to military identities, primarily through the notion of being privileged to impact human lives so profoundly. In line with Figure 11.1, a sense of purpose provided by the army

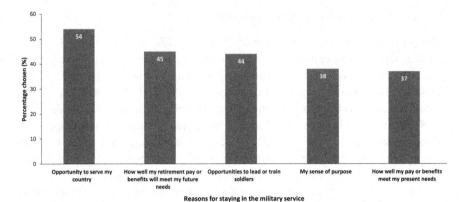

FIGURE 11.1   Top reasons for staying in the military service (adapted from the U.S. Army Department of the Army Career Engagement Survey [DACES] exit Survey of the U.S. Army Public Affairs [Loryana et al., 2021])

prompted senior leaders to remain in the military for longer than an average soldier. It drove the sustainability of their career and enabled them to achieve objective career success. It encouraged them to build and sustain their resilience because they were committed to a higher purpose and saw the value of the military and the importance to themselves and their families. The military, in particular, is fortunate to have a strong inherent sense of purpose. For organizations where a sense of purpose may not be as obvious, efforts to connect individuals to a sense of purpose are likely to deliver benefits, including increased (career) resilience.

The lonely leader and resilience

The final theme identified in our research was how increasingly lonely attaining an elite position within the military was. Loneliness directly impacted perceived resilience because the sources of support built earlier in their careers no longer served them well as senior leaders. Experiences of loneliness in leadership in public positions have been explored to some extent in the literature. For example, Cangemi et al. (2008) explain that leaders in high-trust public serving roles, including the military, are vulnerable to loneliness as they go from one crisis to another without the opportunity to get support and to connect with others. According to Rakip (2013), research on loneliness in leaders confirmed previous literature that points to the need for leaders to redefine themselves in relation to others and themselves. Furthermore, Rakip (2013) explains that a leader's need for confidentiality on classified subjects limits the support that friends and family can provide. Our research validated this notion, highlighting that not wanting to burden family or subordinates led to feelings of loneliness with nowhere to turn. Being a high-ranking military member brings challenges of huge responsibilities, pressure and even less time for the family. Moreover, by acting as role models to subordinates, the camaraderie aspect of the military culture is inevitably lost.

In line with Social Capital Theory (Coleman, 1990), our review underlined social support as a critical aspect of becoming and remaining resilient in facing adversity. A perception existed that a lack of social support and communication with servicemembers contributed to the high prevalence of suicides and mental health issues in the army. Our military leaders indicated that support should come from several different streams: family, other service members, veterans, mental health professionals, and peer support networks. In the absence of support, the interviewed military leaders reported developing their peer support networks as a resource and positive support-seeking activity. By developing alternative positive social support networks, individuals avoided the desire to withdraw and self-isolate, which has consequences for an increased risk of stress and burnout (Treglown et al., 2016). Indeed, Treglown et al. (2016) suggest that burnout and resilience literature indicates the importance of good relationships (family and colleagues) and a positive social network and environment in the occurrence of these.

Schwartz et al. (2021) researched seeking, finding, and accessing informal and formal support for family members of Military-Civilian-Transition Veterans with mental health problems. They identified obstacles to include mental health stigma, caregiver burden, and burnout. Successes of informal support included extended family and friends and online support, and formal support included Military Family Resource Centres and operational stress injury clinics. Despite frustrations and setbacks, pursuing goals including financial aid and receiving counsel and comfort enabled families to demonstrate resilience and resolve. Drawing upon this research, mapping out informal and formal support networks for military personnel and their families, anticipating obstacles and facilitating successes may be a proactive way for organizations to ensure that the dynamic support needs of this community are satisfied. Indeed, in the United Kingdom, the Health and Safety Executive identifies relationships and support as vital in reducing workplace stress (Cousins et al., 2004; Edwards et al., 2008). Therefore, social support in one's career may be the key protective resource that boosts one's career resilience and wellbeing.

Strong peer support networks were seen as one of the most significant pillars of support for senior military leaders. The hierarchical nature of the military, changing the nature of relationships to include a shift away from camaraderie towards increased competition, can impact individuals. Loneliness was a significant aspect of achieving high-objective career success in the military. Our military leaders alluded to how lonely and competitive it is in the army's higher echelons. Loneliness is the discrepancy between the actual and ideal social network Perlman et al. (1984). This underlines the importance of fostering resilience outside one's immediate work environment—finding social support outside the work context was seen as critical for maintaining resilience as a leader.

Although camaraderie—the social support within work—is essential, supporting previous research (Davies, 2015; Seibert et al., 2016), the most crucial pillars of support identified by our research were outside of the military or their immediate troops (Covington et al., in prep). Indeed, an empirical study found that Family-Specific Support was inversely related to Peer-Specific Support (Newcomb & Bentler, 1986). Therefore, our research suggests that leaders may gravitate towards external sources of support when they receive no or little support from within the organization. Furthermore, this seems to be exacerbated by the hierarchical context of the military that results in an increasingly competitive environment as opportunities for promotion significantly decrease and the consequences increase (forced retirement from the military). Whilst it is impossible for the military to avoid competition, research in a non-military context illustrates that competition can be minimised and creativity increased by deliberate organizational policies encouraging individuals to focus on opportunities rather than threats (Steinhage et al., 2017).

Conclusion

This chapter has outlined the concept of career utilising a resilience lens and linking societal changes to the relatively underexplored area of career resilience. Our approach utilised multiple sources of evidence, drawing them together to identify three key themes for understanding how resilience plays a role in the careers of high-ranking military leaders. It is essential to point out that this chapter is not an exhaustive look at the research evidence, nor is it an empirical study. We encourage researchers and practitioners to test the information here empirically. We also believe that these insights have relevance outside of the military, especially for leaders of large corporations operating within a VUCA environment. As we move towards portfolio-based and multiple careers, exploring the various practices that can underpin and support these new models should be encouraged.

Our review suggested that career resilience is a relevant modern concept with utility for individuals and organizations. It aided individuals in continuing their chosen career path in the military by encouraging the building of personal resources (underpinned by high levels of self-belief, self-awareness, and support), perseverance, the ability to adapt to changing circumstances, flexibility, and a spirit of continuous learning. Additionally, it is a concept that organizations could utilise as they adapt their organizational design, culture and practices to foster the adaptability and resilience that the modern VUCA environment demands, providing a vital buffer for when events inevitably occur that may deplete resilience. Furthermore, it invites organizations to consider the contextual factors that may foster a dark side of career resilience as individuals relentlessly pursue their goals.

Wellbeing and mental health emerged as a dominant theme throughout our review, and we expected this to be the case given that career theories reflect the external environment (Savickas et al., 2009). Our research emphasised the importance of facets of EI as a vital career resilience resource, strengthening interpersonal relationships to create a favourable work environment and activating positive social support networks to protect leaders from loneliness and isolation. The military offers a testbed, a natural experiment, where the dynamic nature of career resilience in the context of a unique culture and specific organizational practices (i.e., PCS) can be explored. Resilience is an essential resource for many positive outcomes. Our review posits this is equally true for career resilience, especially when achieved through a symbiotic partnership between the individual and the organization.

References

Acosta, J. D., Becker, A., Cerully, J. L., Fisher, M. P., Martin, L. T., Vardavas, R., & Schell, T. L. (2014). *Mental health stigma in the military*. Rand National Defense Research Institute Santa Monica, CA.

Ahmad, B., Latif, S., Bilal, A. R., & Hai, M. (2019). The mediating role of career resilience on the relationship between career competency and career success. *Asia-Pacific Journal of Business Administration, 11*(3), 209–231. https://doi.org/10.1108/APJBA-04-2019-0079

Akkermans, J., & Kubasch, S. (2017). #Trending topics in careers: A review and future research agenda. *Career Development International, 22*(6), 586–627. https://doi.org/10.1108/CDI-08-2017-0143

Allen, T. M., & Allen-Hampton, T. (2019). A phenomenological study on the perceptions of the veterans transition into the vivilian workforce [Doctoral dissertation, National Louis University]. Digital Commons at NLU. https://digitalcommons.nl.edu/diss/419/

Arthur, M. B., & Rousseau, D. M. (1996). *The boundaryless career*. Oxford University Press.

Arthur, M. B., Hall, D. T., & Lawrence, B. S. (1989). Generating new directions in career theory: The case for a transdisciplinary approach. *Handbook of Career Theory, 7*, 25.

Arthur, M. B., Khapova, S. N., & Wilderom, C. P. M. (2005). Career success in a boundaryless career world. *Journal of Organizational Behavior, 26*(2), 177–202. https://doi.org/10.1002/job.290

Bahtic, M., Prikshat, V., Burgess, J., & Nankervis, A. (2020). Go back to the beginning: Career development and the challenges of transitioning from the military to civilian employment. In *Career development and job satisfaction*. IntechOpen.

Barber, H. F. (1992). Developing strategic leadership: The US Army War College experience. *Journal of Management Development, 11*(6), 4–12. https://doi.org/10.1108/02621719210018208

Barends, E., ten Have, S., & Huisman, F. (2015). The case of medicine. In search of evidence. In M. Rousseau (Ed.), *The oxford handbook of evidence-based management, 2012* (pp. 25–42). Oxford University Press.

Bernstrøm, V. H., Drange, I., & Mamelund, S.-E. (2019). Employability as an alternative to job security. *Personnel Review, 48*(1), 234–248. https://doi.org/10.1108/PR-09-2017-0279

Bowen, G. L., Martin, J. A., & Mancini, J. A. (2013). The resilience of military families: Theoretical perspectives. In M. A. Fine, & F. D. Fincham (Eds.), *Handbook of family theories: A content-based approach* (pp. 417–436). Routledge/Taylor & Francis Group.

Bridges, W. (1996). Jobshift: How to prosper in a workplace without jobs. *American Journal of Health-System Pharmacy, 53*(21), 2671–2671. https://doi.org/10.1093/ajhp/53.21.2671

Campbell, K. N. (2014). Resilience and self-control among Georgia Southern Students: a comparative study between ROTC Students and NonROTC students.

Cangemi, J. P., Burga, B., Lazarus, H., Miller, R. L., & Fitzgerald, J. (2008). The real work of the leader: A focus on the human side of the equation. *Journal of Management Development, 27*(10), 1026–1036. https://doi.org/10.1108/02621710810916286

Carless, S. A., & Bernath, L. (2007). Antecedents of intent to change careers among psychologists. *Journal of Career Development, 33*(3), 183–200. https://doi.org/10.1177/0894845306296646

Carlock, M. M. P. III (2021). The military officers frequent permanent change of station moves: Its effect on readiness and the military family. [Master's Thesis, Marine Corps University of Quantico]. Defense Technical Information Center. https://apps.dtic.mil/sti/citations/AD1177943

Centre for Evidence-Based Management (CEBMa). (n.d.). https://cebma.org/

Chamorro-Premuzic, T., & Lusk, D. (2017). The dark side of resilience. *Harvard Business Review, 16.*

Chin, T., Jawahar, I. M., & Li, G. (2022). Development and validation of a career sustainability scale. *Journal of Career Development, 49*(4), 769–787.

Chudzikowski, K. (2012). Career transitions and career success in the 'new' career era. *Journal of Vocational Behavior, 81*(2), 298–306.

Clarke, M., & Patrickson, M. (2008). The new covenant of employability. *Employee Relations, 30*(2), 121–141. https://doi.org/10.1108/01425450810843320

Clever, M., & Segal, D. R. (2013). The demographics of military children and families. *The Future of Children, 23*(2), 13–39. http://www.jstor.org/stable/23595618

Coleman, J. S. (1990). *The foundations of social theory.* Harvard University Press.

Congressional Research Service (2022, November 22). In Focus. https://sgp.fas.org/crs/natsec/IF10685.pdf

Cousins, R., Mackay, C. J., Clarke, S. D., Kelly, C., Kelly, P. J., & McCaig, R. H. (2004). 'Management standards' work-related stress in the UK: Practical development. *Work & Stress, 18*(2), 113–136. https://doi.org/10.1080/02678370410001734322

Dang, H.-A. H., & Nguyen, C. V. (2021). Gender inequality during the COVID-19 pandemic: Income, expenditure, savings, and job loss. *World Development, 140,* 105296.

Davies, P. (2015). Difficult life transitions: Learning and digital technologies in the military to civilian transition. Centre for Technology Enhanced Learning, Lancaster University. https://eprints.lancs.ac.uk/id/eprint/74292/1/Radical_Futures_Study_Report_Davies_final.pdf

Day, D. V., Fleenor, J. W., Atwater, L. E., Sturm, R. E., & McKee, R. A. (2014). Advances in leader and leadership development: A review of 25years of research and theory. *Leadership Quarterly 25th Anniversary Issue, 25*(1), 63–82. https://doi.org/10.1016/j.leaqua.2013.11.004

De Vos, A., & Van der Heijden, B. I. (2015). *Handbook of research on sustainable careers.* Edward Elgar Publishing.

De Vos, A., Van der Heijden, B. I., & Akkermans, J. (2020). Sustainable careers: Towards a conceptual model. *Journal of Vocational Behavior, 117,* 103196. https://doi.org/doi.org/10.1016/j.jvb.2018.06.011

Demerouti, E., Bakker, A. B., De Jonge, J., Janssen, P. P., & Schaufeli, W. B. (2001). Burnout and engagement at work as a function of demands and control. *Scandinavian Journal of Work, Environment & Health,* 279–286.

Dindial, D. K. (2020). *Preparing for life after the military: An evaluation of the effectiveness of the Resettlement Training Programme (RTP) in the Trinidad and Tobago Defence Force (TTDF).* University of Sheffield.

Domenico, D. M., & Jones, K. H. (2006). Career aspirations of women in the 20th century. *Journal of Career and Technical Education, 22*(2), n2.

Dries, N. (2011). The meaning of career success. *Career Development International, 16*(4), 364–384. https://doi.org/10.1108/13620431111158788

Dunavin, M. K., Lane, C., & Parker, P. E. (1994). Principles of continuous quality improvement applied to intravenous therapy. *Journal of Infusion Nursing, 17*(5), 248–255.

Edmondson, A. C., Kramer, R. M., & Cook, K. S. (2004). Psychological safety, trust, and learning in organizations: A group-level lens. *Trust and Distrust in Organizations: Dilemmas and Approaches, 12*(2004), 239–272.

Edwards, J. A., Webster, S., Van Laar, D., & Easton, S. (2008). Psychometric analysis of the UK health and safety executive's management standards work-related stress indicator tool. *Work & Stress, 22*(2), 96–107. https://doi.org/10.1080/02678370802166599

Elsey, V., Thompson, N., Sillence, E., Longstaff, L., & Moss, M. (2020). Becoming a professional: The five pillars of identification in occupational psychology in the UK. *In Practice: The EAWOP Practitioners E-Journal*, 13, 42–67.

Elsey, V., Van der Heijden, B. I. M. J., Smith, M. A., & Moss., M. (2022). Examining the role of employability as a mediator in the relationships between psychological capital and objective career success amongst occupational psychology professionals. *Frontiers in Psychology: Organizational Psychology*. https://doi.org/10.3389/fpsyg.2022.958226

Feintuch, A. (1955). Improving the employability and attitudes of "difficult-to-place" persons. *Psychological Monographs: General and Applied*, 69, 1–20. https://doi.org/10.1037/h0093689

Fugate, M., Kinicki, A. J., & Ashforth, B. E. (2004). Employability: A psycho-social construct, its dimensions, and applications. *Journal of Vocational Behavior, 65*(1), 14–38. https://doi.org/10.1016/j.jvb.2003.10.005

Haenggli, M., & Hirschi, A. (2020). Career adaptability and career success in the context of a broader career resources framework. *Journal of Vocational Behavior, 119*, 103414. https://doi.org/10.1016/j.jvb.2020.103414

Haenggli, M., Hirschi, A., Rudolph, C. W., & Peiró, J. M. (2021). Exploring the dynamics of protean career orientation, career management behaviors, and subjective career success: An action regulation theory approach. *Journal of Vocational Behavior, 131*, 103650. https://doi.org/10.1016/j.jvb.2021.103650

Hall, D. T. (1976). *Careers in organizations*. Scott, Foresman.

Hall, D. T. (1996). Protean careers of the 21st century. *Academy of Management Executive, 10*, 8–16.

Hall, D. T. (2002). *Protean careers in and out of organizations*. SAGE.

Hall, L. K. (2012). The importance of understanding military culture. *Advances in social work practice with the military* (pp. 3–17). Routledge.

Herrman, H., Stewart, D. E., Diaz-Granados, N., Berger, E. L., Jackson, B., & Yuen, T. (2011). What is resilience?. *The Canadian Journal of Psychiatry, 56*(5), 258–265.

Hill, B. (2017). *The Effects of Deployment on Military Family Roles*. (Doctoral dissertation). The Ohio State University.

Hirschi, A. (2012). The career resources model: An integrative framework for career counsellors. *British Journal of Guidance & Counselling, 40*(4), 369–383. https://doi.org/10.1080/03069885.2012.700506

Hirschi, A., Nagy, N., Baumeler, F., Johnston, C. S., & Spurk, D. (2018). Assessing key predictors of career success: Development and validation of the career resources questionnaire. *Journal of Career Assessment, 26*(2), 338–358. https://doi.org/10.1177/1069072717695584

Hite, L. M., & McDonald, K. S. (2020). Careers after COVID-19: Challenges and changes. *Human Resource Development International*, *23*, 427–437. https://doi.org/10.1080/136 78868.2020.1779576

Hix, W. M., Shukiar, H. J., Hanley, J. M., Kaplan, R. J., & Kawata, J. H. (1998). *Personnel turbulence: The policy determinants of permanent change of station moves*. Rand Arroyo Center.

Hobfoll, S. E. (1989). Conservation of resources: A new attempt at conceptualizing stress. *American Psychologist*, *44*(3), 513–524. https://doi.org/10.1037/0003-066X.44.3.513

Hobfoll, S. E. (2002). Social and psychological resources and adaptation. *Review of General Psychology*, *6*(4), 307–324. https://doi.org/10.1037//1089-2680.6.4.307

Hoge, C. W., Castro, C. A., Messer, S. C., McGurk, D., Cotting, D. I., & Koffman, R. L. (2004). Combat duty in Iraq and Afghanistan, mental health problems, and barriers to care. *New England Journal of Medicine*, *351*(1), 13–22. https://doi.org/10.1056/ NEJMoa040603

Hornor, G. (2017). Resilience. *Journal of Pediatric Health Care*, *31*(3), 384–390.

Hourani, L., Bender, R. H., Weimer, B., Peeler, R., Bradshaw, M., Lane, M., & Larson, G. (2012). Longitudinal study of resilience and mental health in marines leaving military service. *Journal of Affective Disorders*, *139*(2), 154–165. https://doi.org/10.5465/ amr.1983.4284664

Inkson, K. (2015). Contemporary conceptualizations of career. In P. J. Hartung, M. L. Savickas, & W. B. Walsh (Eds.), *APA handbook of career intervention, Vol. 1. Foundations* (pp. 21–42). American Psychological Association. https://doi.org/10.1037/14438-002

Jaeschke, A.-M. C. (2016). *Psychosocial predictors of resilience in a military sample*. West Virginia University.

Jaiswal, A., Gupta, S., & Prasanna, S. (2022). Theorizing employee stress, well being, resilience and boundary management in the context of forced work from home during COVID-19. *South Asian Journal of Business and Management Cases*, *11*(2), 86–104. https://doi.org/10.1177/22779779221100281

Katzell, R. A., & Austin, J. T. (1992). From then to now: The development of industrial-organizational psychology in the United States. *Journal of Applied Psychology*, *77*(6), 803–835. https://doi.org/10.1037/0021-9010.77.6.803

Kaur, R., Singh, H., & Tech, B. (2018). A literature review on the employability and the effects of ex-military personnel in corporate boardrooms. *International Affairs and Global Strategy*, *61*, 50–58.

Kidd, J. M., & Green, F. (2006). The careers of research scientists. *Personnel Review*, *35*(3), 229–251. https://doi.org/10.1108/00483480610656676

Krigbaum, G., Good, C. C., Ogle, A. K., Walsh, M., Hess, R., & Krigbaum, J. (2020). Factors in the transition of career military personnel to the civilian workforce. *TIP: The Industrial-Organizational Psychologist*, *57*(4).

London, M. (1983). Toward a theory of career motivation. *Academy of Management Review*, *8*(4), 620–630.

Loryana, L., Trivette, E. V., & Lathrop, A. D. (2021, June). *Department of The Army Career Engagement Survey First Annual Report*. https://talent.army.mil/wp-content/ uploads/2021/11/DACES-Annual-Report_JUNE2021.pdf

Lyons, S. T., Schweitzer, L., & Ng, E. S. W. (2015). Resilience in the modern career. *Career Development International*, *20*(4), 363–383. https://doi.org/10.1108/CDI-02-2015-0024

Maharajan, K., & Subramani, B. (2014). A critical study on the resettlement problems of air force ex-servicemen in India: Evolving management strategies. *International Journal of Research in Management Sciences*, *2*(1), 13–23.

Mahdiani, H., & Ungar, M. (2021). The dark side of resilience. *Adversity and Resilience Science*, *2*(3), 147–155.

Meredith, L. S., Sherbourne, C. D., Gaillot S., Hansell, L., Ritschard, H. V., Parker, A. M., Wrenn, G. (2011). Promoting psychological resilience in the U. S. military. *RAND Corporation*. https://www.rand.org/pubs/monographs/MG996.html

Mishra, P., & McDonald, K. (2017). Career resilience: An integrated review of the empirical literature. *Human Resource Development Review*, *16*(3), 207–234. https://doi.org/10.1177/1534484317719622

Newcomb, M. D., & Bentler, P. M. (1986). Loneliness and social support: A confirmatory hierarchical analysis. *Personality and Social Psychology Bulletin*, *12*(4), 520–535.

Newman, K. L. (2011). Sustainable careers: Lifecycle engagement in work. *Organizational Dynamics*, *40*(2), 136–143. https://doi.org/10.1016/j.orgdyn.2011.01.008

Parasuraman, S., Greenhaus, J. H., & Linnehan, F. (2000). Time, person-career fit, and the boundaryless career. *Trends in Organizational Behavior*, *7*, 63–78.

Perlman, D., Peplau, L. A., & Goldston, S. E. (1984). Loneliness research: A survey of empirical findings. In L. A. Peplau & S. E. Goldston (Eds.), Preventing the *h*armful consequences of *s*evere and *p*ersistent *l*oneliness (pp. 13–46). National Institute of Mental Health.

Ployhart, R. E., Schmitt, N., & Tippins, N. T. (2017). Solving the supreme problem: 100 years of selection and recruitment at the journal of applied psychology. *Journal of Applied Psychology*, *102*(3), 291–304. https://doi.org/10.1037/apl0000081

Rakip, A. M. (2013). The lonely leader: It's lonely at the top. *An Interdisciplinary Journal*. 105–108.

Reger, M. A., Etherage, J. R., Reger, G. M., & Gahm, G. A. (2008). Civilian psychologists in an army culture: The ethical challenge of cultural competence. *Military Psychology*, *20*(1), 21–35.

Rodrigues, R. A., & Guest, D. (2010). Have careers become boundaryless? *Human Relations*, *63*(8), 1157–1175. https://doi.org/10.1177/0018726709354344

Salovey, P., & Mayer, J. D. (2004). *Emotional intelligence*. Dude Publishing.

Sarrionandia, A., Ramos-Díaz, E., & Fernández-Lasarte, O. (2018). Resilience as a mediator of emotional intelligence and perceived stress: A cross-country study. *Frontiers in Psychology*, *9*, 2653.

Savickas, M. L. (2005). The theory and practice of career construction. In S. D. Brown & R. W. Lent (Eds.), Career *d*evelopment and *c*ounseling: Putting *t*heory and *r*esearch to *w*ork (pp. 42–70). John Wiley & Sons.

Savickas, M. L., Nota, L., Rossier, J., Dauwalder, J.-P., Duarte, M. E., Guichard, J., Soresi, S., Esbroeck, V., & van Vianen, R. (2009). Life designing: A paradigm for career construction in the 21st century. *Journal of Vocational Behavior*, *75*(3), 239–250. https://doi.org/10.1016/j.jvb.2009.04.004

Schneider, B., Goldstein, H. W., & Smith, D. B. (1995). The ASA framework: An update. *Personnel Psychology*, *48*(4), 747–773. https://doi.org/10.1111/j.1744-6570.1995.tb01780.x

Schneider, T. R., Lyons, J. B., & Khazon, S. (2013). Emotional intelligence and resilience. *Personality and Individual Differences*, *55*(8), 909–914.

Schwartz, K. D., Norris, D., Cramm, H., Tam-Seto, L., & Mahar, A. (2021). Family members of veterans with mental health problems: Seeking, finding, and accessing informal and formal supports during the military-to-civilian transition. *Journal of Military, Veteran and Family Health*, *7*(1), 21–34.

Seibert, S. E., Kraimer, M. L., & Heslin, P. A. (2016). Developing career resilience and adaptability. *Organizational Dynamics*, *45*(3), 245–257.

Sewell, P., & Dacre Pool, L. (2010). Moving from conceptual ambiguity to operational clarity. *Education + Training*, *52*(1), 89–94. https://doi.org/10.1108/00400911011017708

Shen, Y., Demel, B., Unite, J., Briscoe, J. P., Hall, D. T., Chudzikowski, K., ... Colorado, O. (2015). Career success across 11 countries: Implications for international human resource management. *The International Journal of Human Resource Management*, *26*(13), 1753–1778. https://doi.org/10.1080/09585192.2014.962562

Southwick, S. M., Bonanno, G. A., Masten, A. S., Panter-Brick, C., & Yehuda, R. (2014). Resilience definitions, theory, and challenges: Interdisciplinary perspectives. *European Journal of Psychotraumatology*, *5*(1), 25338.

Spurk, D., Hirschi, A., & Dries, N. (2019). Antecedents and outcomes of objective versus subjective career success: Competing perspectives and future directions. *Journal of Management*, *45*(1), 35–69. https://doi.org/10.1177/0149206318786563

Steinhage, A., Cable, D., & Wardley, D., (2017, March 20) The pros and cons of competition among employees. *Harvard Business Review*. https://hbr.org/2017/03/the-pros-and-cons-of-competition-among-employees

Sullivan, K. S., Park, Y., & Riviere, L. A. (2022). Military and nonmilitary stressors associated with mental health outcomes among female military spouses. *Family Relations*, *71*(1), 371–388.

Tong, P. K., Payne, L. A., Bond, C. A., Meadows, S. O., Lewis, J. L., Friedman, E. M., & Maksabedian Hernandez, E. J. (2018). Enhancing family stability during a permanent change of station: A review of disruptions and policies. RAND Corporation, https://www.rand.org/pubs/research_reports/RR2304.html

Treglown, L., Palaiou, K., Zarola, A., & Furnham, A. (2016). The dark side of resilience and burnout: A moderation-mediation model. *PloS One*, *11*(6), e0156279.

UK Parliament. (2022, August 23). UK defence personnel statistics. https://commonslibrary.parliament.uk/research-briefings/cbp-7930/

Van Der Heijde, C. M., & Van Der Heijden, B. I. J. M. (2006). A competence-based and multidimensional operationalization and measurement of employability. *Human Resource Management*, *45*(3), 449–476. https://doi.org/10.1002/hrm.20119

Van der Heijden, B., De Vos, A., Akkermans, J., Spurk, D., Semeijn, J., Van der Veldek, M., & Fugate, M. (2020). Sustainable careers across the lifespan: Moving the field forward. *Journal of Vocational Behavior*, *117*.

Vogt, D. (2011). Mental health-related beliefs as a barrier to service use for military personnel and veterans: A review. *Psychiatric Services*, *62*(2), 135–142. https://doi.org/10.1176/ps.62.2.pss6202_0135

Wald, J., Taylor, S., Asmundson, G. J., Jang, K. L., & Stapleton, J. (2006). Literature review of concepts: Psychological resiliency. [Final Report, British Columbia University]. Defense Technical Information Center. https://apps.dtic.mil/sti/citations/ADA472961

Wei, W., & Taormina, R. J. (2014). A new multidimensional measure of personal resilience and its use: Chinese Nurse resilience, organizational socialization and career success. *Nursing Inquiry*, *21*(4), 346–357. https://doi.org/10.1111/nin.12067

Weng, Q. D., & Zhu, L. (2020). Individuals' career growth within and across organizations: A review and agenda for future research. *Journal of Career Development*, *47*(3), 239–248. https://doi.org/10.1177/0894845320921951

Wilson, P. H. (2008). Defining military culture. *The Journal of Military History*, *72*(1), 11–41.

Wolfgang, T. B. (2022). Identity, transition, and high-performing veterans. [Doctoral Thesis, Thomas Jefferson University]. Jefferson Digital Commons. https://jdc.jefferson.edu/diss_masters/22/

World Economic Forum. (2015, June 17). *Who is the world's biggest employer? The answer might not be what you expect.* https://www.weforum.org/agenda/2015/06/worlds-10-biggest-employers/

Zeidner, M., Matthews, G., & Shemesh, D. O. (2016). Cognitive-social sources of wellbeing: Differentiating the roles of coping style, social support and emotional intelligence. *Journal of Happiness Studies, 17*, 2481–2501.

PART III

Enhancing the Resilience Paradigm

Scientific Implications for Future Research

12

REVISITING ASSUMPTIONS ABOUT RESILIENCE EFFECTS

Adaptive Versus Maladaptive Resilience Processes in Organizations

Tisnue Jean-Baptiste, Danielle King,
Nick Banerjee, and Ida Du

Resilience has remained a growing area of emphasis for organizational scientists over the last two decades (King et al., 2016; Linnenluecke, 2017). Drawing from important insights across psychology domains (e.g., child development, Werner, 1995; clinical, Bonanno, 2005, personality, Block & Kremen, 1996), employee resilience research has established its place as an important area of emphasis for leaders in organizations (e.g., Britt et al., 2016). Despite these advances, there are important considerations that deserve more attention. One such consideration is the universally assumed positive nature of resilience. In many cases, "adaptive" is used in the definition of the term, leaving little room for considering times when resilience may not be well-suited for a context or circumstance. For example, Luthar et al. (2000) offered one of the most highly cited perspectives on resilience today and defined this term as "a dynamic process encompassing *positive adaptation* within the context of significant adversity" (p. 1). Similarly, Masten (2001) defined resilience as "a class of phenomena characterised by *good outcomes* in spite of serious threats" (p. 228). In this chapter, we encourage organizational scholars and practitioners to revisit this assumption to consider the value of expanding definitions of resilience to distinguish between adaptive and potentially maladaptive resilience effects (i.e., the relationship between resilience and subsequent outcomes).

The way that we frame resilience effects (e.g., as always good, easy, or "right") has implications for employees' approach to resilience, such as whether they feel they have a choice to change strategies, and/or whether they worry that non-resilience will result in stigmatisation. This framing also has implications for organizational resilience climate (e.g., what behaviours and perspectives are embraced and which are stigmatised), and whether employees are comfortable sharing challenges and seeking support from managers (see Adler, 2013; King & McSpedon, 2022). Adler

DOI: 10.4324/9781003287858-16

(2013) discussed the potential for a "shadow side to resilience" when organizations solely focus on resilience but do not offer needed alternatives, support, and opportunities for structural change. Further, Mahdiani and Ungar (2021) recently discussed "the dark side of resilience" as how functional resilience is based on the degree of resilience, the context, and the type of resilience enacted. To help practically identify and address such concerns, King and McSpedon (2022) outlined the ways that resilience is currently used to exploit employees and has become a term associated with "taking one on the chin" rather than the healthy outcomes that are more closely aligned with the term's original conceptualisations. These points highlight the value in considering, with a more critical lens, the potentially adaptive versus maladaptive nature of choosing to be resilient in the face of significant stressors or trauma. Thus, this chapter extends prior work by presenting a framework for conceptualising adaptive versus maladaptive resilience effects based on resilience outcomes and discusses the utility of that perspective.

In this chapter, we use the recent definition of employee resilience presented by King et al. (2022), grounded in motivation theory, of "continued, self-regulated goal striving (e.g., behavioral and/or psychological) despite adversity (i.e., after goal frustration)" (p. 25). We use this definition in the current framework for two main reasons. First, this definition focuses on what is under an individual's control (i.e., self-regulated thoughts and behaviours). Second, contrary to many resilience definitions in other psychological domains, this definition separates success and wellbeing outcomes from the individual's enactment of resilience. This separation allows for us to consider potential harm to success and wellbeing that may come after one chooses to engage in resilience (i.e., what is here considered a maladaptive resilience process). By using this definition, we offer a more comprehensive perspective on employee resilience that allows individuals to evaluate their post-adversity choices, provides insights about outcomes that leaders can use to determine when to encourage employees to persist (e.g., employee wellbeing post-resilience), and affords organizations greater specificity in what types of resilience effects should be emphasised in organizational missions and value statements.

Because resilience is an on-going process, we encourage future practitioners and scholars to interrogate the outcomes of resilience and to consider these outcomes in organizational strategy development. This approach would entail considering the long-term longevity and health goals of the employee, team, and organization. This chapter begins with an overview of the theoretical goal and stress domains that undergird this adaptive versus maladaptive resilience framework, continues with a detailed presentation of the framework, includes an illustrative example of the framework in practice, and concludes with implications for work of the future. The overall aim of this chapter is to encourage curiosity and greater nuance about the ways we conceptualise resilience effects (e.g., as either healthy [adaptive] versus harmful [maladaptive] in nature), emphasise the value in separating resilience from "success" and "health" outcomes, and facilitate adaptive resilience processes in organizations.

Goals and coping models applied to the resilience domain

Resilience, despite adversity, is necessary to achieve long-term success in any endeavour, and a holistic, perspective on success requires prioritising health (i.e., personal and social wellbeing, Hoyt et al., 2016). Resilience is defined as positive adaptation through self-regulatory goal striving (e.g., behavioural and/ or psychological) after experienced goal frustration (i.e., adversity, King et al., 2022). Motivation is required for employees to complete tasks (e.g., responding to emails, attending team meetings, speaking with a supervisor), and is a key mechanism within resilience (e.g., Cotta & Salvador, 2020; Whitfield & Wilby, 2021). A unique feature of resilience in the motivation domain is that one's actions can only be deemed (potentially) resilient after adversity is experienced (e.g., completing tasks after an experience of discrimination at work, Fisher et al., 2019; Resnick et al., 2018).

An entity must experience goal frustration (i.e., a stressor or failure; King & Burrows, 2021) before the self-regulatory goal striving process is categorised as resilience. Once goal frustration is experienced, an individual, team, or organization decides whether and how they will engage with the goal. Self-regulated goal striving refers to the unit (e.g., individual, team, organization) engaging in goal-oriented activities over time and adjusting to observed changes in circumstances (i.e., feedback, Karoly, 1993). King et al. (2022) present a nomological network structure that incorporates resilience as part of the motivation goal process. That model shows resilience as a possible observed variable post-goal frustration. Resilience is identified by both behavioural and psychological self-regulation processes that occur during the goal-striving process. Goal outcomes are observed after the process of goal striving. In that model, goal process outcomes are distinct variables (e.g., performance and wellbeing) from resilience. This highlights the potential for adaptive (versus maladaptive) resilience by acknowledging that "success" and "health" are factors not necessarily within the control of the entity and do not always result from the experience of enacting resilience (King et al., 2022).

Goal striving is the process that bridges the gap between goals and performance. Specifically, when goal difficulty (i.e., task complexity) is higher, an entity will likely have lower performance (Kanfer et al., 2017). Furthermore, the less time allotted to a task, the greater the level of goal difficulty (Austin & Vancouver, 1996). It has also been shown that overly specific and difficult goal setting may be harmful to an entity, compared to setting more realistic goals. Further Locke and Latham (2002) assert that "…the highest level of effort [occurs] when the task was moderately difficult, and the lowest levels occurred when the task was very hard." We emphasise here that, similar to the notion that there are boundaries to the adaptive nature of goal choices (e.g., goal difficulty level), there are also boundaries to the health of goal pursuit process decisions after adversity.

In addition to considering the role of goal properties on goal outcomes, organizations can simultaneously consider the effect that stress has on employees' performance and wellbeing. Specifically, studies have identified a distinction between adaptive (e.g., mindfulness and reflection) and maladaptive (e.g., catastrophising and rumination) coping. The former is linked to positive psychological wellbeing and the latter is associated with greater emotional distress after difficulty (e.g., Brown et al., 2005; Fischer et al., 2021; Holton et al., 2015; Thompson et al., 2010).

In understanding the relevance of long- and short-term goal setting, balanced goal difficulty levels, and coping strategy choice in goal outcomes, this chapter uses goal and coping theories to form a foundation for the presentation of an adaptive versus maladaptive resilience framework. Specifically, in terms of goals, this work presents the idea that resilience can be viewed as a proximal (short-term) goal outcome that employees aim for that is linked to more distal (longer-term) goal outcomes (e.g., success and wellbeing; see King et al., 2022). Further, in terms of coping, strategies enacted to support resilience may be facilitating or harming more distal goal striving outcomes (e.g., performance and health). Thus, we encourage researchers and practitioners to consider not only whether resilience is accomplished, but also whether the subsequent experiences and outcomes of employees are healthy in nature when determining the adaptive nature and appropriateness of resilience.

Introducing a framework on adaptive versus maladaptive resilience effects

Resilience research has significantly evolved over the years, with a greater focus on adults and work effects in recent years. Initially, resilience studies focused on identifying factors associated with positive outcomes for children exposed to adverse conditions (Garmezy, 1991; Rutter, 1979; Werner, 1995). Specifically, the initial focus was on identifying protective factors (e.g., socioeconomic status, personality, social support; Rutter, 2000). This line of work then led scholars to consider resilience effects in other contexts (e.g., the military) and across levels of analysis (e.g., across the lifespan, across job levels). As the resilience domain has developed, foundational process-oriented research questions have emerged: What are the outcomes/effects of resilience and how do we know whether these are beneficial/desired? The process-oriented approach to resilience allows for consideration of more distal outcomes that emerge after adversity.

In defining resilience, scholars generally agreed on two key features of this concept: (1) exposure to adversity and (2) the experience of "positive adaptation" post-adversity (see Fisher et al., 2019; Luthar, 2006). Further, positive adaptation is operationalised as a "good outcome" and "normal development" under challenging conditions (Masten, 2001; Toland & Carrigan, 2011). King and Burrows (2021) introduced the idea of adaptive enactment of resilience as "assessing the situation and adjusting lower-level goals towards higher-level goal attainment" (p. 106), which counters the notion of resilience as simply "overcoming" or "bouncing back" and begins to expand what is considered adaptive. In line with this conceptualisation, one who decides to alter sub-goal plans may be pursuing the path that is best for maintaining higher-level goal attainment. This idea challenges resiliency narratives of "staying the course no matter what" and showcases a new outlook of "staying the course" and adjusting "the how" when needed.

In a similar manner, we assert that a range of possible goal pursuit experiences post-adversity may be adaptive and healthy, while others are not. As one explores resilience beyond the assumed "positive" conceptualisation, it becomes clear that the designation of a resilient outcome as "adaptive" or "maladaptive" requires time to observe more distal outcomes. Applying this self-regulated and goal-oriented dynamic lens to resilience affords designating resilience as *one* choice, rather than always the *best* choice. This encourages a focus on how one overcomes and how the process of overcoming affects the individual, versus assuming resilience always leads to goal accomplishment and health and, thus, is always adaptive. Individuals may share similar trajectories in their resilience experience yet demonstrate different outcomes (i.e., adaptive, maladaptive; Cicchetti, 2010). Thus, when faced with goal frustrations, it may be most beneficial for one person to disengage from the goal, for example due to the interference of overwhelming emotion-based rumination (Ntoumanis et al., 2014), while others may manage the experience with little interruption to their usual cognitions and behaviours. This perspective encourages clarity in distinguishing what is beneficial from what is resilience, in any situation. At times, these two may overlap, but the assumption that they are always the same should not be universally held.

The idea that resilience may, at times, be maladaptive is a more recent idea. Thus, the resilience domain would benefit from a more complex consideration of how enacting resilience shapes employee and organizational outcomes (e.g., success and wellbeing). There is a widely-held assumption in this domain that everything "good" is resilience, and researchers have begun to challenge this labelling (see Britt et al., 2016). One way that we can do so is by conceptualising what a maladaptive resilience process may entail. Parallel to the consideration of certain forms of coping as maladaptive (e.g., repression and alcoholism; e.g., Brown et al., 2005), we suggest that certain behavioural and psychological outcomes/effects of resilience, too, can indicate maladaptive resilience (e.g., resilience leading to stress and burnout and/or leading individuals away from goal accomplishment). We argue that a "bigger picture"/longer-term perspective on one's resilience process is necessary to categorise resilience effects as adaptive or maladaptive, and that these processes may not be initially or immediately apparent in the resilience experience (i.e., during the initial enactment of resilience).

The potential for a maladaptive resilience process is suggested by theoretical and practical insights. Theoretically, self-regulation theory (Demetriou, 2000) and conservation of resources theory (Hobfoll, 2011), two theories often used in the examination of employee resilience effects, highlight that resources are finite and that resilience requires the engagement of one's resources. At a certain point, choosing to engage in resilience may deplete resources beyond one's capacity, fostering vulnerability rather than wellbeing and success. At times, enacting resilience may create more stress, burnout, loss, and so on, than would goal abandonment. Thus, the resilience domain should consider this possibility, and question the myth of resilience as the assumed best choice in any case by considering the observed relation of resilience to more distal outcomes for the entity enacting resilience (e.g., individuals, teams, organizations). In fact, considering what is more beneficial for success and wellbeing can further our understandings of the value of the resilience domain by encouraging the determination of whether resilience is a choice approached with a clear perspective on longer-term goals (e.g., retention of top talent, organizational growth, and employee wellbeing).

Illustrative examples

Overall, there is value in considering how psychological and behavioural resilience is affecting subsequent employee performance and wellbeing outcomes. *What might this look like in practice?*

Mary is an employee at an insurance company. She has been working there for over 10 years and is accustomed to a hybrid work structure to get her work done. Recently, she was promoted to a managerial role, where she is in charge of overseeing a small group of employees in the customer service department. Employees' tasks include taking phone calls, filing claims, and addressing customer complaints. Mary makes sure that her team is trained to handle calls effectively and efficiently and reach their call quotas. Recently, the company announced its plans to transition to a fully in-person working schedule, in which Mary and her team would be working completely in the office. Mary is not accustomed to reporting to and working in the office every day, and she is still transitioning into her new position. She has performance targets that she must meet in her new role, and she faces multiple work stressors (e.g., time pressure and increased workload) that she must overcome to reach her career goals.

Adaptive Resilience: After receiving the news that her company was transitioning to fully in-person work, Mary initially felt overwhelmed by the change in her work environment as well as her role. However, she reached out to her supervisor after learning about the changes and explained her concerns to them. Her supervisor listens to Mary's concerns and gives her relevant guidance, encouragement, and feedback. Afterwards, Mary is able to reflect on potential benefits of the changes to her workplace environment. Mary attempts to persist in her new role and work structure, and she connects with her team to discuss expectations of their roles and of one another. These steps help Mary's team establish a mutual understanding and work together through the hardships with little disruptions to their levels of stress, performance, or satisfaction. During the next performance review, Mary's supervisor shares that they are impressed by the way that she was able to manage the drastic changes. Mary is able to apply the lessons learned in this experience to her future work to help her meet other work targets as well.

Maladaptive Resilience: After receiving the news that her company was transitioning to fully in-person work, Mary initially felt overwhelmed by the change in her work environment and role. However, after learning about the changes, she reached out to her supervisor and explained her concerns to them. Her supervisor listens to Mary's concerns and gives her relevant guidance, encouragement, and feedback. Afterwards, Mary attempts to persist in her new role and work structure, yet she consistently ruminates on her experience and feels increased self-doubt, unfairness, and decreases in her work satisfaction. Outside of her working hours, the stressors from her work life carry over and negatively impact her wellbeing. This emotional distress leads to irregular sleep patterns, which persist and negatively affect her quality of work. Occasionally, she works during the night to ensure that she is completing all her work tasks, significantly increasing the number of hours she spends on work-related activities. During the next performance review, her supervisor shares that they are overall impressed with her performance. However, Mary knows she is experiencing burnout, decreased motivation, and worry that continuing on this path will further harm her work and personal experiences and outcomes.

In both examples, Mary enacted resilience. Thus, current theoretical perspectives and measures of resilience would categorise the two examples above as equivalent on resilience. However, we encourage a more nuanced consideration of, not only what resilience means but also, what resilience means for the entity enacting it (i.e., what costs are associated with the choice to be resilient), when designating (planned or experienced) resilience as adaptive (or maladaptive)

Implications and future research directions

The concept of maladaptive resilience provides an avenue for new research questions and practical considerations. Rather than focusing solely on positive outcomes of resilience behaviours, questions can be raised about the extent to which resilient behaviours contribute to undesired outcomes. Situational factors could also be explored to determine when individuals are more likely to exhibit resilience at the expense of their wellbeing. Finally, individual differences may reveal how certain characteristics are more often associated with maladaptive resilience.

While this discussion of resilience has focused on the effects of resilience at the individual level, a compelling direction for research is to study interpersonal or intergroup effects of resilience. Using the traditional adaptive approach to resilience, behavioural outcomes and goal enactment by an individual (or group) could positively influence the goal processes of other individuals (or groups). For example, the resilient completion of a project by one entity may allow for progress through improvement and/or implementation for others. In that case, successful enactment of the original goal, "completing the project," is crucial for others to pursue and complete their goals.

In contrast, the proposed inclusion of maladaptive in the framework of resilience allows us to consider how resilient goal pursuit can negatively impact others.

Past research has shown that individual goal pursuits are sometimes accompanied by competitiveness and potential sabotaging behaviours (e.g., Huang et al., 2019). In some instances, the negative effects of resilience on others may even be unintentional. One example is an individual's successful attainment of a promotion at work. The goal of earning a promotion may have required a great deal of resilience, but it could have also prevented another individual who was working towards promotion from achieving their promotion goal. In sum, closer investigation into the effects of resilience on others can provide more clarity about the resilience construct and whether and how one could integrate intentional harms to others into the conceptualisation of maladaptive resilience.

Approaching resilience using an expanded (i.e., adaptive and maladaptive) conceptualisation also encourages researchers to reconsider how they measure resilience. Self-reports are often used and there is a distinction between an individual's capacity for resilience and the demonstration of resilience (Britt et al., 2016). Regarding "capacity for resilience," it may be necessary to critically examine, and potentially re-examine, current scales to consider one's capacity for maladaptive resilience (e.g., including new items that conveys the idea: "I would not give up on my goal, even if it made me extremely stressed and tired at work"). This could lead a new "maladaptive resilience" category of items and require validation studies like those conducted by Cheng et al. (2020). There is also an opportunity to pursue research modelling and measurement of people's awareness of whether resilience effects are adaptive or maladaptive in their experience. This may encourage integration of research from the self-regulation, self-awareness, and also the wellbeing domain that provides insights on whether, when, and how resilience types can be detected in our lived experiences.

Considering "demonstration of resilience," longitudinal data collection can provide particularly useful information for researchers. Such assessments can provide insights about thoughts and behaviours throughout the goal process (i.e., during the goal setting phase, pre-goal frustration, post-goal frustration, at goal completion, and/or post-goal completion). With an adaptive versus maladaptive conceptualisation of resilience, goal abandonment and post-goal frustration abandonment may be evaluated as well. Further, "negative" outcomes (e.g., stress levels, feelings of burnout, maladaptive coping strategies) could be assessed across time to determine rates of maladaptive resilience detection, development, and intervention.

Further, organizations can use a more comprehensive understanding of resilience as potentially adaptive or maladaptive to design interventions for wellbeing and performance. Organizations can change broader cultural norms by promoting adaptive resilience and preventing the creation of an environment and climate that nurtures maladaptive resilience. This includes emphasising the importance of goal completion and positive adaptation after adverse experiences, while also emphasizing employee satisfaction, emotions, work-non-work balance, and health. This could entail the downward adjustment of goals when necessary and sharing the negative consequences of maladaptive resilience behaviours to raise awareness of what to look for and why this is important. In terms of specific interventions, organizations can implement workshops on forms of resilience to influence policy change and employee behaviours. Organizations can also host open discussions regarding adverse employee experiences and potential goal abandonment to shift the assumption that resilience in harmful experiences is the best or only route forward or a marker of employee success and strength.

In tandem, organizational leaders can be trained to identify specific examples of adaptive and maladaptive resilience. Using that knowledge, leaders can adjust assigned and shared goals to accommodate employees and encourage them to reflect on their wellbeing after goal frustrations occur. In turn, leaders may need to re-assign tasks to other team members or themselves when an individual experiences certain adverse experiences (i.e., traumatic life events), as one way to support healthy forms of resilience and a culture that allows space for managing difficulty in healthy ways. Furthermore, leaders can assess the psychological condition of their subordinated and their team's goal processes more frequently to determine whether success and wellbeing are being harmed and when and if changes are needed.

Lastly, employees may use this framework to identify past instances of maladaptive resilience and its effects on their wellbeing. This conceptualisation provides a deeper understanding of the human experience which may serve as a guide for adaptive and maladaptive resilience experience reflection and learning; this should allow employees to evaluate their tendencies and behaviours as one useful form of resilience feedback that can inform future thoughts and decisions. Regardless of organizational, leadership, or team adjustment to adaptive versus maladaptive resilience experiences, employees may also benefit from expressing concerns and explaining negative consequences of past resilience experiences to leaders (e.g., how these decisions increased burnout and reduced productivity). Thus, offering insights into a more functional and healthier route forward.

Conclusion

Overall, this work asserts that resilience may be an adaptive or maladaptive choice made in the goal-pursuit process and that this designation depends upon the effect that the enactment of resilience has on subsequent entity (e.g., individual or team) outcomes (e.g., performance and health). Through grounding this framework in the goal-setting and coping domains, this chapter calls into question the assumed "positive" and "adaptive" nature of resilience to encourage more nuanced conceptualisations and models. Although all enacted resilience may serve as a "positive" accomplishment—in that, by definition, goal pursuit is maintained after adversity—it is here argued that researchers and practitioners should not stigmatise non-resilience as "failure" or "bad" since, in some cases, resilience may harm longer-term outcomes and subsequent goal accomplishment. We encourage more research, practical consideration, and theoretical work on the role of health in interpreting resilience effects and the role of (self- and other-other) wellbeing in deciding how one navigates (and is encouraged to navigate) adversity.

References

Adler, A. B. (2013). Resilience in a military occupational health context: Directions for future research. In R. R. Sinclair, & T. W. Britt (Eds.), *Building psychological resilience in military personnel: Theory and practice* (pp. 223–235). American Psychological Association.

Austin, J. T., & Vancouver, J. B. (1996). Goal constructs in psychology: Structure, process, and content. *Psychological Bulletin, 120*(3), 338–375.

Block, J., & Kremen, A. M. (1996). IQ and ego-resiliency: Conceptual and empirical connections and separateness. *Journal of Personality and Social Psychology, 70*(2), 349.

Bonanno, G. A. (2005). Resilience in the face of potential trauma. *Current Directions in Psychological Science, 14*(3), 135–138.

Britt, T. W., Shen, W., Sinclair, R. R., Grossman, M. R., & Klieger, D. M. (2016). How much do we really know about employee resilience? *Industrial and Organizational Psychology, 9*(2), 378–404.

Brown, S. P., Westbrook, R. A., & Challagalla, G. (2005). Good cope, bad cope: Adaptive and maladaptive coping strategies following a critical negative work event. *The Journal of Applied Psychology, 90*(4), 792–798.

Cheng, M. Y., Wang, M. J., Chang, M. Y., Zhang, R. X., Gu, C. F., & Zhao, Y. H. (2020). Relationship between resilience and insomnia among the middle-aged and elderly: Mediating role of maladaptive emotion regulation strategies. *Psychology, Health & Medicine, 25*(10), 1266–1277.

Cicchetti, D. (2010). Resilience under conditions of extreme stress: A multilevel perspective. *World Psychiatry, 9*(3), 145–154.

Cotta, D., & Salvador, F. (2020). Exploring the antecedents of organizational resilience practices– a transactive memory systems approach. *International Journal of Operations & Production Management, 40*(9), 1531–1559.

Demetriou, A. (2000). Organization and development of self-understanding and self-regulation: Toward a general theory. In *Handbook of self-regulation* (pp. 209–251). Academic Press.

Fischer, R., Scheunemann, J., & Moritz, S. (2021). Coping strategies and subjective well-being: Context matters. *Journal of Happiness Studies, 22*(8), 3413–3434.

Fisher, D. M., Ragsdale, J. M., & Fisher, E. C. (2019). The importance of definitional and temporal issues in the study of resilience. *Applied Psychology, 68*(4), 583–620.

Garmezy, N. (1991). Resiliency and vulnerability to adverse developmental outcomes associated with poverty. *American Behavioral Scientist, 34*(4), 416–430.

Hobfoll, S. E. (2011). Conservation of resources theory: Its implication for stress, health, and resilience. In S. Folkman (Ed.), *The Oxford handbook of stress, health, and coping* (pp. 127–147). Oxford University Press.

Holton, M. K., Barry, A. E., & Chaney, J. D. (2015). Employee stress management: An examination of adaptive and maladaptive coping strategies on employee health. *Work (Reading, Mass.), 53*(2), 299–305.

Hoyt, M. A., Gamarel, K. E., Saigal, C. S., & Stanton, A. L. (2016). Goal navigation, approach-oriented coping, and adjustment in young men with testicular cancer. *Annals of Behavioral Medicine, 50*(4), 572–581.

Huang, S., Lin, S. C., & Zhang, Y. (2019). When individual goal pursuit turns competitive: How we sabotage and coast. *Journal of Personality and Social Psychology, 117*(3), 605–620.

Kanfer, R., Frese, M., & Johnson, R. E. (2017). Motivation related to work: A century of progress. *Journal of Applied Psychology, 102*(3), 338–355.

Karoly, P. (1993). Mechanisms of self-regulation: A systems view. *Annual Review of Psychology, 44*(1), 23–52.

King, D. D., & Burrows, D. (2021). Resilience in the goal hierarchy: Strategy change as a form of perseverance. In *Work life after failure?: How employees bounce back, learn, and recover from work-related setbacks* (pp. 99–108). Emerald Publishing Limited.

King, D. D., & McSpedon, M. (2022). What leaders get wrong about resilience. *Harvard Business Review*.

King, D. D., DeShon, R. P., Phetmisy, C. N., & Burrows, D. (2022). What is resilience? Offering construct clarity to address "Quicksand" and "Shadow Side" resilience concerns. In *Examining the paradox of occupational stressors: Building resilience or creating depletion* (Vol. 20, pp. 25–50). Emerald Publishing Limited.

King, D. D., Newman, A., & Luthans, F. (2016). Not if, but when we need resilience in the workplace. *Journal of Organizational Behavior, 37*(5), 782–786.

Linnenluecke, M. K. (2017). Resilience in business and management research: A review of influential publications and a research agenda. *International Journal of Management Reviews, 19*(1), 4–30.

Locke, E. A., & Latham, G. P. (2002). Building a practically useful theory of goal setting and task motivation: A 35-year odyssey. *American Psychologist, 57*(9), 705–717.

Luthar, S. S. (2006). Resilience in development: A synthesis of research across five decades. In D. Cicchetti, & D. J. Cohen (Eds.), *Developmental psychopathology: Risk, disorder, and adaptation* (pp. 739–795). John Wiley & Sons, Inc.

Luthar, S. S., Cicchetti, D., & Becker, B. (2000). The construct of resilience: A critical evaluation and guidelines for future work. *Child Development, 71*(3), 543–562.

Mahdiani, H., & Ungar, M. (2021). The dark side of resilience. *Adversity and Resilience Science, 2*(3), 147–155.

Masten, A. S. (2001). Ordinary magic: Resilience processes in development. *American Psychologist, 56*(3), 227.

Ntoumanis, N., Healy, L. C., Sedikides, C., Smith, A. L., & Duda, J. L. (2014). Self-regulatory responses to unattainable goals: The role of goal motives. *Self and Identity, 13*(5), 594–612.

Resnick, B., Gwyther, L. P., & Roberto, K. A. (2018). Conclusion: The key to successful aging. In *Resilience in aging* (pp. 401–415). Springer.

Rutter, M. (1979). *Fifteen thousand hours: Secondary schools and their effects on children.* Harvard University Press.

Rutter, M. (2000). Resilience reconsidered: Conceptual considerations, empirical findings, and policy implications. In J. P. Shonkoff, & S. J. Meisels (Eds.), *Handbook of early intervention* (2nd ed., pp. 651–681). Cambridge University Press.

Thompson, R. J., Mata, J., Jaeggi, S. M., Buschkuehl, M., Jonides, J., & Gotlib, I. H. (2010). Maladaptive coping, adaptive coping, and depressive symptoms: Variations across age and depressive state. *Behaviour Research and Therapy, 48*(6), 459–466.

Toland, J., & Carrigan, D. (2011). Educational psychology and resilience: New concept, new opportunities. *School Psychology International, 32*(1), 95–106.

Werner, E. E. (1995). Resilience in development. *Current Directions in Psychological Science, 4*(3), 81–84.

Whitfield, K. M., & Wilby, K. J. (2021). Developing grit, motivation, and resilience: To give up on giving in. *Pharmacy, 9*(2), 109.

13

ROLE OF ORGANIZATIONS TO BUILD RESILIENT EMPLOYEES

Radhika Thanki and D. M. Pestonjee

Organizations have to constantly survive through volatility, uncertainty, complexity, and ambiguity in order to sustain, commonly known as a VUCA world. Organizations had barely cracked this code when the entire world was hit by the COVID-19 pandemic. Significant political, economic, societal, and industrial developments made it difficult for them to foresee future market shifts, and the capability to remodel was seen as vital to success. The experience of disruption led to the stipulation of a new acronym that truly describes the present business scenario—RUPT—which stands for rapid, unpredictable, paradoxical, and tangled.

In the last couple of years, nations, economies, and enterprises have experienced a great deal of change at such a rapid rate that changes have overlapped with one another like waves coming from several sources and smashing in the middle of the ocean. Despite all conceivable study, planning, and calculated future predictions, the unpredictable nature still prevails. Governments and businesses are forced to consider short-term aims while working towards long-term objectives in a way that does not compromise the bigger picture. Since everything is interconnected, it is challenging to ensure that all of the issues are fixed because they are so entangled.

The world economy was still recovering from the financial implication of the pandemic when it was hit by the Russian invasion of Ukraine. This has not only resulted in weaker growth and stronger inflation but it will also have a long-lasting damage to the supply chain, intensifying the policy trade-offs facing central banks around the world.

Various events in the last couple of years have put businesses through rigorous strategic-resilience tests. These crises have exposed weaknesses in the companies' strategic resilience. Coca-Cola, Target, Boeing, TATA Group, and The Times of India are just a few of the many companies with histories dating back more than a century that have weathered several crises, most recently COVID-19. It

DOI: 10.4324/9781003287858-17

is encouraging to see how these and numerous other organizations have risen to the occasion, modifying their operations to safeguard their personnel while still providing for their clients and communities despite the numerous disasters. While some of their rock-solid plans may have failed miserably, some sophomoric ideas might have taken off and produced previously unheard-of growth. But what remains common to most of these organizations is resilience.

Due to the pandemic, businesses have had to demonstrate their strategic resilience. It was a painful waking for many. Today, accelerating digital changes, preventing and mitigating cyberthreats, and establishing stakeholder trust equality are frequently the contexts in which enterprises seek to promote resilience. All of these are essential elements in building strong, future-proof organizations and managing risk. Innovation in business models has become the main differentiator for those who have prospered during the pandemic.

Employees, however, are a crucial component of organizational resilience that are sometimes overlooked. With the advent of the present global crisis, the necessity for employee resilience has become more apparent. The perceived stigma involved with seeking assistance for stress/coping issues as well as with admitting one needs help in the first-place results in an ongoing struggle for the employees. It is vital to give employees the tools that they need to adjust to change so that they can remain focused and productive during and after any turbulence. There can be no resilient organization without resilient employees.

Resilience is a skill that workers can employ to handle stress and turbulence at work. Resilience can have advantageous effects on both at a personal and organizational level when it is developed and maintained well. However, it is vital to distinguish employee resilience from psychological resilience. The former stresses that the organization's responsibility is encouraging and supporting the development of resilience by referring to the employees' capacity to actively respond to, adapt to, and evolve (Tonkin et al., 2018).

The ability of an organization to carry out its duties while promptly recovering from adversity by mobilising and acquiring the necessary resources is referred to as organizational resilience (Hillmann & Guenther, 2021). As a result, an organization's resources and resilience are strongly tied. Human resources, one of an organization's most crucial resources, unavoidably have an impact on organizational resilience.

Organizations could opt for either a reactive approach or a proactive approach to resilience. With initiatives that only support employees after they have encountered difficulties or reached their breaking points, many firms today only address employee resilience in a reactive manner. Such actions are crucial components of the resilience puzzle, but preventive interventions that are part of the organizational culture are probably better suited to deal with the underlying causes of resilience problems and produce better results.

The mental health and welfare of those who are employed, self-employed, or not working have generally declined. Employee burnout, which manifests as a sense of tiredness, mental distance from work, and decreased job performance, has become more noticeable in recent years. Burnout is becoming an increasingly common workplace ailment due to pandemic-related stressors. According to a recent study on employee burnout conducted by Indeed (2021), 52% of employee participants reported having a feeling of burnout, and 67% reported that the feeling had deteriorated over the last 12 months. This has significantly added to the employer's cost, which is evident from absenteeism, presenteeism, and employee turnover.

When an employee shows up to work while sick, they engage in presenteeism and do not work as well as they could. Working while ill has grown more widespread due to the rise in remote employment during the epidemic. Employees may be prone to overcompensate or amplify their online visibility while dealing with mental health issues if they aren't physically present in the office. Even if they might benefit from time off, most people either never or almost never go to work when their mental health is poor.

According to research in the United Kingdom by Deloitte (2022), presenteeism, due to poor mental health, is the largest contributor to employer's cost. This cost of mental health related to presenteeism was about 4 to 4.5 times the cost of mental health–related absenteeism in 2021 for organizations.

One of the reasons why workers might not want to take time off for their mental health is the stigma around it. The accessibility of mental health professionals is also a concern. India has 0.75 psychiatrists per 100,000 people, which is below the optimal ratio of anything over 3 psychiatrists per 100,000 people. This evaluation is very conservative, based on figures showing that there are 6 psychiatrists for every 100,000 individuals in high-income countries. If 3 psychiatrists per 100,000 people is the desired ratio, then 36,000 psychiatrists are needed to achieve that target. Based on the country's present population, India now lacks 27,000 psychiatrists and only generates, on average, 700 each year (Garg et al., 2019).

In such a scenario, organizations will have to step up to proactively help its employees by building the resilience of employees at work. Development of resilience at the workplace has led to a number of benefits for the employees. People in the organization gain from the enhancement of resilience at work in a variety of ways such as contentment at work, employee happiness, organizational commitment, and employee performance (Luthans & Youssef, 2007; Luthans et al., 2007). Current research on resilience indicates that it is favourably related with a variety of behavioural and psychological outcomes such as positive attitude, lower distress, and optimism in thinking (Kumpfer, 1999; Utsey et al., 2008).

Higher workforce resilience, decreased absenteeism from work, fewer mishaps in the organization, better retention of workforce, increased workforce commitment, efficiency and performance, strengthened brand of the organization, effective associations among employees at work, along with self-satisfaction are all favourable results linked to positive psychological wellbeing and considered as business benefits of a healthy workforce (Avey et al., 2010; Bevan, 2010; Harter et al., 2004; Wright & Cropanzano, 2000). With respect to work, it is these favourable results that lead to increased employee engagement, consumer fulfilment, and enhanced productivity, eventually leading to the success of the organization (Harter et al., 2004; Robertson & Cooper, 2010).

Resilience has been shown to be a significant predictor of wellbeing, even in the long term (Barendregt et al., 2015; Davydov et al., 2010; Schultze-Lutter et al., 2016). While resilience of employees at work helps improve their psychological wellbeing and ultimately make the organization resilient at large, the question is what can organizations do to improve the resilience at work of its employees? Organizations today have numerous mental health interventions, few of which are mentioned below:

- Corporate wellness programmes that emphasise work–life balance in terms of no meeting Fridays or pen down days once every quarter. As part of these programs, certain organizations also have wellness sessions that include yoga, meditation, stress management sessions, and so on.
- Awareness programs that emphasise on employees learning more about mental health and its effects in order to break the stigma around it. These programmes encourage employees to come forward not just for themselves but also but also making them more compassionate towards colleagues who are in need of some assistance.
- Screening initiatives help to identify employees who may be at risk for or already experiencing mental health disorders, which enables early intervention and problem prevention.
- Employee assistance programmes include providing counselling services that may be outsourced to mental health professionals and subscriptions to mobile applications that offer some counselling services round the clock.
- Employee wellbeing programmes can include in-house, one-on-one counselling sessions and investing time and resources into employee wellbeing by relieving the pressures that impact them in the first place.

These programs have helped in numerous ways to build the mental health in general and psychological wellbeing in particular of the employees. But organizations will have to become more innovative given the unpredictable nature of the environment we live in that causes poor mental health.

The most common negative aspect of mental health that employees experience at the workplace is stress. Stress occurs when people face demands that are beyond their realm of knowledge or abilities. It can be further classified as acute stress and chronic stress. While there is a general perception that stress is bad, this is not always the case. Stress in its positive form—eustress—can improve health, motivation, performance, and emotional wellbeing.

One's genetic makeup and developmental journey are important in determining their responses to external, environmental, organizational, and interpersonal stressors. These potential sources of stress are always present, but it is the interaction of stressors that governs if an incident will be worrying or otherwise.

According to the Mayo Clinic (2016), stress induces reactions on the body such as a racing heart, heavy breathing, and increases muscle tension. This is a natural response that occurs on a timely basis when there is imminent danger, family issues, or emergency situations. For short-term situations, it is beneficial to our health and can help us cope such situations. Such a response is designed to keep us ready to react in dangerous/emergency situations. When stress becomes regular and persistent, then this very response is injurious to health. Prolonged stress can cause symptoms such as irritability, anxiety, depression, headaches, and insomnia.

Pestonjee and Muncherji (1991) discuss the different ailments that executives are susceptible to, as well as how human resource department interventions may aid in boosting the executive's overall health. Prolonged stress can cause symptoms such as irritability, anxiety, depression, headaches, and insomnia. Cooper and Quick (2017) point out that stress is directly or indirectly linked to 7 of the 10 leading causes of death in all developed nations including the United States and the United Kingdom. In 2019, the World Health Organization designated workplace burnout as a work-related reality in its latest revision of the *International Classification of Diseases* (World Health Organization, 2019).

Natural progression has trained us to adapt to changing environmental circumstances. Our body, for example, adapts to chilly or warm weather, a lack of adequate liquids, and high-altitudes. Similarly, we can get accustomed to both favourable and unfavourable situations so that we experience everything between ecstasy and misery. Our emotional system is utmost sensitive to fresh incidents, and these feelings fade with time.

Interventions at an individual level

Everyone experiences challenges in life, some might be minor, while others would be major with significant impact, such as death of loved one, life altering event, or major illness. The impact of these events might be severe and long lasting for some, and others may be able to move on from major events relatively quickly. While such events trigger several thoughts and emotions, people generally adapt over a span of time. This response to events that enables people to overcome major event is due to resilience. People with abundant resilience are flexible in the way that they respond to stress.

Sharma and Cooper (2016) suggest that stress responses can be due to individual factors and not merely due to external stressors. Such individual factors influence choice of occupation, vulnerability to stress, and ability to cope with stress. Failure to cope with stress leads to burnout. Individual characteristics are developed over a span of time, and arise from differences in demography, personality, education, social setup, and personal expectations.

Researchers agree that resilience is a trait that develops in response to risk rather than something that people are born with. This suggests that, based on reciprocal links between people and their environments, resilience is not a fixed attribute and may be learnt and strengthened at any age (Gillespie et al., 2007). Individuals constantly make efforts to learn from their experiences and strive to become resilient such that their mental health does not get affected. Individuals can work towards various aspects to strengthen their resilience and thus have thriving mental health.

- **Foresight:** This is what motivates people, including their sense of purpose and life direction. Along with a sense of confidence in their ability to accomplish the goals they set for themselves; this also includes their personal vision of what they hope to become. This leads to a sense of self-worth and personal effectiveness, as well as their ideals and capacity for commitment and initiative. These serve as a lighthouse to keep people on the right track throughout time. This is especially crucial in trying times because having a clear vision and goals will make it easier to spot opportunities, choose the best course of action, and emerge from the situation stronger than before. When people have a clear understanding of goals, it is simpler for them to make quick decisions when faced with tough choices. When they make a decision, they are able to stick with it, which makes them feel more confident in their skills.
- **Emotional Equilibrium:** How well one can control emotions in challenging or stressful times can be referred to as emotional equilibrium. People need to be self-aware enough to recognise how they are reacting in certain situations and to use strategies to maintain a positive outlook. People who can keep their cool in stressful situations are better equipped to spot opportunities, continue working towards their goals, and keep their attention on what matters. However, maintaining our composure not only affects our own mental condition but also inspires others, especially when they most need it.
- **Realistic Optimism:** Realistic optimists are certain that they will succeed, but they also understand that they must work hard, plan well, persevere, and use the correct techniques to make it happen. They are aware that they must carefully consider how they will overcome challenges. Their self-assurance in their capacity to do tasks only grows as a result of this practise.
- **Rationalizing:** How confident one is in their capacity to deal with unforeseen challenges and quickly adapt to change depends greatly on their rationalizing skills. This includes the capacity to be resourceful, think critically, recognise possibilities, and adopt an action-oriented mindset to work towards objectives in the best way possible. People who are able to reason persuasively under pressure are better able to maintain concentration, think critically, and be innovative. When times are rough, it also enables people to effectively examine long-term objectives and priorities.
- **Physical Health:** Studies have demonstrated the link between physical health and wellbeing. The most challenging health conditions to manage are those that have a continuing impact on a person's life. People who take an active interest in their health are more likely to be highly aware of the requirements their bodies have for optimal health. Maintaining mental acuity and enhancing brain

plasticity through health investments makes it easier to quickly adapt to varying situations. People can make good use of their time and resources by making sure they form healthy food and exercise habits, as well as restful sleep, in order to assist themselves accomplish their personal health goals.

- **Determination:** This is the capacity to persist through adversity and resume one's course after falling off. This shows a level of toughness that enables people to continue trying and moving forward, regardless of the difficulty—be it a sickness or a setback at work. It's crucial to keep realistic expectations of one's capabilities and knowledge of boundaries when things are difficult. One is motivated to persevere when things get difficult by having faith in one's capacity to handle challenging circumstances. Drawing inspiration from prior successes helps people believe that they can persevere and succeed in spite of the difficulties they encounter.

- **Partnership:** The crucial desire for secure and intimate connections with others that the human brain has is at the heart of partnership. Having a support system made up of friends, lovers, family, co-workers, and even pets can have a significant impact. Collaboration includes being able to manage the perception of others along with self-perspectives so that individuals can stay in a space where they can effectively work with those around them and have meaningful relationships. The key is to expand support network and be open to experience the rewards of supporting others as well. Asking for help can build meaningful and mutually beneficial relationships where individuals can receive and provide support.

- **Gratitude:** People who consistently express appreciation by pausing to think about and reflect on the things they're grateful for feel happier. People acknowledge the goodness in their lives with gratitude. People typically realise that the source of that kindness is at least largely external to themselves during this process. Because of this, feeling grateful also fosters a connection with something bigger than oneself, such as other people, the natural world, or a greater power. Living life with gratitude helps one notice the little wins—getting that right seat on the train, an unfamiliar person helping you put away the grocery bags in car, or the moonlight while lying on the bed at the end of tiresome day. Each of these small moments strings together to create a web of wellbeing. Wood et al. (2010) have shown that gratitude is instrumental in increasing perceived social support and reducing stress levels, if used as an intervention. Mills et al. (2015) found that gratitude is associated with better quality of sleep, less mood disturbances, and better cardiac function among patients with risk of heart failure. A few studies on gratitude have shown its relationship with wellbeing (Emmons & Crumpler, 2000; Fredrickson, 2004; McCullough et al., 2002). In their review on gratitude, Wood et al. (2010) posit that howsoever we look at gratitude, as a moral affect, as a tendency to overvalue the help given by others, as a tendency to count the blessings in one's life, gratitude has a significant and causal relationship with health and wellbeing.

Nowak et al. (2000) suggests that individual stress-management interventions are effective in reducing negative outcomes for individuals only and not necessarily the organization in terms of absenteeism, turnover, productivity, or job satisfaction. The need is to modify stressful features of the working environment as well as help each employee to learn managing stress through improved appraisal and coping skills. The ability to cope improves the quality of life for an individual and, subsequently, the whole organization.

New world calls for new interventions

Why is it that when one hears a particular song, they get transported elsewhere? The same mundane work, which otherwise was taxing, today feels exhilarating? Why is it that sometimes, one feels a sense of calm in the midst of an otherwise tense work schedule? All these moments are nothing other than spirituality. It is during these instants that one feels taken away from their surroundings and yet be present in the moment, where one finds meaning in their work and how the random dots connect to make a whole picture. Spirituality thus becomes part of something like mystical realism where the possibility of attaining is real and yet the path towards achieving the same is quite mystical.

Every individual through their lifetime tries to decode their purpose of their life. When quite young, children formulate their purpose of life in various career options by answering to the unescapable question of "What do you want to become when you grow up?" As individuals grow up, they frame their purpose of life in materialistic achievements such as a vehicle, a house and objects to fill this house, travel, and so on. Lastly, people want their lives filled with deep connections both with themselves and others.

Humans have an innate need to reinvent themselves from their everyday life that helps in the mental and emotional growth of the individual. They indulge in numerous initiatives that result in the desired transformation of themselves, which can lead to a spiritual experience. Anything from practising meditation to listening to music, playing with a child to dancing, or volunteering for a cause to doing daily chores can lead to a spiritual wakening.

So, what is spirituality? It is the ability of an individual to detach themselves from a given situation and combat with the challenges of life while understanding the existence of self and its connection with others. When an individual practices spirituality on regular basis, they experience positive emotions such as contentment, serenity, affection, optimism, wellbeing, and many more. This not only helps decode one's existence but also helps them formulate the objective of each action that was and will be taken during the journey of life.

Our ability to sustain our family and earn a living depends on our work. Our working situation and professional path are impacted by the way that we work. Our work has significant effects on how we identify personally, and it contributes significantly to our sense of self-worth. The principal setting for satiating the need to connect with others has become the workplace due to the collapse of traditional sources of social and community support. Today, many people derive their major sense of self and value from their profession.

People constantly strive to advance from their current state of affairs and desire better health in terms of physical and mental, and every step that people take towards the desired state results in people viewing their actions as more valuable. When people function effectively and use their true potential, they are exposed to positive relationships and work towards valued goals.

People live a life of full of interdependencies. One of the aspects of interdependence is give and take. As people realise their purpose in life, they move from being a taker to giving back to society. It is not possible to only breathe in; one has to breathe out to continue the cycle of life. As people become conscious of their knowledge, time, and resources, they produce more than they consume, giving more than what they take thus, living a purposeful life. As people move towards living a purposeful life, their sense of wellbeing heightens.

As organizations progress towards the development of its employees, they not only concentrate on the individual needs of the employees but also create a culture, a climate of shared goals and values that help employees advance towards their higher purpose. Employees and employers experience work as a spiritual path, as a prospect to nurture and to strengthen the community in a purposeful manner. This suggests that employees and employers attempt to live their values through their work. Organizations that encourage a culture of spirituality at the workplace identify that people have both a mind and a spirit, try to find the meaning and purpose in their work, and yearn to establish a connection with other human beings and be part of a community.

Abraham Maslow was one of the great contributors to workplace spirituality through his hierarchy of needs model, a theory of motivation that argues for self-actualization. A management style that is enlightened is one that sees the other as a way to increase organizational performance and achieve complete intellectual, emotional, and spiritual fulfilment (Maslow & Lowery, 1998).

Webster (2003) claimed that having a spirituality is crucial for people in the workplace because work is not an isolated and autonomous part of life, but rather one facet of a larger self that must be meaningfully integrated with other dimensions. This concept emphasises three fundamental components of workplace spirituality: inner self, meaningful job, and a feeling of community.

According to Genty and Azeez (2017), employees exhibit a greater level of loyalty when workplace spirituality helps provide them reason in life. Pradhan and Jena (2016) suggest that improvement in employees' workplace spirituality improves the connection between the staff and organization.

Dandona (2013) suggests that by applying spiritual practices at the workplace, an employee's desire to work within a community, desire to exhibit compassion towards others at the workplace, and desire to have meaningful work can be nourished.

According to Dutta and Singh (2017), spirituality may help in reinforcing an individual's resilience by helping them draw positive meaning from their experiences, promoting a feeling of coherence and wellbeing. According to Mousa and Alas (2016), spirituality is an important component in fostering employee–employer trust, which has a beneficial impact on the effective functioning of the entire organization. Sharma and Pestonjee (2020) found that spiritual intelligence among leaders helped reduce burnout where burnout was a result of excessive role stress.

Hussain and Khan (2014) mention the following positive aspects of spirituality at the workplace:

- Psychological burnout of employees that is resulting in present work cultures will be replaced by psychological energy conservation.
- Erratic behaviour such as absenteeism and conflict of employees would be replaced by steady and stable behaviour.
- The short-term approach will be replaced by long-term approach.
- Rather than material success, holistic success will be sought.
- Feeling of spiritual and responsiveness; freedom will prevail instead of bondage.
- The sense of completeness will be accomplished instead of alienation and emptiness.
- The focus would be on work commitment instead of reward commitment.
- Job enrichment will be replaced by life enrichment.
- Feeling of compassion, love, trust, and sharing would develop instead of rivalry and repulsion.
- The organizational commitment would be in alignment with self-development.

Employees will try to walk the spiritual path in every walk of their life consciously or subconsciously. With the knowledge of the benefits of a spiritual climate, organizations can consciously make effort towards helping employees in their journey. Pandey et al. (2009) provide a comprehensive list of areas in which organization can work in order to build a spiritual climate for the employees.

- **Meaningful Work:** When employees are facing mental health concerns, they usually tend to ask questions such as "What do I want to do with my life?", "Why do I go to work?", "What is most important to me at work?", which hint at trying to find meaning and purpose in life through work. People who have meaningful jobs feel that they are a part of something bigger than themselves. The tasks that are put in front of them inspire them to work as hard as they can. Meaningful work is defined as having a sense of significance and purpose, both in terms of the work itself and the environment in which it is conducted (Ashforth & Pratt, 2003).

  In such scenarios, organizations can help employees find their purpose by designing meaningful work for them. This can involve identifying the strengths and needs of the individual which are not just professional but also personal in nature. These goals when coupled with the mission and values of the organization can help design work which employees see as meaningful in nature.

Organizations can also help employees see the impact of their work. Leaders can highlight the impact of work done by the employees and thus create a greater sense of meaning. Enabling employees to see the bigger picture plays a role in creating truly meaningful work for employees. Microsoft frequently sends its employees to see how their software in utilised by the end user to understand the effect it has in increasing the productivity and efficiency of the work.

- **Meditative work:** When employees are in the pink of their mental health, they tend to be more efficient and productive. Even during a tense work schedule, they may experience a sense of calmness and feel taken away from their surrounding and yet be present in the moment. Employees may perceive their work to be meditative and become one with their work. When employees have a notion of doing a meaningful and engaging task, it allows them to be fulfilled as a person thus enhancing their psychological wellbeing at work. Organizations can play a vital role in providing a climate that ensures employees can experience meditative work.

- **Creativity:** Innovation at the workplace depends on creativity. Creativity is essential to the experience and development of employees, whether it is through inventive problem-solving or the freedom to choose how work is carried out. We have seen in the past how innovation in business models become the main differentiator for those who have prospered during the pandemic and in the past.

  For organizations to continue innovating, they have to encourage a culture of creativity and imagination among employees. By providing them room to express their creativity, employees are more likely to develop original and creative solutions to problems they face. This desire to find solutions can inspire ideas for novel approaches to tasks and contribute to a more successfully run organization.

  The Students' Educational and Cultural Movement of Ladakh (SECMOL) is a great example to understand the importance of creativity in everyday education. Where 95% of the students were failing high-school, SECMOL worked to change the education system to include imaginative, child-centred, and activity-based teaching approaches to make schooling for children more enjoyable. This has also resulted in rekindling enthusiasm, boosting confidence, and increasing dedication among government school instructors. As a result, SECMOL has evolved into an eco-village where students, employees, and volunteers live, work, and learn alongside one another.

- **Hopefulness:** Philosopher Mary Zournazi states that hope is "built on belief and faith, and the trust that there is a life worth living in uncertain times." Hope is the thin thread that people can hold on to which can eventually help them be pulled out of an otherwise impossible situation. It is a conviction that objectives can be attained, a confidence that effective methods can be devised and paths to goal can be recognised.

According to psychologist Randolph C. Arnau, "a high-hope person tends to have more goals and is quicker to focus on another if they fail." The capacity to hope, even in the face of challenging situations has been shown to be highly related to wellbeing (Ciarrochi et al., 2015; Valle et al., 2006). Organizations that inspire hopefulness among their employees can help build their resilience at work leading to a resilient workplace.

David Waring, co-founder of Fit Small Business, instils hopefulness among the employees by keeping them informed about both the successes and failures of the company, as well as what the plan is for future growth of the company.

- **Sense of community:** Employees with a feeling of security, affinity, and faith in their community have better health. Employees who lack such a feeling, are less motivated to act favourably or associate with others to encourage wellbeing for all. An emotional connect with the members of the organization is often a key factor for ensuring that members stay for the long term. Organizations can create occasions for employees to get to know each other and bond to enhance their sense of community.

Satya Nadella said "what brings people in the office is seeing and connecting with colleagues. 92% Indians said they were motivated to come to work by establishing connections and rebuild team bonds." The work trend index special report by Microsoft says "84% of employees would be motivated to come to work by the promise of socializing with co-workers, while 85% would be motivated by rebuilding team bonds. Employees also report that they would go to the office more frequently if they knew their direct team members would be there (73%) or if their work friends were there (74%)."

- **Authenticity:** Trust and transparency have been key to successful businesses. The importance of being authentic has touched new levels in the pandemic as people are more transparent with each other, especially at workplaces. Authenticity is a means for organizations and leaders to set themselves apart. It's a strategy for creating deep, enduring bonds with both audiences and staff members. Leaders and influencers in the organization practicing the core values of the firm can create a climate which is full of trust leading to an authentic organization.

The founder and CEO of a major food delivery app in India along with his senior management team deliver food on a motorcycle once every quarter while donning the trademark red t-shirt that the company's delivery partners wear. This practice has been prevalent since 2019. This enables the team to understand the concerns at ground level. Employees experience a heightened level of commitment towards an organization that "walk the talks."

- **Respect for diversity:** In order for a company and its employees to function efficiently and harmoniously, diversity in the workplace focuses on attracting, keeping, and developing a diverse and inclusive workforce. Respecting diversity helps in increasing the motivation of existing and new workers. It can also result in an improved range of candidates available for employment, therefore allowing the best to be employed.

An organization becomes more innovative and resilient the more it is receptive to viewpoints from people with various backgrounds. Diversity not only boosts productivity but also generates constructive conflict that encourages thinking and challenges conformity. An organization culture that values diversity fosters a larger range of ideas. Because no two people think alike, a broad group of collaborators can produce a wide range of ideas. Greater creativity is produced by different cultural viewpoints. Better ideas can be produced when there are more employees involved.

Global PC supplier Lenovo has developed its business on the tenet that "different is better," supporting and incorporating diversity into its operations. According to a 2020 study by McKinsey & Company, organizations that value diversity and inclusion are 35% more likely to have superior financial returns than companies that don't (McKinsey & Company, 2020). Additionally, a Deloitte study discovered that inclusion and diversity in the workplace might increase innovation by up to 20% (Juliet Bourke & Dillon, 2018).

- **Concern for family:** Family of employees impact their engagement level in the organization. Initiatives which engage the family of an employee and are cognizant of the family's wellbeing enhance the assurance and appreciation for the organization. Such families are more understanding of the employee's needs, whether they involve extra work hours, more frequent business travels, or other difficulties.

  People are affected by their surrounding even at the organization. Homes have become the new workspace for the last few years and family members share this workspace. It is natural that the family members will affect each other's state of mind more while working from home. The quality of an employee's home life will reflect in their performance at work, and the reverse is also true. Organizations can extend the employee welfare initiatives to include their family members. A comprehensive employee family welfare programme will help attract top talent and provide employees with a better quality of life while developing mutually beneficial relationships.

- **Contribution of the work to community and society at large:** For many, the purpose of life is to serve the society. To be able to follow a passion, in terms of work, and to be able to support towards the betterment of the society in the same organization can be an added advantage. Employees can live a meaningful life when they along with their family members have opportunities to be part of CSR initiatives by the organization which align with their values. Organizations committed to implement CSR activities into their business performance significantly influence the employee's wellbeing.

  Infosys Limited was an early adopter of CSR in India. It has been undertaking most of its CSR initiatives through Infosys Foundation, which was established in 1996, way before CSR was mandated in the country. The company's CSR is not limited to philanthropy, but it includes holistic community development, institution-building and sustainability-related initiatives. CSR programs at Apollo Tyres are designed to be in sync with the national development priorities as well as the United Nations Sustainable Development Goals (SDGs).

Conclusion

Organizations are constantly striving to ensure employee wellbeing, that they feel less stress, and do not get burnout due to the nature of their work. Organizations being a major part of an individual's life can have positive impact on various facets of their life. Favourable impact can be made by improving the spiritual climate of the organization as viewed by the employees.

Organizations can ensure that employees find their work meaningful by aligning the purpose of the organization with that of the employees, and they can ensure that the nature of work is such that employees become one with the task at hand. Organizations can provide opportunities for employees to express their creativity through work and other initiatives and they can provide employees and their family with various opportunities to participate in socially relevant causes.

Organizations can also provide employees with essential skills to grasp the responsibilities and make the employees feel recognised for their work. Such efforts by the organization will lead to improved resilience and psychological wellbeing at work of an employee, which can lead to reduced role stress and executive burnout for the employees.

The recent pandemic has emphasised the significance of mental health. Resources for mental health have an undeniable demand. Employers have agreed to shoulder the burden of offering suitable mental health solutions to workers, and nearly 90% of them intend to increase their investment in 2022, according to an Employee Wellness Report (Wellable Labs, 2022). Since the pandemic started, employees have endured a consistent series of personal and work-related pressures. Companies intend to boost their investments in stress management and resilience tools by 76% in order to aid workers in recovering.

As organizations adopt new ways of working, and as employees become more aware of mental health and its impact on lives and livelihoods, it is important that organizations create a congenial workplace where employees can flourish. For this to happen, organizations will have to create a spiritual climate such that employees discover meaning and determination in life. At the same time, organizations need to constantly be mindful of stress level of employees and assess their coping styles so that the extent of burnout is limited. Without a clear view of the prevalence and severity of burnout within a given company, leaders may underestimate the demand for a burnout strategy or implement ineffective policies. An organization that cares about employee wellbeing and psychological health is likely to reduce the impact suffered due to workplace stress and make employees more resilient.

Employees are the biggest assets and means to achieve organizational goals and achieve global impact. Organizations need to constantly focus on employee wellbeing to enhance employee's contribution and alignment towards organizational goals. Organizations must strive towards enhancing spiritual climate, helping employees discover meaning and purpose in the work they perform, enable employees to express creativity in their work, and participate in socially relevant causes. Such efforts by the organization will lead to improved resilience and psychological wellbeing at work of an employee that when coupled with the right coping strategy can lead to reduced role stress and executive burnout for the employees.

In a world where hybrid working (where remote working and working at an office are balanced) is becoming the norm, focus on employees' wellbeing is all the more important. New ways of working such as hybrid working, remote working, offline working, uberization (gig economy), and so on, have increased the complexity of work environments. Awareness of mental health, and its impact on lives and livelihood, has also led to employees being more mindful of their mental wellbeing. This awareness has led to employees asking for more from organizations—in terms of enhanced work environment—where spiritual climate, meaning, and purpose gain more importance. Pestonjee and Pastakia (2022) discuss the possible trends in general mental health on account of the pandemic on employees in the organization along with their wellbeing while the employees adapt to the post-pandemic working condition. This new and emerging workplace, and ways of working, will have its own challenges in aligning interests of employees and organizations.

As the world grapples through series of changes from great resignation to quiet quitting, from moonlighting to mass firing, it becomes imperative for organizations to question "Are we doing everything right? What is it that needs to change?" As people work on themselves to find the fine balance between work and life beyond work, organizations can play a major role in providing an environment where people and their families can stop their search for contentment and find the same at the workplace, not merely by treating work as worship but emerging as a place of spiritual awakening that helps satisfy their needs to find meaning and purpose in life.

References

Ashforth, B. E., & Pratt, M. G. (2003). Institutionalized spirituality: An oxymoron? In R. A. Giacalone & C. L. Jurkiewicz (Eds.), *Handbook of workplace spirituality and organizational performance* (pp. 93–107). M.E. Sharpe.

Avey, J. B., Luthans, F., Smith, R. M., & Palmer, N. F. (2010). Impact of positive psychological capital on employee well-being over time. *Journal of Occupational Health Psychology, 15*(1), 17–28. https://doi.org/10.1037/a0016998

Barendregt, C. S., van der Laan, A. M., Bongers, I. L., & van Nieuwenhuizen, C. (2015). Adolescents in secure residential care: The role of active and passive coping on general well-being and self-esteem. *European Child & Adolescent Psychiatry, 24*(7), 845–854. https://doi.org/10.1007/s00787-014-0629-5

Bevan, S. (2010). *The business case for employee health and wellbeing: A report prepared for investors in people UK. April*, 36.

Ciarrochi, J., Parker, P., Kashdan, T. B., Heaven, P. C. L., & Barkus, E. (2015). Hope And emotional well-being: A six-year study to distinguish antecedents, correlates, and consequences. *The Journal of Positive Psychology*, *10*(6), 520–532. https://doi.org/10.1080/17439760.2015.1015154

Cooper, C. L., & Quick, J. C. (Eds.). (2017). *The handbook of stress and health: A guide to research and practice*. John Wiley & Sons.

Dandona, A. (2013). Spirituality at workplace. *National conference on paradigm for sustainable business: People, planet, and profit*, 1–9.

Davydov, D. M., Stewart, R., Ritchie, K., & Chaudieu, I. (2010). Resilience and mental health. *Clinical Psychology Review*, *30*(5), 479–495. https://doi.org/10.1016/j.cpr.2010.03.003

Deloitte. (2022). *Mental health and employers the case for investment-pandemic and beyond.* https://www2.deloitte.com/content/dam/Deloitte/uk/Documents/consultancy/deloitte-uk-mental-health-report-2022.pdf

Dutta, U., & Singh, A. P. (2017). Studying spirituality in the context of grit and resilience of college-going young adults. *International Journal for Innovative Research in Multidisciplinary Field*, *3*(9), 50–55.

Emmons, R. A., & Crumpler, C. A. (2000). Gratitude as a human strength: Appraising the evidence. *Journal of Social and Clinical Psychology*, *19*(1), 56–69. https://doi.org/10.1521/jscp.2000.19.1.56

Fredrickson, B. L. (2004). The broaden-and-build theory of positive emotions. *Philosophical Transactions of the Royal Society B: Biological Sciences*, *359*(1449), 1367–1377. https://doi.org/10.1098/rstb.2004.1512

Garg, K., Kumar, C. N., & Chandra, P. S. (2019). Number of psychiatrists in India: Baby steps forward, but a long way to go. *Indian Journal of Psychiatry*, *61*(1), 104–105. https://doi.org/10.4103/psychiatry.IndianJPsychiatry_7_18

Genty, K., & Azeez, O. (2017). Workplace spirituality and organizational citizenship behaviour among Nigerian academics: The mediating role of normative organizational commitment. *Journal of Human Resource Management*, *20*(2), 48–62.

Gillespie, B. M., Chaboyer, W., Wallis, M., & Grimbeek, P. (2007). Resilience in the operating room: Developing and testing of a resilience model. *Journal of Advanced Nursing*, *59*(4), 427–438. https://doi.org/10.1111/j.1365-2648.2007.04340.x

Harter, J. K., Schmidt, F. L., & Keyes, C. L. M. (2004). Well-being in the workplace and its relationship to business outcomes: A review of the Gallup studies. In *Flourishing: Positive psychology and the life well-lived* (pp. 205–224). https://doi.org/10.1037/10594-009

Hillmann, J., & Guenther, E. (2021). Organizational resilience: A valuable construct for management research? *International Journal of Management Reviews*, *23*(1), 7–44. https://doi.org/10.1111/ijmr.12239

Hussain, A., & Khan, S. (2014). *Applied spirituality. Theory, research and practice*. Global Vision Publishing House.

Indeed. (2021). *Employee burnout report*. https://uk.indeed.com/lead/preventing-employee-burnout-report

Juliet Bourke, B., & Dillon, B. (2018). *The diversity and inclusion revolution eight powerful truths*. https://www.deloittereview.com

Kumpfer, K. L. (1999). Factors and processes contributing to resilience: The resilience framework. In M. D. Glantz & J. L. Johnson (Eds.), *Longitudinal research in the social and behavioral sciences. Resilience and development: Positive life adaptations* (pp. 179–224). Kluwer Academic Publishers.

Luthans, F., & Youssef, C. M. (2007). Emerging positive organizational behavior. *Journal of Management, 33*(3), 321–349. https://doi.org/10.1177/0149206307300814

Luthans, F., Youssef, C. M., & Avolio, B. J. (2007). *Psychological capital.* Oxford University Press.

Maslow, A., & Lowery, R. J. (1998). *Toward a psychology of being* (3rd ed.). Wiley & Sons.

Mayo Clinic. (2016). *Chronic stress puts your health at risk.* https://www.mayoclinic.org/healthy-lifestyle/stress-management/in-depth/stress/art-20046037

McCullough, M. E., Emmons, R. A., & Tsang, J.-A. (2002). The grateful disposition: A conceptual and empirical topography. *Journal of Personality and Social Psychology, 82*(1), 112–127. https://doi.org/10.1037/0022-3514.82.1.112

McKinsey & Company. (2020). *Diversity wins: How inclusion matters.* https://www.mckinsey.com/~/media/mckinsey/featured%20insights/diversity%20and%20inclusion/diversity%20wins%20how%20inclusion%20matters/diversity-wins-how-inclusion-matters-vf.pdf

Mills, P. J., Redwine, L., Wilson, K., Pung, M. A., Chinh, K., Greenberg, B. H., Lunde, O., Maisel, A., Raisinghani, A., Wood, A., & Chopra, D. (2015). The role of gratitude in spiritual well-being in asymptomatic heart failure patients. *Spirituality in Clinical Practice, 2*(1), 5–17. https://doi.org/10.1037/scp0000050

Mousa, M., & Alas, R. (2016). Organizational culture and workplace spirituality. *Arabian Journal of Business and Management Review, 6*(3). https://doi.org/10.4172/2223-5833.1000212

Nowak, D. J., Civerolo, K. L., Trivikrama Rao, S., Sistla, G., Luley, C. J., & E. Crane, D. (2000). A modeling study of the impact of urban trees on ozone. *Atmospheric Environment, 34*(10), 1601–1613. https://doi.org/10.1016/S1352-2310(99)00394-5

Pandey, A., Gupta, R. K., & Arora, A. P. (2009). Spiritual climate of business organizations and its impact on customers' experience. *Journal of Business Ethics, 88*(2), 313–332. https://doi.org/10.1007/s10551-008-9965-z.

Pestonjee, D. M., & Muncherji, N. (1991). Executive health: An oft-neglected aspect of HRD. *Vikalpa: The Journal for Decision Makers, 16*(3), 21–34. https://doi.org/10.1177/0256090919910303

Pestonjee, D. M., & Pastakia, T. A. (2022). The post-pandemic workplace: Challenges and prospects. In *Leadership after COVID-19, working together toward a sustainable future* (pp. 361–375). https://doi.org/10.1007/978-3-030-84867-5_21

Pradhan, R. K., & Jena, L. K. (2016). Workplace spirituality and employee job behaviour. *Paradigm, 20*(2), 159–175. https://doi.org/10.1177/0971890716670721

Robertson, I. T., & Cooper, C. L. (2010). Full engagement: The integration of employee engagement and psychological well-being. *Leadership & Organization Development Journal, 31*(4), 324–336. https://doi.org/10.1108/01437731011043348

Schultze-Lutter, F., Schimmelmann, B. G., & Schmidt, S. J. (2016). Resilience, risk, mental health and well-being: Associations and conceptual differences. *European Child & Adolescent Psychiatry, 25*(5), 459–466. https://doi.org/10.1007/s00787-016-0851-4

Sharma, A., & Pestonjee, D. M. (2020). A study on spiritual intelligence in leadership to manage role stress and executive burn out. *International Journal of Management, 11*(10). https://doi.org/10.34218/IJM.11.10.2020.121

Sharma, R. R., & Cooper, S. C. (2016). Contribution of individual and organizational factors in burnout. In *Executive burnout* (pp. 17–62). Emerald Group Publishing Limited. https://doi.org/10.1108/978-1-78635-286-620161002

Tonkin, K., Malinen, S., Näswall, K., & Kuntz, J. C. (2018). Building employee resilience through wellbeing in organizations. *Human Resource Development Quarterly*, *29*(2), 107–124. https://doi.org/10.1002/hrdq.21306

Utsey, S. O., Giesbrecht, N., Hook, J., & Stanard, P. M. (2008). Cultural, sociofamilial, and psychological resources that inhibit psychological distress in African Americans exposed to stressful life events and race-related stress. *Journal of Counseling Psychology*, *55*(1), 49–62. https://doi.org/10.1037/0022-0167.55.1.49

Valle, M. F., Huebner, E. S., & Suldo, S. M. (2006). An analysis of hope as a psychological strength. *Journal of School Psychology*, *44*(5), 393–406. https://doi.org/10.1016/j.jsp.2006.03.005

Webster, J. D. (2003). An exploratory analysis of a self-assessed wisdom scale. *Journal of Adult Development*, *10*(1), 13–22. https://doi.org/10.1023/A:1020782619051

Wellable Labs. (2022). *2022 Employee wellness industry trends report*. https://www.wellable.co/labs/research/employee-wellness-industry-trends-reports/2022/

Wood, A. M., Froh, J. J., & Geraghty, A. W. A. (2010). Gratitude and well-being: A review and theoretical integration. *Clinical Psychology Review*, *30*(7), 890–905. https://doi.org/10.1016/j.cpr.2010.03.005

World Health Organization. (2019, May 28). *Burn-out an "occupational phenomenon": International classification of diseases*. https://www.who.int/news/item/28-05-2019-burn-out-an-occupational-phenomenon-international-classification-of-diseases

Wright, T. A., & Cropanzano, R. (2000). Psychological well-being and job satisfaction as predictors of job performance. *Journal of Occupational Health Psychology*, *5*(1), 84–94. https://doi.org/10.1037/1076-8998.5.1.84

INDEX

Note: *Italicized*, **bold** and ***bold italics*** refer to figures and tables.

Printed in the United States
by Baker & Taylor Publisher Services